ROAD TO REDEMPTION

The Liberal Party of Canada, 2006–2019

BROOKE JEFFREY

Road to Redemption

The Liberal Party of Canada, 2006–2019

UNIVERSITY OF TORONTO PRESS
Toronto Buffalo London

ISBN 978-1-4875-0056-6 (cloth)
ISBN 978-1-4875-1131-9 (EPUB)
ISBN 978-1-4875-1130-2 (PDF)

Library and Archives Canada Cataloguing in Publication

Title: Road to redemption : the Liberal Party of Canada, 2006–2019 /
   Brooke Jeffrey.
Names: Jeffrey, Brooke, author.
Description: Includes bibliographical references and index.
Identifiers: Canadiana (print) 20200307681 | Canadiana (ebook)
   20200307746 | ISBN 9781487500566 (hardcover) | ISBN 9781487511319
   (EPUB) | ISBN 9781487511302 (PDF)
Subjects: LCSH: Liberal Party of Canada. | LCSH: Political parties –
   Canada. | CSH: Canada – Politics and government – 2006–2015. |
   CSH: Canada – Politics and government – 2015–
Classification: LCC JL197.L53 J44 2020 | DDC 324.27106 – dc2

University of Toronto Press acknowledges the financial assistance to its
publishing program of the Canada Council for the Arts and the Ontario
Arts Council, an agency of the Government of Ontario.

Canada Council   Conseil des Arts
for the Arts   du Canada

ONTARIO ARTS COUNCIL
CONSEIL DES ARTS DE L'ONTARIO
an Ontario government agency
un organisme du gouvernement de l'Ontario

Funded by the   Financé par le
Government   gouvernement
of Canada   du Canada

Canada

For Ian, Devon, and Chris

Contents

Acknowledgments

Like its predecessor, *Divided Loyalties*, this book was four years in the making. Since it covers a much shorter period of time this might seem somewhat surprising, but it must be recognized that the circumstances were quite different.

Instead of a party that was spending most of its time as the government before its unexpected fall from power at the end, this book covers a party in opposition for most of the time, with an unexpected return to power at the end. At least that time frame had been my intention. Somehow I was persuaded to put aside my original plan – to end this work with the stunning electoral victory of Justin Trudeau's Liberals in 2015 – and instead to continue on, in order to cover what turned out to be the far more problematic 2019 election. Needless to say, this resulted in a further round of research and interviews, as well as an additional two chapters. This second round was in turn affected by both access to relevant individuals and the type of research required.

Throughout this lengthy process I was fortunate to have the cooperation and encouragement of so many of the key players in this drama from both the volunteer and parliamentary wings of the party. I am once again indebted to the lengthy list of individual Liberals who consented to be interviewed, and who gladly shared their recollections and perspectives on the party's evolution during this time period. Many of them were generous with their time and agreed to several in-person sessions. Others responded to additional questions by email or lengthy phone conversations. Most were prepared to have their comments stand on the record for attribution, although in some cases certain of their remarks were understood to be confidential. (A complete list of those interviewed for the record can be found in Appendix A.) A few individuals consented to interviews on the understanding that all of their contribution would remain off the record, to be used largely as background information or presented as anonymous commentary. This small group included Liberals currently active in government or party posts, as well as some senior public servants. Given the nature of political life, and the fact that my discretion in my previous book undoubtedly contributed to their willingness to participate in the preparation of this sequel, I felt their requests were eminently reasonable. To all of them I would like to extend my sincere thanks for their cooperation, and to the Liberals my appreciation of their important contributions to the ongoing success of the Liberal Party of Canada.

I would also like to thank the many individuals at the University of Toronto Press who have worked so hard, most recently under trying conditions, to make the publication of this manuscript possible. This lengthy list includes my long-time editor, Daniel Quinlan, who once again rose to the occasion and made incisive comments and suggestions that greatly enhanced the organization and content of the manuscript; managing editor Robin Studniberg, whose work in producing this book was a particular challenge during the pandemic crisis; and copy-editor Terry Teskey, who undoubtedly saved me from numerous embarrassing literary lapses and made me appear to be a far better writer than I am.

Finally, thanks are due, as always, to my family and friends, and most of all to my husband, for their ongoing support and understanding, and in particular for allowing me to renege on an earlier promise that *Divided Loyalties* would be my last book. In politics one should never say never.

ROAD TO REDEMPTION

The Liberal Party of Canada, 2006–2019

Introduction

The Conservative Party will be to the 21st century what the Liberal Party was to the 20th, the perpetually dominant party, the naturally governing party.
– Darrel Bricker and John Ibbitson, *The Big Shift*, 2013

The morning after the 2011 federal election, the Liberal Party of Canada was on life support and Liberals across the country were in shock. The once mighty Big Red Machine lay in ruins. The party's traditional support in Atlantic Canada and Ontario had been reduced to a pitiful urban rump, while any hopes for a modest recovery in western Canada were dashed. The party was essentially shut out in that region, holding on to a mere four seats across the Prairies and British Columbia. Adding insult to injury, the New Democratic Party (NDP) under leader Jack Layton was not only the Official Opposition, but had taken many seats away from the Liberals in their traditional Quebec stronghold.

It was a long way to fall for the party that had dominated the federal political scene in Canada for most of the twentieth century. Often described as the most successful political party in the Western world, the Liberals had been in power for so long that legendary Canadian scholar John Meisel once wrote "the line between the government and the Liberal party has become tenuous."[1] Between 1945 and 2000, the party received more votes than any other party in all but four of seventeen national elections, and more votes than all of the other parties taken together in two of those elections.

Unbelievably (at least to many Liberals), in 2011 the party found itself in third place in the House of Commons for the first time in its history. Its thirty-four seats were a record low since Confederation. As one expert on political parties, UBC academic Ken Carty, has stressed, this was also the culmination of a serious and unprecedented series of defeats for the Liberal Party. "In the first decade of the twenty-first century … in four consecutive elections, it failed to win a parliamentary majority. That had not happened since Macdonald's string of Conservative victories had kept the Liberals out of office for most of the last two decades of the nineteenth century."[2]

The situation was so serious that pollster Darrell Bricker and newspaper columnist John Ibbitson predicted the party was finished. They argued its role as the "natural governing party" was being taken over by the new Conservative Party of Stephen Harper, which would be in power for the foreseeable future.[3] Noted Canadian historian Peter C. Newman agreed. In his book on the future of the Liberal Party, published in 2012, Newman predicted the party would soon disappear from the political map of Canada: "They have no power base. Every party must have a power base," he argued, concluding it would be impossible for the Liberals to rebuild on all fronts at once, or in time for the next election.[4] Like many other observers, Newman attributed this electoral disaster to more than the incompetence of the party organization or its unpopular leader. In addition, he argued, this crushing rejection by voters demonstrated that liberalism itself was finished and went so far as to predict "the death of Liberal Canada."[5] A polarized political culture would emerge, Newman said, as the moderate middle championed by Liberals disappeared. The left, in the form of the NDP, would now be the only alternative to the right represented by the new Conservative Party.

Observers of Canada's political scene had heard this apocalyptic story before. In 1984, with the defeat of the Turner Liberals and the election of the Mulroney Progressive Conservatives with their huge majority, the demise of the Liberal Party had seemed a real possibility. NDP leader Ed Broadbent had wasted little time in predicting the end of the "mushy middle" and Liberal hegemony. After all, the party had been reduced to forty seats, a record-breaking low at the time. But, in many respects, the party's situation in 2011 was much worse, exemplified by its mere thirty-four seats and unprecedented loss of Official Opposition status in the House of Commons. Not surprisingly, there were two questions on every Liberal's mind in the aftermath of the shocking 2011 collapse: how had it happened and what, if anything, could be done to prevent the party's demise?

Of course, successfully answering the second question depended greatly on the first. Simply put, Liberals had been in denial for longer than anyone cared to admit. The 2011 electoral disaster was indeed the result of more than the obvious short-term problems with organization or leadership. In fact, the party's implosion was the almost inevitable outcome of a slow but steady decline over several decades, a decline that few Liberals had been willing to acknowledge and fewer still were prepared to confront. Nevertheless, and contrary to the conclusion of Carty, Newman, and others, liberalism itself was *not* on the decline. As subsequent events would demonstrate, the problem was the singer, not the song.

To turn the situation around, then, Liberals would have to admit that they had been trying to get by with shortcuts and ignoring the many underlying problems the party faced. Those shortcuts clearly no longer worked. In many ways they had actually made things worse. They had become part of the internal culture of the party and would be increasingly hard to remedy.

The Liberals actually began to address these problems in the wake of their defeat in 2006. At their biennial convention in December of that year, the Liberals took the first positive steps towards reform of the party constitution at the insistence of a determined few. But progress over the next five years, although measurable, was slow and uneven. It took the near-death experience of 2011 to force a concerted and comprehensive response across the wide range of issues that needed tackling. Still, if initial efforts had not been launched after 2006, those subsequent rebuilding projects could not have succeeded. Similarly, all of the various reconstruction and rehabilitation efforts undertaken by both party leaders and elites over the next nine years were an essential component of the party's eventual electoral success and return to power in 2015. Put another way, the pundits were not wrong about the grave difficulties the party faced in 2011, but they underestimated its ability to reform, rebuild, and rehabilitate itself.

This pessimism is perhaps somewhat surprising given that the party had risen from the ashes before. As Carty noted in his detailed analysis of the party's failings, published in advance of the 2015 election, the Liberal Party's unprecedented electoral success and longevity are not only remarkable, but due in large measure to its well-known ability to reinvent itself.[6] And, as another chronicler of the party, Joseph Wearing, pointed out, this has typically happened when the party is in one of its infrequent periods in opposition. The history of the Liberal Party, Wearing concluded, "has been characterized by a cyclical pattern of decay and renewal, the decay coming after a number of years in power, and the renewal prompted by electoral defeat."[7]

But this did *not* happen between 1984 and 1993, when the party was last in opposition, as would have been expected. The precursor to this book, *Divided Loyalties*, chronicles at length the party's struggles to regroup after the devastating 1984 electoral defeat under leader

John Turner. As that book outlines, the failure to rebuild was due to the unprecedented internal conflict over Turner's leadership, and to his support for the Mulroney government's proposed Meech Lake Accord, which, taken together, preoccupied both the parliamentary and extra-parliamentary wings of the party.[8] As a result, the party's return to power under Jean Chrétien took place without the intensive rebuilding and repositioning exercise that had happened during its previous stints in opposition, most notably during the Pearson years. Instead, the strength of the Liberal brand and the extreme unpopularity of the Mulroney government had proven sufficient for the party to prevail without this renewal.

This renewal also did not take place in a concerted fashion during the first half of the Liberal Party's next stint in opposition, from 2006 to 2011. In this case, the party was burdened with a succession of leaders and interim leaders, and Conservative minority governments, all of which had made any real reform efforts extremely difficult. Recognizing this, Carty – like Newman, Ibbitson and Bricker – questioned whether the party would be able to do so after 2011, or whether it was already too late. He was sure the party's Band-Aid solutions would no longer work and, like the other critics, he doubted the party could tear itself away from these tendencies and reconstruct itself in time to recover before the 2015 election. More importantly, he concluded the party was headed for oblivion in the long term, regardless of whether it made short-term gains in that election.

Even some Liberal sympathizers feared the worst by 2011. Well-known backroom organizers and advisers such as Warren Kinsella and Eddie Goldenberg began to speculate that only a merger with the NDP would allow the party to survive in some capacity and defeat the Harper Conservatives.[9] Others, while rejecting the merger calls, sounded the alarm on the need for the party to undertake serious reorganization and reformation immediately. As one analysis of the disastrous 2011 election concluded, the election of 2015 was likely to be the party's last chance. Referring to the numerous problems it faced in addition to leadership (financial, organizational, technical, and policy issues), the study concluded:

> Whether the party will be able to address these problems remains to be seen. Certainly the experience of the last three election campaigns has demonstrated the futility of shortcuts based on leadership change alone … The Liberal Party should not be counted out on the basis of this election, but nor should its recovery and eventual return to power be taken for granted. Much will depend on the willingness of the Liberal

membership and elites to come together and contribute to the party's rebuilding, and on the party's ability to return to basics and define essential Liberal values in the context of the 21st century.[10]

In the end, and despite the odds, the Liberal Party did just that. It defied the pundits and returned to power in the 2015 election. From a third-place start at the beginning of the campaign, leader Justin Trudeau and his team not only prevailed but delivered a majority government. This book provides the behind-the-scenes explanation for that remarkable recovery. It picks up the saga of the Liberal Party of Canada where *Divided Loyalties* left off, with the defeat of the Martin Liberal government in 2006, and follows the Liberal Party's travails through nearly a decade in opposition.

Martin's defeat, it should be noted, was a surprise to most Liberals as well as pundits. After all, shortly after winning his third electoral majority in 2001, Jean Chrétien was described by political scientist Bruce Doern as "standing astride the Canadian political scene without much effective opposition." Doern also declared that the most important question facing analysts was "the extent to which a one-party state is congealing at the federal level under the Liberals."[11] This expectation was entirely understandable. When Jean Chrétien left office in late 2003, the party enjoyed a solid majority. It stood at 42 per cent in polls, a scenario which Darrel Bricker of Ipsos Reid predicted would easily earn the party a fourth majority government.[12] (Despite nearly two years of internecine warfare, even Chrétien's personal approval rating still stood at 46 per cent, although 48 per cent of respondents also wanted Martin to replace Chrétien as Liberal leader.) Indeed, shortly after Paul Martin assumed the reins of power in December 2003, his team was predicting not only another Liberal victory in 2004, but even greater electoral success in Quebec. This did not come to pass, however. Martin's resulting minority government then turned that marginal victory into defeat in 2006, leaving many in the party with an almost desperate preference for shortcuts over hard choices, and the party unprepared for its return to opposition in increasingly dire straits.

To fully understand the extent of the challenge the Liberal Party faced by 2011, therefore, it is necessary to first examine the origins of each of the party's many underlying problems, almost all of which predated the 2006 defeat. That is the task of the first chapter, which outlines five broad areas in which the party was in serious difficulty for some time, providing context for the remedial efforts that followed.

The following chapters then chronicle not only the various leadership battles and parliamentary crises of the nine-year period in opposition, but also the successive makeshift solutions that were tried, as well as the Herculean efforts of a handful of party elites and organizers to rectify many of these underlying problems under such difficult circumstances. This effort ultimately led to the success of the Trudeau team in preparing the party for the 2015 election. In a campaign for the ages, the Liberals' dramatic return to power conclusively demonstrated the importance of this groundwork and the uncanny ability of the Liberal Party to reinvent itself.

Whether this unexpected victory will lead to another Liberal dynasty is a separate question. As I was completing the writing of this book, the Justin Trudeau government had just been re-elected with a slim minority, a far cry from their resounding majority of 2015. While there were numerous successes during their first mandate, there were also a series of scandals and own-goal gaffes that led to the undermining of the Trudeau/Liberal brand. Perhaps equally significant were the unexpected challenges presented by an American president bent on overturning the global order and the North American Free Trade Agreement, and a series of provincial elections that produced staunch opponents of the Trudeau agenda on issues crucial to the economic well-being and security of Canadians. Certainly the party's electoral machinery, fundraising, and communications skills in the 2019 election were light years ahead of its situation during the 2006–2015 opposition interlude, and have been credited by many Liberal insiders with making the difference in such a tight race. The future of the party and its potential return to political dominance now depends on Trudeau's ability to take advantage of this second chance and redeem himself and his government in the eyes of Canadians.

1 A Party on the Brink

The Liberal Party is broken beyond repair and needs to be completely restructured if it is to survive.

– LPC national director Steve MacKinnon, 2011

The 2011 election forced Liberals to confront some hard truths about the state of their party. Some were obvious and were already on display during the campaign itself. Others were less so. In many cases, the seeds of the Liberals' humiliating defeat were planted years earlier, but were easier to overlook given the electoral successes of the Chrétien era. With the opposition hopelessly split between fringe parties (the Reform/Alliance on the right and the separatist Bloc Québécois in Quebec), the Liberals could – and did – divide and conquer three times over a decade.

But when Stephen Harper succeeded in uniting the right, and creating a winning coalition based on the west and Ontario, without Quebec, the Liberal Party's weaknesses came to the fore. Worse still, in Harper the party had met its match. Disciplined, ruthless, and ideologically driven, Harper was in a different league altogether from the party's earlier nemesis, Brian Mulroney. Harper's ultimate game plan was to supplant the Liberal Party as Canada's so-called "natural governing party." He had the tools to do it.[1] The threat was certainly real. It led some Liberals to consider the possibility that only a "unite the left" movement to bring together all progressives could actually defeat the conservative juggernaut. Others, including many members of the party's mostly voluntary extra-parliamentary wing, redoubled their efforts to make the necessary changes and rehabilitate the party in time for the 2015 election.

As they struggled on, it became clear that they had to address a series of five interrelated problems, none of which alone could resolve their difficulties. As the following chapters demonstrate, each of these five problem areas played a role in the defeats of 2006, 2008, and 2011. And each had roots in the past, albeit exacerbated by the difficulties that began with the party's latest return to the wilderness in 2006. Of these problems, perhaps the most entrenched had become the belief that a change in leadership would solve all of the others.

Leaders and the Liberals' Messiah Complex

If anyone should have known that it was important to learn from past mistakes, it was surely the Liberal Party elites in 2006, having just seen their previous star candidate, Paul Martin, crash and burn. Yet once again they succumbed to the idea of a quick fix, believing the selection of a "winner" as leader would solve their problems and restore the party to its rightful place. The 2006 leadership race demonstrated that the Liberals' messiah complex was deeply entrenched. It also demonstrated that, just as in 1984 with the selection of John Turner, the Liberals' definition of a winner would prove disastrously wrong. Having misplaced their trust in Martin as the heir apparent in 2003, they nevertheless looked for someone similar to replace him.

Given the Conservatives' minority status, the Liberals' hope that their time in opposition would be brief was a major factor driving their decisions. To the dismay of the party elites, however, all of their likely star candidates declined to join the race, an unexpected development that spoke volumes about those presumptive candidates' own views of their chances of ever becoming prime minister. Nevertheless, so great was the Liberals' determination to choose a new leader in anticipation of a quick return to power that the leadership race was called in haste for the end of the year. This haste, in turn, produced a field of seriously flawed contenders and a badly divided party. Unable to agree on their choice, the elites lined up behind two of the most prominent but highly polarizing candidates, Michael Ignatieff and Bob Rae. Meanwhile, a dark horse candidate, Stéphane Dion, came up the middle with the support of the rank-and-file and emerged as the winner. Ironically, in choosing this upstart candidate, the grass roots of the party had succumbed to the messiah complex as well. They had simply concluded that Stéphane Dion, an "anti-politician" and an outsider in the party, was the perfect choice to lead them to victory, rather than the divisive Rae or Ignatieff. But they, too, were wrong, as events would soon demonstrate.

For a brief time, the selection of Stéphane Dion appeared both inspired and timely. His initial appeal quickly faded, however, as his own drawbacks and vulnerabilities became apparent. His lack of political instincts and inability to communicate well in either official language proved a major hurdle with the public, while his outsider status in the party proved to be a major handicap, resulting in his failure to deal effectively with internal party issues or mobilize his troops.

Dion's ignominious defeat in 2008 only encouraged the elites to try again. This time they made no mistake in entrenching their now preferred candidate, Michael Ignatieff, as leader, even bypassing the traditional leadership race to do so. Ignatieff proved that it was possible for the party to fare worse on the hustings with another "winner" leading the charge in the 2011 election. The Liberal Party's obsession with its choice of leader above all other issues had conclusively failed, but would the party be able to avoid the so-called messiah complex now that it was in such dire straits?

This leader-driven focus as the route to electoral success may have been present to some extent in the modern iteration of the Liberal Party. However, the most important secondary factor in the selection of a leader until 1984 – once the top priorities of competence and policy positions had been vetted – had traditionally been "*l'alternance*," that is, the alternation of the party leadership between native English- and French-speaking candidates. In the postwar era this guiding principle had never been abandoned, with the party's leadership dutifully alternating between Louis St Laurent, Lester Pearson, Pierre Trudeau, John Turner, Jean Chrétien and Paul Martin.

But with the departure of Pierre Elliott Trudeau in 1984, the emphasis on leadership candidates' "winnability" arguably emerged as a dominant feature.[2] The first charismatic Liberal leader of the postwar era, Trudeau had been chosen in 1968 to succeed Lester Pearson. The contrast between the two men could hardly have been greater. Pearson, a former bureaucrat and diplomat, projected an image of a kindly but slightly befuddled professor. Trudeau, on the other hand, was a larger-than-life figure whose modern celebrity image appealed to Canadians of the day.[3] Nevertheless, it is important to note that Trudeau also came to power with clearly defined values and beliefs, as well as a high-profile set of priorities that, once implemented, left an indelible stamp on the party and the country. With sixteen years in power, Trudeau was the third-longest serving prime minister in the country's history and the only real figurehead many Liberals had known. Replacing *him* as leader would therefore prove difficult if not impossible, as heir apparent John Turner was to learn first-hand.[4]

To compound the problem, in Turner the elites had chosen someone whose position on many policy issues was at variance with his predecessor. Indeed, with Turner it could be argued that the party had placed winnability above the traditional emphasis on policy positions and liberal values. But while the party elites saw a winner in Turner, the public saw someone who was not Trudeau. Some observers have speculated that Conservative leader Brian Mulroney was initially viewed as a more likely successor to Trudeau in terms of his agenda,[5] although that perception faded once Mulroney was elected. Nevertheless, as Turner biographer Paul Litt has outlined in detail, Turner's short-lived and conflict-ridden term as leader was troubled by numerous clashes with both the rank and file and party elites over policies that were seen as contrary to the Trudeauvian legacy.[6]

After less than six years as leader, Turner resigned rather than face a leadership review that was certain to go against him. Liberals were clearly more impatient for a return to power than they had been in the time of Lester Pearson, who had never achieved a majority government and lost twice to the Conservatives, but remained leader from 1958 to 1968.

Nevertheless Turner's subsequent replacement by Jean Chrétien in 1990 might be seen as a retreat from the growing practice of choosing leaders who were perceived as winners. In reality, though, Chrétien was the exception. As has been outlined elsewhere,[7] one subject that reliably trumps all others as a policy priority for Liberals is national unity. Chrétien was perceived as yesterday's man by many in the party, and he might very well have failed to secure the leadership had it not been for the national unity crisis that emerged after Brian Mulroney's introduction of the Meech Lake Accord. This singular Conservative challenge to the Trudeauvian legacy caused Liberals to close ranks and unite behind Chrétien, the only one of the serious leadership candidates to oppose the accord.

The messiah complex returned with a vengeance upon Chrétien's departure, which was ironic given that, despite early misgivings, he had proven so successful. But after a decade in power, having faced down separatists and delivered three majority governments for the party, he was deemed to have outlived his usefulness, especially by supporters of Paul Martin, who feared electoral defeat if Chrétien lingered. He was unceremoniously dethroned by those supporters in favour of Martin, the man who had originally been seen as the winner in the 1990 leadership race before his enthusiastic support for the Meech Lake Accord had derailed his bid. As the 2003 leadership race to replace Chrétien unfolded, it became evident that Martin's victory this time around was preordained by the party elites. His coronation in Toronto in October 2003 was even more revealing. First, the delegates gave the departing Chrétien standing ovations in recognition of two major and highly popular positions he had taken while in office – introducing the Clarity Act and refusing to take Canada into the American-led war in Iraq. Then, in a remarkable demonstration of their growing ability to separate party policy from the optics of winnability, Liberals selected Paul Martin as their next leader despite the fact that he had opposed both of those seemingly popular positions.

Martin's short and rocky term in office culminated in his ultimate failure in 2006. The Liberals' need for a saviour to lead them out of the wilderness, it appeared, was becoming obsessive. Evidently, understanding that the party now had zero tolerance for leaders who could not deliver electoral success, Martin wasted little time in offering his resignation.[8]

This book takes up the story with the hastily convened 2006 leadership race to replace Martin, and the unanticipated consequences that followed. It chronicles how the party struggled in opposition under three different leaders (and two interim leaders) in less than a decade. To put this in perspective, previous leaders of the Liberal Party of Canada each served, on average, for a decade. Martin lasted less than five, Dion a mere two years, and Ignatieff only three.

Michael Ignatieff literally disappeared after the 2011 defeat, resigning as leader on election night and potentially forcing a fourth leadership contest in less than ten years. Fortunately, the party executive finally concluded that haste did indeed make waste. Their decision to delay the next leadership race to January of 2013 can be seen as an important milestone in the party's road to rehabilitation and restoration.

The messiah complex was only one of many serious problems the party faced, all of which required attention if it was to survive. Understanding the nature and scope of these other challenges highlights the importance of the steps taken to rebuild and restore the party from the 2006 defeat to the electoral victory of 2015. In many cases, it was the party executive and extra-parliamentary wing that took the lead on these issues, though the support of the political leadership was crucial for their success.

Nowhere was this more relevant than in the case of the party's need to modernize its operations and streamline its constitution.

The Myth of the Big Red Machine: Organizational Woes

As the party's national director, Steve MacKinnon, stated in 2011, "the Liberal Party is broken beyond repair and needs to be completely restructured if it is to survive.[9] This blunt acknowledgement of the party's status did not surprise many of its senior advisers. Nor was

MacKinnon describing recent developments. On the contrary, the Liberal Party's operational machinery had been in a state of gradual decline and dysfunction for many years, exacerbated by a constitution that had failed to keep pace with the times.

To be sure, the national party organization was always complicated by the fact that – unlike the Progressive Conservatives and the NDP – it was set up as a federal structure. This meant that the executives of the national party's provincial and territorial associations (PTAs) had considerable clout on the national executive. Moreover, the party's financial situation was extremely complicated due to cost-sharing arrangements among the various levels and the fact that the revenue and expenditure functions were governed by two separate bodies. Because party memberships were arranged through the PTAs, the party still had no national membership list by 1984, which meant fundraising was severely hampered.

In addition, as part and parcel of Pierre Trudeau's drive in the early 1970s to encourage political participation, additional layers had been added to the party's formal structure. While important, measures to highlight the party's openness to diversity, such as the creation of the Liberal Party's Women's Commission, Youth Commission, and Aboriginal Commission, not only increased the complexity of the decision-making process but affected membership rules and delegate and leadership selection as well. At the same time, and somewhat perversely, many grass-roots members of the party were becoming increasingly unhappy with what they perceived to be a massive shift in power and influence to the parliamentary wing and the leader under Trudeau, leaving the voluntary or extra-parliamentary wing with little or no influence on policy or other party matters. This long-standing conflict between the two wings of the party, which tended to be exacerbated when the party was in power, would prove to be a particularly significant issue during the decade under review, a period in which the party was continuously in opposition.

Meanwhile, the party's vaunted electoral machine, which for fifty years had had a reputation as a well-oiled professional organization, had long been able to rely on a dedicated and experienced team of volunteers at the riding level. But it was atrophying at an alarming rate. Many ridings effectively had no organization at all, while in others the "troops" were reduced to a diehard few or were not sufficiently motivated to produce the kind of clockwork organization and seamless effort for which the party had been known in the past. (As party president Alf Apps declared after the 2011 rout, "We lost the ground war. You can't win without boots on the ground.")[10]

Another aspect of the party's growing operational problem was its reliance on outdated campaign practices and technology. While the Liberals were still depending on genteel wine and cheese events and word-of-mouth to bring out volunteers at the riding level for each election, sometimes after the writ was dropped, both the Conservatives and the NDP had for years been using sophisticated computer technology and advanced practices to get out their volunteers and their vote. As famed Progressive Conservative strategist Dalton Camp recounted about his party's campaign director, Norm Atkins: "to walk from the Liberals' headquarters to Norm's offices in Ottawa was to step from the horse-and-buggy age into a jet aircraft factory."[11] Moreover, the Conservatives' state-of-the-art computer system "allowed [Atkins] to communicate policies or strategy to almost all of the riding associations across the country. The same computer system allowed him to raise funds or rally the troops by providing a national membership list."[12]

Not surprisingly, then, the Liberals' national office, which should have been a key factor in election operations as well as providing ongoing support for the extra-parliamentary wing and the grass-roots members, was increasingly irrelevant. This was partly due to the lack of technical resources and also to its drastically shrinking staff and budget. Party president Iona Campagnolo had highlighted this concern shortly after taking office in 1983, and yet the situation deteriorated still further over the next decade.[13]

The simple truth was that the vaunted Big Red Machine existed more in myth than in reality by 1984. The success of the Trudeau era had, in fact, led to national elections being run primarily out of the PMO rather than through the party. The party's problems came to a head with the departure of Trudeau and the 1984 leadership race, in which Trudeau disciple Jean Chrétien was pitted against John Turner, the pick of the party elites. Although Chrétien's loss in that leadership race could be attributed to a number of issues, the fact that Turner championed the cause of party reform and greater input from the volunteer wing of the party – and especially of the youth wing – undoubtedly played a role.

However, Turner's ability to effect change was almost immediately curtailed by the fact that the party lost power in a hastily convened federal election shortly after he assumed the leadership. As mentioned above, that loss was catastrophic and seen by many Liberals as an unforgivable sin. As former Moncton Liberal MP (and Chrétien supporter) Gary McCauley explained, "it was not simply that he lost, but the *way* he lost. He couldn't screw things up that badly and then expect us to let him have another go at it."[14] Unhappiness with Turner's leadership was reinforced by the personal animosity between Chrétien and

Turner supporters. This was so great that for the first time it overrode the well-known and long-standing Liberal tradition of supporting the leader and demonstrating party unity above all, unlike the Progressive Conservatives and their infamous Tory syndrome.[15] The result was that Turner's leadership was in question from day one, and the energy of his supporters was devoted full-time to a fight with caucus and party insurgents throughout the next four years.

Nevertheless, and true to the party's established cycle of defeat and renewal, the 1984 electoral defeat did initially lead to a tentative series of efforts by the party's extra-parliamentary wing to remedy the organizational problems. With the Liberals in opposition for at least one term, as Brian Mulroney's Progressive Conservatives had obtained a massive majority, the party's executive certainly recognized that restructuring and rehabilitation were necessary. Party president Iona Campagnolo swiftly launched the president's Committee for the Reform of the Liberal Party of Canada, declaring: "Our job is to responsibly establish new institutional arrangements to enable the Liberal Party of Canada to meet the challenges of the 80's and a new generation of liberalism."[16] Among other things, she highlighted the party's financial problems, the sorry state of the national office, and the difficulties caused by the lack of a national membership list as well as the lack of regional outreach capacity and failure to engage the grass-roots members.

On receipt of the committee's report in August 1985, Campagnolo then organized a special constitutional reform conference of the party in Halifax in November, with the intent of having party activists discuss the report's recommendations prior to the regularly scheduled biennial party convention in 1986. These recommendations included changes to membership, leadership convention rules, and the structure of the party's revenue and expenditure mechanisms as well as other significant constitutional modifications whose stated purpose was to modernize and streamline party operations.

While there was indeed discussion of the various recommendations at the Halifax conference, for the most part the whole issue of party reform was soon overshadowed by the intense internal conflict over Turner's leadership, which preoccupied everyone until the actual leadership review vote (required by the constitution) was held at the November 1986 biennial convention. As discussed in detail in *Divided Loyalties*,[17] the issue of the party's constitutional and organizational reform also took a back seat at the convention itself, as Turner and Chrétien followers jockeyed for support. Yet as Chrétien confidante Sergio Marchi later commented, removing Turner as leader was highly problematic, since no one would want to take his place given the state of the party.

Certainly Marchi himself had recommended against Chrétien doing so at that point. "The time was simply not right. The party had no money. The organization was in shambles."[18]

Turner's 76.5 per cent support at the leadership review was hard won, but it still bought only a short respite from the internal squabbling. With Prime Minister Brian Mulroney's subsequent tabling of the Meech Lake Accord, and Turner's controversial decision to support that constitutional package, both wings of the party took up an even more intense struggle for supremacy. This struggle included two caucus-led coup attempts (one, unbelievably, taking place in the middle of the 1988 election campaign), all of which made it clear to Canadians that the party was wracked with internal tension and not well positioned to govern.

Money Matters

The financing of political parties has long been an issue in Canada. Canadians have been singled out in the academic literature for their apparent lack of interest in political parties apart from elections, and their seeming belief that those parties will finance themselves. Historically, only a minuscule percentage of traditional Liberal and Progressive Conservative Party members ever contributed financially to those parties.[19] At the same time, by the 1960s, many Canadians were expressing concern that those same parties were dependent on large corporations and a few wealthy but largely anonymous donors.[20] The situation became even more complicated by the 1970s, when the cost of election campaigns increased dramatically as television ads and other media coverage, as well as extensive travel by a leader and accompanying entourage, became the norm.

Pierre Trudeau's Liberal government first tackled the problem in 1974 when it introduced the Elections Expenses Act. This initiative addressed the expenditure side of the equation by limiting the amount political parties could spend during federal elections, on both their national campaigns and the campaigns of their individual candidates. The legislation was intended to accomplish three objectives: to prevent overall spending by parties from spiralling out of control, to provide a reasonably level playing field for all parties during election campaigns, and to introduce some measure of transparency in the spending behaviour of all parties by requiring them to report revenue on a regular basis.

These various measures to control *spending* by political parties had been reasonably well received and were firmly integrated into the political process by the time the Liberal Party found itself in opposition in

2006. One indication of this general acceptance is the fact that the Mulroney Conservatives, in power between 1984 and 1993, made no move to alter these provisions.

On the other side of the equation, Trudeau's legislation also introduced some measures related to the *funding* of political parties. For the first time it provided tax credits to individual Canadians for their donations to a political party. The move was intended to encourage political participation in a country with a traditionally low level of political engagement among citizens, especially in comparison with other Western democracies.[21] This bill also marked the first move towards adopting the European model of public funding for political parties, providing rebates for both the national parties and their individual candidates based on a per-vote formula. These measures, too, became well entrenched in the party system and proved useful in further limiting the amount of money parties needed to raise from other sources.

It soon became apparent, however, that public subsidies alone could not provide sufficient funds for ongoing party operations between elections, particularly given the rapid pace of technological change and the growing perception that parties needed to maintain a high profile at all times. As a result, all political parties continued to develop ways to raise additional revenue.

The traditional dependence of the Liberals and Progressive Conservatives on large corporate donations to bridge this financial gap, and of the NDP's similar dependence on contributions from unions, was well known.[22] But when the Progressive Conservatives were in opposition for nearly a decade, after the 1993 election, they were increasingly unable to attract corporate funding. As a result, they turned to a fundraising process based on membership lists and direct mail appeals, a system that had actually begun under Tory campaign strategist John Laschinger in the late 1970s, but had never before been considered crucial to their ongoing financial viability.

With the advent of the Reform and Alliance Parties in the early 1990s, this emphasis on direct mail as a means of raising revenue – through large numbers of small donations from individual contributors – took on far more importance. Based in western Canada, these new parties had few contacts with corporate Canada but considerable influence with a wide range of special interest groups whose members transferred their allegiance (and funds) to the new parties. Much has been written about the phenomenal fundraising ability of these successors to the old Progressive Conservative Party, and especially of Stephen Harper's new Conservative Party of Canada. As academic and former Harper adviser Tom Flanagan has noted, "the reason for the Conservatives' huge advantage in overall party revenue – and their relative independence from state financing – [is] the party's tremendous success at grassroots fundraising."[23]

By contrast, the Liberal Party's inability to make a similar breakthrough despite spending more than a decade in opposition is a cautionary tale. Having benefited from the fact that it was in power for most of the post-war era, the party had managed to get by with support from its corporate donors and wealthy individuals for so long that there was little sense of urgency about adopting the new model of financing party activities. Suddenly faced with serious financial problems when the party found itself in opposition under leader John Turner, party president Michel Robert attempted to increase revenue through a series of leader's dinners across the country and expanded activities of the Laurier Club, a select venue for wealthy donors. According to Robert, by 1988 these events had become "the single most important source of revenue" for the party.[24] Nevertheless, this revenue was far from sufficient to fund ongoing party activities, and the party's debt load reached a staggering $6 million.

The failure to increase revenue from grass-roots contributors and the near complete absence of corporate contributions forced the party executive to address the shortfall by drastically curtailing expenses at the national headquarters yet again. Meanwhile Robert – who admitted that by 1997 the party was effectively bankrupt – managed to reorganize its debt load with various creditors.[25] Although fears were expressed that the party might not even be able to mount a national election campaign in 1988, this realignment of debt did provide sufficient breathing space. The campaign was respectably but tightly financed. In a sign of things to come, the party was unable to pay for continuous polling throughout the campaign and, at the end, had no money left to fund a final round of media advertisements to counter the last-ditch ad campaign of the Mulroney Conservatives attacking Turner. As several election post-mortems concluded, including the one presented by the party's Strategy Committee Chair, Senator Michael Kirby, the party's lack of funds may well have played a role in the extent of the Liberals' loss if not the actual election outcome.[26]

Nevertheless, Turner's time as leader came to an end and a subsequent leadership race selected Jean Chrétien. Shortly afterwards, Terry Mercer, a professional fundraiser (and future senator) was hired by the party's new national director, George Young, to introduce serious grass-roots funding measures. However, this subsequent effort was only slightly more successful than under Turner. According to Mercer, there were simply too many problems with direct mail for the party to overcome at that time, including the lack of proper membership lists and the diffuse pattern of party organization and revenue sharing. As a result, Mercer too emphasized ongoing corporate contributions and Laurier Club donations, but he also introduced an innovative experiment, national media ads on specific topics. In his view:

> We needed to emphasize specific government policy positions to get any kind of response. The so-called "fish wars" was our first big hit. Our costs were half of our revenues, so there was a 100% return. That's not bad. By contrast direct mail accounted for 5% of our revenue, and we maybe could have increased that to 8% at best, with a great deal of effort.[27]

Despite all of these alternative efforts, the party was only able to fund a fully competitive national election campaign in 1993 by selling its ownership of office space on Laurier Avenue in Ottawa, space that had been purchased with the intention of establishing a permanent national headquarters (with the sale of the venue, the party HQ moved to "temporary" rental quarters on Metcalfe Street where it remains to this day, while the NDP and the Conservative Party each have their own permanent headquarters).

Interviewed several years later, Mercer highlighted what he considered to be another handicap faced by the party when the Liberals were in power. He argued that direct mail campaigns are typically more successful when the objective is to attack or undermine a government policy or action rather than support one. In a sense, then, the Liberals were victims of their own political success. He noted that both the Reform and Alliance parties were not constrained by such a dilemma and suggested that the new Conservative Party (which emerged from various mergers of the right) would not be either, at least as long as it remained in opposition. In addition, as another senior Liberal noted, the Conservatives typically received donations from an astonishing 50 per cent of their membership, while the Liberals were lucky to receive financial donations from 5 per cent of their actual members, making direct mail campaigns with the broader public an even more obvious concern for them.

Certainly the Liberal Party's continued dependence on large corporate donations throughout the 1990s was recognized as a problem by the party executive, who were well aware of the other parties' far superior grass-roots fundraising efforts. "After all, we were hardly going to be in power forever," Lloyd Posno noted.[28] Still, their efforts to introduce direct mail initiatives and obtain grass-roots funding continued to fall far short of their needs or expectations. At the same time, benefiting from the advantage of being in power, the party raised more than enough funds from corporations and wealthy individuals to spend the allowable limit in the 1997 and 2000 elections, so the matter was still not seen as urgent. Meanwhile, two successive party presidents, Don Johnston and Dan Hays, had followed through on commitments they made to rationalize the expenditure management system and eliminate the party's remaining debt. At a minimum, then, it looked as if the party might be moving onto more solid financial ground despite its direct-mail limitations.

Then, in January 2003, an unexpected complication was added to the mix when Prime Minister Jean Chrétien made good on his own earlier commitment to introduce the first legislation dealing with political party finances since the 1974 Trudeau bill. He had made this commitment in spring 2002 when his government introduced an eight-point ethics package to address growing public concern about perceived flaws in the democratic process. He repeated it in June 2002 at the caucus retreat in Chicoutimi, where he also announced he would be stepping down as leader in December 2003. At the Chicoutimi meeting, Chrétien declared that "the real democratic deficit" was campaign financing, which he believed was spiralling out of control and would soon rival that of its American counterparts if strong counter measures were not taken. Moreover, he believed it was only when the Liberal Party was in power and when, as departing leader, he would be seen to have no vested interest that such a bill could successfully be introduced.

This concern about the so-called democratic deficit had also been taken up by his leadership rival, Paul Martin. But Martin had stressed parliamentary reform over electoral reform, and party financing had not been among Martin's top priorities. Nevertheless, Chrétien was somewhat surprised by the negative reaction from some members of his own party that followed his introduction of this legislation.

Chrétien's legislation focused on *contributions* to political parties, eliminating those from corporations or unions and limiting individuals to $5,000. To compensate parties for the inevitable decrease in revenue, he also increased the amount of public funding for them through the rebate system first introduced in 1974. Lastly, Bill C-24 contained regulations governing the financing and activities of constituency associations, leadership races, and nomination contests.

These measures had been suggested for some time, including in the report of the Royal Commission on Electoral Reform and Party Financing that had been tabled a decade earlier. Both Quebec and Manitoba had already introduced limits on contributions to provincial parties. In Europe, virtually all EU member states had provided public funding for political parties for many years, and most prohibited any additional form of fundraising. In this context, it is also important to note that the United States, unlike the democracies of western Europe, does not limit either party expenditures or fundraising efforts. As a result, party politics in that country have increasingly become a free-for-all in which individual congressmen and women are pressured to take specific policy positions by key contributors in exchange for their financial backing, and must spend more than half of their term fundraising for the next campaign. Moreover, leadership contests, as the recent examples of Republicans Mitt Romney and Donald Trump demonstrated, have become the domain of the rich and the super-rich.[29]

This disturbing situation motivated Chrétien to introduce his legislation, which received strong support from many quarters, including the party's former chief financial officers, Lloyd Posno and Mike Robinson. However, party president Stephen LeDrew denounced the original bill as "dumb as a bag of hammers" and even lobbied Conservative and NDP MPs to join him in suggesting a number of amendments that he believed would make the legislation revenue-neutral. Meanwhile, many Liberal MPs expressed serious concerns about their ability to raise funds at the constituency level if the same limitations were imposed there. As a result, the revised version of the bill allowed both union and corporate contributions at the local level to a maximum of $1,000, and individual contributions to national parties were capped at $5,000. In the end, several other amendments were accepted to accommodate MPs' concerns and, although some Liberals – including supporters of Paul Martin – continued to have misgivings, the bill became law in January 2004, in time for the next federal election.

It is not possible to know whether Chrétien's plan would have been successful in the end. Although the $5,000 limit on individual contributions would undoubtedly have left the party in reasonably good shape, most observers agreed that it would still be necessary for the party to improve its grass-roots fundraising efforts quickly if it was to remain competitive. But his plan was not in force for long enough to accumulate sufficient evidence. Instead, with the defeat of the Martin government in 2006, the new Conservative government of Stephen Harper took direct aim at this legislation. Those who knew Harper well were not surprised, citing his ruthless determination to eliminate the Liberal Party as his principal opponent. "He hates the Liberal Party," his former adviser Keith Beardsley stated, "and I would say his aim from day one – and I don't think anyone would disagree – was to break the brand."[30]

Recognizing that fundraising was an Achilles heel for the Liberal Party, Harper moved swiftly to inflict as much damage as possible. In

April 2006, in one of the first acts of his government, he introduced the Federal Accountability Act. An omnibus bill in which measures to amend Chrétien's legislation were buried, it drastically lowered the limitations agreed upon earlier by all parties in Bill C-24. Individual contributions would be reduced from $5,000 to $1,000, and corporate and union contributions were now banned outright even at the constituency level.

It is difficult to overestimate the devastating impact of these changes on the fortunes of all other federal parties, but they were especially serious for the Liberal Party. That impact was evident almost immediately. In the first quarter of 2007, shortly after the Liberals' 2006 defeat, the Conservatives raised more than twice the total of all other parties combined, at $8.9 million. The NDP managed to raise $1.9 million but the Liberals, despite their status as the Official Opposition, could only bring in $1.8 million. Even more revealing was the fact that the Conservatives obtained their funding from more than forty thousand individuals while the Liberals and NDP were only able to obtain roughly ten thousand and thirteen thousand individual contributions, respectively.[31]

The Liberal Party's money problems mounted over the next decade, and it would not be an exaggeration to say that the party was dangerously close to being financially crippled. A lack of financial resources also exacerbated other problems facing it, including its hopelessly outdated approach to election campaigns, discussed above, and its inability to launch outreach programs in the regions, relevant to the long-standing issue of declining support addressed below.

The Shrinking Base

The waning of the party's organizational capacity also reflected the steady decline in its ability to portray itself as a truly national party. The Liberal Party's efforts to define itself as a "big tent" party with something to offer to every region of the country had been successful throughout most of the twentieth century. As a rule, when it did not take a majority of seats in a region, it would finish a strong second, reinforcing the notion that the Liberals were capable of forming a government that would be nationally representative. Even in western Canada, where its platform typically had the least traction, in the second half of the twentieth century it would normally obtain at least 25–30 per cent of the popular vote, making it a credible alternative, particularly as the seats won in the region would generally be split between the Progressive Conservatives and the CCF/NDP.[32]

As Carty has argued so persuasively, however, the Liberals' ongoing electoral success, and the *appearance* of being a national party, masked a steady decline in voter support across the country over several decades. From an average of 52 per cent during the three Laurier victories at the beginning of the twentieth century, the Liberal Party saw its share of the popular vote steadily decline until the three majority victories of Jean Chrétien were achieved with roughly 40 per cent of that vote. The victories also masked a growing and increasingly broad decline in regional representation for the Liberals, which would become obvious in their post-2006 sojourn in the political wilderness. The shrinking base of the party was not only evident in western Canada but, thanks in part to various initiatives of the Harper Conservatives, also accelerating in rural areas and among new Canadians.[33]

Of these, the party's problems in the west were clearly the most long-standing and intractable. In fact, some would argue that the origins of the Liberals' organizational difficulties actually began under Lester Pearson, when the west failed to deliver any seats to the party and caused its minority government status, despite the Liberals' having taken 41 per cent of the popular vote nationally.

Under Pearson's successor, Pierre Trudeau, the party's difficulty with what by now was referred to as "western alienation" continued unabated and actually worsened. This was due, in part, to Liberal policies such as the wildly unpopular National Energy Program. But it was also the result of an increasing tendency on the part of provincial premiers to portray the federal government as the enemy. In the post-war era, that enemy was normally the Liberals who, in turn, possessed few western MPs to defend them.

Yet for a long time the party's growing problem with the west could be largely ignored. This was especially true under Trudeau, since the party's great electoral strength in the rest of the country, and notably Quebec – to say nothing of the first-past-the-post electoral system – rendered this lack of western support electorally unimportant. In the 1980 election, for example, the Trudeau Liberals formed a majority government of 147 seats with slightly more than 44 per cent of the total vote, taking all but one of 75 seats in Quebec but only 2 in western Canada. Indeed, Trudeau was obliged to appoint senators to cabinet to provide representation from western provinces.

Nor did the situation improve under John Turner, Jean Chrétien, or Paul Martin, all of whom were clearly aware of the issue. In his first election as leader in 1984, Turner actually chose to run in the British Columbia riding of Vancouver Quadra, despite having represented a Montreal riding during his time as a minister under Trudeau. Although the election itself was a disaster for the Liberals, Turner did manage to win his seat and elect a few other Liberal MPs to the caucus from that province. Meanwhile, an effort by the extra-parliamentary wing to build linkages (and hopefully electoral strength) in the west resulted in an innovative "twinning" process whereby the ridings of sitting Liberal MPs from the rest of the country were matched with unheld ridings in that region. However, given the lack of financial resources or on-the-ground personnel, little came of this initial effort.

During the early years of the Chrétien mandate, the parliamentary wing attempted to expand on this idea by creating a Western Communications Project run out of the Caucus Research Bureau. Its two-fold purpose was to seek out and develop a network of individuals in the four western provinces to provide input to the caucus on emerging regional issues and, simultaneously, to use the network as a means of communicating Liberal policies and actions to the region. With few western MPs, and extremely limited national media penetration in the region, this alternative method of obtaining and disseminating information in the west was seen as an ideal method for communicating the rationale for Liberal positions, as well as building valuable contacts in advance of the next election. Support for the trial project by the Liberals' small western caucus was initially substantial, but financial considerations and the increasing pressure of other policy issues caused the program to be mothballed in less than two years, abruptly abandoning the many regional contacts that had been established.

During his time as party president during the Chrétien era, Senator Dan Hays of Alberta also attempted to launch a second western outreach program for the party. As he later explained, he saw his tenure in office as being driven by two objectives that he described as "financial consolidation" and "expanding the party's base." Under Hays, the party's debt was eliminated by 1996, one year ahead of his own schedule, but his second objective was far more problematic and ultimately unsuccessful. Once the debt was cleared, Hays introduced a new feature to the party's organization. "Before 1997," he recalled, "there was a trade-off between debt reduction and regional organization. We didn't have much to begin with but we had to let it go. In retrospect, I wonder if we should have tried to keep some of it and reduce the debt more slowly."[34] Hays introduced the concept of full-time, paid party workers operating in Saskatchewan, Alberta, and BC to develop networks, build up party membership, and identify potential election campaign workers. "We had some first-rate people. I thought it was self-evident why we needed to start building our support right away after the election. You can't wait until the next one is due to start doing that kind of spadework," Hays recalled ruefully. However, resistance from the executives of the provincial wings of the party soon doomed the exercise and, like the Western Communications Project, it was abruptly abandoned and the bright young Liberal workers were lost to the party.

Despite this, with Jean Chrétien's unprecedented three successive majority governments, it did appear that the Liberal Party had little to be concerned about. Yet Chrétien himself was evidently aware of the significance of the declining vote share and the party's troubles in the west. After the 2000 election, he announced he would deliberately spend more time in western Canada and told his caucus to temper their criticism of the Reform/Alliance party MPs because "We need these guys."[35] Indeed, with the vote split on the right following the collapse of the Progressive Conservatives in 1993, Chrétien's government effectively won majorities because the Liberals faced no national opposition.

When Chrétien's successor Paul Martin took over in 2004, he wasted little time in demonstrating his concern with Liberal fortunes in the west. Prompted by several of his senior aides who hailed originally from the region, as well as by long-time supporter and Liberal MP Ralph Goodale of Saskatchewan, Martin declared shortly after winning the 2003 leadership race that "no matter what else I do as prime minister, if western alienation is the same as it is at the end of my term as it is now, I will not believe I have succeeded."[36] To that end, he announced that he would delay calling a federal election until the scheduled electoral boundary redistribution could be implemented in 2004. This was a move widely seen to favour the west since there would be an increase in the number of seats in Alberta and BC. (The fact that Ontario would receive an even greater increase apparently escaped many western commentators who approved of the plan.)

Other concrete measures proposed by Martin were less successful. His commitment to outdo Chrétien with a prime ministerial presence in the west led to a number of bizarre proposals, including a semi-annual road show. Another, the idea of a permanent western satellite PMO to be set up in Calgary, led to a farcical situation in which the party's office was bombarded with requests for information about possible job openings until Goodale bluntly stated that this option was not on. At the end of the day, however, the increased attention – and the increased number of party memberships that Martin's aides regularly trumpeted – did not translate into increased votes or Liberal seats in the region. In both the 2004 and 2006 elections, Martin's Liberals took only fourteen out of eighty-eight seats in the four western provinces, the same number as Chrétien in 2000.

This failure to increase their support in western Canada became more significant for the Liberals as their traditional strength in other regions and among various communities also began to decline in the 1990s and contributed to the three successive defeats of 2006, 2008, and 2011. This erosion of support, in turn, was in no small measure related to the party's growing policy confusion on two key fronts, national unity (where attempts to appease soft nationalists in Quebec cost it many seats in that province) and social progress (where the apparent inability to counter the right-wing parable of new Conservatives – that good government is small government, with low taxes and no budget deficits – left it unable to offer compelling platforms that would appeal to many voters in Ontario and the Atlantic). It is to this fifth and final problem that we now turn.

Liberal Values and the Liberal Identity Crisis

It could be argued that almost all of the problems identified above might conceivably have been overcome in any one of the 2006, 2008, or 2011 elections if only the Liberals had been able to present a compelling alternative to the Harper Conservatives. After all, Harper's party was confined to a minority for the first two elections, and even his majority of 2011 was achieved with less than 40 per cent of the popular vote. In fact, it was obtained with only 2 per cent more votes than in 2008 when his party was returned with another minority. In addition, the Conservatives actually lost support and seats in both Quebec and British Columbia in 2011. More importantly, this was the first time that any federal party had formed a majority government without substantial support from Quebec. Instead, the Conservatives had crafted a majority based on a west-Ontario coalition, most notably by taking almost all of the seats in the suburban/exurban region known as the Greater Toronto Area (GTA).[37]

Why, then, were the Liberals unable to take advantage of Canadians' ongoing suspicions about the Conservative agenda and their inherent dislike of Harper personally, issues that had held his party to a minority for the first two of those elections? Harper himself seemed to recognize the voters' reluctance to give him a majority when he unwisely declared during the 2008 campaign that it was safe to do so because he would be constrained by a Liberal-dominated Senate, bureaucracy, and Supreme Court.[38] Yet in 2011, increasingly determined to replace the Harper Conservatives at all costs, voters had turned to Jack Layton and the NDP rather than the Liberals. More ominously still, as Clarke and others have noted, fewer than one in five voters had identified themselves as a supporter of the federal Liberals before the 2011 election, down even from the two in five who did so before the 2008 election. But as Clarke also notes, "the missing Liberals had not been replaced by large groups of identifiers with other political parties."[39] Indeed, long-standing Liberal voters had actually stayed home in droves.

This brings us back to the claim made by Peter C. Newman, that liberalism itself was dead, as demonstrated by the 2011 electoral disaster. Instead, the data outlined by Clarke – as well as the stunning results of the 2015 election – suggest quite the opposite conclusion. It was the failure of the singer (the Liberal Party) and not the song (liberalism) that was at the heart of the party's electoral disasters in the early twenty-first century, the causes of which are examined in this book.

This conclusion, in turn, is one that calls into question policy decisions made by party leaders over several years prior to the 2006 election, decisions that had the effect of undoing much of the Liberals' long history as the party of national unity and social progress, to say nothing of managerial competence.

As LeDuc et al. have outlined,[40] the three key pillars of voters' electoral choice in Canada – once managerial competence has been established – have long been "the party best able to manage national unity," "the party best able to manage the economy," and "the party best able to deliver social progress." Of these three pillars, the Liberal Party has traditionally had the advantage on two (national unity and social progress) while the Conservatives have often been able to prevail when economic difficulties have been the dominant issue.

For the Liberal Party, national unity and nation-building have always been a top priority, and Canadians have long recognized this reality. Moreover, since the time of Laurier, the party's attention to this issue had earned it the consistent support of Quebec voters, providing a crucial stronghold in federal elections (in 1980, for example, Pierre Trudeau was re-elected with seventy-four of the seventy-five seats in the province, despite the presence of a PQ government in Quebec City). While policies such as *l'alternance* and the introduction of official bilingualism helped to ensure the party's continued support among Quebecers, the rest of the country recognized the party's ability to "manage" Quebec and to create compelling symbols of national identity. More recently, this was perhaps most clearly demonstrated by Pierre Trudeau's vigorous rejection of Quebec nationalism and dominant role in defeating a Quebec separatist referendum. Similarly, his subsequent introduction of the Charter of Rights and Freedoms in a constitutional reform package provided Canadians with one of their most important symbols of Canadian identity.[41]

Trudeau's later opposition to the Mulroney Conservatives' proposed Meech Lake and Charlottetown Accords ("*Canada* is the distinct society") was demonstrably the tipping point in public opinion. The morning after the Charlottetown referendum was defeated, *Globe and Mail* journalist Jeffrey Simpson recognized this fact when he declared "the Trudeau vision won."[42]

Yet as mentioned earlier, Liberal leader John Turner had supported Meech Lake while in opposition during the Mulroney era, which proved to be his undoing and, at least temporarily, that of the party as well. Although his "soft" nationalist Quebec advisers such as MP Raymond Garneau and communications director Michelle Tremblay convinced Turner that support for the deal was essential for the party's continued success in that province, this proved to be a serious mistake. The decision cost Turner both caucus and grass-roots support, and the ensuing widely publicized internecine warfare cost the party votes. After Trudeau's seventy-four seats in Quebec in 1980, the Liberals under Turner fell to seventeen seats in 1984 and then, despite his support for Meech Lake, to a record-low twelve seats in 1988. By contrast, after Turner was replaced as leader by Meech Lake opponent and Trudeau acolyte Jean Chrétien, the party's fortunes in Quebec improved to nineteen, twenty-six, and thirty-six seats respectively in the three elections under Chrétien's watch.

This was particularly significant since Chrétien, like Trudeau, had been obliged to defend Canadian federalism and national unity in another Quebec sovereignty referendum in 1995. Subsequently, Chrétien introduced the Clarity Act, which was highly popular in both Quebec and the rest of Canada, as part of his ten-point plan to reassert a federal presence in Quebec and decrease support for separatism (this so-called Plan B, it should be noted, was shepherded by Chrétien's intergovernmental affairs minister, Stéphane Dion).

The plan paid off. When Chrétien left office in late 2003, polls consistently showed support for separation in Quebec had fallen to its lowest levels since the 1970s. Separatist premier Lucien Bouchard resigned, saying that there were no "winning conditions," and his successor, Bernard Landry, declared that there would not be another referendum in the foreseeable future. Noted Quebec journalist Chantal Hébert wrote that "the Chrétien agenda is even more popular than elsewhere in the country" and "the Bloc will be fighting for its life" in the upcoming 2004 election.[43]

Canadians might well be forgiven, then, for being confused about the party's national unity stance when Paul Martin, who replaced Chrétien in late 2003, once again inexplicably took the side of soft nationalists and repudiated the Trudeau vision (as one senior Liberal commented, "If it had not worked for Turner, why would he think it would work for him?"). Martin, it will be recalled, was among the small minority of Liberals who supported Meech Lake and opposed the Clarity Act. As leader, he promptly accepted a number of soft nationalists as Liberal candidates in that province, including some who had voted yes in the last Quebec referendum. Among them perhaps the most astonishing was Jean Lapierre. A former Liberal MP who left the party in high dudgeon after Jean Chrétien's leadership victory and the failure of Meech Lake, Lapierre had actually been the co-founder of the Bloc Québécois with Lucien Bouchard. Retired from politics for several years, he was nevertheless brought back by Martin and was even appointed the leader's Quebec lieutenant and left to run the party's 2004 campaign in that province. Despite high expectations of increased Liberal representation, the party's seat count fell by nearly half, from thirty-six to twenty-one, and then plummeted to a record low of ten in 2006. The party's Quebec fortress was lost for the next nine years in opposition as it struggled to reaffirm its ability to manage the national unity file in the eyes of Canadian voters.

Similarly, the Liberals' longstanding advantage as "the party best able to promote social progress" had also taken a beating in the years leading up to the 2006 defeat. While the Progressive Conservatives had never held the advantage there, the NDP had often challenged the Liberals on this front. The Liberals' tactical response had been nothing short of brilliant on many occasions, appropriating and implementing some of the NDP's best ideas. Most Canadians, however, were only concerned with the result, and the NDP received little or no credit because voters knew that the vast majority of the programs of the welfare state were implemented by Liberal governments.

However, with the return to power of the Chrétien Liberals in 1993, the party faced a conundrum. The Mulroney Conservatives, who had been in power for nine years, had drastically increased both the deficit and the national debt, despite having been elected on a platform of fiscal responsibility. Combined with the effects of a global economic downturn, this left the country's finances in rocky shape and the party of social progress facing difficult choices. Many in Chrétien's cabinet were highly resistant to the idea of spending cuts despite increased pressure from international organizations to trim the country's debt-to-GDP ratio. Ultimately, Chrétien's government accepted the need for austerity and actually eliminated the deficit in four years. But this economic "success" came at a cost to social program funding, and was achieved in large measure by downloading some of that cost to the provinces.

This atypical Liberal agenda did not go unnoticed. It took the remainder of Chrétien's time in office to restore the Liberals' credentials in this area with the premiers and the general public. This was accomplished by an aggressive program of spending, the so-called deficit dividend, primarily through increased funding for existing social programs and the introduction of a number of popular new ones such as the Child Tax Credit, the Millennium Scholarships, and Canada Research Chairs.

Here, too, Senator Keith Davey's famous dictum that the Liberal party should always "run from the left but govern from the centre" must be kept in mind. This approach had resonated with generations of Liberals and served the party well at the polls. Much of the party's credibility as a competent manager of governmental affairs flowed from the fact that Canadian liberalism had always been seen to value moderation and balance as much as tolerance, consultation, and compromise. Far from representing a "mushy middle," the Liberal party's approach was seen by the average Canadian voter as the ideal type of political compromise – the epitome of politics as the art of the possible. In the case of the Chrétien government's cuts to social programs, for example, the saving grace had been Chrétien's decision to trumpet the use of the deficit dividend after 1997 for two purposes: half for new spending on social programs, and half for further debt reduction, a "balanced" decision that proved extremely popular and afforded the party considerable protection from attacks by opponents on either the right or left.

The Liberals' moderate and balanced approach had been represented within the party itself, where it was home to both so-called social and business Liberals. Traditionally, Liberal prime ministers had always taken care to ensure that their cabinets contained a good representation from both wings of the party in order to maintain that continued balance, as demonstrated by the appointment of John Turner, a business liberal, as finance minister under Pierre Trudeau and by the presence of Paul Martin in the same capacity under Jean Chrétien.

With the arrival of Paul Martin as leader in late 2003, this balance appeared to be in doubt. Not only was Martin's newly appointed cabinet missing any strong proponents on the social liberal side (almost all of whom had been deliberately overlooked because of their support for Chrétien), Martin himself was seen as a business liberal. This was particularly significant since, as Jean Chrétien noted on more than one occasion, "We have had leaders from both camps and one has been conspicuously more successful than the other."[44] Simply put, past election results suggested that Liberal leaders who appeared to be more socially progressive, such as Pearson, Trudeau, and Chrétien, had been far more successful at winning elections than those chosen by the party from the business liberal wing, such as Turner and Martin. Yet this hard-earned knowledge also appears to have been lost on the party and its elites in the years spent in opposition under the Harper Conservatives.

Last but hardly least, the Liberal Party in the twenty-first century was confronted with a new challenge to its philosophical underpinnings – the far-right economic and social conservatism of the Harper Conservatives. For a variety of reasons, the Liberal leadership of the day appeared to be unequal to the task of defending and adapting liberalism in this new context. Nowhere was this more evident than in the party's inability to respond to the new conservative mantra of shrinking government, lower taxes, and the elimination of deficits. A succession of Liberal politicians attempted to square the circle without refuting or even addressing these key underlying conservative economic assumptions. The result was a series of Liberal platforms that lacked credibility, and a party that seemed unable to adapt its philosophy to new realities, something that had been its traditional strength in the past.

And so, in the aftermath of the 2011 election, this lengthy list of ongoing and new problems facing the party caused many supporters and objective critics to conclude the writing was on the wall. The party had passed its "best before" date and could not possibly hope to rebuild and rehabilitate itself, far less recoup its losses, in time for the next federal election a mere four years hence.

Yet that is exactly what happened. What follows is the story of that remarkable turnaround, achieved against all odds, culminating in a historic campaign in 2015 and the beginning of a new Liberal era under Justin Trudeau.

2 Unanticipated Consequences: The 2006 Leadership Race

It was a no-brainer. The four leading candidates were an American, an NDPer, a college dropout, and the Man Who Saved Canada.
– Mark Marissen, interview with author, 2018

Dion campaign manager Mark Marissen's description of the choice faced by Liberals in the 2006 leadership race may well have been the most blunt, but his opinion was shared by almost all of Stéphane Dion's key supporters. Expressed in somewhat more diplomatic terms by Dion's campaign co-chair Don Boudria, a former Liberal MP and Chrétien cabinet minister, "Ignatieff was not Canadian enough and Rae was not Liberal enough."[1] These shared impressions reveal the primary reason why neither of the two media "favourites" was able to win the leadership in the end. As Boudria said, "there were just too many people who would never consider them. They were nobody's second choice."[2]

An equally important reason why many chose to support Stéphane Dion was revealed by Marissen's emphasis on Dion's role as minister of intergovernmental affairs under Jean Chrétien. His description of Dion as "the man who saved Canada" succinctly demonstrates the ongoing importance of the national unity issue for many Liberals. Don Boudria similarly referred to Dion as "my hero" and "Mr. National Unity." A long-serving Ontario MP, Boudria was joined by former Quebec Liberal MP Eleni Bakopanos and campaign co-chair Dahlia Stein of Montreal in explaining that their support for Dion was based first and foremost on the latter's role as "the national unity minister" and "the architect of the Clarity Act." Similarly, Andrew Bevan, his future chief of staff, described Dion's appeal for him as being based in no small measure on "his commitment to Canada."[3]

Nor was this rationale for supporting Dion limited to Liberals in central Canada. Saskatchewan Liberal leader David Karwacki, for example, declared that he was supporting Dion because "his performance as a minister has been exemplary, particularly on the separatist file. I think he has gone after separatists in an unwavering way. He came to the aid of the country, really, when that needed to happen, and I think he did a very good job there."[4] Anti-free trade activist David Orchard ultimately chose to support Dion for much the same reasons. The prominent Saskatchewan farmer, a two-time candidate for the leadership of the Progressive Conservative Party, specifically stated that his decision to move to the Liberals and "help elect Stéphane Dion" was based on the latter's "role in the Clarity Act and the national unity file" as well as his environmental record and support for the Wheat Board.[5] Orchard's long-time campaign manager Marjaleena Repo agreed that Dion's record on national unity was easily as important as his support for environmental policies. She added that the two issues taken together made Dion an easy sell for the anti-Harper, old-school Progressive Conservatives in western Canada whom she and Orchard had mobilized once again, but this time to elect a new Liberal leader.[6]

Yet the odds were clearly stacked against Dion at the outset, and all of Dion's closest advisers and organizers knew it only too well. To begin with, hardly any caucus members supported Dion's candidacy. As his co-chair Don Boudria explained, "We had nobody. We had less than nobody."[7] Dion also had very shallow roots in the party, no money, no pan-Canadian network, and not even the semblance of a campaign organization. Indeed, in March 2016, when the party executive announced the leadership convention would be held in Montreal on 2–3 December of that year, few if any Liberal insiders expected Dion even to enter the race. As one delegate who ended up supporting Dion on the third and deciding ballot at the convention was heard to exclaim, "If you had told me nine months ago that I would be voting for him I would have laughed and said 'don't be ridiculous.' No one could have predicted this."

The Unexpected Candidate

The party executive may have announced the start of the official leadership contest in March 2006, but the race to replace Paul Martin had actually begun long before. For some, it began even before he snatched defeat from the jaws of victory in the January 2006 election that saw Stephen Harper obtain a slim minority. It was not supposed to end that way. Martin was expected to lead the party to another majority, having taken over the reins from Jean Chrétien in December 2003. But instead of an even larger majority, based on an anticipated resurgence of support for the party in Quebec (which did not materialize), his shaky performance in the 2004 election led to a Liberal minority and a steady decline in popular support as his government lurched from one crisis to another, many of them self-inflicted. The 2006 election merely put an end to this downward spiral.

Whether Martin's failure was due to the poisoned chalice he had been handed by Chrétien in the form of the sponsorship scandal (as some of his followers maintained), or whether it was the result of hubris and incompetence on the part of his closest advisers (as others argued) remains a moot point. But everyone agreed that it was a humiliating defeat that did not sit well with Liberals of all stripes.

After Martin stepped down, however, there were many more-experienced and well-known leadership hopefuls than Stéphane Dion waiting in the wings. Some could see the writing on the wall and began organizing behind the scenes well before the party's 2006 defeat. One senior organizer even raised the possibility of Michael Ignatieff's return to Canada, and eventual assumption of the leader's mantle, as early as October 2004.

Once again Liberals appeared to be looking for a saviour to lead them out of the wilderness. The long list of candidates frequently cited by party pundits included Liberal heavyweights from both the social progressive left (Brian Tobin, Allan Rock, Martin Cauchon) and the business right (John Manley, Frank McKenna) wings of the party. Virtually no one expected all of these serious contenders to demur, especially given the Harper Conservatives' tenuous grasp on power. But that is exactly what happened. One by one the heavy hitters declined to enter the race for a variety of stated reasons. Many observers believed their real reasons were an unwillingness to serve as Opposition Leader, or their knowledge that the party was broke and in no shape to contest another election in the foreseeable future.[8]

This startling development was followed by a brief period in which such unlikely individuals as Belinda Stronach, the recently converted Liberal MP who had crossed the floor from the Conservatives the year before to become a minister in the Martin government, were reported to be considering a leadership bid. These candidacies did not materialize either. Soon there was mounting concern that a "succession gap" was emerging. However, Liberals' fears were put to rest as a field of no fewer than eleven candidates eventually emerged to compete for the brass ring.

At first blush, only two, Bob Rae and Michael Ignatieff, were seen as potential winners. Both men had significant support from party elites (such as Senator David Smith and former party president Alf Apps for Ignatieff, and former senior Chrétien advisers John Rae and Eddie Goldenberg for Rae) and went into the race with substantial caucus backing (Ignatieff began the race with the support of a remarkable forty-nine MPs, while Rae counted twenty-six). The remainder of the field were often described as second-string candidates hoping to position themselves for a cabinet post in the next Liberal government. They included relatively unknown backbench Liberal MPs Joe Volpe, Caroline Bennett, Hedy Fry, Maurizio Bevilaqua, and John Godfrey, as well as former hockey great Ken Dryden and former Conservative MP Scott Brison, along with Toronto lawyer Martha Hall Findlay.

Perhaps the most striking aspect of Rae and Ignatieff's perceived front-runner status was the fact that they were outsiders who had only recently joined the Liberal Party.[9] Ignatieff, a well-known public intellectual and academic, was a newly minted Liberal MP who had literally spent the previous three decades outside the country. Within the space of a year he had returned to Canada, joined the party, and won a seat in a Toronto-area riding in the 2006 election. Rae, meanwhile, was a former NDP MP in Ottawa who had moved to provincial politics and become the NDP premier of Ontario. A lawyer by training, he returned to private practice in Toronto after his government was defeated in 1995 by the Harris Conservatives. He, too, had only recently become a member of the Liberal Party.[10]

For many Liberals, the fact that neither man had been involved in the vicious internecine warfare of the past fifteen years between the Martin and Chrétien camps was a huge advantage, enough to overcome what might otherwise have been seen as some serious drawbacks to their candidacies. Moreover, the decision by Paul Martin's inner circle of advisers to either refrain from participating in the leadership race in any way, or to spread themselves out amongst the various candidates and work alongside Chrétien operatives in a "bipartisan" approach, was seen as a positive gesture that went a considerable way towards putting the whole ugly episode behind them. True, there were those who saw Ignatieff as a stalking horse for Martin on the right wing of the party. Others inevitably viewed Rae, whose brother John had long been a key Chrétien adviser, as the former prime minister's choice and the preferred option of the party's left wing. Nevertheless, both men were seen as star candidates with sufficient gravitas and public name recognition to become the party's next messiah, and the media treated them as such.

That this narrative ultimately did not prove accurate, therefore, must be attributed to factors other than the party's longstanding internal feud or a philosophical conflict between the right and left wings of the party. In fact, it was the entry into the race of two more "outsiders" that sealed the fate of Rae and Ignatieff, since neither of the newcomers carried the significant baggage of the two supposed front-runners. Equally important, unlike Ignatieff and Rae, both men were also seen as solid choices on the national unity file. For the grass roots in particular, this made them seem like more realistic "winners."

The first, Gerard Kennedy, was the former director of food banks in Edmonton and Toronto. A life-long Liberal, Kennedy had become a highly successful minister of education in the Liberal government of Dalton McGuinty in Ontario. He had also come within a hair's breadth of winning the provincial leadership race of 1996 before losing to McGuinty on the fifth ballot. He was widely seen as both a charismatic politician and a skilled political operator with a well-oiled campaign machine and a formidable team of advisers and organizers from Queen's Park. Nevertheless, his resignation as education minister in April 2006, in order to seek the federal party leadership, had come as a surprise to almost everyone and had forced a re-evaluation of the potential front-runners.

The second perceived outsider was none other than Stéphane Dion, a former minister in the governments of both Jean Chrétien (intergovernmental affairs and national unity) and Paul Martin (environment). In Dion's case, the "outsider" label was obviously a perplexing one for many. As the architect of the Clarity Act and a staunch defender of Canadian federalism, he had earned much respect from rank-and-file Liberals in the Chrétien era. Similarly, as the environment minister who chaired the UN Conference on Climate Change (COP-11) in Montreal the previous year and saved the Kyoto Accord from oblivion, he had won the admiration of leading Canadian environmentalists, including Elizabeth May. How, then, could he be seen as an outsider in this leadership race?

The simple fact is that Dion was an outsider to the Liberal Party, and almost everyone in the party's elite knew it. In fact, for many of them, he was an outsider to politics. Originally an academic in Montreal with no connection to the Liberals, he had been appointed directly to cabinet by Jean Chrétien after the harrowingly close 1995 Quebec referendum campaign, *specifically because he was known as an ardent federalist*. As a result, Dion entered politics without contesting an election or winning a seat in the House of Commons. Then he was given Saint-Laurent-Cartierville, one of the safest Liberal seats in the country, to run for the party in the 1997 election.

When the Martin-Chrétien wars subsequently heated up, Dion remained uncommitted (some would say oblivious) throughout. As a result, he was astonished to learn that he was being dropped from cabinet by Martin[11] as soon as the latter became leader in December 2003 ("Had he not done a good job? Was that not enough?" Dion asked his advisers. Surely Martin would call at the eleventh hour to say he had made a mistake?).[12] He was equally surprised to discover that the Martin forces were opposing him for the Liberal nomination in his own riding in the lead-up to the 2004 election. Given the wholesale purge of sitting MPs (those who had supported Chrétien as well as those who had *not supported Martin actively enough*) taking place across the country to widespread media coverage, Dion's surprise demonstrated an almost other-worldly lack of political sense. Although he put up a vigorous defence of his candidacy, many Liberals attributed his eventual success in retaining the nomination to the Martinites' prudent decision to withdraw their opposition to him, as a conciliatory gesture in light of the public backlash that had resulted from their earlier ruthless treatment of Sheila Copps.[13]

Nevertheless, during the 2004 federal election campaign, Dion was the butt of much criticism from Paul Martin's chosen Quebec lieutenant, Jean Lapierre. Lapierre was the former Liberal MP who left the party after the failure of the Meech Lake Accord and co-founded the Bloc Québécois with Lucien Bouchard. In an interview during the campaign, Lapierre described the Clarity Act as a "worthless" piece of paper, a remark that caused Dion to respond once again with incredulous disbelief, to the delight of Quebec media looking for controversy.[14]

Lapierre was asked to step back from the campaign[15] when the party's numbers in Quebec plummeted during the election, but the damage had been done. The party suffered a loss of seats rather than the "huge majority" that Lapierre and several Martin aides had been predicting in the province. Martin's government was reduced to a minority that could fall at any minute. In this context, Dion, one of the few remaining Quebec MPs, was grudgingly readmitted to cabinet but only as environment minister, a much less prestigious position than he had previously held. Though he distinguished himself in that portfolio with his dogged determination to secure an agreement in Montreal, he remained an enigma to most Liberal party insiders. Viewed by almost everyone as a man of honour and integrity, he also continued to be seen as a single-minded "policy wonk" with little aptitude or interest in politics. Or, as one of his closest advisers said, he had "the political instincts of a turnip."

Perhaps the most telling evidence of Dion's lack of political sense can be found in the response of his own advisers when he told them he was considering a run for the leadership. One of them noted the obvious – that he had no organization, no network, and no money. He replied that surely money was not the important thing. Asked by another how he thought he could win despite these drawbacks, Dion replied, "We'll all go to the convention. I'll give a big speech – *my best speech* – and everyone will vote for me."[16] This combination of naivety and intellectual arrogance was a feature of his character that some of his supporters found refreshing ("On the plus side, he could be presented as an anti-politician"), while others despaired.[17] Certainly these characteristics were well known to his caucus colleagues, few of whom were his friends, and bolstered his outsider image. Nor did Dion benefit from what might have been seen as the imperative of "*l'alternance*" to choose someone from Quebec. As *Le Devoir* reported sarcastically about the growing list of potential contenders to replace Martin, "Même Dion serait de la course" (Even Dion is planning to run).[18]

At the same time, it was Dion's very clear position as an outsider in terms of the party elites, the "old guard" of the party whom the grass roots were increasingly inclined to mistrust, that led many organizers to join his campaign. He was, as Andrew Bevan said, "someone whom we could see would 'do politics differently' and not give in to vested interests, in addition to being untainted by the Chrétien-Martin feud."[19]

The Dion Campaign "Machine"

Given his lack of support by the party elites, and the many other organizational problems outlined above, the obvious questions are how Dion managed to acquire a campaign team at such short notice, and what strategy they chose to pursue in their attempt to back their dark-horse candidate. Once again, the answers are instructive.

As Dion's director of parliamentary affairs at the time, Jamie Carroll was one of a handful of senior advisers to whom Dion confided that he was thinking of running. After consulting with other prominent Dion aides, Carroll told Dion that they were sceptical of his bid, not only because of the practical problems his run would pose, but also because "we are all pretty sure you are not prepared to do" what was necessary if he was to have any hope of winning.[20] With that Carroll handed Dion a list of 250 names of prominent party members and told him he should call them to see if there was any support for his candidacy. Somewhat to Carroll's surprise, Dion faithfully did just that. His report back suggested that there might indeed be a possibility of crafting a winning campaign strategy, one that would see Dion selected leader because he was everyone's second choice.

Still, the launch of Dion's campaign was hardly auspicious. As Don Boudria recalled, the meeting at the Palais de Congrès was enough to cause many to reconsider whether a run was possible. "Even the small room we had booked was too big. There were fewer than fifty people."[21]

Over the course of the next several weeks – "We were so far behind everyone else," Carroll complained, "we had to think outside the box all the time"[22] – Dion was sent on a series of trips to consult any local or provincial movers and shakers in the party who were willing to meet with him. In British Columbia this proved to be a turning point. Dion attended an event hosted by former Chrétien and Martin organizer Mark Marrissen, a political heavy hitter in that province, and his then wife, former provincial cabinet minister Christy Clark. As mentioned above, Marrissen was attracted to Dion because of his record on the national unity file, and pleasantly impressed when he met the former unity minister in person.

In short order, Carroll had convinced Marissen to become Dion's campaign manager. Carroll himself had agreed to serve as the deputy campaign manager. The combination of Marissen and Carroll (who had worked in the Martin PMO and was also considered a strong organizer with excellent contacts and political sense) was seen as an impressive gain for Dion, who until that point had been little more than an after-thought in anyone's considerations, including the media's.

When news of Marissen's involvement leaked out,[23] the response was largely positive in the sense that many insiders were convinced Marissen's credentials would enhance the credibility of Dion's candidacy. One commentator declared, "This is really big news ... Dion told me that he's been having problems raising money and getting big-time organizers to sign on to his campaign." Another declared it was "a very big development, and one that I imagine could make Dion into a king-maker, if not a really serious contender."[24]

While no one else considered him a "serious contender" either, Dion had at least succeeded in raising his profile. A variety of other well-known organizers from both the Chrétien and Martin camps were soon on-board, including Brian Klunder, Tim Murphy, and Herb Metcalfe. Soon after both Andrew Bevan and Brian Guest, who had been support-ing MP John Godfrey's candidacy, joined the Dion organization when Godfrey withdrew barely a month into the campaign due to health issues.

As time and Dion's standing in the race progressed, he received fundraising help from Stephen Bronfman, Marc de la Bruyere, and Rod Bryden, a former president of the party's Ontario provincial wing. Moreover, he had received a loan of $300,000 from a Liberal in his riding,[25] which allowed his campaign team to expand beyond their shoestring organization. Carroll had also brought in his then partner, Megan Meltzer – a former professional development officer at the party's national headquarters – to begin raising money across the country and to assume overall responsibility for finances.

Still, the lack of finances continued to hold back his campaign while the front-runners, and especially Michael Ignatieff's campaign, were awash in contributions and even able to conduct polling, a notoriously expensive proposition. Nevertheless, the party's decision to limit each candidate's expenses to $3.4 million (a move taken in response to the astonishing $10 million spent by the Martin campaign in 2003 despite its certain victory) undoubtedly helped level the playing field between the two front-runners and the rest of the field to some extent, but was well above the $1 million that had been recommended by party officials and a figure far beyond the Dion campaign's reach.[26]

Thinking outside the box was one of Marissen's specialties, and he proved this once again when Dion held a press conference in early August to announce that he would run a minimum of 33 per cent female candidates in the next election if he became Liberal leader, increasing that number to 50 per cent in successive elections. That innovative (and inexpensive) commitment resulted in the declared support of fourteen current and former female parliamentarians, a huge boost to Dion's tiny caucus contingent. Despite this surge in support, however, it should be noted that Dion's caucus support, which eventually stood at seventeen on the eve of the convention, was among the lowest of the leadership candidates, surpassed by even non-MP Gerard Kennedy (nineteen) to say nothing of Bob Rae (twenty-six) and Michael Ignatieff (forty-nine).

A second important gain for Dion came from an even more unexpected source. David Orchard, a former leadership candidate for the Progressive Conservative Party in 2003, met with Dion in Montreal on 9 March 2006 to discuss his possible support for Dion's candidacy. Orchard, it will be recalled, had negotiated a signed agreement with Peter MacKay ensuring the latter's victory at that earlier convention, an agreement that guaranteed there would be no merger of the PCs with the Canadian Alliance. To Orchard's dismay, MacKay reneged on his commitment and turned the party over to Stephen Harper in less than six months.[27] Three years later, Orchard had joined the Liberal Party and was considering throwing his support behind Dion.

The significance of this offer became clear when Orchard confided that he had been approached by representatives of virtually all of the serious leadership camps requesting his assistance.[28] As the campaign heated up, Bob Rae personally spoke with Orchard seeking his support.

Orchard recalled the 19 June phone call in which Rae told Orchard that he had "a unique position in the country's affairs" and "a remarkable organization for anywhere in Canada."[29] However, Orchard was not convinced. As he later explained, in addition to Rae's questionable positioning on the national unity file, he was concerned that Rae would be unable to deliver Ontario to the Liberals in a federal election because of his unpopular stint as an NDP premier there, a period that was still remembered unfavourably by many voters.[30]

In the end, Orchard decided to back Stéphane Dion. Not surprisingly, Dion made a special trip to Saskatoon to announce Orchard's support. The press conference, held on 16 August at the Bessborough Hotel, received national coverage. Orchard declared "Stéphane's commitment to a tolerant, bilingual country that defends the institutions that have been built over time – Canadian institutions that make us what we are – on all these fronts it gives me great pleasure to support him."[31] Dion in turn noted that over the course of his leadership travels, "I have had people speaking to me about David in every province I went, telling me, 'We hope you and David will work together.'"[32] In a move that would come back to haunt him, Dion also promised that Orchard "will play a very important role in the campaign. We didn't discuss yet which role it will take, but I'm very pleased he's coming to the team."[33]

One national columnist declared that Orchard's support was "yet another coup for Dion" and that "Dion has put himself in the top tier of candidates" with his "focused" campaign and "stronger-than-expected" support.[34] At a minimum, it was clear that Orchard's backing would enhance Dion's candidacy where he was weakest, namely in the west and, specifically, in rural ridings. This strategy had the added advantage of allowing Dion to pick up delegates in ridings where membership was low, since all ridings were entitled to send delegates to the convention. Some observers speculated that Orchard's support could translate into more than one hundred delegates for Dion, but spokesmen for other camps downplayed this development and stated that they did not expect it to produce more than thirty or forty at the very most.

Those who knew Orchard demurred. As Adam Campbell, president of the Alberta wing of the federal Liberals, said of him, "I think people underestimate [him]. I think they go around thinking they're a quaint bunch of amateurs ... but there's an organization there. They know how to work conventions. They've done it twice before."[35] Their plan was to convince the Red Tories who had supported Orchard in the past to follow him to the Liberal Party, in order to become delegates to the convention and back Dion. Both Orchard and his campaign manager, Marjaleena Repo, stated that they could not say how many of the individuals on their estimated thirty-five-thousand-member database could be delivered to Dion. However, as Repo later commented, they had swung into action almost immediately after Orchard made his decision, and well before the cut-off for new members to be eligible to vote in the leadership.[36] Both the Saskatchewan and Alberta party offices reported a dramatic upswing in membership applications, most of which appeared to be coming from former Progressive Conservatives, but no actual numbers were available.[37]

Behind the scenes, Marissen, Carroll, and campaign chair Don Boudria were quietly building support in a number of other niche markets Marissen had targeted, believing they had been overlooked by other candidates and could be fertile ground for Dion's campaign. Marissen later noted that one of their most successful efforts had involved tracking down ex officio delegates other than sitting MPs – the former MPs, cabinet ministers, and other privy councillors, as well as party executive provincial and territorial appointees (PTAs), who were automatically delegates to the convention. "We painstakingly tracked down every one of them that we could and made sure they were aware of Stéphane's platform and his near-universal second choice status," Marissen recalled.[38] Statistics demonstrated that this tactic also paid off. Dion finished second among committed ex officio delegates, with the support of 20.4 per cent or 137 before the convention began. Interestingly, it was Gerard Kennedy who finished a close third in this market, supported by 17.3 per cent or 112 such delegates, suggesting that his team had also decided to target this area.

The numbers for Dion and Kennedy are even more significant when contrasted with those of Michael Ignatieff, whose first place support among ex officio delegates (at 231 or 35.4 per cent) was heavily dependent on his support among sitting MPs, and Bob Rae, who finished a rather distant fourth in this category with the backing of only 13 per cent or 88 delegates.[39] None of the other leadership candidates registered meaningful support among these delegates. Perhaps equally important were the 400 ex officio delegates who went into the convention undeclared, and which voting results suggest swung to Dion as ballots progressed.

A third area of strategic concentration was, of course, Dion's environmental policies and credentials. However, there was no evidence of a concerted move by environmental activists to sign up with the party in order to cast a vote for him. The idea of launching such an appeal had apparently been briefly considered but rejected as unlikely to prove effective. Many in the environmental movement preferred to remain determinedly non-partisan while others had forged close links with the NDP or Green Party. In addition, the appeal to environmental interests within the Liberal Party was not uniquely Dion's domain. Gerard Kennedy's youth component was strong, and it was with the youth delegates in both camps that this issue resonated the most. Nevertheless, Dion did obtain the public support of the Green Party's former deputy leader, Tom Manley, another announcement that garnered some public attention.[40]

Dion also participated aggressively in the leadership debates organized by the party over June and July, obviously thinking to make an impression with potential delegates. Campaign chair Don Boudria felt that his candidate had, in fact, won several of them.[41] At the same time, the one candidate with the most to lose, Michael Ignatieff, did not do well. At a minimum, he needed to justify his front-runner status with a good performance and justify his decision to support Stephen Harper's extension of Canada's presence in Afghanistan, an outrider position taken by only one of the other leadership candidates, Scott Brison. As columnist Chantal Hébert noted, he failed on both counts.[42] However, the debates were poorly attended and not well organized. With so many candidates, little of relevance in terms of individual candidates' positions could emerge. Moreover, since the major networks had refused to carry the debates, few people actually saw them. As one report noted, "the 11 leadership candidates bored their audience with consensus and politeness" and the format "virtually ensured no actual debate would take place."[43]

Nevertheless, the debates may have had some impact with dedicated Liberals who followed them. As the so-called Super Weekend approached, public opinion polls were showing Dion in a surprisingly strong position for someone who had been given no chance only a few months before. In early September, one poll showed Michael Ignatieff, the presumed front-runner, was indeed in first place, but with only a slim lead. At 19 per cent, he was hardly pulling away from the pack. A second, more comprehensive poll conducted by EKOS Research from 17 to 24 September revealed that Bob Rae and Ignatieff were essentially tied for first place at 25 per cent, while Dion and Kennedy were close behind, at 17 per cent and 16 per cent, respectively. Newspaper reports routinely began speaking of the "top four." Even more significant was the finding that Ignatieff was the second choice of only 19 per cent while Dion and Rae were tied at 27 per cent.

The Super Weekend Revelations (29 September–1 October)

Under the Liberal Party constitution in force at the time, delegates to the leadership convention had to be selected fifty-nine to thirty-five days before the convention itself, and only members who had joined the party at least ninety days before the delegate selection meetings could vote for delegates. This meant that all of the leadership camps had been preoccupied to this point with signing up new party members whom they expected to support them. As mentioned above, this is what made David Orchard's contribution of new Liberal members – a large swath of former Progressive Conservatives in the western provinces – so significant for Dion's chances.

Lacking the support of the party elites or caucus members, Dion's team had also spent considerable time recruiting new party members across the country. This of course was in addition to their efforts in seeking out the huge number of ex officio delegates who would automatically be at the convention and were not part of the Super Weekend calculations. Since all delegates except the ex officios were bound to vote for a specified candidate on the first ballot, the results of that first vote at the convention were likely to mirror the results of the Super Weekend. After that, if no candidate reached the minimum necessary for a first ballot victory, there were no guarantees.

Even before the voting began it was clear that no candidate would come close to the 51 per cent needed to win on the first ballot, as Paul Martin had done in 2003. But when the voting was completed the weekend of 29 September to 1 October, Michael Ignatieff – the assumed front-runner – had the support of only 1,377 delegates or 29.3 per cent, a far cry from the minimum 35 per cent that Liberal insiders and even members of his own team had been saying he would need on the first ballot in order to avoid being overtaken in successive ballots. Bob Rae finished second, with 943 (20.1 per cent), while newcomer Gerard Kennedy finished a surprising third with 820 (17.5 per cent), ahead of Stéphane Dion, who also surprised many observers with his fourth-place finish and 754 committed delegates (16.1 per cent).

Ignatieff was clearly the front-runner and the media continued to view him as such, but they also began to speak more often of the "front four." Although this meant that in principle more attention would be paid to Kennedy and Dion, in reality this was not the case. Media coverage continued to be focused on Ignatieff and Rae. Given that the front-runner at delegated conventions typically has gone on to win a leadership race, this was perhaps not surprising. Indeed, according to one study, of thirty-five such races held in Ontario and at the federal level since 1958, the candidate who finished in first place on the first ballot won twenty-eight times, or 80 per cent of the time.[44] And in four of the seven exceptions to that scenario, the eventual winner finished in second place on the first ballot. However, the average first-ballot vote received by those front-runners was over 36 per cent, or far more than Ignatieff or Rae had received.

Evidently this Super Weekend result was viewed negatively by Ignatieff's team. When a debate for the four front-runners was proposed by the Canadian Club and the Empire Club of Toronto (a long-standing tradition) almost immediately after the Super Weekend results were known, Rae, Kennedy, and Dion agreed but Ignatieff declined to attend. A spokesman for Ignatieff said he would not attend unless all of the eight remaining candidates (four had withdrawn by this point) were allowed to participate, although the clubs said he also offered to come and speak individually without other candidates present.[45] Privately, a senior member of Ignatieff's team later confided that they were becoming increasingly worried about his lack of knowledge of Canadian events and his tendency to "go off message," which they felt they simply could not afford at that point.

Ignatieff's team were right to worry, as the developments the following month clearly demonstrated. To almost everyone's surprise, national unity had become a major issue in the race, and it would soon culminate in a dramatic showdown in the House of Commons.

The Quebec Nation Resolution Realigns the Race (22–27 November)

One area in which Michael Ignatieff's lack of first-hand knowledge of Canadian politics proved to be crucial was the national unity file. It soon became apparent that, having lived abroad for decades, he lacked an understanding of the tumultuous Mulroney era of constitutional reform proposals that was personal rather than academic. This quickly proved to be hugely problematic for his candidacy.

Given that Ignatieff had recently ventured into the minefield of Middle Eastern politics with unfortunate results, including the resignation of his Toronto co-chair Susan Kadis,[46] one might have expected him to be more circumspect in pronouncing on controversial issues. This proved not to be the case. When Prime Minister Stephen Harper flatly refused to rise to a challenge launched by Quebec PQ leader Andre Boisclair at a St Jean Baptiste Day rally in Quebec City, demanding that the federal government recognize Quebec as a nation, the matter might well have quietly disappeared. But Ignatieff promptly jumped into the fray. Not only did he agree with Boisclair that Quebec was indeed a nation, but he proposed that recognition of this "fact" should be entrenched in the constitution. In the ensuing furore, the Quebec wing of the federal Liberals (whose executive strongly supported Ignatieff) immediately proposed a draft resolution for their upcoming policy conference in which the party would recognize Quebec as a nation "within Canada" and "constitutionalize" this recognition. Needless to say, Ignatieff supported the resolution.

This soon led to a chaotic situation in a Liberal Party that still bore the scars of the Meech Lake/Charlottetown conflicts.[47] Regardless of which side individuals had taken in those debates, almost everyone wanted to put the whole issue behind them. Or, as former Chrétien minister Dianne Marleau said, they wanted to avoid "this stupidity we've gotten ourselves into."[48] Few could believe Ignatieff had voluntarily reopened the wound. For many Liberals, "Ignatieff was implicitly questioning the entire legacy associated with Pierre Trudeau."[49] For them this was completely unacceptable, and it cost him support in the race.

Various members of the caucus and the party's federal executive attempted to intervene to water down the resolution, and in the end it was confined to a workshop, where it quietly expired. Meanwhile, interim leader Bill Graham had intervened in caucus "to prevent a train wreck" after several of the leadership candidates publicly expressed differing views.[50] Notable among them was Bob Rae (an architect of the Charlottetown Accord when he was NDP premier of Ontario), who stated in September that he supported the concept in theory but believed it was far too difficult to implement since it would require a constitutional amendment. This produced a scathing response from Ignatieff. "Other candidates have said recognizing Quebec as a nation in the constitution is too difficult," he declared. "Yes, it is difficult. But we must do it."[51]

The other political parties could hardly believe their good fortune. Bloc Québécois leader Gilles Duceppe immediately threatened to table a resolution in the House of Commons declaring Quebec a nation, but without qualifying conditions. Just as this latest salvo was being absorbed by the shell-shocked Liberal caucus, the prime minister upped the ante by tabling his own version of the resolution, which recognized Quebeckers as a nation within Canada. Now the cat was definitely among the pigeons. With all but two of the leadership candidates (Kennedy and Hall Findlay) in caucus, this was a potentially explosive situation. Bill Graham called a special emergency caucus meeting to discuss the matter, urging everyone to vote in favour of the resolution to demonstrate party solidarity, but his plea fell on deaf ears. On 27 November, when the matter came to a vote in the House, some fifteen Liberal MPs, including leadership candidates Ken Dryden, Joe Volpe, and Hedy Fry, voted against the motion (it passed by a margin of 266 to 16). More significant still was the fact that the majority of leadership candidates in the Liberal caucus, including Ignatieff, Rae, and, surprisingly, Stéphane Dion, voted in favour. Although he had opposed the Quebec wing's motion, Dion had circulated an alternative option for several weeks within the caucus, and claimed that the wording of Harper's resolution closely resembled it.

Dion's campaign chair, Mark Marissen, an ardent opponent of Meech Lake and Charlottetown, later confided that he had advised Dion not to support the motion but that, too, had fallen on deaf ears. "He's not really a Trudeau Liberal," Marissen said. "Yes, he's a strong federalist, but he's also a product of the Quebec intelligentsia."[52] Carroll agreed, noting Dion's enthusiastic support as Jean Chrétien's intergovernmental affairs minister for the Social Union Framework Agreement (SUFA), a deal that had been forced upon the federal government by the provinces after the 1995 referendum. It represented a far more decentralized vision of federalism than most Trudeauvian federalists approved. "Of course SUFA never really went anywhere so it wasn't important in the end and was soon forgotten."[53]

Still, Dion's speech explaining his decision to support the motion was painfully convoluted. Seemingly torn between the logical academic rationale for voting against it (as several prominent academics had noted, neither the Quebecois nor the province of Quebec fit any recognized political definition of a nation)[54] and the apparent political imperative to support it, he spent considerable time attempting to distinguish between the two. An obviously uncomfortable Dion declared that the motion recognized Québécois as a nation only in the "sociological" sense, not the legal, and that the resolution was in any event strictly "symbolic" and would have no practical consequences. "Symbolic is something we Canadians need to handle better," he concluded.[55] This view of Quebeckers as a nation like Acadians or Aboriginal Canadians, however, was not well received by Quebec elites, the very group he presumably had been trying to placate.[56]

No doubt Dion's speech would have surprised many of his supporters elsewhere but, luckily for him, apart from Quebec it was hardly noticed outside the House of Commons. This was primarily because the media focused on the dissenters and, most dramatically, on the surprise resignation of Harper's own intergovernmental affairs minister, Michael Chong. Unlike Dion, Chong had *not* been consulted by the prime minister on the wording of the motion and was not pleased. Ironically, it was left to Chong to defend the Trudeauvian vision of Canada in Parliament. He did so with wording that took direct aim at Michael Ignatieff, who, as an academic, had introduced the terminology of "civic" (good) and "ethnic" (bad) nationalism. "I believe in one nation, undivided, called Canada," Chong told reporters afterwards, adding, "I believe that recognizing the Quebecois as a nation, even within a united Canada, is nothing else than the recognition of ethnic nationalism."[57]

One person outside of official Ottawa who had followed the debate closely was Gerard Kennedy. Although he was not able to cast a vote because he was not an MP at the time, Kennedy was determined to make his views known. He called a press conference in Toronto the day of the vote, in which he denounced Harper's introduction of the resolution as "irresponsible, politically inspired, treating this country like a political trinket," and declared "we need and should expect better" from a prime minister. Kennedy went on to state that he opposed the contents of the resolution as well, categorically rejecting the use of the term "nation" as Chong had done, and stating that he would have voted against the motion if he had been able to do so.[58]

It was a defining moment in the campaign. Kennedy had not only positioned himself as a Trudeau Liberal, but had provided some unhappy Rae and Ignatieff supporters with a reason to look again at his candidacy. The move also cemented the commitment of former Liberal MP Charles Caccia, whom many observers had expected to support Dion. For Caccia, a former environment minister under Pierre Trudeau and influential chair of the Environment and Sustainable Development Committee under Jean Chrétien, the logical choice might well have been Dion. Instead, as someone who had vigorously opposed both Meech Lake and Charlottetown, the tipping point for Caccia was Kennedy's firm stance on the national unity issue.[59] Nor was he alone. Other left-wing social Liberals such as Sheila Copps and Terry Mercer, who might also have been expected to support Bob Rae, had moved to Kennedy because of his strong stand on centralist federalism.

Most significant of all, Kennedy's stand against Harper's resolution reinforced the decision of a promising young Liberal who had not yet entered politics himself – Justin Trudeau – to support his leadership bid. Trudeau's move would have immediate consequences in terms of Kennedy's support, but it would also be important in the development of future relationships in the party. It was through Kennedy, for example, that Trudeau met many of the individuals who would later become key organizers during his own leadership bid in 2015, and eventually go on to staff his PMO or accept posts in his first cabinet. Similarly, it was the first in a series of events that stoked the barely concealed personal enmity between Trudeau and Dion.[60]

Announcing his support for Kennedy a day earlier, Trudeau was front and centre in providing comments about the resolution on the day of the vote. "Some people these days are wrapped up in this idea of a nation for Quebec," he said, concluding "this stands against every-thing my father ever believed."[61] He later reinforced this position in an interview with *La Presse*. "My problem with the idea of special status for Quebec, or the constitutional recognition of Quebec as a distinct society, or the recognition that the Quebecois form a nation, is that it creates divisions in society and groups within groups."[62]

Nevertheless, Trudeau, like many supporters of both Kennedy and Dion, stressed that there were a number of other reasons to choose one of those two men, rather than Ignatieff or Rae. Apart from their obvious baggage, he suggested neither of the latter had the experience or vision necessary to lead the Liberal Party: "The party needs bold leadership and there is really one choice and that's Gerard."[63] Even more interest-ing was Trudeau's concern about the state of the party and its need for reform, which he believed Kennedy – as the next generation as well as an outsider – would be able to accomplish. "This has been a party that has drifted away from the grassroots toward the corporate donorship that has always worked but no longer works in Canada right now ... We need to be really brave about taking a fresh look and listening to people and sharing the power and the privilege of power that the Canadian people keep granting the Liberal Party."[64]

Certainly Trudeau was not alone in this view. This was also an important factor in the support Kennedy received from some of the newer members of the federal caucus, such as MPs Mark Holland, Scott Simms, and Navdeep Bains. For them – as Liberals who had just arrived in Ottawa without any involvement in the Chrétien-Martin feud – the lingering toxic atmosphere they encountered there was a mystery. Mark Holland recalled:

> It made us all very uncomfortable. Our primary concern, as with so many of the delegates, was to open up the party. We wanted to let go of past bat-tles, but we also wanted to have the membership take back the levers of power from some of the elites who had held them for so long. We saw this race as an opportunity to create a new vision for the party, and to bring about a new way of doing politics. Gerard was very much the man to do that.[65]

In keeping with this theme, a small minority of the party elites were working on a number of reform measures in advance of the biennial convention, which had already been scheduled for late November/early December in Montreal. For them, this convention was seen as a make-or-break scenario for the party if it ever hoped to recover and regain its status as a truly unified party and one capable of governing.

Party Rebuilding Begins

If the heavyweights who declined to run for the leadership of the party were not prepared to do the heavy lifting on party reform and rebuilding, the party executive was. At a meeting of the executive in March, the December event was simply expanded to include a leadership convention as well, with the leadership vote taking place on 2 December. But there was no question that the constitutional reform issues already planned for discussion at the convention would still be dealt with. This was to be the third attempt at constitutional reform since 1982, a point the party's national director, Steve MacKinnon, was quick to underline. Referring to any progress that had been made in the past twenty-odd years as "baby steps," MacKinnon stressed that only major change would be enough to right the good ship Liberal in 2006. "The Liberal Party is broken beyond repair and needs to be completely restructured to survive," MacKinnon declared.[66]

Party president Mike Eizenga agreed. Eizenga made it clear that he and MacKinnon were planning to push through a raft of constitutional reforms at the convention. To begin this process, at the same executive meeting Eizenga also announced the creation of a Red Ribbon Task Force on constitutional reform of the party to be composed of both parliamentary and extra-parliamentary party members, with expert assistance from veteran Liberals Jack Graham and Andy Scott. The mandate of the task force was clearly spelled out: "to evaluate how the current operational and decision-making structure of the party can be streamlined and made more efficient."[67]

Then in May Eizenga delivered an address to the annual meeting of the federal party's Ontario wing in which he hammered home the need for reform. This was the first in a series of presentations he made to riding associations and party meetings across the country designed to win delegate support long before the convention. Noting such obvious problems as the fact that the party executive consisted of seventy members, making decision-making "cumbersome and expensive," Eizenga later recalled that he stressed the time was right and there might not be another chance. "We were not just in opposition," he said, "we were in a scenario where there could be another election at any time and we were far from battle-ready."[68] At the time he told listeners that the party "is institutionally unable to provide us with an electoral advantage,"[69] citing three basic functions of any political party at which the Liberals were failing: "policy development, revenue generation, and election readiness." And he backed up his statements with facts and figures, producing charts comparing the Liberal Party's situation unfavourably with that of its chief competitor, the new Conservative Party of Stephen Harper.

The Red Ribbon Task Force reported in August. Not surprisingly, it submitted a comprehensive list of twenty-four recommendations for constitutional reform. "A Party for Everyone, A Party Built to Win" concluded with a call to arms: "We strongly urge the national executive to oversee ... the drafting of constitutional amendments" that would be put before the Montreal convention delegates for approval. Recognizing that such amendments would require the support of at least 66 per cent of these delegates, something that had been difficult if not impossible to obtain on previous occasions when party reform had been attempted, the task force nevertheless insisted that it was necessary to make every effort to do so. "The Liberal party belongs to all of us," they said, "and we must collectively agree to change it."[70]

Among the report's many recommendations were a major redistribution of responsibility between the national office and the PTAs, creation of a truly national membership list, reduction of the national executive to twenty members, creation of a Council of Presidents of local riding associations that would meet once per year, and creation of a permanent election readiness committee, a national revenue committee, and a management committee of the national executive. In addition, representational bodies such as the controversial seniors and youth clubs would only be recognized if their membership exceeded fifty. Several suggestions for minor reforms to the leadership race process were also made and, more importantly, the report raised the option of replacing the existing structure entirely. Rather than a convention with delegates, it proposed a one-member, one-vote alternative for consideration by Montreal delegates.

Eizenga and MacKinnon spent the fall travelling across the country speaking with Liberals about the proposals. For Eizenga, this was an essential factor in the eventual success of his reform package. "You couldn't simply place all of this before delegates at a convention and expect them to agree. We needed to do a lot of preparatory work. And we were extremely lucky because we had the full support of [interim party leader] Bill Graham, who was instrumental in selling the package to caucus members and leadership candidates."[71] Graham himself spoke at the convention in favour of the proposals, stating that he wanted to be the first party president who could say that he was a member of the Liberal Party of Canada, rather than simply a member of a local Liberal riding association.

In the end, their efforts paid off. At the convention, delegates passed almost all of the proposed recommendations by a margin of 90 per cent, far beyond the 66 per cent that was needed. Only the option of replacing a delegated convention with a one-member one-vote leadership race was rejected by the Montreal convention delegates, which was hardly surprising. For Eizenga, this was a gratifying success, and one that he later confided he saw as his legacy as president. "During my term," he said, referring to MacKinnon and Graham as key partners in the effort, "we put the basic structure in place to move to where we are now. Because of them we are in a very different place today." Eizenga also noted that the party's situation in 2015 was "beyond what we envisaged" and stressed that he was very impressed with what had followed from his early efforts.[72] MacKinnon concurred. "After Chrétien introduced C-24, it was imperative that we obtain donor data and a national membership list. We needed to become a data-driven party, with a coherent central party structure, or we were doomed. The changes we put in place in 2006 allowed us to begin to do that. In some respects, the 2015 victory is the inevitable result of the changes that began in 2006."[73]

But if the reform convention unfolded smoothly, the same could hardly have been said for the leadership race taking place at the same time, a race that appeared to produce an unanticipated leadership result.

The Leadership Convention "Upset"

As every backroom organizer knows, a leadership race is like any candidate nomination battle at the riding level, or indeed like an election. The name of the game is numbers and, once you have them, getting them to actually show up and vote. The Super Weekend demonstrated what the first ballot result would look like but, because no candidate had sufficient numbers of supporters to win on the first ballot, the race was wide open. Still, this was not commonly understood by most Canadians, nor apparently by many in the media. They continued to follow closely the every move of Ignatieff and Rae to the exclusion of almost everyone else, and saw the final result as unexpected.

Meanwhile, editorial opinion was clearly split. While the *Toronto Star* endorsed Bob Rae on the eve of the convention, *Le Devoir* chose Michael Ignatieff. One clue as to the eventual outcome might have been seen in the decision of the *Globe and Mail* and the *Montreal Gazette* to endorse – albeit reluctantly – Stephane Dion. As the *Globe* put it, "each of the [main four] contenders boasts attributes of leadership, and each reveals areas of weakness and vulnerability … not one of them is perfect."[74]

The editorial's analysis of the two front-runners dismissed them out of hand for the reasons already discussed – insurmountable baggage as an unpopular NDP premier or as someone who had been out of the country for decades. It was much kinder to Gerard Kennedy who, it declared, "is the kind of talent the Liberals need to rebuild the federal party. He is a strong communicator (at least in English) and a formidable organizer, and he stands unequivocally for change and renewal. He has infused the campaign with much needed energy."[75] At the same time, it noted Kennedy's two fatal flaws – a lack of sufficient competence in French and the lack of a national profile.

Yet arguably the most important development in the Liberal leadership race took place behind the scenes. Gerard Kennedy and Stéphane Dion had many things in common, including their views on federalism and national unity (Dion's "sociological" musings notwithstanding), their concern for the environment, and their essentially left-wing "social liberal" perspective on issues. Even more than that, though, they were both determined to bring about the kind of change in the party, and a new vision of politics, about which Justin Trudeau had spoken earlier. To do that it was essential that they prevent either Bob Rae or Michael Ignatieff (and their old guard supporters) from becoming leader at all costs, a view shared by the vast majority of their delegates. Looking at the results of the Super Weekend, strategists in both camps realized that together they would have a real possibility of stopping the frontrunners. Of course, each man and his organizers believed they would be the one to carry on the good fight with the help of the other, who would withdraw from the race and endorse him.

Representatives of Dion's team (Andrew Bevan and Herb Metcalfe) approached Kennedy's organizers (Katie Telford and David McNaughton) to suggest discussions, which then took place on several occasions and culminated in a breakfast meeting between the two men in Montreal. Kennedy later recounted how "odd" he had found the discussion with Dion, whom he later described as being both "detached" and "argumentative" – even about what they should eat.[76] Nevertheless, the two men realized that they had much in common and agreed that they would be willing to strike an informal alliance to further that end. According to several of his senior advisers, Kennedy was not interested in "cutting a deal" in the conventional sense. "There was no quid pro quo. He was very clear that this was precisely the type of old school politics that he was trying to replace."[77] However, the two teams continued to liaise closely through the four interlocutors in the hopes of arriving at an agreement that whoever was about to be eliminated, or finished in fourth place on the third ballot, would throw their support to the other. To that end, and behind the scenes, Bevan and Kennedy's policy adviser, Rob Silver, worked on a written policy plan that the two leaders saw and agreed upon, although it was never made public.[78]

The two men met again at Kennedy's campaign office at the convention centre several hours before the first ballot, to reinforce this understanding. Kennedy, clearly the more politically astute and experienced of the two, was most insistent that Dion indicate he believed Kennedy was the best choice for leader after himself, so that there would be a firm commitment to the deal. His major concern was that Dion would wait too long to decide to withdraw, allowing one of the two front-runners to win. In the end, however, there was no written agreement and no precise deal, but the pair shook hands and agreed to keep in close contact as the votes progressed. For Kennedy, the informal "entente" was made somewhat easier by his belief that he would be the one in third place on the first ballot.

This was not an unreasonable assumption. With his formidable team of organizers from Queens Park, Kennedy had mounted an impressive campaign for the top job of the federal party in which he was an admitted outsider, and he had done so in a remarkably short period of time. Not only had he finished in third place, ahead of Dion in the Super Weekend, he had actually finished in second place in Canada outside of Quebec, ahead of Bob Rae in Ontario and in first place in BC and Manitoba. He had also signed up more new members than any other candidate.[79] Moreover, his team knew the importance of getting out the vote and his supporters were widely recognized as being among the most committed.

No candidate could ever take this for granted, as Orchard organizer Marjaleena Repo pointed out.[80] The further delegates had to travel to the site of the convention, and the less enthusiastic they were about their candidate, the less likely they were to actually make the expensive and time-consuming trip. And it was here that the "Orchard factor" proved decisive. Stéphane Dion arrived at the convention with 750 potential delegates, not 600, thanks to the organization of Orchard and Repo, who delivered all of the 150 delegates they had acquired for him in western Canada to the convention centre in Montreal. Dion's own organizers also delivered an impressive 90 per cent of their delegates to registration in Montreal, something most other candidates could not hope to match. And then, of course, there were the ex officio delegates whom Dion and Kennedy had courted more than the front-runners had done, although these delegates' preferences would not be known until the first ballot was counted because they were not obliged to publicly commit their votes.

The Dion camp was cautiously optimistic heading into the convention, believing they at least had a shot at the brass ring. As Mark Marissen recalled, his team had fanned out and made contact with delegates in each of the other camps to pitch Dion as their second choice, and "there appeared to be a real drop in support for Ignatieff, which we thought was very encouraging. We suspected he was going down for the count."[81] Dion himself continued to tell anyone who would listen that he was going to win. As one Kennedy organizer confided, Dion appeared to believe that he would win because he had the best policies, suggesting that Jamie Carroll and Mark Marissen's attempts to educate their candidate in the ways of realpolitik had not been successful.

But disaster struck on the first night of the leadership race, when the candidates delivered their convention speeches. Both Kennedy and Rae delivered polished and engaging speeches that inspired their supporters, although Rae was criticized by some for using little French. Many observers described Kennedy's speech as a "barn burner." Michael Ignatieff's speech was described by some analysts as the best of the evening but it failed to impress many delegates, a victim of an overwrought delivery or, as one delegate would presciently put it, "trying too hard. The words were good but he wasn't convincing. He just didn't seem authentic" (in an apparent attempt to demonstrate messianic leadership qualities by association, Ignatieff's speech contained numerous references to Pierre Trudeau).

By contrast, Dion's speech epitomized his tendency to argue using Cartesian logic rather than emotion, in this case focusing on the concept of a "third pillar of environmental sustainability." (As Jamie Carroll later noted, this was symptomatic of Dion. "He insisted on writing his own material and generally ignored any political advice.")[82] Worse still, he went on for far too long. Music started to play, drowning out Dion's words, and then his microphone was actually cut off when he refused to stop speaking after a warning. Even then, as his organizers watched in horror, Dion stubbornly continued to speak until he had finished his prepared remarks, although almost no one could hear him. Some of his team blamed his problems on an overly long introduction by supporter Glen Pearson, who had not agreed to rehearse his remarks in advance. Andrew Bevan recalled sitting in a booth with headphones, listening to the introduction and realizing Dion's speech would be too long, and also knowing that Dion would never make accommodations and cut it short.[83] Don Boudria admitted, "We were all very down, we thought it was fatal."[84] Mark Marissen confessed that he was sure the speech had been "a disaster, the kiss of death," while Jamie Carroll and several other members of the team retired to his hotel room to drown their sorrows.[85] Dion himself realized he had made a mistake politically, and apologized profusely to his team and the speech authors after the fact.

Yet the next morning the results of the first ballot were extremely positive. As Carroll later recounted, unbeknownst to them, it turned out that
the first ballot voting had been completed before the speeches began,
and so had not been affected by Dion's bizarre behaviour. To no one's
surprise, Michael Ignatieff finished in first place, with 29.3 per cent of the
votes cast. Bob Rae was a distant second, at 20.3 per cent, and Stéphane
Dion and Gerard Kennedy were virtually tied at 17.8 per cent and 17.7
per cent, respectively. Dion, however, had received the most unassigned
(ex officio) ballots by a wide margin, at 1.8 per cent as opposed to the 0.2
per cent for Rae and Kennedy, and none for Ignatieff.

At this point, Dion's team redoubled their efforts to remind all of
those delegates from other camps about Dion's place as "everyone's
second choice," a move that Don Boudria believed was a key factor
in their ultimate victory.[86] He argued that Kennedy's support in Quebec was almost non-existent and that this alone made Dion the preferred second choice. It was also at this point that Dion's organizers
unveiled what many saw as a brilliant tactic, handing out green scarves
for supporters to wear. The original idea had come from a Toronto public affairs and communications specialist, Susan Walsh, and had been
taken up by another member of the Dion team, Brian Guest. This had
been a hard-fought issue behind the scenes, with Marissen arguing that
Liberals always wore red and all they needed was Dion's name on the
scarf, while Guest argued for green as a symbol of Dion's environmental
priorities.[87] Walsh explained that her experience had been largely with
leadership campaigns in the Progressive Conservative Party, where
individual candidates all had distinctive colours for their campaigns,
and the furore over the green option surprised her. As she also noted,
though, "if you are a little campaign, you need to look bigger, and this
will help do the trick."[88]

In the end, a compromise was reached where the green scarves – as
well as green signs, hats, and T-shirts – were kept under wraps until
the second ballot (to pay for this compromise, the Dion campaign had
to forego hosting a hospitality suite, normally a standard feature of any
leadership campaign). But, as Brian Klunders pointed out, the sacrifice
paid off. The distribution of the scarves to Dion supporters on the floor
of the convention caused a stir, particularly as former candidates such
as Martha Hall Findlay and Joe Volpe chose to join the Dion camp wearing the scarves. Ironically, Dion was unaware of the plan and, because
he is colour blind, wondered what all the fuss was about until his wife
explained that his delegates were now wearing green. "It made a real
visual impact in the hall and it created momentum, no doubt about it,"
Marissen admitted.

Meanwhile, Andrew Bevan recalled making the announcement that morning at the hotel that Dion and his team would be travelling to the convention in Findlay's bus, a sure sign, in his view, that the corner had been turned and the contest was now Dion's to lose. This momentum accelerated after the results of the second ballot became known. To the surprise and considerable disappointment of Gerard Kennedy and his team, he remained in fourth place on the ballot and Dion's lead had grown more than his. From a virtual tie on the first ballot, the two men were now separated by 2 percentage points, at 20.8 per cent for Dion (a 3 per cent increase) to 18.8 per cent (a 1 per cent increase) for Kennedy. Although there was no way to determine the accuracy of the claim, there was much speculation at the time, and afterwards, that some of the Kennedy delegates had agreed to "temporarily lend" their support to Martha Hall Findlay, the only woman in the race, mistakenly assuming it would be only a symbolic gesture and not affect the outcome.

Although Ignatieff's support appeared to have peaked, it had not collapsed, and Rae received the biggest increase of all. His organizers were even beginning to approach Kennedy's delegates to convince them to switch their vote, although their pleas fell on deaf ears. Still, as Mark Holland recalled, "I knew we were in deep trouble after the first ballot, never mind the second. I realized virtually every argument that we had made about Gerard as the voice of change could now be transferred to Dion."[89] After much reflection, and some heated discussion with his inner campaign team, Kennedy decided to withdraw from the race early and hopefully make more of an impact, fearing that otherwise either Rae or Ignatieff might acquire enough support to pass the 50 per cent mark. He immediately moved to the Dion camp, donned a green scarf, and urged his supporters to do the same.

This move on Kennedy's part caught almost everyone, including the other candidates, by surprise. But it had the desired effect. To the chagrin of the Ignatieff organizers, who had thought they would obtain the support of the Kennedy youth vote, Kennedy delivered a remarkable 95 per cent of his delegates to Dion.[90] As a result, on the third vote Dion ended up in first place with 37 per cent and Bob Rae was eliminated from the ballot. The real race was over.

Not everyone conceded this point. The Ignatieff team put on a surprising show of strength in advance of the next vote. Printed leaflets asking "Ignatieff or Dion? Who Will Beat Harper?" were distributed widely by their volunteers, a spur-of-the-moment feat that obviously required both considerable funds and an impressive war machine. Ignatieff supporters were also strategically mobilized to concentrate outside the voting room and overpower other camps with raucous chanting of Ignatieff's name.[91] Nevertheless, on the fourth and final ballot Dion won with 54.7 per cent of the votes to Ignatieff's 45.3 per cent.

As the behaviour of both the Rae and Ignatieff camps demonstrated, they continued to believe it was possible for either of their candidates to win, something that still perplexed Gerard Kennedy weeks after the convention. The front-runners may not have known of the unofficial agreement between the two men, but how could they not see the obvious synergy between the two outsider camps and, of course, the numbers? "Why didn't people think this was a likely vote? Together we had more delegates than the other guys. So why would people be surprised?"[92] In addition, as Mark Holland pointed out, there should have been no surprise about the fact that Gerard could deliver his delegates: "They were here for a reason." When asked by other camps why he thought they could deliver their votes to Dion, Holland replied, "Our delegates won't allow us to do anything else."[93] (By contrast, many believed it was unlikely that Dion would have been able to deliver so many of his delegates to Kennedy, especially among those who came from Quebec.)

The numbers also suggested it was the generational divide that especially benefited Dion. Some 35 per cent of the delegates were under twenty-five and more than half were under forty. As Liberal pundit John Duffy noted, there was no green power sweep of the convention that propelled Dion to victory. But "environmental concern is a generational issue par excellence. Dion's and Kennedy's youthful delegates intimately shared the concern."[94] This, in turn, likely made the merger of the two camps easier to effect, as did the remarkable loyalty of Kennedy's delegates. As senior Ignatieff organizer Ian Davey admitted, this was a turning point – a "key moment" – in the race.[95]

After Dion's victory was announced, a joyful and enthusiastic scene erupted on the convention floor. At least, that is how it appeared. As Marjaleena Repo recounted, the trip home with the delegates that she and David Orchard had recruited from western Canada was an exhilarating one, in which many people spoke with amazement of their ability as grass-roots members "to make a difference,"[96] despite the preferences of party elites. After all, their man had gone from a third-place tie at slightly less than 18 per cent on the first ballot to take the prize, something that had never been done before, at least in the Liberal Party. The immediate disappointment of the new generation of young Liberal MPs such as Mark Holland and Navdeep Bains, who had supported Gerard Kennedy, was tempered by the knowledge that the change they had been looking for in the way the party operated could still be achieved through Dion.[97] Indeed, media reports for the next several days began painting Dion as an anti-politician whose environmental fervour could potentially change the dynamics of federal politics under Stephen Harper and rejuvenate the Liberals.

But all was not well in some camps. Earlier, Dion organizers had attempted to speak with Rae after his third-round removal from the ballot to see if he would support their man. In a preview of things to come, a clearly furious Rae walked away, leaving it to his brother and former Chrétien organizer, John, to make it clear that this would not happen. A similar and allegedly more hostile exchange occurred between John Rae and Michael Ignatieff.[98] In the end, Rae released his delegates and did not indicate his support for anyone.

Virtually all of the Liberals' Quebec party elites had flocked to Ignatieff on the final ballot, a fact that was not missed by many observers. Despite evidence to the contrary, these Quebec delegates were convinced that Dion would not sell well in Quebec in an election because of his role in the Clarity Act and his strong opposition to Quebec separatism. Instead, these delegates – many of whom had supported Paul Martin – opted for the leadership contender whose views on federalism were most similar to Martin's in the apparent belief that this would increase their chances of restoring the party's dominance in the province. Even left-wing social liberals like Martin Cauchon and Denis Coderre joined the Ignatieff ranks at the end, although in their case the issue of "*l'alternance*" no doubt loomed large as well. As francophone Quebecers, they realized that by electing Dion the delegates would likely have ensured the next Liberal leadership race would be handed to an anglophone from outside Quebec, forcing the two men to wait much longer for any potential bid they might consider making.

The next day Dion hosted a lunch for his losing fellow candidates along with their spouses and senior aides. Publicly, the theme of party unity was promoted by all of the candidates as they arrived and were questioned by reporters. Once assembled and beyond the view of the cameras, several members of the Dion team recalled that Michael Ignatieff was still very gracious in defeat. By contrast, Bob Rae remained cool and aloof throughout. One Dion aide described Rae's mood as "toxic." According to several of those present, although Rae was clearly unhappy with Martha Hall Findlay, whose vote he believed he had been promised, he was primarily directing his wrath at Gerard Kennedy, whom he viewed as the architect of his defeat, and especially at one of Kennedy's key advisers who was present,

Katie Telford. Although Dion attempted to smooth the troubled waters, it was apparent that much more tact and diplomacy would be necessary to assuage ruffled feathers. Unfortunately, diplomacy was not Dion's strong suit, and the early promise of Liberal renewal quickly evaporated.

3 The Dion Era: Disappointment and Disarray

I am the leader of the Liberal Party 100%. You are either not the leader or you are the leader. There is no in-between.

– Stéphane Dion, 3 December 2006

I am a quick learner. We don't have a lot of time, as you know. We may be in an election at any time.

...

I don't want to rush an election. I want to be ready for an election. I know this government will have a lot of difficulty to go through its neoconservative agenda.

– Stéphane Dion, 4 December 2006

Stéphane Dion may have been an unexpected choice as Liberal leader, but in the immediate aftermath of the December 2006 leadership race Canadians appeared ready and willing to give him a chance. A Strategic Counsel poll conducted the day after the vote showed the Liberal Party ahead of the Conservatives for the first time since the Martin Liberals' defeat in January of that year. The Liberals were at 37 per cent support versus 31 per cent for the Conservatives, with the NDP trailing at 14 per cent while the Bloc polled 11 per cent and the Green Party 7 per cent. Even more encouraging for the Liberals was the fact that most of the gains came from the NDP and Green Party, and in Ontario. But the most significant result was clearly in Quebec, where an impressive 62 per cent of respondents thought the Liberals had made a good choice (contrary to the apparent views of the party's elites in that province) as compared with 55 per cent in the rest of the country.

However, any hopes that grass-roots delegates, rather than the elites, had been able to discern the most promising new messiah to lead the party out of the wilderness were quickly dashed. Dion faced a rocky road almost from the beginning, and things deteriorated with astonishing speed. By February 2007, another Strategic Counsel poll gave the Liberals only 29 per cent, an 8 per cent drop in support that placed them far back of the Conservatives, a position they would continue to occupy until the 2008 election. Dion, who had initially seemed so keen to challenge Harper to an election, proved less enthusiastic as he became aware of the difficulties he faced. While many of Dion's challenges were grounded in the party's pre-existing problems, such as lack of money and organization, he would do little to address them. Many more would prove to be of his own doing. Among those, the problems caused by his inability to build bridges, consult, and take advice from others were apparent almost immediately.

For any leader with little caucus support, and faced with the inevitable unhappiness of disgruntled leadership losers, party unity would naturally be a top priority. Certainly everyone else in the Liberal Party was acutely aware of this. And so, apparently, was Dion, at least in the beginning. On several occasions he told his advisers he was determined to avoid a continuation of the Chrétien/Martin feud and would make every effort to include other camps in his plans.

The morning after the convention, as they arrived at the special lunch that Dion had organized, virtually all of the defeated candidates made some allusion to this. Perhaps the most forthright was the kingmaker, Gerard Kennedy, who told reporters, "People need time to lick their wounds … It's going to take a real effort when the cameras are off to pull everybody together. I think Mr Dion is up to this task. He's going to invite other people's perspectives and make use of them. He understands that in some ways he doesn't have a choice. We all have to find a way to make this work."[1]

At first it looked like Dion had understood that message. He promptly found roles for all of the defeated candidates to play, although in one important respect this did not go as he originally planned. His initial decision to appoint Michael Ignatieff as policy chair, to prepare the platform, had to be abandoned when Ignatieff refused the offer and demanded the deputy leader post instead. Nonplussed, Dion felt he had no choice but to comply. According to Mark Marissen, Ignatieff's explanation was that he "wanted a broader role" and felt that Dion had already developed most of the platform, but Marissen was already sceptical of hidden agendas.[2] This scepticism proved well founded. Instead of Rae, who had been the most visibly unhappy in the immediate aftermath of the leadership convention, Ignatieff and his team proved to be the major problem for the leader in terms of loyalty.[3] Ignatieff soon began travelling across the country to raise his profile, while his team in Quebec began planning various events. One of the MPs who supported Dion later stated that, in his view, "Ignatieff's people undermined Dion during his entire time in office," a view shared by many of his caucus colleagues but categorically denied by Ignatieff.[4]

Meanwhile, Rae (who did not join the caucus until March 2008, when he won a by-election in the riding of retiring Liberal MP Bill Graham) was unaware of this contretemps, and accepted Dion's first offer to him – of policy chair – quite happily. He also suggested Scott Brison as co-chair, a request Dion quickly approved. (These appointments would later pose a serious problem as well, since Rae and Brison did not share Dion's priorities, and Rae in particular did not see the necessity of a formal Red Book – the official Liberal platform made famous by the Chrétien Liberals – which Dion was expecting.)

Gerard Kennedy, who would not be able to join the caucus until the next federal election because the riding in which he planned to run was held by the NDP, was appointed special adviser on election readiness. Martha Hall Findlay, also not in caucus until the same March 2018 by-elections that saw Rae elected, was given responsibility for policy outreach, which inevitably put her on a collision course with Bob Rae. (Here, too, problems would emerge before the next election, as Dion's decisions to appoint his own candidates and directly intervene in policy development would render much of their work meaningless.)

Caucus Discontent

As for the caucus, there were few people in it who had supported Dion. It remained deeply split, with significant groups of Ignatieff and Rae supporters never fully recognizing Dion's legitimacy: "He got 17% on the first ballot, for Pete's sake. How could this have happened?"[5] Even with the presumed support of those who had campaigned for Kennedy, he would still only have the automatic goodwill of far less than half of his colleagues. Moreover, his team knew only too well how divisive the Martin takeover had been, excluding anyone who failed to show sufficient allegiance. Dion publicly indicated he was intent on avoiding even the appearance of such exclusion. Declaring that he didn't care why any of his fellow MPs had supported someone else, he insisted "they should come to me and explain what they want to do to win the next election ... This race has seen a lot of success with the bottom-up philosophy, and we'll win the election the same way."[6]

But there was no bottom-up process in sight. Although Dion constantly spoke about his team approach, it soon became clear that inclusion on his team did not mean acceptance of other viewpoints. He expected the members of his team to be loyal foot soldiers, as he had been, and to not question his decisions once made. This soon led to accusations that he was in fact autocratic in his management style, an accusation that looked increasingly well founded. After barely four months in charge, he was routinely challenged, often publicly, by MPs who felt their views were being ignored.

Dion's decision in early April 2007 to strike a "non-compete" agreement with Green Party leader Elizabeth May in a riding in Nova Scotia for the next election was a case in point. Although there was some public support for the idea, it predictably caused consternation in caucus ranks, as the party had never before failed to field a candidate and many MPs believed this was a betrayal of Liberal voters in the riding. (The fact that May had little chance of winning the riding, while her agreement not to run a Green candidate in Dion's safe riding was meaningless, did not make the situation any easier to bear.) But the most serious concern was raised by the six Nova Scotia MPs with whom Dion spoke by telephone the night before he announced his decision. All six had understood his call was intended to canvass their views, and all six rejected the idea out of hand. Dion then reiterated his view that it was an excellent idea, and when one MP repeated that he was under the impression this was to be a consultation, Dion informed them that he would be announcing the move the next morning and ended the call. "They get called for their input and then their opinion gets not listened to," one disgruntled MP said. "That's really frustrating for MPs but it's not a surprise because Dion had practically zero caucus support."[7]

The situation deteriorated still further when it was learned that Dion and his House leader, Ralph Goodale, had instituted a "secret," by-invitation-only tactics committee meeting at 7:30 each morning because the regular 8:30 meeting had become too heavily attended, cumbersome, and, most important, unwilling to take direction. Not surprisingly, perhaps, news of this secret meeting quickly leaked, causing a further outcry. The increasing unrest led to embarrassing leaks from caucus and to growing questions of loyalty.[8]

Dion's difficulty accepting advice was well known to some of his closest advisers, one of whom suggested that it was "a more serious problem than simply thinking he was the smartest person in the room. He had real problems relating to others and almost no ability to empathize" with individuals.[9] This theme was repeated by several other confidants and advisers. Former MP Marlene Jennings, for example, stressed that she saw Dion as a man of honour and integrity who genuinely believed he could make a difference in politics, but she nevertheless noted that his intellect and policy knowledge were undermined by his "stubborn streak. He only listened to caucus when he was forced to and he rarely changed his mind on something once it was made up."[10] Karen Redman, former Liberal MP and party whip under Dion, agreed: "Resistance [about a policy] from politically savvy colleagues was irrelevant and would not faze him."[11] In addition, Jennings noted, Dion was not able to breach the political divide with some of his colleagues because he often had difficulty connecting with people on a personal level. "Being able to make that human connection and develop friendships easily, even if they're only facades, if it's, you know, only a diplomatic friendship. Those are not things Stéphane does easily."[12] These views were shared by veteran political insider Peter Donolo, who noted, "if the most important element in political success is EQ [emotional intelligence], that's kind of like the one ingredient that he was missing, but he made up for it in pure intellect and in integrity and determination."[13]

As one of his advisers recalled, Dion had few personal relationships or meaningful interactions with individual caucus members. One critic pointed out that there was never a line-up to see the leader outside of his Centre Block office in 409-S. "This was unheard of. Usually there would be a long line of supplicants waiting to get a leader's ear at all hours of the day." At the same time, Dion's wife, Janine Krieber, also a political scientist and a former instructor at the College Militaire St Jean, began to host lunches for small groups of caucus members at the parliamentary restaurant, a move the media interpreted as an attempt (albeit controversial) to enhance Dion's caucus credibility.[14]

The Leader's Office as a Work in Progress

In such a situation, it was crucial for Dion as leader to be surrounded by a group of experienced, competent, and politically astute advisers, as Marlene Jennings noted when she encouraged him to run.[15] Years later, Don Boudria ruefully recalled that Dion had asked him to work in the Office of the Leader of the Opposition (OLO) for a year or so in order to help set up the office. But Boudria had made it clear from the beginning that he did not want a job if Dion won, and he refused to change his mind. "I was wrong. I should have stayed," he confided. "There just were not enough experienced people around him, and no one who could speak truth to power, and there were problems immediately."[16]

Interestingly, at the morning-after luncheon, Dion had asked the defeated candidates for their advice on a range of issues. Bob Rae had cautioned against making the classic mistake of both Paul Martin and Brian Mulroney of "dancing with the ones that brung you."[17] This advice came too late. Dion had already appointed his key supporters Marcel Masse, Rod Bryden, and Herb Metcalfe as his transition team. Masse would soon become Dion's principal secretary in the new OLO. Another key supporter, Jamie Carroll, would be appointed acting chief of staff. Shortly afterwards, another senior adviser, Andrew Bevan, assumed the role of chief of staff, while Masse's deputy principal secretary was to be Paddy Tornsey, a former MP from Ontario who was among the first of the ex officio delegates to support Dion after his pledge to appoint more female candidates.

Andre Lamarre, Dion's communications adviser during his entire time as a Chrétien minister, became director of communications, and Geoffroi Montpetit, who had handled policy for Dion throughout his time in Ottawa, accompanied him. In fact, many of Dion's trusted team from his cabinet days at both Intergovernmental Affairs and Environment, almost all of whom were francophone Quebecers with an academic rather than political background, were recruited to make the move to the OLO. His caucus liaison, meanwhile, was one of his few caucus supporters from Quebec, former MP Eleni Bakopanis. In a nod to the two candidates who had handed him the leadership, Dion also engaged Kennedy staffer Katie Telford as policy secretary and director of stakeholder relations, while Martha Hall Findlay's policy adviser, Elliott Hughes, was assigned to run the Ontario desk. After much discussion, Ignatieff's adviser Brad Davis was named deputy director of strategic communications under director Robert Asselin, another Dion staffer.

Meanwhile, Jamie Carroll, one of Dion's more senior and experienced advisers and someone known for being able to stand up to Dion, had not been part of the transition team, nor did he have the role he anticipated in the OLO. As Megan Meltzer recalled, "There is no one who relates to Stéphane the way Jamie does … [he] can tell him when he has done something wrong or silly, and Stephane knows this. Jamie was the only one who told Stephane the truth one hundred per cent of the time."[18] After less than a month as acting chief of staff, Carroll was replaced by Andrew Bevan. Though he was offered the position of deputy chief of staff, he served in that role for only a short time. Carroll later indicated that he believed he had been assured the position of chief of staff by Dion, and was not enthusiastic about taking the lesser post.[19] Instead, after discussion with Bevan and Dion, Carroll took up the post he was offered of national director at the party's headquarters, where he felt he could make a real contribution to the reform efforts that had been started at the convention and prepare for the next election, which could occur at any time.

This issue was in fact one of two that divided the senior OLO staff from the beginning. Some, notably Andrew Bevan, wanted to proceed almost immediately to bring the government down and force an election, believing the polls were favourable and might not get better. Others, notably Mark Marissen, were opposed to this plan and felt the party apparatus was not ready.

This, in turn, was the source of the second internal division in the OLO, with some Dion supporters believing that the old guard as represented by party officials were not to be trusted. Not only were they concerned that "the party" might not have the best interests of the leader at heart, they also believed the old guard and campaign veterans were more fixated on money and election readiness than was wise. "We could negotiate a line of credit if we had to. And it's often easier to fundraise during a campaign. We also had all the build-up of the convention with potential new workers and sources of funding. And the other opposition parties were in no better shape than we were," one of them explained.[20] Another said, "They never accepted that Dion could win. They wanted him gone but, failing that, they wanted to save the furniture. They were not going to spend any more than they had to."[21]

Whether an early election would have made a difference to Liberal fortunes is, of course, impossible to determine. There can be little doubt, though, that Dion's image, and the party's fortunes, declined dramatically over a short period of time. Many blamed "the OLO" for these problems. In just a few months, caucus members were regularly complaining that the leader's office was inefficient and the whole system was bordering on chaotic. "Who's in charge?" one Dion supporter asked unhappily. Another described it as "a circus." Requests to the Liberal Research Bureau would be referred to the Leader's Office, which, in turn, forwarded these requests to the House leader's office, where they would often be told to try the Research Bureau.[22] Critics attacked the communications unit in particular for producing unclear or overly complicated press material and adding to Dion's image woes (as well-known journalist and former Turner communications director Ray Heard once commented, "They always go for us first. They can't admit it's the leader, and we are the obvious scapegoat. Then, if that doesn't work, they want a wholesale change of personnel in the OLO. Of course, sometimes they're right").[23]

It did not take long for major changes to be made. By 8 May, a press release indicated that communications director Andre Lamarre was being shuffled out of OLO to make room for Nicolas Ruzkowski, an Ottawa-based communications consultant who had never been involved with Mr. Dion, but who had worked for other Liberal ministers and in the Liberal election war room. Meanwhile, veteran backroom strategist Herb Metcalfe was brought on board to handle political strategy and the tactics committee. As one *Globe and Mail* article put it, "the policy wonks who have surrounded the former university professor are now making way for political tacticians."[24]

By October 2007, after the by-election disasters discussed below, Dion's numbers were plummeting and his office was undergoing another reorganization. Well-regarded former Chrétien aide Johanne Senecal was hired to replace Andrew Bevan as chief of staff, where she was allegedly expected to "impose order" on the operation.[25] At the same time, it was clear that her appointment and that of other Quebec francophones to the OLO was a direct response to the Outremont loss (of which, more later) and its fallout, which many Quebec party organizers blamed on a lack of francophone presence in the OLO. Bevan, meanwhile, became principal secretary and retained authority for policy and communications advice as well. The short-lived tenure of Nicolas Ruzkowski as director of communications ended when he was replaced by another former Chrétien staffer, Leslie Swartman, who had also worked in that position for former immigration minister Sergio Marchi and as chief of staff to transport minister Jean Lapierre. By the time he was defeated in the 2008 election, less than two years after his election as leader, Dion's OLO had been a revolving door for two chiefs of staff and four directors of communications.

Even as critics complained about the lack of experience in the OLO, a scenario evolved that was uncannily similar to that which had plagued John Turner. Dion's office was increasingly criticized for its failure to hire representatives from the various leadership camps, despite the examples given above. Even more significantly, it was often described as being top heavy with Martin operatives. This latter accusation made little sense unless the field was expanded to include formal election readiness posts and the party headquarters, but it was indicative of the growing unease within the party about Dion's leadership. "After all, these were the guys who led us to a minority in 2004 and defeat in 2006," one MP recalled, presumably referring to Murphy, Alboim, and Guest. "They never actually won anything."

This perspective was widely shared among the newer MPs who had come to the caucus in 2004 or 2006. Dion may not have listened to caucus members, but the previously optimistic new MPs were also becoming increasingly discouraged by who he *was* listening to, and the apparent influence that some of the old guard seemed to have with

Dion behind the scenes. For them, this lack of progress in setting a new course for the party was most disconcerting given that they had hoped for such a change when they campaigned for Dion or Kennedy. Instead, there was a growing sense that some of Dion's more "erratic" decisions were being made after he listened to advice provided by a number of these prominent Liberal advisers of the old guard, such as Senator David Smith, even though they had no formal role to play in the decision-making process. Accusations also flew that some of the advice Dion was receiving was not designed to help him, but to bring about his early demise and replacement as leader well before the next election.[26] Another MP who had observed this behaviour concluded that Dion's lack of political instincts was a potentially fatal flaw. "You have to know in politics who you can trust and who you can't, and he didn't seem to be able to do that."

Caucus unease grew exponentially over the course of 2007, partly because of Dion's decisions concerning candidates for by-elections, and partly as a result of the Liberals' dismal performance in the House of Commons.

By-election Blues

Party unity, and the leader's political judgment, were called into serious question mere months after Dion assumed the leadership when a series of by-elections were announced by the prime minister, the first three of which were to be held in Quebec on 17 September 2007.

Although the Liberals did not have high expectations for two of the Quebec ridings, which were held by the Bloc, they did not expect to do as badly as they did. In the first case, in Saint-Hyacinthe Bagot, the Bloc predictably retained the riding but the Liberals not only finished in fourth place, they received fewer votes than in the 2006 election, well behind the NDP. In Roberval-Lac-Saint-Jean, the Bloc's victory in 2006 had been by a narrower margin than in the past. In this by-election, the Conservatives were successful, giving Harper another seat to enhance his minority.

But it was in the third riding, Outremont, where Liberals were shaken to their very core. This was a riding that they had held continuously since its creation in 1935, a riding that had been represented for many years by well-known Liberals such as Marc Lalonde, Lucie Pepin, Martin Cauchon, and, more recently, Jean Lapierre. It was considered one of the safest Liberal seats in the country and the seat a young Justin Trudeau hoped to represent when he announced in the spring of 2007 that he was planning to enter politics. Also interested in Outremont was former astronaut Marc Garneau, who ran in a suburban Montreal riding and lost his seat in the 2006 general election. Both were prevented by the leader.[27] (Garneau subsequently made sufficient waves that Dion handed him the uncontested nomination in Liberal-safe Westmount, but continued to place roadblocks in the way of Trudeau, who in the end was denied an appointment [allegedly because he needed to prove himself] and forced to run for the nomination in the very unsafe riding of Papineau.) Instead, on 18 July Stéphane Dion intervened and appointed an old friend and fellow academic, Jocelyn Coulon, as the Liberal candidate in the riding. Although Coulon had an impressive resume, he lacked any political experience and was widely seen as being even more "academic" than Dion. Party insiders were speechless but vowed to do their best.

According to Jamie Carroll, the problem was with both the organization (or lack of it) and the candidate's own lack of political experience. In his view, the party was in very real danger of losing:

> I don't know where the Coderre/Ignatieff team were – they were supposed to be looking after this. We sent three workers to help out, we offered money and support, but it was hopeless. When [the party HQ workers] got there, they discovered the situation was chaotic. There did not seem to be anybody in charge, and no one was doing any of the usual things, including the candidate.[28]

Carroll and Gordon Ashworth met to discuss the situation and agreed that Dion should consider having Coulon step aside in mid-campaign. "I met with [Dion] and warned him that he was going to wear this," Carroll recalled, "but he wouldn't budge."[29]

In the end, in one of the most dramatic upsets in modern Liberal history, the party not only lost the riding but paved the way for the election of an NDP candidate, Tom Mulcair. This defeat would have long-term consequences for the party in that province as, for the first time, the NDP could claim to be a viable alternative to the Liberals with voters who rejected the separatist Bloc and the right-wing Harper Conservatives.

Dion was indeed widely blamed for this stunning defeat. In Quebec a minor revolt broke out in Liberal ranks (or, as one Dion adviser put it, "the elites freaked out"). The former Liberal MP for Outremont, Jean Lapierre, told reporters it was Dion's 14 per cent standing in the polls in Quebec that had caused the defeat.[30] Others blamed the leader's stubborn determination to appoint an inappropriate candidate against the advice of senior party officials. Some Dion supporters speculated that the Ignatieff camp had actually planned the defeat in order to demonstrate Dion's inability to win in Quebec. Meanwhile, Marcel Proulx,

Dion's Quebec lieutenant, took responsibility and resigned, leaving Dion to try to replace him. More embarrassment followed as both a furious Denis Coderre and Liberal MP Pablo Rodriguez refused Dion's offer of the post. In the end he appointed Liberal senator Celine Payette, a controversial choice among party elites.[31]

The fallout from the disaster included changes to the leader's office, as discussed above. The internal party quarrel also had a significant impact on the party's future electoral fortunes in Quebec. While the party elites may have been wrong about Dion's initial image with the average Quebecois voter, it was now clear to everyone that he was not perceived as a leader by his own party elites, and hence whatever credibility he might have had as a strong leader was destroyed with the broader public.

After this debacle, one might have expected Dion to be more cautious in the use of his power to appoint candidates, particularly if they were not representative of minority groups, since that had been the original purpose of the party's constitutional resolution.[32] Yet this was not the case. Apparently unmoved by the furore in Quebec, Dion did not hesitate to invoke his ability to appoint a candidate when four more by-elections were announced by the prime minister for 17 March 2008. And here, since all four ridings were currently held by Liberals, it was imperative that the Liberals retain their seats.

This proved a simple enough proposition in Toronto Centre where, as mentioned earlier, Bob Rae successfully replaced retiring Liberal veteran MP Bill Graham. The same was true of Willowdale, where the popular Liberal MP Jim Peterson had represented the riding for most of the past two decades and his replacement, Martha Hall Findlay, was easily elected. Somewhat more problematic was Vancouver Quadra, John Turner's old seat and, more recently, that of Chrétien cabinet minister Stephen Owen. With Owen's retirement, the riding was retained for the Liberals by the high-profile candidate Joyce Murray, a former provincial environment minister under BC Liberal premier Gordon Campbell. But the margin of victory was very narrow, causing concern in Liberal ranks.

This anxiety was largely eclipsed by the disaster that loomed large in Desnethé–Missinippi–Churchill River. With the resignation of Liberal MP Gary Merasty, the riding had opened up and David Orchard, a key lynchpin in Stéphane Dion's victory, hoped to be the Liberal candidate. "I did not ask to be appointed," he said, "I wanted to win after a fair and contested nomination." As he later recounted, "I have farmland in the riding, I know the Aboriginal community leaders there very well, and it seemed like a good fit."[33] Orchard agreed with Mark Marissen's claim that there had been no specific quid pro quo when Orchard offered to work for Dion's leadership campaign. However, there was "certainly an understanding that I would play a role" if Dion were elected; "he said it himself at the press conference."[34] More importantly, Orchard had spoken with Dion about his plan to run there in the summer of 2007 and Dion had encouraged him to run. Dion had even introduced Orchard and one other contender as the two candidates vying for the nomination when he visited the riding. "I spent three months driving twenty thousand kilometres around the riding signing up five hundred new members," Orchard recalled. "It was pretty clear that I would win. Then, out of the blue, over the Christmas holidays, Dion announced, *from Bali*, that he was appointing Joan Beatty as the Liberal candidate."[35]

Beatty, a Cree/Métis woman from southern Saskatchewan who was a sitting NDP cabinet minister in Regina at the time, had only recently been re-elected in a November provincial election. But she abruptly resigned her post to run in the distant northern Saskatchewan riding to which she had no known connection. "I had no advance warning," Orchard said. "And I later learned that [lone Saskatchewan Liberal MP] Ralph Goodale had told Dion that I was OK with this!"[36] Goodale later claimed that Orchard knew Dion might appoint a woman, to which Orchard replied, "Mr. Goodale's statement is completely and utterly false."[37]

Not surprisingly, Dion's decision was not well received in the riding or by the local Liberal riding association, and a very public feud erupted. According to Métis leader Jim Durocher, "Liberals in the riding feel betrayed ... [and] angry that Central Canadians think they know what works in northern Saskatchewan."[38] This became news even in central Canada, and a *Globe and Mail* editorial described the situation as "an unholy mess that could cost the Liberals the riding."[39] Both Aboriginal leaders and the riding president publicly called on Dion to reverse his decision, but his office informed them it was "final." Trying to broker an end to the ugly dispute, former Turner aide Doug Richardson, a prominent Saskatoon lawyer, arranged for Orchard to meet with Dion in Ottawa at the opposition leader's residence, Stornaway, with Ralph Goodale present. "Stéphane was surprised when I said I had not agreed to the Beatty announcement in advance," Orchard recalled. "But his only offer was that I run in Toronto Danforth, against Jack Layton!"[40] Calling the offer "ridiculous and insulting," Orchard left without any agreement having been reached (he later campaigned successfully against Beatty for the nomination in the 2008 general election, which he lost by a narrow margin despite the Dion campaign's disastrous showing).[41]

Meanwhile, Dion attempted to defend the appointment as a way of increasing the number of women candidates,[42] but others pointed out that this appointment was unlikely to prove helpful in increasing either the number of women candidates or sitting MPs. "You have to pick and choose your fights," one of Dion's former advisers said, "and that definitely was not one of them. He should never have gotten involved. How was he going to inspire loyalty after what he did to Orchard? The man may have been a bit of a loose cannon, but if Dion was going to take Orchard's delegates then he was obliged to let him run."

Many of Orchard's supporters, including Shoal Lake chief Marcel Head, promptly began a campaign to discourage Liberals from voting in the by-election. The tactic appeared to be effective, as turnout fell from nearly 60 per cent in the last federal election to barely 25 per cent. In the end, Beatty suffered a humiliating defeat to the Conservative candidate, Bob Clarke, and the Harper Conservatives added another seat to their minority.

Despite these by-election additions, however, Harper's government was technically clinging to power with the smallest minority in Canadian history – only 143 MPs or 40 per cent of the seats in the House. With seventy-seven seats, the Liberals could easily have defeated them if the Bloc (forty-nine seats) and NDP (thirty-seven) had joined forces with them, but they did not. In fact, by mid-2007, the Harper Conservatives had not only been in power far longer than the longest previous Conservative minority government (six months, nineteen days), but longer than the average minority government of any party (one year, five months).

A major factor in their longevity was the situation unfolding in the House of Commons, where the Conservatives were pushing ahead with an aggressive agenda and – as many observers watched in growing disbelief – the Liberals appeared to be unable to find their footing.

The Liberals' Unprecedented Performance in the House

To begin with, communication proved a problem for Stéphane Dion during Question Period (QP) in the House of Commons. As John Turner had in his tenure as Leader of the Official Opposition after the 1984 Liberal loss, Dion tried to read his questions from a prepared text. Like Turner, he was widely mocked for this practice until he finally abandoned it. Unlike Turner, though, Dion's problem was not simply an aversion to the televised sessions. Derek Ferguson, the former journalist running the Liberal Research Bureau, was charged with preparing Dion for Question Period, a challenging task. The very idea of attacking and using theatrics in the House, it seemed, was beyond the Liberal leader. In addition, his difficulties with English were becoming a significant concern, and many of his early supporters were surprised by this. Mark Marissen, David Orchard, and David Karwacki, who had not known Dion before they agreed to support his campaign, each commented that they had had no difficulty understanding him in one-on-one conversations when they first met him, and did not originally think his English was a problem at all.[43] However, his closest advisers noted that his accent, already strong, became much thicker when he was under pressure. Furthermore, they worried that, because there were so many francophones in the OLO, his English-speaking skills might actually be diminishing.[44] Worse still, the situation was exacerbated by the presence of Michael Ignatieff, the public intellectual so comfortable in front of the cameras, who shone in QP.

Dion was soon signed up for English elocution lessons, something that had also been tried with Jean Chrétien with very little success. Yet Chrétien somehow managed to communicate well in his flawed and accented English, primarily due to his knack for using short words and shorter sentences, and offering up homespun analogies (many voters would remember his image of a car gently rocking back and forth in a snowdrift as a metaphor for Canadian federalism, for example). Although Dion's speech coach, Mary Houle, noted that he had an excellent vocabulary, she identified a problem with intonation and pitch, his sentences often rising at the end and conveying the impression of uncertainty.[45] Another analyst noted that, unlike Chrétien, Dion had an unfortunate tendency to try to speak in English as he would in French, in the lengthy and complex sentences typical of an academic. This more than anything proved to be his undoing.

But Dion's communications problems paled in comparison with the various problematic decisions he made in the first few months of his term, all of which called into question his political judgement. They began just days after he took over as leader, when the Martin Liberals' same-sex-marriage legislation faced a government motion. During the 2006 election campaign Stephen Harper had attempted to placate the religious right in his own party by promising he would table a motion asking MPs, in a free vote, if they wanted to re-open the debate. Most analysts believed that Harper realized such a vote would almost certainly be defeated. On 7 December, the motion came up for the vote, less than a week after Dion had won the leadership. Dion had originally promised Scott Brison that he would deliver the Liberals in a whipped vote, a move that soon proved unwise. It became apparent in caucus that this decision was highly controversial, particularly as Harper was allowing a free vote. In the end, whip Karen Redman convinced Dion to do the same (although she had first tried pointing out that the motion would not only fail but had no legal force, and the courts in any event would continue to support the constitutionality of the legislation, she recalled that – tellingly – it was her appeal to Dion to consider his position if the issue had been the Quebec referendum that finally convinced him).[46] The final vote was 175 to 123, with 12 Conservatives, including six cabinet ministers, voting *against* the motion, and 13 Liberals voting in favour.

Ironically, the issue of whipped votes would soon re-emerge as a huge problem, but not in the way most observers – or whip Karen Redman – would have expected. Initially, Dion had had some success in the House, first by introducing a motion on a Liberal opposition day demanding the Harper government "reaffirm" its commitment to the Kyoto Protocol on the environment. The motion, supported by the NDP, passed easily on 5 February 2007. Similarly, the Liberals and the NDP combined to defeat a Conservative proposal to extend some provisions of the Anti-Terrorism Act for a further two years, arguing that they represented an unnecessary constraint on civil liberties.

However, as both parties were aware, there was no political consequence to defeating the government's proposal, since such a defeat would not be considered a confidence vote. Typically, only money votes – votes on a budget or the legislation flowing from it – would automatically be considered a confidence vote that would bring down a minority government. Otherwise it would be necessary for an opposition party or the government to specifically declare in advance that they were considering a vote on a particular piece of legislation as a confidence vote. With the election of Dion as leader, and his enthusiastic early comments about an imminent election, many observers were expecting the Liberals to take advantage of their situation to bring down the government with such a non-confidence vote at an early opportunity. That this did not prove to be the case was a surprise in itself, but the mechanisms the Liberals used to actively avoid the calling of an election were even more unexpected.

Their problems began early on when it became clear that Stephen Harper was planning to govern as if he had a majority. This highly unusual move, in turn, was based on the political calculation that the opposition parties did not want to be seen forcing another general election so soon after Harper's January 2006 electoral win. Before the Liberals seemed to know what had happened, they found themselves boxed in by the other opposition parties. Both the NDP and the Bloc responded to Harper's bravado by making it clear that they would vote against the government's proposals whenever they pleased. It would be up to the Liberals to decide whether the government fell or not. This, of course, was something most of Dion's caucus believed they could not allow to stand, and there were a number of tactics they could have employed to turn the tables if they had wanted to.

The result was that, on some occasions, Liberals voted with the government, on some they indicated they would revoke legislation of which they disapproved when they eventually formed the government, and on others they simply absented themselves from the debate. Plainly put, it increasingly appeared to everyone, including the media and the general public, that the Liberals were terrified of provoking an election. Worse still, the image of them abstaining from votes proved embarrassing politically, as the prime minister and the other opposition leaders took turns attacking the Liberals for failing to live up to their responsibilities as the Official Opposition.

Dion was under increasing pressure from party organizers to delay an election because they had no money, no campaign organization, and no candidates. Added to which, Dion himself did not have a platform. Nevertheless, a number of other procedural options were recommended by legendary Liberal procedural adviser Jerry Yanover and another veteran adviser to the House leader, Richard Wackid. Both men argued strenuously against the selective abstention option, but Dion refused to consider their alternatives.[47]

Matters came to a head with the Throne Speech of 23 October 2007, when the House of Commons returned after Parliament had been prorogued on 4 September. The speech contained several controversial proposals, including a withdrawal of Canada's commitment to meet its emissions-reduction targets under the Kyoto Protocol and a plan to extend Canada's military mission in Afghanistan by an additional two years. These were matters on which the Liberals had already expressed themselves and that they would normally have rejected out of hand. In an astonishing move, the entire Liberal caucus sat in the House and abstained in the final vote. Moreover, it came to light that this was a "whipped" vote. As Karen Redmond recalled, she was asked not only to tell her colleagues not to vote, but to ensure they were present for it anyway. "It was an ill-conceived and very bad idea," she said. "Of course it was resented, and it eroded morale."[48] Nevertheless, in caucus she defended the move as a loyal soldier, telling her colleagues "we've got to stick together. This is a decision that we have made."[49]

Although they complied, many of her colleagues were furious. As one new Liberal MP loudly declared, "I did not run for office in order to stay in the Lobby [or sit in the House] and not vote!" It was not that all of Dion's caucus was determined to bring down the government. On the contrary, many of his MPs had revised their thinking about forcing an early election in light of the falling Liberal polling numbers over the course of 2007. But they continued to believe there were other ways of handling the situation. Dion demurred.

Responding to this extraordinary development, parliamentary procedure expert C.E.S. Franks believed it was the first "whipped abstention" in Canadian history. "I have never heard of it before," he said. "I think it sets a precedent. Certainly it reflects the current state of the Liberal Party ... At some point the Liberal Party stands for something or it doesn't."[50]

Meanwhile, House leader Ralph Goodale defended the Liberal abstention as essentially unimportant. "There has never been a government in this country ... that has been defeated on a Throne Speech," he told reporters. "A Throne Speech is an entirely symbolic gesture. It carries no legal consequences." Had he stopped there, the wily Liberal veteran might have defused the situation. Unfortunately, he continued, uncharacteristically offering more detail than was necessary and a rationale that would come back to haunt him. "What's important is the legislation that flows during the session of Parliament, and we will consider each one of those pieces of legislation on their merits. If they don't pass muster, we'll vote against them."[51]

The problem was that the Liberals did not find *any* legislation to be sufficiently egregious that they would reject it, and spent most of the fall finding new ways to allow Harper's bills to pass. In early February the entire Liberal caucus walked out of the House of Commons rather than vote on a Conservative crime bill that the government had declared it would consider a confidence motion. Then, in early March, they struck a deal with the Conservatives that allowed them to support the proposed extension to the Afghan mission, a measure that had been mentioned in the Throne Speech, and then voted in favour of the modified plan that the government also gave notice would be considered a confidence motion.

On the Throne Speech, there had been some consideration given to the idea of the Liberals' front bench – leader and shadow cabinet – symbolically voting against it, while the rest of the caucus abstained – but with more than two dozen MPs involved in that plan, and no idea how attendance would shape up with the other opposition parties, they feared it was entirely possible they might bring down the government accidentally. As a result, even that fig leaf of visible opposition was rejected. This was not the case in late February 2008, when the Dion Liberals again abstained several times on the votes on the Harper government's budget. Perhaps in response to the earlier widespread criticism concerning their handling of the Throne Speech, and undoubtedly in anticipation of how this abstention would be perceived on a money bill, the Liberals did allow some of their front bench – Dion, the House leader, whip, and eight others – to vote against it, while the rest of the Liberal benches were empty.

Both Dion and his finance critic, John McCallum, also made it clear that they might vote against other implementation legislation flowing from the budget, and word began to spread that the Liberals might be preparing to pull the plug on the Conservative minority. "We have said that we would not bring down the government at this time," McCallum told reporters, "but come April or May circumstances may have changed. Later on in the session all options are open," he declared. Sounding unusually aggressive, Dion agreed. "If they do something that we Liberals consider aggravating the situation that they have created ... we may decide, indeed, to trigger an election."[52]

Dion contacted Mark Marissen, his election campaign chair, to see what the campaign's situation was at that point, as he was eager to proceed. Marissen flew to Halifax to meet with Dion and his chief fundraiser, Senator James Cowan of Nova Scotia. Marissen, along with campaign director Gordon Ashworth, had prepared a status report that showed the party was completely unprepared to fight another election, something to which Cowan readily agreed. Among other things, Marissen noted, the lack of money to fund a campaign was a crucial problem. At the briefing, Dion appeared shocked and then furious. "You have put me and the caucus on our knees!" he exclaimed, and walked out the door.[53]

Money Matters

When Jean Chrétien introduced Bill C-24 on political party financing in 2003, the Liberal Party was still heavily dependent on donations from corporations and wealthy individuals. This was despite some considerable effort over the past ten years to expand its ability to raise money from individuals through direct mail and other techniques. As a result, virtually every analyst agreed that the Liberals would be the hardest hit by Chrétien's new rules. But many Liberals argued that this could be a good thing, because it would provide the necessary impetus for the party to finally move into the twenty-first century with its fundraising.

While this would have been difficult, it should not have been life-threatening. When Paul Martin took over from Chrétien in December of that year, the party's situation was not bleak. The Liberals were in power (making it easier to raise money), the party's debt had been eliminated, and there was sufficient money to fight the next election campaign. According to public opinion polls, there was every reason to believe that the Liberal Party would continue to be in power for several more years. In addition, with the changes to Chrétien's original draft legislation that were made after opposition and internal party concerns were raised, the final version of the bill was one Liberals – including initially strong opponents such as party president Stephen LeDrew – believed would be revenue neutral. This, in turn, was partly because individual contributions had been capped at a "reasonable" $5,000, and also because of the substantial increase in the publicly funded per-vote subsidies that the legislation promised each party, in order to make up for the anticipated shortfall caused by the elimination of corporate and union contributions at the national level.

Then the unthinkable happened. Paul Martin came close to losing the 2004 election and, within little more than a year, the party was obliged to fund another election campaign. This time Martin did lose to Stephen Harper's new Conservative Party. Following that second campaign, the party was once more in debt. A costly leadership campaign siphoned off more money that otherwise might have been contributed to the party. Even then the Liberals might have been able to recover if the situation had been relatively normal, one in which elections were held once every four years. But it was not. The Conservatives were in power with only a slim minority, meaning that yet another election might be called at any time, and the party would have to be ready.

Although the December 2006 convention had adopted Mike Eizenga's proposed changes, which included starting to compile a national membership list for fundraising purposes, these changes would take time and had yet to be fully implemented. Worse still, Stephen Harper had recognized the seriousness of the Liberals' situation and took action to ensure that it became much worse. Among the measures buried in one of the Harper government's first pieces of legislation, the Federal Accountability Act, was one that reduced the individual contribution amount from $5,000 to $1,000 and eliminated corporate and union contributions at the local level.

This had a devastating impact on the Liberals. The bill was passed in December 2006 and the Liberals' total revenue declined dramatically in 2007, and again in 2008. While some of the decline could undoubtedly be attributed to Dion's problematic leadership and the Liberals' low standing in the polls, experts agreed that the abrupt changes in contribution levels also played a huge role.[54] In 2007, as mentioned above, the Conservatives raised more than twice the total of all other parties combined, at $8.9 million. The NDP managed to raise $1.9 million but the Liberals, despite their status as the Official Opposition, could only bring in $1.8 million. Even more revealing was the fact that the Conservatives obtained their funding from more than forty thousand individuals while the Liberals and NDP were only able to obtain roughly ten thousand to thirteen thousand individual contributions, respectively.[55] By April 2008, even as Dion and McCallum spoke of bringing down the government, Elections Canada revealed that the Liberals had raised only $846,129 from 10,169 individual contributors in the first quarter, while the NDP raised $1.1 million from 13,329 contributors and the Conservatives had amassed more than five times the Liberals, at $4.95 million from 44, 345 donors.[56]

Perhaps even more significant was the fact that by 2007 only the Bloc was more dependent on public subsidies than the Liberals. In 2008 the Liberals relied on the subsidy for 60 per cent of their total revenue, while the NDP stood at roughly 48 per cent and the Conservatives at slightly more than 30 per cent[57] (these figures would become critically important after the 2008 federal election, as we will see in the next chapter).

In contrast to the other parties, the Conservatives were awash in funds. In fact, they had far more money than they could legally spend given the limitations of the 1974 Trudeau legislation, which had been specifically designed to level the playing field among political parties. Already in the 2006 election the Conservatives (and notably campaign director and later senator Doug Finley) had devised a plan that came to be known as the "in and out" scandal, in a devious attempt to spend some of their excess money. The chief electoral officer accused the Conservatives of violating Trudeau's legislation by diverting national funds to local riding associations and then redirecting the money to the national campaign. The scandal continued to plague the Conservatives throughout their first minority term, with all opposition leaders raising questions about it in the House. The prime minister and other cabinet ministers consistently stonewalled in their replies, denying any wrongdoing. Then, in April 2008, agents of Elections Canada and the RCMP raided the party's headquarters and confiscated relevant material under the glare of television cameras, reminding Canadians of the issue. However, the Conservatives continued to employ a number of stall tactics, and it would take several more years for the matter to finally be resolved. In 2012, the party and Senator Finley struck a plea bargain admitting guilt and agreeing to an established set of facts related to "fraudulent practices" including "false or misleading" expense documents submitted to Elections Canada, and paid nearly $250,000 in fines.

This lengthy delay, of course, meant that the matter had little or no impact on the 2008 election or even that of 2011.

Meanwhile, the Conservatives were actively looking for other ways to legally spend their considerable resources and quickly found one in the so-called permanent campaign. The spending limitations of the 1974 legislation only covered the election period since, at the time, no one expected a political party to have sufficient resources, or interest, to spend money outside of that period. Now one party did. Following the lead of the Republicans in the United States, the Conservatives began to make extensive use of so-called attack ads and did so far in advance of an election being called. As Liberal communications expert Peter Donolo later noted, Dion "was really the first kind of victim of the American style of politics that Harper adopted in Canada, which is very much about destroy your opponent. He's not your opponent, he's your enemy."[58]

In fact, the Conservatives launched not one but three extremely expensive waves of aggressively negative advertising against Stéphane Dion long before the launch of the 2008 campaign. The first came less than a month after he was elected leader in December 2006, when a flurry of ads depicted him as "not a leader" and "not worth the risk." As Woolstencroft and Ellis wrote:

> Nowhere was the Conservatives' toughness or their approach to perpetual campaigning better demonstrated than in their relentless twenty-month airwave assault on Stéphane Dion ... In January 2007 they purchased some of the most expensive TV advertising time available (during the Super Bowl broadcast) to run an ad featuring a clip of Michael Ignatieff's challenge to Dion during the Liberal leadership debates over their party's environmental record. Dion's response of "Do you think it's easy to make priorities" [with the accompanying photo of him shrugging and looking helpless] suitably captured the Conservatives' preferred image of him as weak, indecisive and unwilling to make tough decisions.[59]

This was followed by a second wave of negative ads after the tabling of the March 2007 budget, when the Conservatives thought an election might be imminent, and a third in the fall of 2007, when Dion was again considering the possibility of bringing down the government.

As journalist Ira Basen has outlined in some detail,[60] the Harper ad campaigns were significant not only for their unprecedented expense and timing: they were a "textbook example" of a new political tool called "framing," a relative of the commercial marketing tool known as "branding." In the United States, framing had already been used to great advantage by political spin doctor Karl Rove, who managed to save the campaign of George W. Bush in part by framing Democratic candidate John Kerry, a decorated war hero, as a dishonest coward. The "Swift Boat" ads that Rove orchestrated are legendary, and "swiftboating" has now passed into the lexicon as a term for an act that discredits someone or something through inaccurate but effective framing. Political pundits now routinely repeat the maxim "Frame yourself, or others will establish the frame for you." As Canadian political scientist Alex Marland has described in detail, such branding has now become common in Canada and not only serves to discredit the individual targeted, but also provides a favourable contrast with an opposing political actor.[61]

In Dion's case, this was quintessentially true. He was essentially a blank slate with the general public after his unexpected December victory; the Conservatives managed to hang the "not a leader" frame on him in just a few months through their relentless depiction of him as incompetent and weak. At the same time, by inference the ads reinforced the notion that Stephen Harper as prime minister and Conservative leader was both strong and highly competent.

According to several of his advisers, Dion was ambivalent about the ads. HIs well-known inability to believe that good policy would not always prevail over political manipulation in a contest for public opinion was being sorely tried by the attacks, which he saw as unfair and misleading. After the fact there was also considerable disagreement in the party's inner circles as to whether the party was willing to expend money countering the ads, despite Dion's repeated requests that this be done. Several of his closest advisers insisted that these requests were rebuffed out of hand, with the explanation that there was simply no money available in the pre-writ period if the party were hoping to finance a national campaign. "They told us there would be time during the campaign to launch a series of good ads to counter this. We told them it would be too late." Yet at least one party insider claimed they did offer to fund a (limited) response, an offer that was refused as unnecessary,[62] suggesting at a minimum that once again internal communications in the Liberal organization were part of the problem.

Public opinion polling showed that the ads were extremely effective. Dion's approval ratings plummeted over the course of the year. At the same time, however, it must be noted that the ads could not have been successful had it not been for the substance he added to the Conservatives' frame with his uninspiring performance in the House, his difficulty expressing himself in English, and his inept handling of several by-elections. Changing the frame certainly would take money and time, and the Liberals had neither. (By contrast, the Conservatives' use of attack ads was much less successful against a more credible and popular opponent, as I outline below.)

The Party in Disarray

Stéphane Dion was not a party man, but many party insiders had expected him to pay more attention to the party once he became leader. This simply did not happen, which was perhaps even more surprising as he himself had recognized that reform was necessary and that an election might take place at any time.

An early indication of his lack of interest came with his failure to respond to the lengthy and detailed letter that Tom Axworthy, party policy guru and former senior adviser to Pierre Trudeau, had sent him shortly after the December convention. The letter outlined the various recommendations of the thirty-two task forces of the party's Policy Renewal Commission, which Axworthy had chaired. Those recommendations had been tabled at the convention but literally ignored in the frenzy of the leadership race, to Axworthy's dismay and that of all the various party noteworthies and experts who had laboured on them throughout 2006. In his accompanying letter, Axworthy stated:

> I both insist that the Party should follow through on its commitment to use this product of the volunteer wing of the Liberal Party to assist ridings and activists in their policy work, and I suggest a plan for the months ahead that would see the party commit to a thinkers' conference, extended policy discussions in the ridings, an email vote by the whole membership on platform priorities, and the use of the new Council of the Presidents to give legitimacy to the platform effort. My argument is that party renewal and success in the next election go hand in hand.[63]

As Axworthy later confided, Dion never replied to the letter or followed through on any of the recommendations.[64] Despite the fact that an election could occur at any time, he seemed determined to ignore the ground work already accomplished on the policy front by the thirty-two task forces, and instead charged several of his former opponents for the leadership with the task of creating a platform from scratch.

True, on the organizational front he had quickly appointed senior leadership campaign advisers Mark Marissen and Nancy Gerard as his election campaign co-chairs. But then he had left matters largely up to Marissen, who made more than 120 flights from Vancouver to Ottawa and elsewhere in an effort to organize the campaign and recruit troops.

Nevertheless, Marissen's distant base was seen by many as a problem for efficient organization, and Marissen himself had suggested adding Senator David Smith for his central location in Toronto as well as his expertise.

Within the OLO, a significant disagreement emerged as to who should be involved in that campaign. For many of Dion's original supporters, intent on having the party do things differently, it was obvious that new blood should be brought on board to run the show. The problem, as Andrew Bevan later noted, was that there had been no attempt by the party to encourage the training of a new young cadre of party organizers and managers. "The top Martin people were obviously out," he recalled, "and that really left only the old guard from the Chrétien era" if not the era of Trudeau. "Marissen had already brought on Smith. When Marissen suggested Gordon Ashworth, who obviously had extensive experience, no one was very happy but there was really no alternative," another senior Dion adviser agreed.[65] And so, Gordon Ashworth was brought on board as campaign director along with long-time Liberal pollster Michael Marzolini, both of whom were seen as Chrétien-era Liberals. Rounding out the top echelons were Tim Murphy and Elly Alboim from the Martin campaign. On the other hand, the party's national director and one of Dion's closest aides, Jamie Carroll, would also serve as the deputy campaign manager. But, as Marissen had stressed in Halifax in his meeting with Dion in the spring of 2008, all of these senior operatives argued the party was in no shape to fight another campaign at that point.

Meanwhile, at the party headquarters, Jamie Carroll had assumed the role of national director in December 2006 with a clear agenda in mind. First and foremost, he wanted to clear up a backlog of receipts that had not been issued, prepare for an election, and get the party's finances in shape, and that meant understanding and perhaps changing the HQ organization, as well as implementing the 2006 convention results. He quickly realized that he and the party headquarters would have to deal with new groups – such as the Council of Presidents – and, more importantly, that the recent changes meant the provincial associations would get the lion's share of the per-vote subsidy. Despite this, he felt progress was being made. Brian Klunder, another Dion campaign worker, had been put in charge as director of memberships (obviously a new position resulting from the changes), and "he actually got all the provincial associations onside and online with a national membership list, a national set of membership rules, and a national membership fee. This was no mean feat."[66]

Carroll was not as successful with the revamping of the Federal Liberal Agency of Canada (FLAC), which continued to cause problems. He was concerned with finding competent members, but others – such as new party president and senator Marie Poulin – were concerned with representation and wanted to bring in more members from the west, more women, and more francophones. Everyone agreed the two sets of concerns were not mutually exclusive, but the additional constraints delayed the rebuilding process more than expected.

At the same time, the party's lease on its office space was about to expire, and Carroll was obliged to spend time arranging a deal so that they could stay in the same place as a matter of necessity with an election in the offing. He later indicated he would have preferred to go elsewhere, but under the various constraints it was better to simply sign the lease.

"Money was a huge problem, or rather the lack of it," Carroll admitted.[67] He soon found out that the party had not been paying all of its bills for several years, and there were surprising consequences. "The leader could not stay at a certain hotel chain because the party's credit was not good, nor would a certain grocery chain deliver groceries to Stornoway. That's the level of difficulty we were in," he said. "In the end, we let go most of the existing fundraising staff and started over."

Carroll's term as national director was a controversial one for a variety of reasons, including the perception by many in the party management that, at twenty-nine, he was too inexperienced to run the national office. In the end, however, his mandate was cut short by the same fallout from the by-election disaster in Quebec that saw Johanne Senecal replace Andrew Bevan as chief of staff. The unhappy Quebec wing of the party had been pressing Dion and the party's management committee to introduce more bilingual-imperative positions at the party headquarters. Carroll's response, as reported publicly by Quebec president Robert Fragasso, had been to state that if he hired more francophones he would also have to hire more Chinese Canadians.[68] Carroll, furious, issued a denial in which he said his comments were taken out of context. "I was suggesting we needed to reach out to ethnic communities the way the Conservatives were," he later explained. In addition, he noted that the remarks, and the management committee meeting, had been confidential.[69] He also pointed out that members of the management committee agreed to increase the number of Quebec francophones at headquarters and maintain the party's commitment to bilingualism. "Any suggestion that I believe otherwise is quite simply a misrepresentation of the facts," his statement said. Meanwhile, several others who had been present at the meeting disputed Fragasso's interpretation as well. "[Carroll] talked about the need to reach out to all ethnic groups in the country, but not in comparison with anybody or any groups. He didn't say anything that would have been insulting to anybody," according to Derek Wells, the Nova Scotia president.[70]

But the controversy did not go away. On 28 September, Dion was forced to defend his handpicked incumbent, one of his closest advisers, while rumours swirled in Liberal circles that the Quebec wing was deliberately targeting Dion appointees. Those rumours gained traction when Deputy Leader Michael Ignatieff also called for Carroll to be fired, despite the numerous clarifications and denials that had been issued. By 2 October, it was reported that the leader was planning to "reassign" Carroll to quell the growing revolt, at the same time that a shuffle was about to take place in his own office. Carroll subsequently sent a confidential letter to the party executive in which he threatened to sue for defamation, but that letter was also leaked to the press and Carroll felt it was impossible to continue in the post. He officially resigned on 10 October 2007, and later reached a confidential financial settlement with the aid of lawyer Andrew Davis. But considerable damage had been done to the leader as well as to Carroll's reputation.[71]

The search for a new national director began immediately and ended quickly with the appointment of Greg Fergus, a former ministerial aide and past president of the federal Young Liberals. Fergus was appointed on 22 October, less than two weeks after Carroll's departure, in keeping with the ongoing concern of many Liberals that an election could occur at any time. To that end, he essentially picked up where Carroll had left off. Referring to the recent controversy and leaks, Fergus indicated his first task was to hold the operation together. "The leadership race was over. We needed to put that behind us and focus on the task at hand. More importantly, we needed to circle the wagons and point our guns outward."[72]

It was under Fergus that the Victory Fund originally suggested by Senator Poulin was implemented, with assistance from Herb Metcalfe and Brian Klunder. He also felt it was necessary, given the party's minimal resources, to let go individuals with no election experience in order to build a stronger team for the upcoming campaign. "We built a great team," Fergus claimed, "in spite of the challenges." It included Heather Chiasson on election readiness, Jim Anderson as deputy director, Daniel Lauzon in communications, and Brian Klunder and Adam Smith on fundraising.

Fergus had been in the position for less than six months when another major change occurred as Marie Poulin abruptly announced her resignation as party president in early April, 2008, due to health reasons.

This forced the party's national executive to select her replacement, as per the party constitution. They quickly chose Doug Ferguson, at the time the party's national vice-president (English) who had much-needed experience, having served on the party executive in the past and as chair of the Organization Committee under Chrétien, and had instituted the well-regarded Liberal University to "professionalize" the party's efforts at the riding association level.

Perhaps equally important, Ferguson had supported Dion's candidacy for the leadership – in large measure due to the fact that he was "an outsider and someone who would support party reform" – and confided that after Dion's election he left Montreal "full of optimism" about the party's future prospects. In fact, Ferguson was in the position of vice-president because he had supported the earlier initial reforms of Mike Eizenga and Steve MacKinnon, and believed he could help make a difference by implementing those reforms, as well as bringing back the Liberal University, which had been discontinued under Paul Martin. "The Liberal Party was built for the twentieth century," he later stated, "and we needed to modernize from the ground up. We were a party of silos – the caucus, the headquarters, the PTAs, and the riding associations – and we had almost no way of communicating across them."[73]

As Ferguson recounted, he never anticipated becoming president and realized immediately that he would have his hands full:

> I knew what had to be done, but there just was not enough time. We had almost no troops on the ground in some regions of the country. In Quebec, virtually nothing seemed to be happening. The constitution requires that PTAs hold at least one annual meeting, and they had not even done that. I know they were strapped for cash but this was crazy. I had to threaten to suspend them before they took action.[74]

And, of course, the party still did not have a complete national membership list. Not surprisingly, Ferguson would later list the implementation of the party's "Liberalist" as one of his chief accomplishments.

Both Ferguson and Fergus emphasized that they worked well together and shared a common vision of what was required. "I remember Greg telling me he couldn't believe we had no data," Fergus recalled saying, "and I understood immediately. We need to be the party of mass memberships and mass fundraising, and we can't do it without the data." Shortly afterwards, Ferguson, a lawyer by profession, attended a legal conference in Atlanta and met individuals familiar with the voter identification technology used in American elections. This was quickly followed by a trip to the Democratic National Convention in Denver, where he became familiar with the social media techniques made famous by the Obama team. However, once again, the lack of lead time prevented further work on this. "It was August of 2008 and we all knew that Harper would drop the writ any day," Ferguson recalled. Fergus admitted that no one had any illusions as to the likely outcome. "We all knew the numbers. With those polls our job was to hold the party together and do the best we could to support the leader. At headquarters we developed a type of gallows humour to get us through."[75]

The Election Call

The party's difficulties were in direct contrast to the aggressive tone that the Liberals had taken in the House of Commons in the spring of 2008, threatening once again to bring down the Conservative government. For Stéphane Dion, tired of appearing weak and indecisive, the need for a positive policy position seemed obvious. On 19 June he unveiled his Green Shift document, a comprehensive approach to sustainable development and the environment, which he and his caucus spent much of the summer trying to sell to Canadians while Stephen Harper spent an equal amount of time disparaging it. By the end of August, the Liberals were still far behind the Conservatives in public opinion polling, at anywhere from 24 to 29 per cent as opposed to the Conservatives' 37 to 39 per cent.

Despite the passage of Bill C-16 in early May (Harper's own legislation that instituted fixed election dates beginning on 19 October 2009), he evidently decided that there would never be a better time to take advantage of the Liberals' weak showing. On 7 September the prime minister went to Rideau Hall to request that Governor General Michaëlle Jean dissolve Parliament, and the 2008 election was underway. It would appear to be one of the least well-organized Liberal campaigns in living memory, one in which the leader and the Green Shift would play prominent roles and eventually be perceived, rightly or wrongly, as an albatross around the party's neck.

4 The Green Shift and the 2008 Election Debacle

Making a carbon tax the key plank in our appeal to the electorate is a vote loser, not a vote winner.

– Liberal pollster Michael Marzolini, confidential memo to the Liberal Campaign Committee, obtained and cited by the *Toronto Star*, 29 April 2008

Even after Stéphane Dion had been Liberal leader for nearly eighteen months he still believed that ideas were more important than tactics, strategy, or even people when it came to winning an election. According to one MP who had been a loyal supporter, "Despite all the evidence to the contrary, Stéphane believed that he won the leadership because of his comprehensive 'three pillars' platform, and he was convinced he would win the election the same way." It was also clear that nothing would change Dion's mind on this fundamental point. By the spring of 2018, after a disastrous few months of by-election dramas and internal party squabbles in Quebec, he was determined to put his beliefs into practice.

Stung by criticism that neither he nor his party stood for anything because of their passive behaviour in the House of Commons, Dion decided it was time to remind Canadians of exactly where he stood on what he considered to be the most important issue of the day, the environment. This idea had been strongly recommended to him by policy adviser Andrew Bevan, who felt that it was the one remaining asset that Dion could exploit to his advantage. "I had argued in January 2007 that we should go for an early election. When that idea was rejected we saw what happened" as the Conservative ads convinced Canadians Dion was "not a leader" and the problems in the House and with the by-elections reinforced it. "Our numbers were good in the early days. We were practically neck and neck with the Conservatives. But over time they fell badly and I thought this was his only chance to recoup some of his standing with Canadians."[1]

The idea began when a small group of senior advisers and MPs met in Toronto for a brainstorming session that Derek Ferguson had organized. In addition to Andrew Bevan, Johanne Senecal, and Jeremy Broadhurst of OLO, the group included MPs John McCallum, Ralph Goodale, Dominic Leblanc, and Bob Rae. "We had no pre-conceived plan, we were looking for a 'big idea,'" one of them recalled, "and of course with Stéphane's pre-existing identification with the environment it came up often as a possibility." Another of those present noted that Rae was an enthusiastic participant, and highlighted the difference between his approach and that of Michael Ignatieff. "Bob was as helpful and supportive of Dion as he could be, whereas Michael was absent, yet again, and tended to simply avoid this kind of consultation with the leader as much as possible."[2]

As a result of that meeting Bevan prepared a lengthy memo to Dion in which he outlined both the challenges facing the leader and the Liberals in the next election, and the possibility of highlighting an environmental policy – a green tax shift – as their best chance of overcoming these problems and actually winning. "It is indeed a massive ... change that should not be undersold. It is complex and substantive ... it is also innately engaging, exciting and cutting edge." Bevan argued that it could be sold to voters as a plan with economic and social advantages as well. "Canada will have much lower tax rates, poverty would be reduced substantially, Canada will be a leader in fighting climate change and pollution."

Recognizing that such a "bold, comprehensive change" would be "too much to explain during a writ alone," Bevan made it clear that such a plan could only work "if allowed enough time to resonate with Canadians" and if "a successful communications and logistical plan can be produced and implemented." To that end his memo envisaged a "clear five-month plan" on what the shift would mean for Canadians, with carefully modelled examples, and a clear five-month plan on who (in caucus and in the party) should help the leader take the message and its various elements to Canadians.[3]

It was not difficult to convince Dion. He saw the environment as being fundamental to the party platform for the upcoming election. He was also prepared to make a radical departure from the standard practice of "keeping your powder dry" until the writ was dropped in order to promote it. (Of course the rationale for waiting was that other parties would not have time to analyse your plans and develop credible criticism.) It was a risky gamble but perhaps Dion's only chance, as Bevan implied. If his warnings about implementation had been heeded, the possibility of success might arguably have been somewhat greater. But in the end, a comprehensive communications strategy was evidently lacking. And due to a variety of other problems, some of which were beyond Dion's control, the result was catastrophic for the party's fortunes in the federal election that fall.

The Green Shift's Failure to Launch

Work on the Liberal platform had been proceeding for some time, with consultations and platform "outreach" under Martha Hall Findlay, and behind the scenes in the OLO and Liberal Research Bureau, where materials were being prepared by veteran staffers such as Marjorie Loveys and Eugene Lang. But the work on the sustainable development plank was hived off and quickly became the domain of the leader. Andrew Bevan called upon the services of Michael McNair, an environmental economics expert working in OLO at the time, and together they crafted the document that came to be known as the Green Shift for Dion's consideration. He then added his own input and, to a considerable extent, held the pen on the final document.

When it was ready Dion presented his Green Shift plan to his caucus. One MP recalled that there really could be no doubt Dion had been deeply engaged in its development, since it was "detailed, comprehensive and masterful. At the same time it was hugely complex and difficult to explain."[4] This would prove to be an understatement. Another member pointed out that there had been "absolutely no discussion or consultation" with caucus on the plan. "It was just presented as a fait accompli." The vast majority of MPs, by now concerned about their personal electoral fortunes in light of consistently poor public opinion polls, urged Dion to either cancel the plan entirely or fold it into a larger and more vote-friendly package. As Karen Redman recalled, she told Dion it was "good public policy but bad politics," a view echoed by many of her colleagues.[5] Predictably, Dion rejected this criticism as irrelevant. If it was good policy then Canadians would accept it. The fact that he would need his caucus to help him sell this plan to Canadians apparently was not part of his calculations.

Meanwhile, media reports revealed the extent of the plan's perception problems with the Canadian public. They quoted extensively from a mysteriously leaked memo that the Liberals' party pollster had written to the campaign committee after testing the plan with focus groups. According to Michael Marzolini, "the policy is complex, confusing and cannot be adequately explained or defended in a few sentences much less a ten-second clip." Worse, Marzolini went on to predict (correctly as it turned out) that, unchanged, "every potential argument in favour of the Green Shift is comparatively weak, vague and ineffectual, when compared to expected attacks from the Tories, which are effective, sticky and have traction." As a result, he recommended the same approach that the caucus had tried with Dion. "It is our recommendation," Marzolini wrote, "that if a carbon tax shift absolutely must be part of our platform – and we do not recommend this at all – that it only be part of a larger environmental strategy involving actual popular proposals."[6]

Dion's chief of staff, Johanne Senecal, responded to Marzolini by demanding additional focus group work to determine what line of argumentation *would* work to convince Canadians, and to overcome likely Conservative attacks. After all, she said, "[Dion] is putting his political career at risk here."[7] In addition she wrote to the campaign committee – Marissen, Smith, and Girard – to advise them that more focus group work would be necessary before the document could be released.[8] As a result, the launch of the Green Shift was delayed twice. At one point Liberal consultant Rob Silver also was brought on board briefly to prepare a detailed communications plan, but most of his recommendations were ignored as well.[9]

Undaunted, Stéphane Dion finally announced his Green Shift on 19 June 2008 to considerable media fanfare. In his remarks he stressed that his overall objective was to make it clear that it was possible to promote both a sustainable environment *and* a prosperous economy. In what would prove to be the clearest and most concise description of the Green Shift's overall contents, Dion told reporters it was intended to "cut taxes on those things we all want more of – such as income, investment and innovation – and shift those taxes to what we all want less of – pollution, greenhouse gases and waste."[10] To that end there would be cuts to the lowest income brackets, an additional universal child tax benefit, and increased benefits for seniors and low-income families to offset most of their additional costs for home heating fuel and other consumer goods. At the same time there would be a new carbon tax on fossil fuels (other than gasoline, which Dion noted was already taxed) based on consumption. The supporting documents went out of their way to emphasize that "the bulk of their plan would be paid for by large industrial emitters,"[11] while the tax cuts would render the whole package revenue neutral.

Initial media response to the plan was quite positive. *A Montreal Gazette* editorial the following day declared "Dion's Plan Offers a Sincere

and Honest Challenge to Canadians," and was typical of the favourable press coverage.[12] Several well-known environmentalists, including
David Suzuki, also made supportive comments, and polls in the immediate aftermath of the announcement showed a slight improvement in
the party's fortunes. Dion set out on a cross-country tour to promote
the Green Shift and "get Canadians to know me." His MPs were also
instructed to fan out across the country to their respective ridings and
promote the plan.

But this positive reaction proved to be short lived. As Michael Marzolini had predicted, this was a very complicated proposal and the lack
of Andrew Bevan's proposed five-month window, along with a convincing communications strategy, caused enormous problems from the
beginning. As one of Dion's former caucus members later stated, "You
need a really good salesman to pitch something like that, and Dion was
no salesman. He would get down into the details and talk forever, and
lose everyone's interest." Don Boudria, who described the Green Shift
as a "brilliant document but a political disaster," agreed. He recalled
an event in Alexandria, Ontario, his former riding, where his son was
the Liberal candidate. "Stéphane spoke for more than thirty minutes
about the Green Shift, when we were expecting him to speak on the
economy and go after Harper. By the end no one was listening." Boudria also commented that "If Chrétien had been the leader he would
have rejected it [the Green Shift] right away. Even he could not have
sold that plan at that time."[13]

Another former MP recalled, "it was mentioned at the door every-
where I went in my riding, and I had no simple answers." In fact, individual MPs tied themselves in knots trying to explain the plan, which
was far more complicated than Dion's opening remarks had suggested,
even though they were provided with briefing notes and talking points.
Even a prepared video seemed to have been lost in the wash once the
summer recess sent the MPs to their respective ridings. In short order
the media had collected numerous contradictory statements from supposed Liberal spokespersons.

By the time the writ was dropped there were other negative considerations over which they had no control. To begin with, the economy
was not doing well and was about to become much more volatile as
the effects of the 2008 financial crisis in the United States were felt. In
addition, oil prices were skyrocketing. And, as campaign co-chair Mark
Marissen noted, it was a mistake to assume that the Green Shift would
be successful because it had worked in BC for Premier Gordon Campbell. "He could do it because he had a very different situation there, and
I tried to make this clear."[14]

There were significant regional implications to the plan as well. In western Canada, where David Orchard was now the Liberal candidate for the 2008 general election (having defeated Joan Beatty in a hard-fought open nomination battle), the situation could hardly have been worse. "It [the Green Shift announcement] was a complete surprise to me. And trying to explain a fuel tax in northern Saskatchewan was pretty much impossible. In the end I believe it was fatal to my campaign."[15] Dion evidently recognized that it would be a hard sell in Alberta, but he tried to convince supporters during a visit to the Calgary Stampede by assuring them that companies would benefit in the end from a movement towards renewable energy. Meanwhile, both Alberta premier Ed Stelmach and academics such as Peter McCormick, a political scientist at the University of Lethbridge, compounded Dion's problems by arguing that his proposal reminded many Albertans of the Liberals' infamous national energy program from the early 1980s. "It's going to be a hard sell in Alberta because Alberta feels it's being made the target again," McCormick said.[16] The plan also fell on stony ground in many rural areas of central Canada as well as in the north. For a party attempting to rebuild its support outside of urban areas, this was a very difficult proposition.

Still, all of these problems paled in comparison with the Green Shift's treatment at the hands of Stephen Harper and the Conservatives. Having been handed a golden opportunity to take the plan apart piece by piece, over the entire summer, they proceeded to do so with gusto. And their attacks, while not always accurate, were hugely successful. Harper himself began by dismissing the whole plan as economic folly during a campaign-style appearance in Saskatoon the following day, even though he had not actually seen the details.[17] Despite the various tax cuts included in the plan, and the Liberal pledge that it would be revenue neutral, Harper persisted in describing the Green Shift as a "tax grab" that Canadians could not afford. Then he deliberately designated Finance Minister Jim Flaherty and Industry Minister Jim Prentice to take the lead on the file, while Environment Minister John Baird was nowhere to be seen.

Opinion polls quickly began to reflect growing public confusion, and then widespread rejection of the plan. Simply put, the Conservatives had successfully "framed" the Green Shift. Several Dion advisers asked the party to allocate funding to counter the attack. In the end party president Doug Ferguson agreed to spend roughly $500,000 on ads, but he admitted this was hardly sufficient. "We would have needed millions and we just didn't have them. It was already hard to spend this amount outside of the campaign period and we really shouldn't have. It meant there would be less for later."[18]

By the time the writ was dropped on 7 September, the Green Shift was proving so unpopular that Dion was forced to explain that the plan "was never the party's central election campaign plank." Instead, he described it as the "foundation" of the platform, on which all planks were built. Moreover, he accused the media of having mistakenly described it as the platform centrepiece. "You have said it was," he said in surprisingly aggressive tones, "never me."[19] Speaking to reporters on a Manitoba farm, the leader also announced the Liberals would commit an additional $1.2 billion to help farmers, fishermen, and truckers (those who believed they would be most hard hit by the plan) to "adjust" to the shift. Adding insult to injury, the farmer on whose land Dion was making the announcement later told reporters he had difficulty understanding the plan and thought the Liberals should "back away" from it.[20] Stephen Harper responded to the news by declaring "He's shifting his Shift," and Conservative ad campaigns promptly appeared showing a photo of Dion shrugging, with the caption, "What Green Shift?"

The Shaky Campaign Start

In late August Stéphane Dion also announced that the Liberal Party was ready to fight an election whenever the prime minister decided to call one. On paper this looked to be the case, at least in some key respects. Certainly people had been put in place in all of the key positions. Veteran campaigner Doug Kirkpatrick would be the leader's tour director. On the plane Andrew Bevan would be in charge, Gavin Menzies would serve as wagon master, Katie Telford was on board and, along with Andrew Bevan, would be responsible for policy. On the ground Jonathan Goldbloom, who had spearheaded Bob Rae's leadership campaign, was in charge of the war room, which would also be staffed by a number of Michael Ignatieff's team. As Andrew Bevan noted, the full platform was ready and drafted to complement the Green Shift, along with briefing notes and media kits for each plank.[21]

However, the party had nowhere near the money required to run a national campaign, and a much larger line of credit than hoped for had to be arranged to fund it. And Greg Fergus and Doug Ferguson knew that the organization at the local and regional levels was not in place, nor had all the party's candidates been nominated. Despite the planned array of personnel in Ottawa, it soon became apparent that some members of the Ignatieff camp in particular were, as one wag put it, "missing in action."

Unfortunately, a series of events in the early days of the campaign soon put paid to Dion's claim that the Liberals were ready. Accustomed to the party's professionally run campaigns and well-oiled Big Red Machine, Canadians of all political stripes looked on in amazement as problems beset Dion's campaign from day one. While some could be attributed to the party's ongoing problems, others were caused by the self-inflicted wounds of the leader. Still others were thrust upon them by outside forces beyond their control. As one senior adviser put it, "we fought an entire election with one hand tied behind our back."

It began with the Liberals' difficulty in obtaining that most basic item of an election campaign, the plane for the leader's tour. The Liberals had always used planes provided by Air Canada, and had expected to do so again. But as they began what Kirkpatrick had assumed would be the routine negotiations to lease an Airbus 319 in the summer of 2008, a monkey wrench was thrown into their plans by the airline itself, which abruptly announced that it had only one plane to lease. Nor did Air Canada agree that the Liberals had first claim on it. Instead it seemed the party would have to enter into a bidding war with the NDP. It was a war the cash-strapped Liberals could not win. And so at the last minute they unexpectedly found themselves looking elsewhere for another plane. Doug Kirkpatrick, the veteran tour director, was livid: "They knew money was a problem for us, but this was unheard of. We all felt – and certainly I felt – betrayed." Not everyone shared Kirkpatrick's view that this had been unavoidable. Some Dion supporters believed the party brass could have afforded the plane but chose not to spend the money on what they saw as a lost cause. Others believed that Kirkpatrick had simply been incompetent. Still other Liberals, both in the Dion camp and across the party, defended Kirkpatrick and were quick to point out that Duncan Dee, the company's executive vice-president and chief administrative officer, who was in charge of the negotiations, was a prominent supporter of the Harper Conservatives and had contributed money to their party since 2006. Adding insult to injury, he had once been a staffer for Liberal cabinet minister Sheila Copps. Rumours flew in Liberal circles that this contretemps had been deliberately orchestrated to embarrass them. (As Rob Silver and Doug Kirkpatrick separately pointed out several years later, rightly or wrongly the Liberals' conviction that they were sabotaged was reinforced when Dee received a three-year patronage appointment to the board of trustees of the Canadian Museum of Civilization shortly after.)[22]

Obliged to make do with whatever they could locate on such short notice, the Liberals finally secured the use of a thirty-year-old Boeing 737 that they leased from Air Inuit. For the first few days of the official

campaign they were forced to wait in Ottawa while the plane was read-
ied for their use. Then they travelled by bus to Montreal and Toronto for
events, and picked up the plane there. But their travails were not over.
Within days the plane made an emergency landing due to a generator
problem, and the tour was grounded once more.

Nor did the leader personally have a stellar first week. After a difficult question-and-answer period at one campaign venue, Dion told
an astonished group of reporters that his problems with English were
caused by "an inherited hearing ailment that caused him to have a difficulty to isolate sounds."[23] The following day all of his events were
cancelled as he underwent an emergency procedure to repair a cracked
tooth. Not surprisingly, by the end of the first week of the campaign the
Liberals were rapidly becoming a subject for political cartoonists.

Nevertheless these setbacks need not have been a disaster. As Peter
Donolo commented, "It's not fatal, it's not the end of the world, but it
does [risk becoming] a symbol. You've always got to make light of your
own setbacks in politics and not take it too seriously."[24] Dion appeared
to take this advice seriously, calmly telling reporters it was an inconve-
nience, nothing more.[25]

The Invisible Ground War

Unfortunately, the campaign's problems were only just beginning. As
Doug Ferguson noted, the party had lost many workers during the
Martin/Chrétien wars,[26] and this could not be overcome quickly, let
alone with a problematic leader. Two days after the writ was dropped
one journalist wrote that the Liberals' presence on the ground appeared
to be "wafer thin," even in ridings with an incumbent Liberal MP.[27] The
lawn signs of local candidates for other parties, including the Greens,
appeared out of nowhere, but the Liberals were invisible. Many Liberal
candidates *never* received any campaign materials (such as brochures or
copies of the platform) from headquarters, despite having had to pay
for them in advance, as was customary.

Meanwhile, the leader's tour was described by one of the senior
advisers as a "comedy of errors." Another described the absence of any
overall plan. "The first ten-day schedule was scrapped by the leader
after he apparently lost faith in the ground team that had set it up."
This in turn resulted in an increasingly ad hoc set of "events looking for
a reason." The media, for example, reported critically on an event held
at a high school in rural Ontario where Dion unveiled a "meat safety"
plank, rather than the party's extensive education plank that instead
was unveiled in Moncton several days later.

The situation was made far worse by the fact that Dion was proving to be a micromanager. "He insisted on signing off on every comma," one disgruntled staffer recalled. In one instance, a planned "meet-and-greet" in a coffee shop was converted, only hours before it was scheduled, into a major platform announcement by the leader that required not only a larger venue but far more people. Not surprisingly, there were not enough people in the cavernous room that was finally located for the purpose, causing the media to remark on what they saw as the public's apparent lack of enthusiasm for Dion. In another instance, a frantic Liberal advance team repeatedly called the "tour" to find out when the leader – already very late – would be arriving at a scheduled platform announcement at a farm in southwest Ontario. Dion, it transpired, was sitting on a bus nearby but unwilling to proceed until he had rewritten entirely the material he had been given.[28]

A frustrated Doug Kirkpatrick later described what he saw as a "total lack of discipline" on the leader's tour that he had never encountered before, despite his extensive experience with many other Liberal campaigns. According to Kirkpatrick, it was only when senior adviser Herb Metcalfe was on the plane that it was possible to impose order, but Metcalfe could not be there all the time. Campaign director Gordon Ashworth put it more succinctly. "The people on the plane seemed to think they were running the campaign. This never works."[29]

Needless to say, those on the plane disagreed. They saw Kirkpatrick and Ashworth as part of the problem, representing the old-party elites and the interests of the party establishment rather than the leader. "There are often rifts between 'the plane and the ground,'" one adviser noted, "but this was beyond the pale. The leader felt he had no friends on the ground." As the campaign progressed, and the dysfunctional relationship between the ground and the plane grew, the tour organizers simply "stumbled from one day to the next" with no idea what to expect. Suggestions for events from regional coordinators were ignored. Planned events were cancelled. Others were held but with the tour arriving late or leaving early. By now, many on the Liberal campaign trail were simply hoping to survive the remaining weeks until election day. Unfortunately, the media were only too well aware of this situation, and such incidents became the nightly news rather than whatever message had been planned for the day.

The Lost Liberal Message

By the end of the second week of the campaign the polling numbers had moved very little. The Liberals decided to release their full platform at this point, hoping for a turnaround, but this too proved to be a non-event. The fully costed and substantial document – *Richer, Fairer, Greener: An Action Plan for the 21st Century* – offered a more comprehensive version of the Green Shift as well as detailed proposals on health care, education, infrastructure, and child care. It also reiterated the Liberals' commitment to offer major tax cuts for most Canadians. Yet the plan fell on deaf ears. As one former MP said, "It was like a tree falling in the forest. No one heard it, so it didn't happen."[30]

Actually, this was not strictly true. The message may have been heard but rejected, the result – at least in part – of more work by the Harper Conservatives in framing that Liberal message. Having already discredited the Green Plan per se, most notably by describing it as a "tax grab," they had then begun to portray the Dion Liberals as the "tax and spend" variety, long before the entire platform was released. The reality of the Liberal plan's tax cuts was simply lost in the wash. Moreover, and in spite of the Chrétien/Martin Liberals' impressive record of eliminating the deficit and introducing prudent fiscal forecasting, Harper's team managed to convince Canadians that it was the *Liberals* who had been profligate, not the Mulroney Conservatives. At one point an incredulous Stéphane Dion told a reporter "We have no lessons to learn from this man!"

Perhaps the unkindest cut of all was saved for the Conservatives' criticism of the platform's costing. Once the document was released Harper, Flaherty, and Kenney immediately claimed that Dion's numbers "didn't add up." Dion, his shadow cabinet finance critic John McCallum (a former bank VP), and House leader Ralph Goodale all responded vociferously that they did, but to no avail. Even a full-page ad showing a letter signed by one hundred economists, all of whom concurred with the Liberals' numbers, did little or nothing to change people's minds, which had already been made up by the Conservatives.

Some observers, and a few Liberal MPs, also noted that the platform, while comprehensive, emphasized the environment and other specific planks but did not outline an overarching Liberal vision for the country. Nor did Dion speak of Liberal values that were driving the elements of the platform, something that these critics felt was a serious omission. One veteran campaigner later complained, "Here we were fighting an election against the most right-wing government the country had ever seen and, yes, we were attacking them, but not explaining how we were fundamentally different. And we seemed to be mesmerized by their narrative of lower taxes and no deficits."

Another reason for the platform's lack of impact was undoubtedly the public's low image of the messenger. Of course, part of Dion's problem was that the Conservatives had already defined him for Canadians almost as soon as he became leader. The Liberals had not been able to respond to those "not a leader" ads at the time, with the party arguing yet again that they simply could not afford to do so. They needed to save what funds they had for the campaign itself, not the pre-writ period.

Despite this, the Liberal ad campaign focused primarily on the leader. Since that leader's personal approval rating at the start of the campaign stood at 10 per cent, much lower than Stephen Harper (32 per cent) and Jack Layton (18 per cent), but also trailing his own party (27 per cent), this decision was more than a little surprising.[31] Even more surprising was the decision to try to use the ads to make Dion appear informal and ordinary. Many showed him relaxing with his family and their dog Kyoto. Others showed him skiing, bicycling, or engaged in other outdoor activities, and all of them had him casually dressed. Ironically, the Conservatives were employing the same tactic to "humanize" their man, portraying Stephen Harper wearing a light blue cardigan and speaking directly into the camera in a folksy "fireside chat" motif. These images may very well have been useful to Harper, who otherwise was widely seen as rigid and formal, but in Dion's case many observers argued that a more prime ministerial pose was exactly what was needed.

This was even more noticeable since the party lawn signs that finally appeared in some ridings featured the name of the local Liberal candidate and the Liberal logo, but made no mention of the leader, a stark contrast with the high-profile Martin and Chrétien signs of earlier times. While it was certainly true that the Liberals' ad campaign was a low-budget one, the content could have been quite different at no extra cost. Internally a debate raged about the need to highlight some of the more prominent members of caucus, and to promote some Liberal MPs and candidates as future cabinet ministers in a Liberal government. Still the polling numbers stubbornly remained the same.

It was in this discouraged frame of mind, then, that the Liberals approached the televised leaders' debates, for which prominent Martin/Ignatieff supporter Tim Murphy had been preparing Dion.

The Brief Success of the Leaders' Debates

By the time the leaders' debates took place – the first in French on 1 October and then in English the following day, public expectations of Dion's performance were extremely low. Moreover, the "debate over the debates," as Jack Layton described the wrangling among parties as to whether the Green Party's Elizabeth May would finally be included, had distracted voters from the serious issues to be covered.

In the end the format, which did include a place for May and therefore involved five leaders, was a new one in which everyone was seated at a table rather than standing at individual podiums. This had the effect of limiting individual interventions, a situation made worse in Dion's case because May's presence was a two-edged sword: she constantly agreed with him but also put forward more ambitious goals than the Liberals. Few serious exchanges between any two leaders were possible, and the conversation was sometimes impossible to follow as key words were drowned out by a chorus of interventions.

Despite these constraints, Stéphane Dion surprised everyone with his effective, measured, and knowledgeable performance. Many believed he had won the French debate, in which both May and to some extent Harper were sidelined by the other three fluently bilingual leaders. In English Dion proved to be equally effective, and actually managed to isolate Harper in an exchange on the economy. Harper appeared to be taken aback by the concerted attacks of the other four leaders, who focused on his cavalier advice to Canadians to invest in stocks during the downturn, and his government's lack of action to address the growing crisis. In this context Dion's intervention, in which he outlined a Liberal five-point economic recovery plan, appeared positively masterful, even though the plan did not contain many new initiatives. Moreover, in a one-on-one exchange Dion turned to Harper with an incredulous and obviously genuine look on his face and then turned to the cameras and spoke directly to Canadians. "Don't listen to this man," he urged, after Harper had once again misrepresented the Green Shift and its tax plan.

For a brief time it appeared that Dion's debate performance may have struck a chord with Canadians anxious about the economy. The Liberals' polling numbers improved and it began to look as if this could be a horse race. The Conservatives, who had believed quite correctly at the outset of the campaign that a majority was within their grasp, now saw it slipping away. They had already suffered from earlier remarks by Harper about "rich galas" that had cost the Conservatives support in Quebec. Bloc leader Gilles Duceppe railed against the Conservative cuts to cultural programs there as "cultural genocide," and was gaining increasing voter sympathy there. Now the Liberal campaign organizers were switching from the environment to the economy as they detected Harper's Ontario Achilles heel, and quickly added venues for John McCallum and Ralph Goodale to follow up with repeated references to the Liberal economic plan that Dion had outlined during the debates.

But this late mini-surge soon proved unsustainable. To begin with, Harper and his senior cabinet ministers quickly regrouped. Having seen their falling numbers after the debates, they recognized the error of their ways and soon promised a variety of measures to allay the public's fears. Harper also committed to unveiling the Conservative platform on 7 October, after pressure from the leaders in the debate the night before to do so, and assured Canadians that it would contain appropriate measures to address the growing economic fallout.

While this response no doubt helped to stem the Conservatives' declining support, a second development unquestionably saved the day for them and sealed the Liberals' fate. While Harper was in damage control mode, Stéphane Dion was making his way to Atlantic Canada for a tour of the region and a series of media interviews that everyone hoped would enhance Liberal fortunes.

The Fateful Interview

It was in Halifax on 9 October that Dion encountered another unexpected setback, one that arguably stalled whatever momentum he and the party may have been experiencing at the time. In a taped interview that afternoon with CTV Atlantic News anchor Steve Murphy, to be shown on the 6 p.m. news, Dion requested that Murphy's first question be repeated, and the interview restarted three times. This was because he found the question extremely unclear, and indicated that he wanted to be sure he had understood Murphy's intent. (Online and informal surveys quickly showed that most viewers agreed with Dion that the question was convoluted and difficult to follow.)[32] Murphy agreed to the "restart" without comment. The interview then continued as planned. At the time Dion's accompanying communications aide, Sarah Bain, saw nothing out of the ordinary and was not concerned with how the interview had gone. In fact, she thought it had gone rather well.

Only a few hours later she, and those on the leader's plane, were alerted to the fact that CTV was playing not only the interview, as expected, but also the three false starts, contrary to standard practice and what they believed had been agreed upon. In fact, the restarts were being highlighted. The overall effect was to make Dion look incompetent, and commentary suggested that his problems with understanding English were significant. It was later learned that the decision to show the restart clips had been taken by CTV's senior political correspondent Mike Duffy after he had seen an advance copy of the full tape, and it was shown nationally on "Mike Duffy Live." Stephen Harper immediately commented on the material and suggested it reflected negatively on Dion's ability to govern.[33]

Astonished and dismayed, Dion's team could do nothing to compensate for the highly damaging video, which was then rebroadcast repeatedly across the country. "This was just before the Thanksgiving weekend," Andrew Bevan recalled, "and we knew that this was when most voters would make up their minds. The election was the following Tuesday [14 October]!"[34]

Liberals and many other Canadians were incensed by the treatment of Dion, but many more were convinced by the tape that the Liberal leader simply was not up to the task. As Patrick Boyer, a former Conservative MP and well-known expert on electoral and constitutional law, later wrote, "The damage that Mike Duffy inflicted on Mr. Dion's campaign was measurable. Mr. Harper's campaign was faltering but [after the clip aired] he won the October 2008 general election and formed another government, still a minority but with an increased number of seats." Moreover, referring to Duffy's long-standing and widely known efforts to obtain a Senate seat under at least four previous prime ministers, Boyer concluded, "Two months later, on December 22, the reinstated prime minister gave "the Senator" [Duffy's nickname] his most cherished Christmas present ever, a real seat in the Senate of Canada."[35]

The Canadian Broadcast Standards Council (CBSC) received thirty-nine complaints about the broadcast. Some twenty-one of these provided sufficient grounds to allow the CBSC to proceed with its investigative process. Although the network attempted to defend its decision to abrogate its agreement with Dion and allow the restarts to be shown, following receipt of the broadcaster's response to that process at least four complainants were still unsatisfied and requested a formal ruling by the council. In its written decision, the CBSC issued a detailed and thoughtful critique of the network's handling of the affair and especially the behaviour of Duffy. It agreed that the initial question was extremely ambiguous and difficult for even native English speakers to understand, and also confirmed that the practice of allowing restarts was commonplace, rather than unusual as CTV had tried to claim. In the end the ruling found that CTV had violated broadcasting codes and at least one section (8) of the Journalistic Code of Ethics, concluding that Duffy's decision to show the restarts was "not fair, balanced or even-handed."[36] Unfortunately for Dion and the Liberals, that ruling was issued on 12 January 2009, long after the election was over.

The Final Verdict

The Liberal campaign team were in no doubt about the eventual outcome of the campaign. Their only question was how many more seats they would lose than in 2006. But they were afraid to tell the leader, whom Greg Fergus described as "a trouper," and who continued to believe it was possible for the Liberals to win a minority. Finally on election night Andrew Bevan and Johanne Senecal broke the news to him that he would not be the next prime minister. According to Bevan, this was not only a surprise but one that Dion found very difficult to accept.[37]

Doug Ferguson recalled being in Montreal that night because he was concerned that the leader might resign immediately during his concession speech, as Paul Martin had done, and he wanted to be there as president to avoid any procedural confusion. But when he arrived at the campaign suite in a hotel in downtown Montreal he found everyone except the leader, who watched the results unfold alone in another room with his wife. In the end Ferguson was barely in time to catch up with the Dions as they made their way down to the lobby for that speech, and he had no time to speak with the leader in advance and no idea what he would say in the face of this significant loss.

The results were certainly not encouraging. Having entered the campaign roughly ten points behind the Conservatives, the Liberals finished in almost exactly the same place. But it cost them. At 26 per cent, their electoral showing was at its lowest level since the first election after Confederation. They were now reduced to seventy-seven seats in the House of Commons from their pre-writ standing of 103. Many veteran MPs had lost their seats, including whip Karen Redman and two other long-serving Ontario MPs, Bonnie Brown and Diane Marleau. Perhaps even more devastating was the fact that NDP MP Tom Mulcair, who had won the fateful by-election in Outremont, was able to hold his seat, becoming the first NDP MP in Quebec to be elected in a general election.

Regionally there were serious implications as well. The party had lost seats in BC and Manitoba, and even two seats in Atlantic Canada that the Liberals had held for years. Even more ominous, they had lost seats in Ontario outside of Toronto to both the NDP and the Conservatives. One analysis of the election results highlighted both the crumbling support of the party outside of large urban centres across the country, as well as the need for the party to seriously tackle its growing list of structural problems, many of which were on display during the campaign. "The stakes have rarely been higher and the next few years will be crucial for the Liberals: their claim to the title of natural governing party is at stake ... A number of tremors in the Liberal heartland suggest a tectonic plate movement could be possible if the Liberals are not able to reinvent themselves in time."[38]

On the other hand, a number of Liberals were delighted that their situation was not worse. The Harper Conservatives had, after all, been held to a minority and a marginal increase in popular support, having gained only sixteen seats. In Quebec, where the Bloc had played a key role in denying the Conservatives a majority, both Marc Garneau in Westmount and newly minted MP Justin Trudeau in Papineau had held onto or retaken their Quebec ridings for the Liberal Party. Trudeau's victory was particularly noteworthy since he had been denied Outremont by Dion and then been forced by the leader to compete in a nomination for Papineau, proving to everyone that he was a political winner. Similarly, Gerard Kennedy had defeated the NDP incumbent, Peggy Nash, in the Toronto riding of Parkdale-High Park, another impressive victory. In Quebec, the Liberals had finished in second place with fourteen seats, well ahead of the Conservatives and the NDP, whose fourth-place finish produced only Mulcair.

Conservatives were not overjoyed with the results either. They had hoped for a majority, and many felt it had been somehow squandered during the campaign. Moreover, Stephen Harper's plan to forge a winning coalition of the west and Quebec had faltered, with his party all but shut out in that province not by the Liberals but by the Bloc. As academics Faron Ellis and Peter Woolstencroft concluded, "The Liberals had been bloodied, were maybe even on their knees, but had not been knocked out ... The results indicated that even when competing against an underfunded and organizationally weak competitor with an ineffectual leader, it seemed the Conservatives still had work to do if they planned to replace the Liberals as Canada's natural governing party."[39]

When Dion delivered his concession speech he looked stunned, but indicated he intended to stay on as Liberal leader and Leader of the Official Opposition. This was something neither Ferguson nor other members of the party establishment had expected. Soon, "delegations of Liberal insiders began shuttling back and forth between Ottawa and Toronto to meet with Dion and convince him that it was in everyone's best interest that he step down."[40]

A week later Dion called a press conference to announce that he would resign. but would stay on as leader until the party was able to mount another leadership convention, probably in the spring of 2009. This was a compromise that again surprised the elites but almost everyone felt was reasonable and respectful of Dion's role as leader. With a convention already scheduled for Vancouver in May 2009, and an executive meeting planned for November 2008, it was not difficult to see how the leadership convention would be arranged.

The fact that this was not what happened in the end was due primarily to the actions of the Harper Conservatives once they returned to Ottawa and resumed governing, and Dion's response to them. Having described the Liberal campaign as "one of the most incompetent in living memory," political columnist Jeffrey Simpson went on to bluntly sum up the party's troubles following their defeat. "The party is weakened financially, beaten politically, and split intellectually," he concluded.[41] He also concluded that "Dion is history," whether "sooner or later." As it turned out, it would be sooner.

The Coalition Debacle

When the fortieth Parliament opened on 18 November 2008, the returning Liberal MPs were not a happy group, but they had accepted that the Conservative minority government was stronger than before and there was little they could do. As a result they were prepared to oppose what they could and wait for the leadership convention in May of the following year. So, too, the supporters of leadership hopefuls Michael Ignatieff and Bob Rae were resigned to waiting until then. All of that changed, however, when Finance Minister Jim Flaherty tabled his economic update on November 27.

The Conservatives apparently had little to offer in the way of economic stimulus, and as a result decided that they would use the statement to demonstrate that politicians and bureaucrats in Ottawa were "tightening their belts" in sympathy with Canadians who were experiencing the economic downturn. The opposition parties could hardly believe this was the extent of Harper's response after his wake-up call in the election. For all three opposition parties (Elizabeth May having lost her bid for a seat, there were no Greens in the House) the lack of concrete measures in the update to address the growing economic crisis was seen as scandalous. In addition, and for the NDP especially, Flaherty's plan to "temporarily" deprive public servants of their right to strike, and female public servants of their right to pursue "equal pay for work of equal value" claims, was anathema.

But for all three opposition parties, the final straw was Flaherty's plan to eliminate the $1.95 per-vote public subsidy that had been put in place by Jean Chrétien to compensate them for the loss of revenue caused by his limitations on contributions from individuals, and the elimination of corporate and union contributions. This was a serious miscalculation on Harper's part. According to several sources, he believed the NDP would support the measure – and hence the economic statement, which would have been a confidence vote – because it would cripple and likely destroy the Liberals but only seriously inconvenience the NDP. Moreover, he did not believe any of the opposition parties would dare to force another election barely two months after the last one. He was wrong.

As Flanagan and Jensen have explained, the Liberals were more dependent on the public subsidies than anyone else, but both the NDP and the Bloc would also have been very seriously impacted.[42] Both Flanagan – a former Harper adviser – and Gerry Nichols, a well-known right-wing conservative commentator, took issue with Flaherty's plan and described it as not simply overly partisan and mean-spirited but undemocratic, as it would have the effect of destroying effective opposition parties.[43] The unintended consequence of Flaherty's drastic measure therefore was an unprecedented meeting of the minds among the three opposition parties, who were prepared to take their own drastic measures to prevent this from happening.

Conventional wisdom has it that the Liberals initiated the dramatic response to Harper's plan to eliminate the subsidies, namely, a plan to defeat the Conservatives in a non-confidence vote and replace them with a coalition government of the Liberals and NDP. But it was the NDP, and *not* the Liberals, who initiated the process. The shell-shocked Liberals were focused inward, preoccupied with the upcoming leadership race. The NDP, meanwhile, had already considered the possibility of bringing down the Martin minority in 2004, going so far as to approach both the Harper Conservatives (the Official Opposition at the time) and the Bloc Québécois. On 9 September 2004, after secret negotiations, they even sent a jointly signed letter to the governor general indicating that the three opposition parties would be prepared to cooperate and form a government if Martin's should fall, rather than resorting immediately to another election.[44] (When this 2008 plan started to fall apart – and Harper denied the accusation that he had agreed to this earlier venture in 2004 – Bloc leader Gilles Duceppe released the 2004 letter with Harper's signature.)

And so, faced with a Harper minority government after the 2008 election, NDP leader Jack Layton returned to the charge. This time he asked members of his negotiating team from that earlier coalition foray to approach the opposition Liberals about a similar plan. Layton adviser and future NDP party president Brian Topp, who served as a lead negotiator on the deal, immediately made contact with several key Liberal organizers as well as other NDP strategists.

What followed was a complicated series of interactions that saw the Liberals in some disarray about their response as it became increasingly clear – to the NDP negotiators as well as the Liberals' authorized spokespersons – that leadership agendas were diverting attention from the main purpose.[45] While the idea was initially rejected by Stéphane Dion, some of his key advisers were inclined to consider the option, in part as a way of salvaging his leadership, and he soon saw the advantages of this as well. Meanwhile the NDP negotiators, led by Brian Topp, were also pursuing the issue with Michael Ignatieff's representatives because they were concerned that no deal with the Liberals would be possible without his support, since he was seen as the likely successor to Dion. Conversely, Bob Rae and his supporters, only too well aware of the negative outcome of the NDP-Liberal accord in Ontario (in which they merely agreed to support the Liberal minority government, not join it in a coalition)[46] and still hoping to prevail in the spring leadership race, were initially keeping their heads down, although Rae later became a champion of the accord.

From the beginning of the negotiations it was clear that internal conflict raged within the ranks of senior Liberals privy to the discussions. Many key players were concerned that a successful plan to orchestrate a coalition government would lead to Dion's becoming prime minister, something many of them considered completely unacceptable. Others, and notably Ignatieff's strategists, wanted to arrange for the defeat of the Conservatives, but only with an agreement on the part of the NDP to support the Liberal government that emerged, rather than having them becoming part of a genuine coalition government with NDP ministers. This view was also shared by some of the initial negotiators for Dion, such as Marlene Jennings, who argued that too many Liberal caucus members would never accept the idea of a coalition if it meant NDP MPs would be given cabinet seats while they themselves languished on the back benches.

As later recounted by Topp,[47] all of these emerging issues led Layton and his advisers to conclude that a deal would need to be struck with Dion, not Ignatieff, and sooner rather than later. As a result, their representatives met frequently over the course of the following three days to hammer out an agreement that would see them form a coalition government. Liberal emissaries Herb Metcalfe, Ralph Goodale, Katie Telford, Marlene Jennings, and Johanne Senecal met with their NDP counterparts, including Brian Topp, Anne McGrath, BC MP Dawn Black, Allan Blakeney, and Ed Broadbent, at various hotels in Ottawa. Behind the scenes, both Roy Romanow and Jean Chrétien were also frequently consulted. Then, when basic details had been worked out about cabinet

representation (sixteen Liberals, seven NDP), institutional appointments, and a policy agenda, the negotiators met with Bloc representatives Francois LeBlanc and Pierre Paquette. While the Bloc would not be
part of the coalition, it would agree to support the coalition government
for a specified period of time (eighteen months) once it was satisfied
with the policies being put forward in the package that the Liberals and
NDP had crafted.

On 1 December, Harper having cancelled Opposition Day in the
House of Commons, the coalition parties announced that they would
hold a press conference in the Railway Committee Room of the Centre
Block later that afternoon to symbolically sign their agreement. Their
plan, they said, was to bring the government down when the economic
statement was brought before the House as scheduled on Thursday
morning, 4 December.

As someone noted who was present at the courtesy meeting that
Dion had held earlier in the day with Rae, Ignatieff, and Dominic LeB-
lanc (the publicly announced candidates to replace him as leader),
after Dion explained the situation and asked for their support "Ignatieff, who was sitting directly across from Dion, immediately looked
him straight in the eye and said 'What are your intentions?' Obviously
he was still worried that this deal would make Dion prime minister
and then perhaps there would be no leadership race next May." Dion
assured Ignatieff that he would stick to his commitment to resign when
a new leader was chosen.

In the national caucus that followed, party president Doug Ferguson
specifically reiterated this point with MPs when his turn came to speak
on the deal, which he supported. "I told them the leadership train has
left the station. We are going ahead in May." According to several of
those present, it was this categorical reassurance, as well as the strong
support for the deal provided by Bob Rae, that played a key role in
its acceptance.[48] By the end of the meeting the mood in the room was
euphoric. "It was not simply that they would have a chance to be in
power once more," Ferguson said. "It was that they were going to be
able to get rid of a prime minister, and a party, that they all thought was
doing real damage, perhaps unprecedented damage, to Canada."[49]

Unfortunately for them the euphoria was premature. As many
observers pointed out after the fact, the coalition's decision to broadcast their intentions well in advance of the scheduled non-confidence
vote may very well have been the fatal flaw in their plans, regardless
of what later transpired. Nevertheless, there were also many pundits,
and senior Liberals outside of Parliament, who questioned the political wisdom of the whole plan. Some Liberals even declared they were

secretly glad when it eventually failed. Criticism of the deal centred largely on the fact that it would result in Stéphane Dion, perceived as the weakest Liberal leader in living memory, becoming prime minister, and the Liberal Party, which had been solidly defeated in an election only weeks earlier, being back in power.[50] As one former Liberal MP fumed, "What planet are these people on? How did they imagine this was going to fly with the public after we were just handed our worst defeat since Confederation?"[51]

Harper Turns the Tables

While the political costs of the plan might well have been significant for the Liberals a coalition was, of course, an entirely legitimate exercise in a parliamentary democracy. Coalitions had occurred often in other countries with Westminster model systems, such as New Zealand, India, and Australia, and would soon emerge in Britain after the 2010 defeat of the Cameron government. However, it was not a practice that had been used much in Canada, especially at the federal level.

When word of the opposition meetings and their purpose began to leak out the Conservatives initially appeared to be petrified. In the House of Commons, and in press comments, Finance Minister Jim Flaherty began to offer concessions. He indicated there would be stimulus measures in his budget, which he would exceptionally table in late January rather than the usual end of February. Then he said that he would be willing to bend on the removal of the right to strike. Finally, he suggested that even the scrapping of the subsidies might be up for discussion, or at least they could be phased in over time rather than all at once to soften the blow.

Several of his closest advisers have indicated that Harper himself was deeply depressed and sure that he was about to lose power.[52] For a short time he was all but invisible in Parliament. But that passive retreat by Harper soon changed. Apart from his natural combativeness and resilience, he was no doubt helped by the NPD themselves, who had mistakenly invited Conservative MP John Duncan to participate in a conference call about the plan on 28 November, instead of their own MP, Linda Duncan. While a minor debate raged over what the NDP subsequently alleged was "eavesdropping," Harper prepared his lines of attack. By 1 December the Conservatives began a new framing exercise in which there were two key messages for Canadians.

The first was Harper's argument that the presence of the Bloc Québécois meant that the government of Canada would now be in the control of separatists, even though the agreement signed by the three parties clearly stated that the Bloc was only going to support the coalition and not be part of it. This led to calls of "treason" by Conservative back-benchers in the House and charges by Harper and others in his cabinet that Dion was not really a federalist. (There were even claims that the Liberal leader had refused to have a Canadian flag behind him during the press conference, a patently false accusation that infuriated Dion.)

Ironically, this particular line of attack should have come as no sur-prise to the NDP coalition partners since Brian Topp subsequently admitted that it was the first response he received when he had earlier informed a Conservative "friend" who was "close to the prime min-ister's thinking" about the emerging plan. "You're going to run the government with separatists?" the friend replied to Topp's "heads-up" on 27 November.[53] As Topp himself conceded, he did not pay serious attention to that response, having assumed that Harper's desire to win over Quebec nationalists as part of his long-term Conservative support plan would prevent him from taking that unpopular short-term option. Several of the Liberal participants agreed that concern over Duceppe's presence at the press conference – something he himself had cautioned might be a problem – was given little or no thought.

Harper's instincts proved correct, however, and particularly in west-ern Canada numerous public opinion polls demonstrated that this line of attack was highly persuasive.[54] Moreover, the Liberals' traditional strength as the party of national unity was seen, even by many grass-roots Liberals, to have been placed in jeopardy by the plan, regardless of whether the Bloc was an actual member of the coalition.

The second Conservative framing line was that the very concept of a coalition was undemocratic. Rather than a legitimate exercise in a parliamentary democracy, it was portrayed by Harper and his team as a type of coup d'etat. Using their apparently bottomless financial resources (even in the aftermath of a general election campaign), the Conservatives soon had radio ads airing that declared, "Dion thinks he can take power without asking you, the voter. This is Canada. Power must be earned, not taken."[55] Although eminent parliamentary schol-ars such as David E. Smith deplored the lack of understanding of the Westminster system that these ads reflected,[56] it was clear from polling results that this argument also was highly effective with the general public.[57] (Following the hung parliament of 2010 in Britain – the first in the post-war era – a parliamentary committee was tasked with examin-ing the experience of coalition governments elsewhere in the Common-wealth in anticipation of the Cameron-Clegg coalition. Not only did the committee conclude that the Canadian example was not helpful, since it had failed, but the committee's report specifically noted that Canadians in general displayed a shocking lack of understanding of their system of government).[58] Perhaps even more surprising was the fact that Harper's rejection of a coalition this time was accepted by many Canadians despite the fact, as Gilles Duceppe had demonstrated, that Harper himself had seriously considered forming one a few years earlier.

By 2 December, in light of the growing success of Harper's concerted attacks, the opposition parties were the ones becoming concerned. What if Harper did not table the bill and there was no chance for them to table their non-confidence motion to bring down the government? Fearful that he was now planning to delay the vote or even prorogue Parliament rather than face such a vote, the Liberals and the NDP wrote letters to the governor general assuring her that Harper had lost the confidence of the House, but that they were ready to attempt to govern rather than forcing her to call another election. Almost everyone remarked that Michael Ignatieff's signature was last on the list of Liberal MPs provided by Dion to show party solidarity. (Ignatieff's only significant public comment on the deal during that time was half-hearted support for a "coalition if necessary but not necessarily a coalition.")

The prime minister then requested television time on the night of Wednesday, 3 December to speak to Canadians about the "parliamentary crisis." Both Jack Layton and Gilles Duceppe were to be given time to speak as well as Stéphane Dion, although he was expected to appear first. Since Dion insisted on doing a pre-recorded speech rather than a live appearance like the others, it was agreed that the tape of the Liberal leader's comments would be delivered to the TV studio by 7 p.m.

What followed was a public relations nightmare for the Liberals for which the fault, as one of their MPs later declared, could only be laid at the feet of the leader. The recollections of several of those present in the leader's office are identical. Dion insisted on rewriting the material he had been presented by his staff, especially the French version. He worked on the speech for more than an hour and neither Johanne Senecal nor Marlene Jennings could convince him to stop, despite the fact that their communications officers and cameraman told him time was of the essence. They made it clear that they needed sufficient time to properly prepare a tape of his speech before it was delivered to the studio, and that additional time would be needed at that end to ensure compatibility and resolve any other technical concerns. In the end there was not nearly enough time. More than thirty minutes late, a hastily prepared tape was delivered to the studio, which simply played it as it was. In it, both the sound and visuals were blurred; adding insult to injury, the amateurish appearance of the video was highlighted by a book visible behind the leader's head with the words "hot air." The extremely poor quality of the Liberal message shocked viewers across the country and added to the widespread perception that both Dion and the party were out of their depth.

Not surprisingly, Stephen Harper did not table the motion on the economic statement, nor did he wait for the House to resume the following morning. Instead, early on 4 December he crossed the road from his residence at 24 Sussex to Rideau Hall and asked Governor General Michaëlle Jean to prorogue Parliament. After lengthy consultation with a number of constitutional experts, she agreed. For better or worse the Liberals' brief chance to form a government had passed, and it would not come again for nearly a decade.[59]

In addition, the debacle marked the end of Dion's stint as leader. He immediately came under intense pressure to resign from both the parliamentary and extra-parliamentary wings. Former Chrétien minister John Manley took the exceptional step of writing an op-ed in the *Globe and Mail* calling for Dion's immediate resignation, declaring that "the first step for my party is to replace Stéphane Dion as leader with someone whose first job is to rebuild the Liberal party, rather than leading a coalition with the NDP.[60] Barely a week later, on 8 December, Dion announced his resignation would take place as soon as a successor was chosen. "As the Governor General has granted a prorogation, it is a logical time for us Liberals to assess how we can best prepare our party to carry this fight forward," he said in the statement released at the time. "There is a sense in the party, and certainly in the caucus, that given these new circumstances the new leader needs to be in place before the House resumes."

With the House scheduled to resume on 26 January 2009, this resignation – although welcomed by most Liberals – would present yet another problem for the party, since it would not be possible to hold a standard leadership convention in that time. The decision on the next leader, therefore, would require an "outside the box" method that in the end might diminish the legitimacy of the successor.

5 Third Try: The Ignatieff Solution

The timing of my entry into politics was not of my choosing but I thought, as one does, that I could turn circumstances to my own advantage. I had taught Machiavelli but I had not understood him. I thought I could master time, only to discover that it would master me.

– Michael Ignatieff, *Fire and Ashes*, 2015

In the summer of 2006, when I was campaigning for the leadership of my party, I appeared before the Montreal business community [and] one of the leaders asked me whether I could explain … why I wanted to be prime minister. The question caught me by surprise. I answered that it was the hardest job any country has on offer. I wanted to see if I was up to the challenge. I can still remember the chill my answer spread over the crowd. I learned then that I had the wrong answer to the question of what my political life was to be for.

– Michael Ignatieff, *Fire and Ashes*, 2015

Barely six months after Paul Martin had finally taken over from Jean Chrétien after years of internecine warfare, the first "messiah" chosen by the party to replace the veteran prime minister had faltered badly. To the surprise of the elites who had arranged his coronation, Martin and his team had turned what everyone expected to be a fourth Liberal majority into a tenuous Liberal minority. For some, the writing was already on the wall. They did not even wait for the second, and final, humiliation that Martin suffered in 2006. While he was still prime minister they were giving serious thought to whom they would select as their next protégé to succeed him.

This was not the first time such a move had been contemplated. Alf Apps, a prominent Toronto lawyer, had once been president of the Young Liberals and had introduced the incendiary Resolution 40 at the party's 1982 biennial convention. Although he later insisted that the resolution had been designed to address the dysfunctional aspects of the party organization, at the time it was widely seen as a personal attack on Prime Minister Pierre Trudeau by those who would prefer to see former finance minister John Turner assume his role. "The issue of party reform had been building for years," Apps stressed, "but the Coutts nomination fiasco was the catalyst."[1] The resolution itself denounced the role of "non-accountable, non-elected members of the party who have informal direct roles in advising the government which totally bypass the democratically elected executive of the party." The resolution was defeated, as was the party's heir apparent, Turner, in the 1984 election. It was left to Apps and three other prominent Young Liberals, Terry O'Leary, David Herle, and Peter Donolo, to travel to Montreal to try to persuade businessman Paul Martin Jr. to run in the next election and then throw his hat in the ring for the leadership. Donolo chose Jean Chrétien instead, but O'Leary and Herle worked loyally for Martin for many years.

Needless to say, Martin's career did not work out as hoped. And so by December 2004, disillusioned with the performance of his hand-picked choice, Apps decided it was time to try again. He arranged a small gathering of Liberals in the boardroom of his office at the law firm of Fasken Martineau, to meet an internationally known public intellectual, Michael Ignatieff, who was in Toronto delivering a speech. Ignatieff had actually been on Apps's list of potential successors to Martin for some time. Apps's colleague Dan Brock, who attended the event, recalled that Ignatieff seemed to be interested in the proposition, and indicated that he had always felt that he was a Liberal, but no commitments were made.[2]

Then in 2005, as Martin's Liberal minority faltered, Apps persuaded Brock and his friend Ian Davey to make the trek to Boston, where Ignatieff was living at the time, to speak with him again and convince him the time was right to return to Canada and enter politics. Davey, known to many Liberals primarily as the son of legendary backroom fixer Senator Keith Davey, had actually been involved in politics in a variety of functions for many years, including with the Liberals' Red Leaf advertising campaign in 1988, yet he was widely (and in his view quite mistakenly) viewed in Liberal circles as a neophyte. Similarly Brock, a senior lawyer with Fasken Martineau in Toronto, had been Justice Minister Irwin Cottler's senior aide during the brief Martin government. Brock later explained that he had no defined views on the matter beforehand but thought the prospect looked intriguing and, in the end, he was convinced by the one-on-one meeting with Ignatieff. In particular, he thought it would actually be helpful to have someone who had been away from Canada for so long, as he would not be identified with any of the fierce internecine battles that had taken place within the Liberal Party for more than a decade.[3]

These "men in black," as Michael Ignatieff later described them,[4] had in fact decided on a Canadian-born academic who had lived abroad for decades, mostly in London, and was now ensconced in a teaching position at Harvard. Ignatieff was a well-regarded scholar who had written extensively on issues of diversity, political integration, and human rights,[5] and considered the legendary Isaiah Berlin to be his mentor. He was the number one choice of this small group of disaffected party elites largely because he was someone they believed could be presented as the second coming of Pierre Trudeau. He was an intellectual, he was charismatic, and he was a fresh face for the party; yet for many other Liberals at the time Ignatieff was not viewed as a fresh face but as an outsider whose connections to Canada, never mind the Liberal Party, were tenuous at best. Still, in 2004 the three emissaries had a plan to address such concerns. All they needed was time. Unfortunately, fate intervened and the future leader of the Liberal Party was caught in its web, forcing them to act before they were ready. Whether this was as significant a development as Ignatieff himself believes, or whether his leadership would still have been doomed, remains a moot point.

The Next Messiah

The original plan for Michael Ignatieff's entry into politics made sense. It was to be gradual and measured. First he would move back to Canada, then he would run in a safe Liberal riding and become an MP. After a few years he would run for the leadership of the party, which Martin by then would have vacated, or if things unexpectedly improved for the party, he would serve in the cabinet of a Martin government. As Ian Davey recalled, "I told him this will allow you to find out if you like it [politics] and it likes you."[6]

But events overtook them. Before anyone could find out the answer to that basic question, Ignatieff had been thrown in at the deep end. After a carefully orchestrated speech at the party's March 2005 convention in Montreal, which was intended to be his first political exposure (a speech given at the invitation of party president Mike Eizenga), Ignatieff had returned as planned to Harvard. Originally he was going to move back to Canada after classes were over in December 2005 and look around for a riding to contest. This task was made harder by the fact that Paul Martin's key advisers, Tim Murphy and David Herle, saw him as a threat to their man and did not offer to help him find a riding or nominate him as a star candidate. He was on his own.[7] Luckily for him, the team that the original men in black had begun to assemble had been working behind the scenes to orchestrate his nomination in the riding of Etobicoke-Lakeshore, a solidly Liberal riding held at the time by MP Jean Augustine. With the fall of the Martin minority in November 2005, Ignatieff was obliged to make his move immediately.

Augustine announced her resignation on 25 November and pledged her support to Ignatieff for the nomination. Still it was not easy. The Liberal riding association expressed its displeasure with a parachute candidate and someone whose more recent publications had included a defence of waterboarding.[8] President Ron Chyczij stated, "I don't think he's the candidate for this riding. He's offended a large portion of the electorate by his past writings."[9] Chyczij was referring to comments in the candidate's earlier book *Blood and Belonging*, which Chyczij and many others in the heavily Ukrainian Canadian population of the riding considered derogatory. But the hundreds of protesters gathered outside the hotel where the nomination meeting was to take place one night in December were, instead, furious with the Liberals for having selected a man they viewed as supporting the use of torture and the Iraq war of George W. Bush. Inside, order was maintained by the unusual presence of Liberal party president Mike Eizenga himself. At the end of the day Ignatieff did become the Liberal candidate for the riding, and then he was plunged into the actual election campaign. On 23 January he became the riding's Liberal MP, defeating his closest Conservative rival by nearly five thousand votes. But the party lost, and Ignatieff would find himself on the opposition benches when Parliament reconvened under the Harper minority.

Barely eight weeks later a Liberal leadership race was underway, resulting from the immediate resignation of Paul Martin on election night. Despite his lack of experience, Michael Ignatieff was widely described by the media as the front-runner. Ignatieff had the overwhelming support of the old-school party elites, including David Smith, Elvio DelZotto, and David Peterson in Toronto, the official party apparatus in Quebec including president Robert Fragasso and former Martin ministers Liza Frulla and Jean Lapierre, and the vast majority of MPs in the House of Commons.

Still he did not win. In fact, the grass roots of the party repudiated not only Ignatieff but the large team of party veterans who supported him. But, as he himself recounted later, while the grass roots were hopeful of a new start, the old guard were convinced that Stéphane

Dion would not succeed and their chosen candidate would have another chance.

> My leadership team predicted that Dion would not survive another election and so they urged me to wait my turn ... We agreed to keep our leadership ambitions out of sight. Parties rightly punish plotters, or at least those whose plots are too public.[10]

So Ignatieff became deputy leader, shone in the House of Commons in Question Period, and spent much of his time touring the country and giving speeches to Liberal associations, thereby building up support. When Dion (the second, albeit "grass-roots," messiah) lost in 2008 as predicted – and by a worse margin than expected – Ignatieff and his team were ready, whether the party was or not. He and his supporters were expecting a leadership convention in Vancouver in May, but the prorogation debacle that forced the sudden resignation of Stéphane Dion threw everything into confusion. What should the party do now?

And there lay the rub. The party most certainly was not ready for another leadership race, never mind in December rather than May. Both expensive and time consuming, it would take up far too much of the scarce resources left to the party. This was particularly true since the executive knew that their income from the per-vote subsidy, on which they depended so heavily, would fall dramatically in 2009 because of their poor showing in the 2008 election. And then there was the problem of Harper's minority. He had succeeded in putting off the nonconfidence vote by proroguing Parliament, but that was a temporary measure. He would have to come back to Parliament in late January and table a money bill. What if the Liberals and/or the other opposition parties found it so unpalatable that they were forced to defeat it? Could they realistically go into another federal election with only an interim leader? And who would that be?

Ignatieff Takes Charge

All of these problems crossed president Doug Ferguson's mind in the space of a few minutes after Dion's second resignation announcement on 8 December. "I felt the caucus was right that we could not go into an election with an interim leader. On the other hand, I knew it was impossible to hold a standard convention. But we needed to ensure that there was a process that was seen to be as fair and democratic as possible."[11] Then a decision was made to hold the leadership selection process on 17 December, since it would be almost impossible to organize one after

Parliament recessed for the Christmas break, and this exacerbated an already difficult situation.

Ferguson asked national director Greg Fergus to draw up a list of possible options, which he did. In the end the national executive believed only two of the three Fergus presented were feasible. Either there would be a country-wide, one-member/one-vote election (which is what had been proposed by Eizenga at the 2006 convention and rejected by delegates), or there would have to be some type of electoral college election. If the latter, it would involve voting by MPs and senators, defeated candidates, and riding association and club presidents. (It would also favour Ignatieff, with his huge advantage of caucus support.) Ferguson personally preferred the former, but more executive members preferred the electoral college option, and the decision was made easier when the PTAs of Quebec and BC rejected the universal vote by saying they simply could not set it up in time. "I was very disappointed by their refusal," Ferguson recalled, "but there really was nothing we could do."[12] For some, the refusal of Quebec was more than disappointing: it was considered highly suspicious. "We knew Ignatieff's supporters preferred the electoral college option," a Liberal senator who was supporting Bob Rae noted, "and we figured this was a deliberate move to shift the odds in the leadership race."

While the party was deliberating, the caucus and the media were speculating. Since Stéphane Dion had announced in late October that he would resign the following May when a new leader was selected, many names of possible contenders had already emerged. Some, including Gerard Kennedy and Martin Cauchon, declined because they were still financially encumbered by the previous race. Others, such as Frank McKenna, Brian Tobin, and John Manley, ruled themselves out a second time for a variety of career and personal reasons. Still, many Liberals once again concluded that another key factor in these veterans' decision to abstain was their ongoing belief that the party could not win the next election. But three candidates were still left who did come forward to throw their hats in the leadership ring – Ignatieff, Bob Rae, and New Brunswick MP Dominic LeBlanc, son of the former governor general and Trudeau minister Romeo LeBlanc.

Although LeBlanc was widely considered a dark horse who was primarily in the race to provide an Atlantic presence, Rae was clearly in it to win. By the end of October he held a conference call with sixty "key" supporters. "Our campaign will be stronger, better organized than it was last time, and we're going to win," he told his listeners.[13] However, when it became clear that prorogation had changed the political landscape and the party would prefer a permanent leader right away, LeBlanc withdrew in favour of Ignatieff, saying that there was clearly no time for him to mount a credible campaign. This left only Bob Rae, who already had at least some semblance of a campaign organization in place, as did Ignatieff.

It is unclear how much of a threat Rae would have been to Ignatieff's plans had there been a one-person/one-vote decision by the executive. Rae obviously believed that his chances of winning were good under that scenario, and he argued vociferously for it. "I think that it's in the interest of both Mr. Ignatieff and me to have a process that's democratic," Rae told reporters on 8 December. He rejected the idea of Ignatieff being appointed and said the party's grass roots needed to be consulted. A "coronation," he warned, "is something that outrages people. That's a very widespread feeling" among the Liberal grass roots.[14] In the end the national executive disagreed. They announced that the vote would be the electoral college model, although they also stressed that in May in Vancouver the delegates would have a chance to "confirm" the new leader.

The following day, after the electoral college option was announced, Rae folded his tent. In another conference call that morning he told supporters he was withdrawing and would back Ignatieff because he could not mount a viable campaign under the circumstances. Several were upset, including Senator Celine Hervieux Payette, who declared, "This will destroy the Liberal Party, I'm devastated by what this will do to the party, they don't understand anything about democracy."[15] Nevertheless Rae told them he would support Ignatieff wholeheartedly, obviously keeping in mind the criticism that had followed his refusal to back any of the other candidates in the 2006 leadership race when his own candidacy had failed. This time, despite the fact that the earlier race had destroyed the relationship between the two men, Rae was gracious in defeat, telling reporters "I learned how to count a while ago. I drew the conclusion it was time to pack it in." Then he offered Ignatieff "my full and unqualified support. He has been a colleague for more than 40 years. I call upon my friends and supporters to do exactly as I am doing today."[16]

The vote proved anticlimactic. Ignatieff received more than 90 per cent of the ballots cast. And so Michael Ignatieff, who had only returned to Canada and joined the party two years earlier, was now in charge of the fate of the Liberal Party of Canada. The irony of this was not lost on many observers. The elites had rejected the grass roots' choice of messiah because he was an outsider, and now they had chosen an outsider themselves, one with less experience than Stéphane Dion.

The Leader's Office: Déjà vu All Over Again

One of Ignatieff's first tasks was to organize his office as the Leader of the Official Opposition. This proved to be a challenge. And like Dion, he encountered problems and criticism almost immediately, although in Ignatieff's case some new wrinkles were added to the mix. Since funds are allocated to the offices of opposition leaders on the basis of representation, the total budget of Ignatieff's OLO would already be considerably less than for Dion, who had a caucus of nearly thirty more MPs. And because the staff of a leader's office are not public servants but are hired by the individual leader, their positions are not secure in the event of a change at the top. As a result, given the precarious nature of their positions, such staff are entitled to clearly spelled out severance and separation packages.

In Ignatieff's case, a decision was made to lay off all eleven senior Dion aides immediately in December. The total cost of this mass dismissal (roughly $350,000) resulted in a serious shortage of funds for the OLO to hire replacement staff. "They don't have the money to pay the new chief of staff," one Liberal insider confided to the *Hill Times*. "They are facing some challenges but the situation will improve after the new fiscal year starts [on 1 April 2009]."[17]

Like Dion, Ignatieff too was inclined to dance with "the ones that brung him." (Of course in his case, his very limited knowledge of the party and its established specialists limited his options more than most.) Not surprisingly, all three of the men in black soon found a place in the new hierarchy. Ian Davey became Ignatieff's chief of staff, replacing former MP Paul Zed who had occupied the post on a temporary basis while the finances were sorted out. Dan Brock, meanwhile, was named Ignatieff's principal secretary a few months later. And Alf Apps became the president of the party. (Another Toronto acquaintance of Ignatieff, professional fundraiser Rocco Rossi, was personally asked by Ignatieff to serve as the party's national director.) Other key figures in OLO included Jill Fairbrother, a Toronto communications consultant (and Ian Davey's partner) who had first worked for the party on media relations in the 1988 federal election campaign with Doug Kirkpatrick, and had been active on Ignatieff's 2006 leadership campaign. She served as deputy director of communications in the Ignatieff OLO while Sachin Aggarwal, an up-and-coming young Toronto lawyer who had worked on both Ignatieff's riding and leadership campaigns, was appointed director of operations and then deputy chief of staff. Perhaps not surprisingly given the lack of funds, many of the remaining staff were in fact young and inexperienced, albeit enthusiastic. They included speechwriter Adam Goldenberg, who admitted he had never been involved in politics before the 2008 campaign,[18] and Mark Sakamoto, another young Toronto lawyer who served as director of operations.

As the astute reader may have noticed, virtually all of Ignatieff's senior aides hailed from Toronto, like the leader himself. This heavy concentration in one urban locale was already the source of considerable discussion among critics within the party, who began to speak disparagingly of the "Bay Street Brain Trust." In their view this lack of regional representation was especially serious at a time when the Liberals clearly needed to expand their appeal to the regions and rural areas. And Ignatieff, still new to Canada as well as Parliament, would need advisers familiar with those regions, especially the west and the Atlantic.

This regional concern was heightened by the issue of the OLO's lack of a francophone presence and the fact that so many of the senior staff – unlike the leader himself – were unilingual. As Jill Fairbrother recalled, it was expressly stated that she would be complemented by a francophone communications director, and yet this never materialized.[19] At the same time she pointed out to the media that 24 per cent of OLO staff at the time came from Quebec, while 19 per cent were from Toronto.[20] This, however, did little to appease Quebec party elites. As one disgruntled MP stated, "Considering the importance of Quebec in the next election, one has to wonder how come there is not even one senior Quebec adviser in the OLO. They should have at least three or four."[21]

It was Quebec's concerns that in the end brought down Ignatieff's first OLO. In a scenario uncannily reminiscent of the situation under Stéphane Dion regarding by-elections, Ignatieff and his original team ran afoul of the Liberal elites of that province over candidate nominations. The leader had appointed veteran Liberal MP Denis Coderre as his Quebec lieutenant in January 2009 and tasked him with recruiting some star candidates in the province, in addition to getting the party on an election-readiness footing. Coderre, well known as an organizer, was making progress. However, he was also attempting to replace several sitting Liberal MPs, including Raymonde Falco, Bernard Patry, and Stéphane Dion, to make room for some of his star candidates. Not surprisingly, this caused considerable friction, and all three MPs vigorously rejected Coderre's suggestion that they step down. Word of this growing internal dispute had begun to leak out when the matter escalated dramatically because Coderre also had the riding of Outremont in his sights. His plan to appoint a Hydro-Québec executive, Nathalie Le Prohon, was approved by the leader, but the riding association opposed it vociferously. Instead, they unanimously supported the nomination and return of their former MP, Chrétien justice minister Martin Cauchon, who did not run in the 2004 election under Paul Martin.

Soon the Coderre-Cauchon feud became national news. Ignatieff first defended Coderre's move, suggesting Cauchon would be found another riding if he would like one, but this option was immediately rejected by the former minister. In the end, Ignatieff gave in and allowed Cauchon to run in an open nomination in his old riding. (Although he won the nomination handily, Cauchon subsequently went down to defeat against Tom Mulcair in the next election.) Meanwhile Coderre, furious, resigned as Quebec lieutenant and as the party's defence critic. As one CTV commentator noted, "The most important thing here is nobody can win power in this country if they can't govern their own party."[22]

In an interview a few days later, attempting to make amends for some of his initial comments, Coderre told his interviewer, "Don't get me wrong – I still have confidence in Michael Ignatieff. The reality is that he will have to make some changes around himself and take some decisions."[23] Former Liberal MP Jean Lapierre, who succeeded Cauchon in Outremont before stepping down under Stéphane Dion, agreed. "He [Ignatieff] is the one that shook hands with [Nathalie Le Prohon] and then was influenced by his Toronto crowd to change his mind and he didn't even inform his lieutenant or his Quebec team," he said.[24] The potential damage was even more significant given the Liberals' need to retake their lost seats in Quebec if they were to have any hope of returning to power. As Stephen Harper's former communications adviser commented, "You can't change the leader, but you can change the staff."[25]

Barely two weeks after he had written a memo to Ignatieff called the "Turnaround Plan," Ian Davey learned that efforts were being made to recruit Jean Chrétien's highly regarded former director of communications, Peter Donolo, presumably to help out with the restive caucus. But two days later an astonished Davey learned from television that, instead, he had been fired and Donolo would be replacing *him*. Although several people shared his disbelief that someone he had spoken to every day for five years would fail to inform him personally ("Michael wouldn't do that to you, they all said") Davey never received any formal notice from Ignatieff. "Of course he had every right to replace me, but I found it incredibly callous and hurtful that he did not feel the need to speak with me himself."[26]

Ignatieff, who had been pressured by senior caucus and party officials for some time to make changes in his office, told reporters that Donolo would be starting as his new chief of staff immediately, and praised his "wealth of experience." At the same time, he said, "Ian Davey has my gratitude for his enormous service in building this OLO team, and I am grateful for his continuing counsel."[27] (After the 2011 defeat, Ignatieff acknowledged in his autobiographical account of his time in politics that it was "an ill-handled changing of the guard that left bitterness in its wake.")[28] Shortly afterwards both Fairbrother and Brock left the OLO of their own volition, followed closely by Mark Sakamoto. Another twelve staff were let go as Donolo attempted to impose his personal imprint on the office and create a "disciplined and determined" team.[29] As he wrote in a 17 November memo outlining the various changes:

> As with any winning effort, to succeed we must work as a team, a disciplined and determined team. To that end I am very pleased to announce the new senior staff complement in the OLO. This is a very seasoned group of proven individuals with a wide breadth of experience in politics and the wider public sphere. Moreover, as you will see from the organization chart (attached), the emphasis will be, as it must, on clear lines of authority and responsibility as well as accountability for execution and results.[30]

The "new and improved" OLO unquestionably contained many seasoned veterans who were well known and highly regarded in the party and familiar with the internal workings of caucus. They also demonstrated a balance among the various camps that still existed within the party, and enhanced the visibility of Quebec. Quebecers Jean-Marc Fournier (principal secretary) and Mario Lague, a former public servant and adviser to Paul Martin (director of communications), were quickly engaged. They were followed in short order by Pat Sorbara, a veteran organizer for former Ontario premier David Peterson (chief operating officer), Jeremy Broadhurst, a former policy adviser to Dion and Bill Graham (director, Legislative Affairs), and Brian Bohunicky, a former senior policy adviser to two Chrétien-era ministers and to Ignatieff (director, Liberal Caucus Research Bureau.) In addition, and of particular note, popular former MP and whip Karen Redman was engaged as caucus liaison, and long-time party worker Heather Chiasson took on the post of party liaison. Only Sachin Aggarwal of the original team remained in place, as director of operations, although some – such as Broadhurst and Fournier – had already been working in OLO but were transferred to other responsibilities. Meanwhile Warren Kinsella, the Toronto-based former Chrétien adviser who had been expected to direct war room activities for the next election, had been spending up to three days per week in Ottawa. He, too, announced that he was returning to Toronto.

A further round of cuts also occurred in early 2010, managed by Pat Sorbara, a move that apparently was intended not only to further increase efficiency but also to reduce the overall cost and size of the OLO (which had reached ninety-five individuals at one point) in advance of the next election. According to Lisa Kirbie (the former chief of staff to Liberal senator Grant Mitchell), who was working in the OLO's political operations division at the time and who was one of those let go, the third round of cuts were equally poorly handled and resulted in at least one successful lawsuit.[31]

Almost everyone agreed the Donolo-led OLO was more efficient and better organized, but none of these changes was able to achieve the hoped-for result of enhancing the leader's public image. His personal approval ratings were actually decreasing at an alarming rate. This in turn led to a steady stream of leaks from caucus and sniping from Liberals in other leadership camps. But the majority of the caucus remained supportive. As one resigned Liberal MP stated, "We really want him to succeed because we know we can't change him before the next election."[32] Others believed, as his advisers did, that Ignatieff would become far more popular once he had greater exposure, and especially after the writ was dropped. However, there were ominous signs that, once again, the Conservatives may have managed to shape Canadians' image of the Liberal leader before he could do so himself.

The Framing of Michael Ignatieff: Money Talks?

Just as they had done in the case of newly elected leader Stéphane Dion, the Harper Conservatives wasted no time in beginning an advertising offensive to try to define Michael Ignatieff for Canadians before he had a chance to do it. In his case the ads began in early January 2009, before Parliament even resumed and he had a platform as Leader of the Official Opposition.

With their huge financial advantage, and no legislation preventing them from spending it outside of the writ period, the Conservatives blanketed the airwaves with two main messages. Michael Ignatieff was either "just visiting" (in which they targeted his long absence from the country) or "he did not come back for you" (in which they seemed to suggest he was really a carpetbagger who had returned because of personal ambition and a thirst for power). Few Canadians over the age of twelve were not familiar with those two ads, which were shown at expensive times and in costly venues to maximize their coverage.[33]

Since there could be little doubt that the earlier ad campaign against Dion had been highly effective, many observers began to question why the Liberals did not respond to this Conservative offensive immediately. The Liberals insisted publicly that it was not a lack of money that prevented them from defending themselves. The party's newly appointed national director, former fundraiser Rocco Rossi, assured the media that money was not the issue. In fact, he suggested there was a silver lining in the ads, since infuriated Liberals were being encouraged to give even more to the party. For his part, Ignatieff first claimed that his party was going to take the high road, and then also dismissed the ads as irrelevant. "Is that serious government? Is that serious politics?" he asked Liberals at a fundraising dinner in May.[34] Unfortunately the answer was irrelevant as well. Whether or not the ads merited the label of "serious," they were effective. And, as Rocco Rossi later revealed, it was indeed a lack of money that prevented the party from striking back quickly and hard.[35] As Ignatieff himself later admitted, "They had made me the issue and I knew I had to make them the issue. In speeches in the summer of 2009 I attacked ... but no matter how I tried to widen out the issue beyond me it didn't work ... I was still 'just visiting.' The press wasn't listening and our party didn't have the resources to launch a campaign of our own."[36]

One indication that some Liberals were taking the ads seriously could be found in the actions of Liberal senator Denis Dawson. He tabled a bill in the Senate that would limit such advertising in the pre-writ period, something made easier by Stephen Harper's own fixed election date legislation. Dawson also proposed that any such spending in the three months immediately preceding the start of an election campaign would have to be counted as part of a party's election expenses, which, it will be recalled, were already limited. The bill was harshly criticized by the Conservative government and notably by democratic reform minister Stephen Fletcher, who railed against the bill as "undemocratic, unCanadian, unworkable and intellectually corrupt." Not content to stop there, Fletcher added, "The ads are obviously hurting the Liberal Party and this is just an irrational, hypocritical reaction to them."[37]

In the end the Liberals did fund a few ads in the fall of 2009, but they were almost universally panned as ineffective. Ignoring entirely the arguments of the Conservative ads rather than rebutting them, they inexplicably focused on the leader standing in the middle of a forest, casually dressed, and ended with the vague phrase "We can do better." Canadians were not persuaded. And when Ignatieff began to speak of forcing an election once more in January 2011 the Conservatives struck again, with an even more devastating (and technically inaccurate, since Ignatieff had opposed the coalition idea) set of ads claiming "Ignatieff and his ruthless coalition. He did it before and he'll do it again."

Clearly the ads had an impact. Pollster Nik Nanos specifically stated that "the negative attack ads launched by the Conservatives did their job." In November 2010, a Harris Decima poll found that 64 per cent of Canadians, and fully 59 per cent of Liberals, wanted the party to replace Ignatieff as leader. By the end of February 2011 the bottom had fallen out of Ignatieff's personal approval ratings, which were now down to 13.6 per cent.[38] As one party insider noted, there was no possibility that the Liberals could counter those ads. While the Conservatives ran 1,600 ads in the weeks before they tabled their budget in February, "We had 131 and the NDP had ... 25 or something. It was a massacre."[39]

Of course the ads, and the money that funded them, are only one part of the equation. Like Dion, Ignatieff had presented a relatively easy target for the Conservatives to attack, even if the approach was different. And, as numerous observers pointed out repeatedly over the course of the two years in which Ignatieff failed to respond – either with his own ads or in speeches – he had actually had many other opportunities to refute the Conservatives' points and he failed to do so. Certainly his leadership confirmation at the party convention in Vancouver in May 2009 was one. It afforded him a golden opportunity to use his acceptance speech, and the national audience watching, to lay out his reasons for coming back to Canada and wanting to lead the country. But, as the business leaders in Montreal learned, he did not have a ready answer then, nor had he crafted a convincing one in the interim. (By contrast, the Conservatives' attack ads were an abject failure when addressed promptly and cleverly by Ignatieff's successor.)

For the rest of the summer of 2009 Ignatieff was practically invisible, surfacing publicly only once (after the obligatory Calgary Stampede appearance in June, which failed to impress) and, worse still, that appearance was in Britain. He was there to deliver the keynote speech at a conference honouring his mentor, Isaiah Berlin, a signal honour that the Conservatives managed to turn into a public relations disaster for the Liberals, reinforcing their "just visiting" label.

The following summer, with Peter Donolo in charge, the Liberal leader made a dramatic and highly visible cross-country tour by bus. The Liberal Express, as it was called, was designed to expose Ignatieff to the fundamentals of election campaigning, at the same time that it was supposed to expose Canadians to "the real Michael Ignatieff." Media coverage was almost universally positive. Liberal insiders considered it an unqualified success. Yet the party's standing in the polls barely moved – up perhaps 2 per cent at most – while the Conservatives' standings held steady despite a summer rife with problems for them, including the long-form census cancellation, the G20 spending, and G8 security issues.

Some disgruntled caucus members concluded Ignatieff simply did not have the royal jelly. "He just doesn't seem able to connect with Canadians," one lamented. Early supporter Dan Brock agreed. "The longer he was there, the worse he seemed to get," Brock admitted. "He never developed any political instincts."[40] Still others pointed to his ongoing failure to address the reasons for his return to Canada, or to outline his overall vision for the country. According to Brock, this was because after more than two years "he was not sure" why he had come back, and as a result "he really had no vision."

Moreover, when he was asked what he had learned from the tour, the leader promptly listed the ways in which Canadians were unhappy with the Harper government. "We don't trust this government," he said they told him. "They want us to hold them to account this fall. And that's what we're going to do."[41] But many Liberals, and especially the social Liberals on the party's left wing, wanted to know how the party was going to position itself as the real alternative to the Conservatives, rather than the NDP. Ignatieff's newly appointed Quebec lieutenant, Marc Garneau, stressed publicly that more was needed. "We've got to say not only why this is wrong but what we would do instead."[42] Frank Graves of Ekos concurred. When the pollster was asked what one thing the Liberals needed to do, he immediately said, "They need to talk about values ... they need to connect the values to concrete, costed choices."[43] Yet, as many in the caucus and the party were now only too well aware, this was a significant challenge for Ignatieff.

Policy Problems and the Caucus

The division between left-leaning social Liberals and right-leaning business Liberals has always existed. For the most part, this division has caused few problems since all Liberals, regardless of their place on the party's philosophical spectrum, are reliably centrist when compared with the Conservatives on the right and the NDP on the left. Put another way by former senator Jack Austin, protecting the centrist view is a sacred trust of Liberals, particularly in times of great change and upheaval, when the more simplistic views of the left and right may seem more appealing with their apparent offer of certainty.[44] But it is necessary for each generation of Liberals to explain this centrist vision to voters, rather than taking their understanding for granted, a point American liberal and scholar Robert Reich reiterated during the rise of right-wing conservatism under Reagan and Bush.[45] In the face of the most right-wing conservatism of the post-war era that Canadians were experiencing under the Harper government, the need to outline how Liberal values differed was even more essential and should, in fact, have been relatively easy to do.

At the same time, the happy co-existence of business and social liberals in the Liberal Party has been predicated on the expectation that they would be of relatively balanced representation in both the caucus and the cabinet, although within the party the predominance of social liberals among members was generally recognized. Whenever this balance has been disturbed, as happened under John Turner (a business liberal) when his caucus was overwhelmingly composed of social liberals, difficulties can arise fairly quickly. And it was something Liberal MPs were beginning to realize had happened again under Michael Ignatieff. Indeed, some of the predominantly social liberal caucus members were wondering whether he was just a business liberal or actually a liberal at all.

The situation was made worse by the fact that Ignatieff had appointed his supporters (many of whom had also supported Paul Martin) to almost all of the important caucus posts. Whip Rodger Cuzner and the chair of the Tactics Committee, Albina Guarnieri, also lacked sufficient gravitas to gain solid support from their colleagues, while some of the better known and more experienced MPs were conspicuous by their absence from any of these posts.

One result of this was an embarrassing defeat of the Liberals' own motion by the Liberals themselves. Foreign Affairs critic Bob Rae had introduced the motion supporting maternal health care and criticizing the Harper government's decision to exclude family planning from government funding. But although it had the support of all opposition parties, it was defeated because some pro-life Liberal MPs voted against it and other pro-choice MPs who supported it did not show up to vote. Many criticized Cuzner for failing to tell either Rae or the leader that they did not have the numbers.

Similarly, Ignatieff had pleaded with his caucus to support his position opposing a Conservative measure aimed at eliminating part of the gun registry, but eight Liberal MPs nevertheless supported the motion.

On other subjects Ignatieff was not on the same page as his caucus from the beginning, and the situation worsened when it appeared that he was making policy statements on the fly without consulting caucus. Only a few weeks after the two embarrassing developments mentioned above, he was forced to backtrack and "clarify" his position on user fees in medicare after he appeared to support Premier Jean Charest's plan to charge such fees.

A few months later he once again had to apologize and explain himself to caucus after he initially had agreed to a bipartisan motion of the Conservative government concerning the tightening of refugee determination rules. Similarly, he was determined to support the government's planned extension to the Afghan mission, despite advice to the contrary from Ian Davey and Warren Kinsella[46] and widespread caucus resistance. "They [the Conservatives] should take the fall for the body bags," one disgruntled MP said. Another MP confided that Ignatieff "is more conservative than his caucus, especially on external affairs," and this was particularly important since "we get elected in cities and if we tilt to the right on this stuff we are going to lose our base."[47] But Bob Rae, somewhat surprisingly, was insistent that the Liberals should support this move, and Ignatieff agreed.[48]

Clearly Ignatieff needed to learn more about the country and the challenges it was facing. One attempt to improve this situation was the Thinker's Conference organized by the party and the leader's office in Montreal in early March 2010. (Stéphane Dion, it will be recalled, had rejected Tom Axworthy's idea of holding such a conference.) "Canada at 150: Rising to the Challenge" was described by the leader as an attempt to "determine what Canada should look like in 2017 and mapping how to get there."[49] Many outside experts spoke at the conference on a wide range of issues, to generally favourable reviews. But it was unclear how this input would be assimilated by the party or the leader. In his closing remarks Ignatieff seemed to agree with almost every proposal concerning initiatives in health care, post-secondary education, pension reform, and protection of the environment. On the other hand, he ignored the message from former Bank of Canada governor David Dodge that it was imperative the Liberals prioritize their issues and then decide how to pay for any programs – whether through decreased spending elsewhere or increased taxes, although Dodge did not mention the possibility of running a deficit. Instead, Ignatieff seemed to suggest that cancelling the Harper government's proposed corporate tax cuts would provide sufficient revenue, a point experts categorically rejected. Dodge had also indicated that he believed the Liberals had failed to criticize many of the Conservatives' policy options sufficiently, and were leaving themselves open to future difficulties if they were elected. Perhaps the most sombre note to the proceedings was introduced by former foreign affairs deputy minister Bob Fowler, who clearly agreed with Dodge and concluded his remarks with the warning: "I believe to a significant extent the Liberal Party has lost its way, at least in policy terms ... and is in danger of losing its soul."[50]

Party Rebuilding in Slow Motion

While these difficulties were unfolding within the parliamentary wing, the extra-parliamentary wing was busy trying to resolve some of its own ongoing problems. To that end the national executive, clearly recognizing that these problems were quickly becoming intractable, appointed a three-member Change Commission to consult widely with the membership and report back in a timely fashion. Their mandate was to explore the current problems with nine key areas of concern – finances, community engagement, rebuilding riding associations, making better use of technology, improving the party structure; improving internal communications, strengthening the policy process, and outreach. Overall, the objective was to "strengthen and empower our party's grassroots ... The end result will be a more open and democratic party – united around Liberal values – better able to compete and win."[51]

The commissioners began the consultation process – "En Famille" – with a series of nine questions for discussion in an online forum, each of which was chaired by a Liberal MP who had prepared a brief discussion paper on the topic. (Interestingly, one of those MPs was Justin Trudeau, who was the facilitator for the section posing the question "How can LPC improve the party's internal communications? What do members want to hear from the party?" In all, some 2,065 party members participated in the process.

The three commissioners – national party president Doug Ferguson, MP Carolyn Bennett, and Quebec party president Brigitte Garceau – presented their final report in April 2009, in advance of the Vancouver convention. Entitled *Advancing Change Together: A Time to Act*, the report was a comprehensive, detailed, and masterfully presented strategic plan for the party, which even included a timetable of deliverables.

It also highlighted areas in which some progress was beginning to be made, as for example in the case of the national membership list, which had now been modified to the highly successful Liberalist. Similarly, the report noted that the new leader had shown considerable interest in the party (as opposed, presumably, to the inattention of Stéphane Dion), and had focused on the fundraising issue.

But there was simply too much to do and too little time to do it. As Doug Ferguson later recounted, "I knew what had to be done. We just couldn't do it that fast." Perhaps more importantly, despite the concern over finances, there was a real conflict between the need to do the immediate things required to ensure the party was ready to fight an election at any time, and the things that would require – according to the Change Commission's own timetable – more than a year or even two. As Ferguson later confided, "In retrospect, holding Harper to a minority for five years was actually an obstacle to reform for us. It took the 2011 debacle, and the Harper majority, to arrive at a consensus with the leader and caucus that party reform would have to take top priority."[52]

His successor agreed. When Alf Apps was acclaimed as party president at the May 2009 party convention in Vancouver, he believed he did not have time to pursue the medium- or long-term recommendations since "we thought there would be an election any day, and certainly by the fall."[53] (But after the election, Apps would launch his own set of reform recommendations, "A Roadmap to Renewal," which continued the drive to update the party for the twenty-first century.)

This view that only short-term issues could be addressed at the time was also shared by MP Navdeep Bains and his co-chair, former national director Steve MacKinnon, whom Ignatieff had appointed to head a "Renewal Committee" that would implement further items related to the party's reform process. But these items, as Bains explained, were "plumbing and engine-room stuff" geared to the next election.[54] Criticism of the party's modest goals was minimal, although one young Liberal activist – Ryan Androsoff of Saskatoon – represented the views of many western Liberals when he wrote that the party should adopt a resolution in Vancouver to put considerable resources into regions and ridings where the party was weakest. "If there is one thing above anything else that we need to do," he wrote, "it's get boots on the ground, get organizers out to regions where we don't have seats, particularly in western Canada."[55] Bains's response was that the administrative and by-law changes being proposed would in the end lead to greater party efficiency, which in turn would ultimately achieve the same objective. "We are going to centralize administrative functions and use those savings to put more workers back in the field," Bains said. "We want more boots on the ground."[56]

At the convention the only "major" element of party reform was the adoption of the earlier Eizenga proposal to eliminate delegated conventions entirely for future leadership selection, in favour of universal suffrage of members, something that now proved not only non-controversial but irrelevant to the pressing issues of the day, such as fundraising and operational capacity.

As mentioned above, Michael Ignatieff had appointed Rocco Rossi as the party's national director in early 2009, replacing Greg Fergus, precisely because he was an experienced professional fundraiser, and increasing party revenue was the leader's top priority. Rossi's early efforts were indeed productive, although it must be kept in mind that his success corresponded with Ignatieff's initial honeymoon with voters. The party's annual revenue in 2009 increased from roughly $6 million the previous year to $9.5 million, while the number of individual donors increased to 37,876. At the same time, the Conservatives had raised $21 million in 2008, suggesting the Liberals still had a long way to go.

Rossi pointed out that the Vancouver convention had made money for the party and that the party was slowly reducing its debt load. But he also emphasized that successful fundraising required a sophisticated database, which the party had until recently lacked. Without it, grassroots fundraising was virtually impossible. With it, he noted, it was possible to target the party's message, something that had allowed him to be successful elsewhere. "Not for profit does not have to equal 'for a loss,' he quipped."[57]

At the convention Rossi had led a fundraising workshop for Liberal activists, based on the newly purchased software system Doug Ferguson had discovered in the United States and that had been used so successfully by Barack Obama's team. Much was riding on the Voter Activation Network (VAN) system that would allegedly help the party keep track of potential supporters and donors, using the new Liberalist national membership list. With it, the Liberals believed they would soon achieve a state-of-the-art ability to micro-target their supporters, something the Conservatives already had been able to do for more than seven years using a similar program, their Constituent Information Management System (CIMS).

However, after barely a year in the post Rossi unexpectedly left the party to run in the mayoralty campaign of Toronto.[58] His sudden departure did little to help Ignatieff's image, especially when it was learned that the former fundraiser had complained to officials at a lunch at the US embassy that "he knows his own mind, and the only person whose opinion he really cares about is his wife, Zsuzsanna."[59]

Rossi was replaced as national director by Ian McKay, an international financial adviser with an MBA who was also a lifelong Liberal, having run (unsuccessfully) as a federal candidate in his native BC and having served as a policy adviser to three Liberal cabinet ministers during the Chrétien era. However, McKay soon encountered the problems faced by any political party when trying to solicit money while the party's and the leader's fortunes were plummeting in the polls. In 2010, total revenue fell to $6.6 million, while the Conservatives raised $17.4 million.

To Force an Election or Not?

Holding Harper to a minority had certainly been the preoccupation of the caucus and party organizers, and it became increasingly difficult to do as time passed. Many observers believed that Michael Ignatieff's best chance would have been to force an election shortly after he became leader. By 2010 Bob Rae was telling anyone who cared to listen that the Liberal Party was fast losing credibility and would need to pull the plug soon if it was to have any hope of salvaging the situation. At the same time Canadians could have been forgiven for thinking that Michael Ignatieff was an opportunist if they were paying attention to his various warnings that the government was about to fall in the two years prior to the 2011 election.

He had already cried wolf twice. His first effort was tied to the Conservatives' 27 January 2009 budget, when he told Canadians the Liberals were going to issue report cards on the government's progress and would bring it down if not enough was done to address his economic concerns. This attempt actually backfired as the Conservatives issued their own reports showing how well they had done. His second warning to the government, the widely mocked "Time's Up" announcement launched at the special caucus meeting in Sudbury in fall 2009, led to a rapid and drastic decline in support for the party when the Liberal non-confidence motion failed because the NDP supported the Conservatives in the House of Commons. (Interestingly, many observers believed that this second failed attempt was the primary reason for the major reorganization that took place shortly afterwards in Ignatieff's OLO, building on the pre-existing pressure from Quebec Liberals, since it was widely believed that Ian Davey and his team had suggested this tactic. But as Davey later recounted, they had not known about it in advance. "We were appalled. None of us thought it was a good idea."[60] Instead, this decision had been taken by the leader after a meeting with senior caucus members a few days earlier, in which Bob Rae had told him, "You can't be half pregnant. Either we're taking them on or we're not. And if we are, then say so."[61]

This second failed attempt led to the hiring of Donolo and Sorbara, who were given a year to set the OLO house in order and stabilize the situation, but it also led to a collapse in the leader's confidence as the polls worsened. Despite the success of the Liberal Express in restoring that confidence, and preparing Ignatieff for the rigours of an actual election campaign, there were still those depressing polling numbers that refused to budge.

Nevertheless, by the spring of 2011 it seemed clear to the caucus that they were in the best position they could hope for in order to bring about an end to the waiting. The Harper government's lengthy record of obstruction, abuse of power and, most recently, contempt of Parliament led them to believe that they could tackle Stephen Harper successfully on the issue of trust in government. What Michael Ignatieff described as a "cascade of abuse"[62] – including examples such as the muzzling of government scientists, public criticism of Supreme Court decisions, and blatant disregard for the findings of various parliamentary watchdogs, as well as the unprecedented use of closure and a second prorogation to limit the damage on the Afghan detainees file – had recently culminated in two major scandals in early 2011. One was related to the highly problematic actions of international cooperation minister Bev Oda and the other to the government's refusal to provide information on the costing of two important measures in its February budget. Both issues had been widely covered in the media and uniformly criticized by academics, think tanks, and interest groups as flagrant violations of parliamentary democracy.[63]

In the first instance, the minister had been publicly accused of lying to a parliamentary committee and retroactively altering a departmental memo she had signed. Although she was strongly defended by Harper, the possibility of Oda's being found in contempt of Parliament loomed large in the spring of 2011. Moreover, she had already lost the battle in the court of public opinion. Even staunch Conservative supporters had stated that she should resign. As Lorne Gunther so succinctly put it, "She lied to the House, so she must go."[64]

Meanwhile, and almost simultaneously, the government's continuing and categorical refusal to provide costing numbers on either its proposed super-prisons or its purchase of F-35 fighter jets – both measures included in its February budget – had led the Commons Procedure and House Affairs Committee to issue a majority report recommending the government be found in contempt of Parliament for violating parliamentary privilege. The speaker, Peter Milliken, concurred. In a scathing ruling that found the Harper government had breached parliamentary privilege and was indeed in contempt of Parliament, Milliken declared, "This is a very serious matter that goes to the heart of the House's undoubted role in holding the government to account."[65] Not only was this an unprecedented ruling in Canada, it was the first time any government in the Commonwealth had been found guilty of such behaviour. Not surprisingly, Ignatieff and his team felt they were on solid ground with their approach.

On 25 March the Liberals moved a motion of non-confidence in the government. In debate before the vote, Liberal leader Michael Ignatieff stated confidently, "We are the people's representatives. When the government spends money the people have a right to know what it is to be spent on. Parliament does not issue blank cheques."[66]

The motion was supported by all opposition parties, and the Harper minority government fell. Two days later the federal election that they had forced got underway. As Michael Ignatieff told reporters, he believed the election "issue here is one of trust. How can Canadians remain trusting of a government guilty of such flagrant abuse of power?"[67] Unfortunately, for Ignatieff and the Liberals, he was wrong.

6 The Near-Death Experience: The 2011 Election

We believe that the moment has come for Canadians to make a choice here between the responsible, progressive, compassionate choice of the Liberal Party or the irresponsible and undemocratic path of the Conservative government.
                                    – Michael Ignatieff, 23 March 2011

What were they thinking?
                                    – Ipsos pollster Darrell Bricker, 18 May 2011

Stephen Harper decided when to pull the plug on his first minority government, despite many threats by the Dion Liberals to do it themselves. But as we have seen, it was the Ignatieff Liberals who decided when Harper's second minority would come to an end. And their decision on timing was made when they believed they had the advantage in terms of framing the election question.

During the fall of 2010 the Liberals had raised a number of possible topics, the most frequent being "Are you better off?," a question they had asked during the summer 2010 Liberal Express tour. However, the failure of that trial balloon to spark voter interest or lead to a favourable uptick in the polls had led them to reject it in favour of the theme of "families, not jets and jails" following the tabling of the Conservatives' budget in February 2011. It was only with the speaker's historic ruling in late March 2011, finding the Harper government as well as minister Bev Oda were in contempt of Parliament, that they changed course once more. The next election, the Liberals decided, would be about the arrogant, undemocratic, and possibly corrupt Harper government.

On the surface this seemed like a reasonable assumption. Canadians had been exposed to a series of parliamentary scandals. Taken together, these various offences had led pundits and academics in Canada and internationally to denounce the Harper Conservatives' autocratic behaviour in scathing terms.[1] Noting that no government in a parliamentary democracy had ever been found in contempt of Parliament before, Alberta political scientist Lori Thorkalson wrote, "No other legislature among what Winston Churchill termed the English-speaking peoples would ever tolerate such treatment. And since Westminster-style Parliaments tend to be weaker than others, our House of Commons could [now] be described as the weakest of the weak."[2] The government's unprecedented behaviour led all of the opposition parties to denounce the Harper Conservatives' disdain for the rules, and gave the Liberals their rationale for defeating the government.

"Who do you trust?" would be the election question, one on which the Liberals were confident they would be the first choice of voters. With that decision made, they wasted little time in tabling a non-confidence motion in the House of Commons and sending Canadians into another election.

In public the Liberals projected a degree of confidence that was somewhat surprising given that polling numbers did not bear this out. A dozen polls conducted between early February 2011 and the day the writ was dropped in late March all showed a gap of more than ten percentage points between the Liberals and the Conservatives.[3] Campaign director Gordon Ashworth had urged the leader to delay the election call for this very reason, maintaining that it was better to wait for improved numbers before casting the dice.[4]

But Ignatieff personally was tired of waiting, and many of his closest advisers believed he would surprise and impress during the campaign itself. True, conventional academic wisdom has long held that campaigns matter,[5] just as it has shown that the governing party is the one most likely to lose ground during an election campaign. But the gap between the Liberals and the governing Conservatives in this case was substantial if not insurmountable.

Another cause for concern might have been the campaign launch. Ignatieff appeared confident at the press conference after the non-confidence vote he had triggered, stressing the agreed-upon line that the upcoming election would be about trust, and the inability of Canadians to trust the Harper government. Initially this session went well, and Ignatieff looked pleased. However, as the conference was drawing to a close one reporter asked him whether he would be willing to form a coalition with the NDP in order to defeat the Conservatives, if the result of the election was yet another minority. Ignatieff was ready. "There's a Blue Door and a Red Door in this election," he intoned decisively, apparently thinking this would end the matter. It did not. Confused, several journalists asked him what exactly he meant by this. Looking somewhat less confident, Ignatieff indicated that he had been perfectly clear. The only alternative to the Conservatives was the Liberals. No one else could form a government. Not the NDP, not the Bloc, and not the Greens. Voters had but two choices. When several journalists insisted he had not answered the question, Ignatieff repeated his "red door, blue door" line and hastily exited.

As Peter Donolo later confirmed, the line was Ignatieff's own, and he obviously had thought it would end any possible discussion of coalitions.[6] If he had said at the time that he would never consider such a move, the issue might have gone away. But he did not. Instead he waited two days before issuing a statement saying that he would not consider forming a coalition under any circumstances. This hesitation was puzzling to many observers, who knew that he had opposed the idea under Dion and had been the very last member of caucus to sign the Liberals' letter to the governor general on the subject. Moreover, virtually everyone knew that Canadians now overwhelmingly believed the Conservatives' argument that Dion's coalition plan was anti-democratic and practically a coup d'etat. No sensible politician would admit to giving it any consideration. Perhaps most troubling was the fact that Ignatieff's hesitation allowed the Harper Conservatives to continue their fearmongering among Canadian voters, arguing that they needed a "strong stable majority" to prevent such an undemocratic outrage.

Still, the mood in caucus was cautiously optimistic. They were sure that they were on the right track by stressing Harper's own undemocratic behaviour. Privately, there was widespread consensus that a majority was out of the question, but a minority Liberal government was within the realm of possibility and, in any event, the party would definitely gain ground and be better positioned for next time.

The Party and Election Readiness

One reason for this apparent confidence was the state of the party apparatus. In comparison with the situation in 2008, the Liberals were in far better shape. Alf Apps, Ignatieff's personal choice as party president in 2009, insisted that he had worked diligently "from day one" to ensure the party's election campaign machinery was up and running to the extent possible, at the expense of other reform issues, which, like his predecessor Doug Ferguson, he felt obliged to put on hold.[7] Communications between the party headquarters and the field had improved considerably and the new state-of-the-art Liberalist computer software was being applied. Although there was still a shortage of troops due to the

leftover resentment from the Martin-Chrétien era of internecine warfare, more volunteers were coming forward every day and more ridings
were beginning to establish credible election operations. But Apps also
felt that he was operating in a vacuum. Among other things, he had
virtually no meetings with the leader, a man he himself had recruited.
"The leader failed to understand the importance of the party," Apps
stated.[8] Again, this was perhaps hardly surprising since Ignatieff had
spent no time in the Liberal Party before becoming an MP and leader.
On the other hand, those in the OLO were now experienced veterans
such as Peter Donolo, and coordination between the party headquarters
and the leader's office began to take place at lower levels.

According to Donolo, for once money was not *the* major concern of
the campaign.[9] True, the heady increase in revenue in the first year
of Ignatieff's leadership in 2009, under national director Rocco Rossi,
had fallen off badly in 2010 under his replacement, Ian McKay, despite
the latter's recognized expertise as a professional fundraiser. Many
observers blamed the drop in contributions on a lack of enthusiasm
for the leader among grass-roots Liberals and the general public.
Certainly Ignatieff's personal approval ratings had plummeted in
the year since the convention. This lack of resources had seriously
limited the party's ability to respond to the Conservatives' negative
pre-campaign advertising. Nevertheless, sufficient funds had been
husbanded for the campaign, and the party was able to spend the
maximum allowable.

Of course, the shambles that was the 2008 leader's tour automatically made Ignatieff's campaign appear highly competent by comparison. Nevertheless, the party was far more prepared than in 2008 by
any tangible measure. A plane was engaged, and an experienced group
of veterans were assigned to the leader's tour. In addition to Donolo,
who served as senior adviser, Brian Bohunicky was onboard as policy
adviser, Leslie Church was director of communications, aided by Dan
Lauzon and Michel Liboiron as media contacts, and Adam Goldenberg
continued in his role as speechwriter on the tour.

On the ground, campaign director Gordon Ashworth had made it
clear that he was in charge, and people were cooperating. This time,
instead of the party's national director, Ian McKay, it was Ignatieff's
chief operating officer, Pat Sorbara, who served as deputy campaign
director. Toronto executive Bob Richardson was handling the Liberals'
advertising campaign (traditionally known as Red Leaf), and a series of
ads were ready to go. Ignatieff's director of legislative affairs in OLO,
Jeremy Broadhurst, took over the running of the war room, and Heather
Chiasson handled candidate liaison. Former broadcast executive Glenn

O'Farrell had agreed to handle debate prep, and once again Michael Marzolini would serve as the party's pollster.

Together with national campaign co-chairs David Smith and Luci-enne Robillard, the senior members of the campaign committee had examined the various problems that plagued the leader's tour in the previous election, and adopted a deliberate strategy designed to avoid those pitfalls. In addition, the campaign committee decided on an aggressive approach to the tour, in which Ignatieff would begin by vis-iting a number of seats held by the NDP, Bloc, and Conservatives, seats that the Liberals believed they had a chance of winning. This was in direct contrast to the Dion tour, which had focused almost exclusively on ridings the Liberals already held and were concerned about retain-ing. This defensive approach had not gone unnoticed. As one observer concluded, Dion "spent the beginning of the 2008 campaign sending the very strong message that the Liberals were in trouble on their own turf."[10]

An official plan of platform plank announcements also had been drawn up and a variety of official engagements planned for the first two weeks. All went off seamlessly. Unlike the spectacle of Dion speak-ing to half-empty rooms, Ignatieff's events were usually jam-packed. Field workers actually competed to see who could arrange for the most bodies at an event. Communications between ground and plane went smoothly as well, suggesting once again that a far more professional organization was in place than in 2008.

The Early Campaign's Encouraging Showing

The first two weeks did indeed go well for the Liberals. Liberal insiders felt their optimism had been justified when the early polls suggested a modest increase in popular support for the party of 3–4 per cent. Much of the credit could be given to the stabilizing influence of Peter Donolo and the organizational skills of Pat Sorbara. In addition, as veteran strategist Warren Kinsella noted, the party's new and improved image was the product of work by two senior backroom organizers who had been preparing the groundwork for several months before the writ was dropped:

> If the Liberal Party of Canada ends up doing better than expected in Campaign 2011 – and so far the Grits are doing much better than anyone thought they would – they should give Bob Richardson and Gordon Ash-worth a great big thank you ... From the time of their arrival in Ottawa, Richardson and Ashworth have firmly taken control ... The pair have

given the Liberal Party's efforts a maturity and strategic sense that, until just a few weeks ago, it simply didn't have.[11]

Then there was the unexpectedly strong, at times exceptional, performance of the leader himself. After his stumble out of the gates on the coalition issue, Ignatieff quickly picked up steam and was soon surprising even his handlers with his impressive performance. It was obvious to everyone that he was enjoying his encounters with the crowds organized for his various events, and even more obvious that he could ad lib when necessary if given the chance. "At one point we decided to let him have more unscripted encounters, since he did so well with them. I guess it was all his experience as a television personality."[12] He also appeared relaxed and engaged, something that Stephen Harper – who could not perform without a teleprompter and was being kept in a bubble during the campaign by his handlers – did not.

One benefit of the leader's surprisingly good showing in the first few weeks was that the constant sniping from the sidelines of the party came to a halt. Seeing that Ignatieff was doing so much better on the hustings than they had expected, Liberal volunteers and candidates were clearly energized. As one journalist put it, "Ignatieff's confidence on the road" was "motivating them to work harder for a leader they believe is now an asset rather than a liability."[13]

Similarly, there was no question that the Liberals had a comprehensive and detailed platform ready for distribution. Advance notice of many of the main themes had been communicated by the leader in the months leading up to the election call, stressing the concept of intergenerational fairness and including a series of planks devoted to providing additional benefits for Canadian families. This was the substance of the "families, not jails and guns" slogan they had used earlier in the House of Commons, to criticize the Conservatives' heavy emphasis on retribution in their latest budget.

It was in Oakville, one of the ridings held by the Conservatives that the Liberals had targeted as vulnerable, that Ignatieff unveiled the first plank in his election platform. Speaking to a crowd at Sheridan College, Ignatieff introduced the Liberals' "Learning Passport," a plan specifically designed to provide assistance to low-income students and their families to pursue post-secondary education, and to encourage all Canadians to participate in "life-long learning" by offering targeted assistance for training and retraining.

This was the first of many planks that, taken together, constituted what Ignatieff referred to as the "family pack." For the next several days the Liberals followed the example of the Conservatives in 2008 and unveiled a plank a day. Over the next week they unveiled specific planks on child care, the Canada Pension Plan and Guaranteed Income Supplement, aid for disabled Canadians, and assistance for caregivers in the so-called sandwich generation who were supporting aging parents and young adults. Additional planks addressed Aboriginal education and an education benefit for returning veterans.

There were also planks on democratic renewal, addressing concerns raised by the Harper government's contempt for Parliament and its rules and procedures. In addition, there were proposals for internet voting and a "people's question period," and a commitment to restore the Court Challenges Program cancelled by the Harper government. In foreign affairs the platform committed a future Liberal government to reallocating funds currently spent on the Afghan mission to development aid once the mission ended. Similarly, a number of specific projects, such as a new bridge in Montreal and federal assistance for sports buildings in several cities, was to be funded through a reallocation of funds in an existing infrastructure program. A modest $265 million was to be invested in environmental technology to reduce the impact of the oil sands, and a commitment was made to consider the implementation of a cap-and-trade program similar to ones already in force in Europe.

The theme of intergenerational fairness that Ignatieff had raised in his remarks on the release of the platform was intended to be an updated take on the underlying Liberal value of "equality of opportunity," a concept that had served generations of Liberal leaders so well, and that Liberal icon Tom Kent had publicly urged Ignatieff to emphasize in his platform.[14] But after the initial launch, this broader rationale for the platform, and for the Liberal "vision," was lost in the details and never mentioned again.

Instead, Ignatieff and his team were careful to stress that their platform was fiscally responsible. To pay for their new initiatives they proposed not only to reallocate existing funds but to "slash" government advertising and consultants' fees, reduce the size of cabinet, and eliminate a tax break on stock options over $100,000, as well as increasing the corporate tax rate by 1 per cent. "We've made very cautious assumptions here," Ignatieff said at the press conference unveiling the platform. "We owe it to the Canadian people to give them responsible, prudent fiscal management."[15]

Since a decision had been taken more than a year before the writ was dropped that there would be no major tax increases or large deficits in their platform to pay for whatever platform was eventually approved, the Ignatieff Liberals had effectively limited their options before they began to make policy decisions. But this decision had not been without its detractors. Some of the social liberals in caucus had been extremely concerned that there was virtually no big-ticket item for them to trumpet and capture voters' imagination. Nor was there a plainly stated vision for the future of the country. Meanwhile, business liberals had insisted that the platform as a whole, whatever it contained, must demonstrate that there were no "tax and spend" liberals for the Conservatives to criticize. Everything must not only be fully costed but its funding sources must be explained. In the end, the result was the modest but solid platform that was indeed more difficult for the Liberals' adversaries on either the right or left to criticize.

Still, initial response to the platform was quite positive, not only among the various non-governmental organizations who represented many of the targeted groups that would benefit, but also with the media. CTV reporter Craig Oliver was particularly positive in his assessment. He saw the document as "a statement of principle" and "a template, a touchstone they can use as a reference point in the coming weeks on every campaign issue that comes at them."[16] This may well have been what the Liberals intended, but it did not come to pass. The leader was extremely familiar with the platform and all of its items. But his reference to only one or two specific planks at each public event, coupled with a detailed explanation of them, did not create any sense of the whole document or its underlying principles.

Meanwhile, the polls did not reflect the positive reaction to Ignatieff's strong performance at public events, or the positive response that individual Liberal candidates were finding at the door. Nor did there appear to be much public recognition of the Liberals' platform, despite the hype first accorded to its release. The general public, it seemed, remained either uninterested or sceptical. It would fall to the leader during the mid-campaign debates, then, to try to ratchet up the attention of the large number of voters who seemed to be sitting on their hands or had yet to make up their minds.

The Leaders' Debates Change the Game

If the 2006 Liberal leadership race debates, with their cumbersome format and lengthy list of candidates, had demonstrated anything, it was that Michael Ignatieff – to almost everyone's surprise – was not a particularly skilled debater, at least in a political forum. This was perhaps the reason why his handlers had declined to have him participate in the "front four" debate organized by the Empire Club in Toronto during that race, since both Bob Rae and Gerard Kennedy were known to be quite adept and even Stéphane Dion had shown up well.

Certainly Ignatieff's team had realized his weakness in this area, and had done their best to address it early on, in preparation for the leaders' debates during the campaign. The practice of conducting mock debates, using other individuals as stand-ins for the real adversaries a leader would face during the traditional televised debates, has become well entrenched, especially since the disastrous performance of Conservative leader Kim Campbell (who had refused to participate in such debate preparation) in the 1993 election. Yet Ignatieff evidently did not feel he was in the same situation. He told advisers he had been "a championship debater at university and had spent his life as a TV journalist."[17]

Despite his reluctance, debate prep began in earnest in 2010, more than a year before the election. In Ignatieff's case, provincial Liberal cabinet minister Dwight Duncan was engaged to portray Stephen Harper, and he pursued the Conservative leader's anticipated line of attack against Ignatieff with vigour. But Ignatieff's obvious distate for the exercise became palpable, and in the end the number and frequency of such practices declined as he found other, more pressing matters to occupy his time.

Perhaps it would have made no difference to his performance in the real debates. Evidently this is what Ignatieff believed, since his only comment on the debates in his autobiographical account stated that they "did not do me any good" and concluded, "I see now that we were so consumed by the run-throughs of our mock debates that we failed to settle on a basic strategy."[18] Many observers, and no doubt members of his Liberal team, would have disagreed.

The two debates, one in English and one in French, were held on 12 and 14 April, or roughly halfway through the campaign. At that point the Liberals had made little further progress in the polls, but neither had the NDP. The election was, for all intents and purposes on hold, a non-event. In this situation the debates had the potential to play a more significant role than might otherwise have been the case. Despite the noteworthy exceptions of 1984 and 1988, few such debates have ever featured a so-called knockout punch. But there is always the potential for error in what is essentially an unscripted format, and the Liberals were hopeful.

For the Conservatives, it was crucial that they have their man avoid any mistakes, since they knew he was not popular and could only maintain the party's hold on power by avoiding potential pitfalls. As a result, Harper was urged by his handlers to keep his well-known temper in check, avoid any confrontations with the other leaders, and say as little as possible, the classic front-runner strategy.[19] Since the Liberals had been hoping to provoke Harper into an angry outburst, this was not good news.

With Elizabeth May excluded from the debates this time, there were only four leaders participating in the event, making Harper's task somewhat easier. He did manage to follow the script his advisers had given him, and Ignatieff's repeated efforts to draw Harper out with pointed criticism of his government's behaviour and handling of issues were unsuccessful. And, while Harper used his time to outline various elements of his party's platform, the Liberal platform was not mentioned at all by Ignatieff in the English debate and only appeared as one item – the "Learning Passport" – in the French debate, a reference whose meaning and significance were lost on most of the audience.

Meanwhile NDP leader Jack Layton, who was participating in his third leaders' debate, remained calm and smiled frequently during both debates, a marked contrast to the aggressive behaviour and negative comments of Ignatieff. One of his few attack lines, however, was far more successful than even he must have anticipated. Ignoring Stephen Harper in favour of Ignatieff most of the time, Layton at one point accused the Liberal leader of a poor attendance record in the House. "If you want the job you have to show up for work," Layton said. Ignatieff appeared stunned by the accusation. Although this comment had been on the NDP website for some time, he appeared to have no ready-made response. This was particularly surprising since he could easily have explained all of the other work he had been doing instead, and since Layton's attendance record was hardly any better. But the art of the "pivot," so important in politics when under attack, was not in Ignatieff's repertoire.

Perhaps equally important was Ignatieff's failure to take advantage of opportunities that were afforded him to make his case about why he had returned to Canada and wanted to be prime minister, something he had repeatedly failed to do throughout his two-plus years as leader in response to the "just visiting" theme of the Conservative attack ads. These ads had certainly not been forgotten by the public. As Liberal MP Mark Holland later recalled, when he was canvassing door to door during the election more than one constituent told him, "If he [Ignatieff] can't stand up for himself, how can he stand up for me, or for the country?"[20]

Similarly, in the French-language debate Ignatieff failed entirely to take advantage of a golden opportunity provided by Bloc leader Gilles Duceppe to expound on his vision of liberalism and liberal values. The moment came (and went) when Duceppe was responding to a comment made by Stephen Harper about his conservative values. Duceppe quickly replied that he did not share Harper's values; then he quite remarkably went on to state that the last time he had shared the same values as a federal leader was when Lester Pearson had been in power. As one analysis later concluded:

> With Ignatieff scheduled to speak next, viewers might well have expected Ignatieff (a self-described Pearsonian Liberal) to build on that unexpected statement to highlight Liberal values, his own values and the values reflected in the Liberal platform. Instead, Ignatieff returned to the theme of trust and lack of confidence in the Harper government.[21]

The morning after the second debate, the results of Angus Reid's focus group evaluations confirmed what Ignatieff apparently already knew. The events had done him no good. Worse, they had hurt him and helped Layton. Harper had emerged relatively unscathed but no better off either. In Quebec, it was clear that Harper was not popular, but this was hardly news. In the rest of Canada, all three opposition leaders had suffered from their tendency to attack Harper and each other, but Layton much less so than the others. "The level of annoyance grew markedly when the leaders attacked each other," the Reid focus groups demonstrated, and Ignatieff had done that far more than Layton. For the Liberals, this was clearly a lost opportunity to make their case as the real alternative to the Conservatives, and they would pay dearly for it.

The Liberals in Free Fall

After the debates very little went well for the Liberals. They had been expecting those debates to jump start their campaign, and that had not happened. In fact, nothing seemed to be working. Certainly not the platform, which had been all but forgotten by the few voters who had ever been aware of it. This, in turn, was particularly galling since Stephen Harper had not yet released the entire Conservative platform and had made it clear he would only do so a few days before the end of the campaign. The Liberals' own platform, of course, had been public for weeks, and the prime minister along with various Conservative cabinet ministers had been chipping away at its proposals, as had the NDP.

Immediately after the debates the Liberals decided to focus more on the leader, who was performing so well, by showcasing him in a series of additional ads that they would have to stretch to pay for. Then they were handed what they saw as an ideal opportunity to do just that, with Michael Ignatieff's entirely unscripted performance at a campaign rally in Sudbury on 15 April. At the town hall in Sudbury Ignatieff ignored his prepared text on the Liberal platform and began by asking if anyone in the room liked singer Bruce Springsteen. He went on to say that one of his personal-favourite Springsteen songs was "My City of Ruins," in which the line "rise up" occurs. "And I began thinking about it today on my way here. Because we're in a funny place in this election campaign right now." Then he went on to list the litany of Conservative misdemeanours, from contempt of Parliament to throwing out the long-form census, and lamented the fact that Canadians seemed to be shrugging and saying, "so what?" Building on that theme, he captured the imagination of the enthusiastic crowd, who began clapping as he called for Canadians to rise up. Soon the entire audience was on its feet chanting that message. The Liberals on the plane viewed the footage of the event and decided that it would be the centrepiece of their new ads. They even hoped to have it up and running on YouTube shortly.

But this would not turn out to be the positive move they had anticipated. For one thing, it reinforced the concerns of the Angus Reid focus groups that the Liberals, and Ignatieff, were more intent on criticizing the Conservatives than on putting forward their own positive vision. One account of the fallout from the ads suggests that, unbeknownst to the Liberals, the Conservatives who saw this new clip online actually responded enthusiastically themselves. According to Paul Wells's detailed analysis of the 2011 election results, Jason Litaer, Harper's war room director, tweeted "with any luck this will go viral." Another Conservative war room source told Wells, "You've got Stephen Harper on the one hand saying we need a stable government, and then you've got a guy yelling at people to rise up?"[22]

The Liberals' situation deteriorated still further after Bloc leader Gilles Duceppe made his own unscripted intervention at the Parti Quebecois convention on 17 April. For some time the Bloc and PQ had been operating quite separately, but on this occasion Duceppe evidently felt he needed PQ support to hold onto all of his seats in the province. "Before we are Pequistes or Bloquistes we are all sovereignists," he told the crowd. "We have only one task to accomplish. Elect the maximum number of sovereigntists in Ottawa, and then we go to the next phase, electing a PQ government."[23] Like the Liberal crowd in Sudbury the partisans in the room loved Duceppe's comments, but not everyone else did. Many in Quebec were tired of the endless separatist-federalist battles and had assumed from his platform that the Bloc would be spending its time putting forward concrete policies to benefit the province, not plotting a separatist hegemony. His decision to raise the spectre of mutual cooperation on separatism in his keynote speech would soon prove to be a costly mistake. Nanos polls showed support for the Bloc falling from nearly 39 per cent to barely 30 per cent in less than a week. That lost support, moreover, was not going to the Liberals or Conservatives but to the province's new favourite son, Jack Layton, "le bon jack."

By 19 April, Marzolini's internal polling showed that the NDP had pulled ahead of the Liberals. As one party worker put it, voters were beginning to think that they *did* have an alternative to the red and blue doors. And since Harper had won his two minority governments with less than 40 per cent of the vote, it was clear that far more than half of the population was determined to find an alternative to deny him a stable majority.

As support for the Bloc in Quebec collapsed in favour of the NDP for the first time ever, Ontario paid attention. By 25 April pollsters were detecting a landslide of popular opinion away from the Liberals, and towards the NDP, until it became a full-fledged avalanche. The Liberals were caught in the crossfire, attempting to defend themselves simultaneously on their left and right flanks. As one insider confided, they were all glad that the campaign had only one week left to run, or they feared they might be reduced to the plight of the old Progressive Conservatives in the 1993 election, reduced to two seats.

It did not come to that, but the result was unprecedented for Liberals. The party finished in third place, and lost its status as the Official Opposition. From the previously low seventy-seven seats under Dion, they had now been reduced to a humiliating thirty-four, or ten less than the previous record of only forty-four under John Turner in 1984. They had lost seats in every region of the country, and had seen their long-time Quebec stronghold fall to the NDP for the first time ever. In effect, the Liberal Party had been reduced to an urban rump with support in only four or five major centres and the Atlantic region. Many long-serving Liberal MPs in previously untouchable ridings had fallen to the NDP or the Conservatives, especially in ridings with large populations of new Canadians, another previous Liberal stronghold. Incredibly, some ninety-two Liberal candidates (or 30 per cent) did not even qualify for the partial reimbursement of their election expenses by Elections Canada, having received less than the threshold of 10 per cent of the vote in their riding. Even the leader had lost his seat, and Michael Ignatieff had resigned the following morning, leaving the party with yet another leadership race to organize. This disastrous situation was what led Peter Newman to declare the party was finished, since they had no power base left from which to begin any rebuilding.[24]

What Went Wrong?

Party president Alf Apps was among the first to indicate what he felt had gone wrong during the campaign. "We lost the ground war," he said. "We failed to mobilize our voters, especially in Ontario."[25] Apps argued that previously committed Liberals had stayed home in droves rather than vote for Ignatieff and could not bring themselves to vote for the NDP. The election results appeared to bear out Apps's conclusion about Liberal apathy. Voter turnout across Canada was very low, and subsequent analyses concluded the vast majority of those "lost" votes would normally have gone to the Liberals, notably in Ontario.[27] As a result, many Liberal seats in that province were lost to the NDP by small margins. One StrategyCorp study noted that more than a million more voters turned out to vote in Ontario in the 2015 federal election, and another five hundred thousand more showed up at the polls in BC and Quebec, all areas in which the Liberals increased their support dramatically in that later election. Yet only in Ontario and Nova Scotia was the Liberals' 150 per cent increase in voter support in 2015 accompanied by a slight decrease in voter support for the Conservatives, suggesting those votes had not gone elsewhere in 2011.[28]

Yet others – who did not dispute the fact that large swathes of previous Liberal voters had indeed stayed home, especially in Ontario – argued that the "ground war" had actually gone quite well and could not be the reason for this phenomenon. In their view, the party's new sophisticated voter identification technology had been a success, albeit limited in the sense that it could only do so much given that it had been recently acquired and the party lacked the masses of data necessary to make it truly effective. And, while no one disputed the ongoing lack of regional organizers and field workers in the west, the party workers and volunteers in Ontario had been more numerous than in several previous elections and had been deployed efficiently. Local candidates and canvassers at the doors, and grass-roots Liberals attending Ignatieff's fiery rally speeches, all continued to question how the election results could be so disconnected from their own direct and positive experiences. The party may not have "won" the ground war, they argued, but they had done well, and they certainly did not do as badly as the results implied.

Of course, party workers and candidates can only meet a finite number of voters, just as the leader could only reach a fixed number of listeners at rallies. As journalist Susan Delacourt argued, one explanation could be that there was a major disconnect between the ground and air wars. "A campaign that feels so good on the ground, by all accounts, has been getting zero bounce on the airwaves. And now ... the Liberals are getting knocked around in this campaign for their lack of resources – not on the ground but in the air."[29]

And it is here, once again, that the importance of the Conservatives' ability to frame the Liberal leader for Canadians at such an early stage takes on such importance, as does their ability to seize on specific aspects of an individual's personality or history and magnify or distort these aspects to create their preferred image. Ignatieff himself referred to this phenomenon in his autobiography, stating that he had been "swiftboated." As several Conservatives later admitted, rather than their portrayal of Dion as weak and indecisive, they deliberately framed Ignatieff as strong but self-interested, an arrogant, out-of-touch, and opportunistic figure who was only in politics for the power.[30] In this sense, the Conservatives' use of attack ads, and their ability to do so relentlessly between election campaigns because of their far superior financial resources, may well have made the actual conduct of election campaigns much less relevant. Certainly this was the view of veteran strategist Warren Kinsella, who argued after the election that perhaps "campaigns don't matter" anymore because of these new dynamics.[31]

Rocco Rossi had argued internally that the Liberals could not afford to respond to the Conservatives' ads, but it was also true that many of Ignatieff's advisers did not believe they would be so lethal. That was the position of Gordon Ashworth, although he may well have been influenced by the need to ensure adequate funding for the actual campaign. Then too, several of Ignatieff's key advisers assumed that the Tories' ads about Dion had been effective because they were closer to reality. Bob Rae, for instance, predicted in early 2009 that any prospective Conservative ads attacking Michael Ignatieff would backfire. "I think the circumstances are very different. You can sometimes try and play the same movie twice but it doesn't always work the second time ... I just think the appetite in the country for this is almost nil and I think the Conservatives risk really angering people."[32]

Perhaps Dan Brock summed up the insiders' general outlook best, at the same time demonstrating how new and exceptional the Conservatives' "permanent campaign" strategy was at the time, and how little was known about the implications:

> I don't think we really understood how effective it would be if done over a sustained period of time between writ periods. We thought Canadians are going to say "You shouldn't be doing this." And that's exactly wrong. Canadians are too busy living their lives. They pay a little bit of attention to politics, and if that little bit of attention is dominated by a particular

message, effectively delivered and repeated over and over again, that message is going to sink in. And it did.[33]

This perspective was borne out by the comment of pollster Nik Nanos quoted above that "the negative attack ads launched by the Conservatives did their job." Or, as both Conservative strategist Allan Gregg and Liberal Warren Kinsella had said repeatedly, negative ad campaigns do work and must be countered.[34] (At the same time, both men agreed that the way in which such ads are successfully countered can vary considerably.)

But the crucial loss of Liberal voters' support also could be seen as symptomatic of the larger problem the party faced in this election. Pollster Darrell Bricker of Ipsos, for one, argued that the Liberals had no chance of winning the election even before the writ was dropped, for a variety of reasons. To make the point, he titled his presentation on the 2011 election results at the annual meeting of the Canadian Political Science Association "What Were They Thinking?" In his view, the Liberals' decision to force an election when they did was a fatal error, and the confidence they displayed at the beginning of the campaign, in the face of such negative polling numbers, was misplaced to say the least. It was not simply that they were so far behind in the polls, although that alone should have given them pause. As Bricker demonstrated in painstaking detail, the Liberals were also trailing in public opinion on almost every indicator that might have had an impact on the election result. According to his Ipsos findings, fully 57 per cent of voters believed Canada "was on the right track" going into the campaign, and some 45 per cent believed Stephen Harper deserved to be re-elected. On the question of who could best manage the economy, the Conservatives led the Liberals by more than 20 points, at 47 per cent to 23 per cent.[35]

In addition, it appeared that the Liberals had identified the wrong question as the one to hang their hats on. "Trust in government" placed a distant fifth on a list of voters' priorities, with health care and the economy taking the top two spots. As Carleton university political scientist Jonathan Malloy observed, the Conservatives had correctly concluded that they could dismiss the opposition criticism of their behaviour as simply partisan wrangling, since "public reaction [to their behaviour] has been modest, and largely confined to huffy professors and committed partisans."[36] Worse still, even on the question of trust the Liberals were not the first choice of the electorate as they had expected. Adding insult to injury, voters placed Stephen Harper first, at 39 per cent, while Jack Layton ran a close second at 34 per cent and Michael Ignatieff finished a dismal third at 19 per cent.

When asked whom they preferred to lead a coalition government if the election produced another minority, fully 59 per cent of respondents preferred Jack Layton compared to only 27 per cent for Michael Ignatieff. As Bricker concluded, the 2011 election, "more than any other over the past decades, was about leadership, and in that regard alone the Liberal disadvantage going into the campaign was likely impossible to overcome."[37]

But this, too, was not the whole story of the Liberals' 2011 election disaster. While Bricker's numbers suggest that Liberals had no chance of winning the election he, like Mike Marzolini, would also argue that they were not doomed to finish in third place either. An additional factor was at play that caused the party to fall so precipitously and so far.

The more fundamental problem was what the party had on offer during the campaign in a concrete sense. The "family pack" platform was not a bad platform. It contained many appropriate, reasonable, and well-crafted proposals. But it was never presented as more than a collection of disparate items, and was therefore easily ignored or forgotten. After the party's ignominious defeat, Steven MacKinnon, a former national director of the party who had run (unsuccessfully) as a Liberal candidate in a Quebec riding, wrote a devastating but insightful article in *Policy Options* recognizing this crucial point. When asked by a voter "Why are we having this election?" he had first launched into an explanation of the Learning Passport as part of the family pack.

> "You're the Liberal Party. And we're having an election so you can bring in a 'family pack.' Is that it?" she said. That's when it hit me. The Liberal Party of Canada, in response to the most bewildering and troubling economic times in a generation, had aimed very low indeed … Unsurprisingly, Canadians took a pass. Sensing an unambitious Liberal option, they opted for clearer prescriptions on the left and the right. As Liberals we must never make the same mistake again.[38]

Some observers have argued that the most important challenge the Liberal Party faced in the 2011 election was to explain liberal values and how they differed from those of the Harper Conservatives or Jack Layton's NDP, a task that should have been easy but proved insurmountable.[39] Indeed, for many of those involved in the trenches the idea of Liberal values or, more dramatically, a Liberal "vision" for Canada was not something that was even discussed. Yet countless advisers over the years since the 2006 defeat had stressed the need to promote those liberal values that Canadians identified with the party, with Canada, and with the federal governments run by Liberals, if the party was to continue to be seen as the natural governing party. The result of the party's failure to do so for more than a decade, as one poll conducted by Abacus Data revealed during the campaign, was that 54 per cent of respondents believed the Liberals "would promise anything" to get elected, far ahead of all other parties, including the Conservatives. At the same time the Liberal Party had by far the lowest score (10 per cent) of all parties on the statement "stands for clear principles," where the Conservatives received 23 per cent, the NDP 32 per cent, and the Bloc 39 per cent.

For left-wing Liberal insiders, the problem in 2011 was epitomized by Mr. Ignatieff, a business Liberal. "There are all kinds of problems ... but they could be overcome to a very large degree if the party had the courage to chart a clear, values-based progressive course," one senior Liberal confided. But that would not happen under Ignatieff, he argued, because "Ignatieff is basically a conservative dressed up as a progressive."[40]

In addition to the Ignatieff Liberals' failure to identify the underlying Liberal values motivating their policy choices, there was the party's ongoing willingness for more than a decade to accept the neoconservative narrative of small government, low taxes, and balanced budgets. Ignatieff epitomized that approach in his statements regarding the Liberal platform, which was "modest" precisely because it was based on the assumptions that taxes could not be raised nor could deficits be justified. The platform, he insisted, "must be fiscally prudent and disciplined." Put another way, "moving this party any further to the left means you abandon the commitment to fiscal responsibility and deficit control." Even so, plans to pay for several of the larger planks in the platform were frequently criticized by the media, and Conservatives, because they were based on the cancellation of tax cuts that had already been implemented, or spending cuts that were optimistic in the extreme. In short, Canadians were presented with a package that was only moderately interesting and not fiscally credible after all. Taken together, the lack of liberal values and the willingness to accept a conservative narrative on public finances had proven fatal once again.

One analysis of the Liberals' prospects after the 2011 debacle pointed out that, despite improvements, the party continued to have problems with fundraising and organization, and its regional reach was extremely limited. Its position as a third party in the House of Commons meant that the OLO and Research Bureau would receive considerably less funding than before, and it would have more difficulty attracting media attention through Question Period. With yet another leadership race on its agenda, its resources would be stretched to the limit. Its revenue from public subsidies would also be severely reduced because of the per-vote formula, and even this, of course, would presume that public subsidies would actually continue, something that would now be in doubt with Stephen Harper's newly acquired majority. Coupled with the party's long-standing inability to craft an alternative parable to that of the neoconservatives, its future did indeed look grim.[41]

On the other hand, even the Conservatives admitted that the Liberal brand was still strong and the party still could call upon the services of a core group of experienced veterans. The losses in Ontario were by narrow margins, and many observers saw the "Orange Crush" in Quebec as a temporary phenomenon caused by the popularity of Jack Layton, rather than a shift in support to the NDP.[42] Perhaps most importantly, polls definitely did not suggest that there had been a massive shift in public opinion to the right or left. As this analysis concluded, it remained to be seen whether the party and its elites would learn the correct lessons from this devastating rejection by voters for the third time in a decade, and set about to correct its many serious shortcomings. "The Liberal Party should not be counted out on the basis of this election, but nor should its recovery and return to power be taken for granted. Much will depend on the willingness of the Liberal membership to come together and contribute to the party's rebuilding, and on the party's ability to return to basics and define essential liberal values in the context of the twenty-first century."[43]

7 Rebuilding and Renewal: Trudeau and the Liberal Way

Canadians have sent Liberals to the political woodshed on three previous occasions – 1930, 1958 and 1984. Each time, the party was seen as arrogant, out of touch and out of date. Liberals bounced back from their defeats by doing two things: reaching out to new people with new ideas, and modernizing their organization. Once modernized, the party earned its way back to governing Canada – for 22 consecutive years the first time, for 21 almost-consecutive years the second time and for 13 years the last time this happened.

– LPC president Alf Apps, quoted in *Globe and Mail*, 13 January 2012

With the Liberal Party finishing in third place in the 2011 election and losing its status as the Official Opposition – the party's worst showing ever – it would not have surprised anyone if the knives had come out immediately. Indeed, after a third humiliating defeat in less than five years, a lengthy period of angry finger-pointing, accusations, and counter-accusations by party activists could quite reasonably have been expected to follow. In this, at least, the Liberals were now seen by many observers to be little different from their former counterparts, the Progressive Conservatives, who were far more used to ending up on the losing side of elections. The "Tory syndrome" of infighting and leader assassinations was a well-established phenomenon in Canadian politics for decades,[1] and speculation was running rampant that the Liberals were now the new victims of this syndrome.

However, in the case of the 2011 election debacle, any Liberals who were anxious to allocate blame found themselves with a conundrum. It was pointless to criticize the leader, who had had a much better campaign than anyone expected. In any event there was no need to remove him, since Michael Ignatieff had already voluntarily departed and returned to academe. Nor was there much to criticize about the campaign itself, at least in comparison with the disastrous 2008 campaign, which had nevertheless produced a better result. In short, there was really no option for Liberals at this point but to consider the underlying problems that had brought them to this sorry pass. Their trouble was much deeper than one election campaign, and it was time to finally acknowledge the extent of those problems and address them as a priority. At the same time, with Stephen Harper's solid majority, it was also possible for the Liberals to turn their full attention to these problems, since they could be reasonably certain that no election would interrupt them for the next four years.

Another factor mitigating against lengthy infighting was, of course, the damage that had already been done to the party's brand during the Chrétien-Martin era of internecine warfare. This undoubtedly provided a cautionary tale about the perils of undermining your image of party unity and managerial competence with voters. And for a party whose every leader since Edward Blake in the 1880s had become prime minister until these two back-to-back disasters of the twenty-first century, the failures of Dion and Ignatieff were not only crushing but unthinkable for most Liberals. Certainly it forced them to understand how serious the situation was. (If they did not, there was plenty of expert commentary to make it clear to them.)

But perhaps the most compelling reason for party loyalists to pull together, despite their differences, was the recent fate of the Progressive Conservative party. If there was ever any doubt it was now abundantly clear that no party, no matter how venerable or successful, was too big to fail. Reduced to a mere two seats in the House of Commons in the 1993 election, the once mighty original party of Confederation had undergone a slow and painful demise, culminating in the 2003 "merger" of the party with the radical new western Reform/Canadian Alliance Party. The result was the creation of a new right-wing Conservative Party in which the tail was wagging the dog and former Reformer Stephen Harper, not Progressive Conservative Peter McKay, was the leader.

Several pundits offered discouraging analyses for the Liberals as well. Peter Newman was quick off the mark, publishing a book in November 2011, a mere six months after the election, predicting the death of the Liberal Party and of liberalism itself.[2] His pessimistic tome was followed by another negative report, authored by columnist John Ibbitson and pollster Darrell Bricker, which made very similar arguments. According to the authors of this second damning account, Canadians were undergoing a massive demographic and cultural shift that would not only result in the death of the Liberal Party, but also entrench the new Conservative Party as the "natural governing party" for decades to come.[3]

Liberals were not immune to these negative viewpoints. As party president Alf Aps stated, "The reality of the May vote has not only placed the longer-term health of the Party in question, it has also precipitated an immediate existential crisis for many Liberals. Once regarded as vigorous, vibrant and confident, Canada's former 'natural governing party' is suddenly now widely seen as tired, stale and troubled."[4] With this type of prognosis, one might have expected many Liberal stalwarts to take a lengthy hiatus from party activities. That this did not happen is a crucial factor in the party's eventual success in the next election.

As Harmel and Janda[5] have demonstrated, change "does not just happen" in political parties, which like any large organizations are naturally conservative and instinctively resist efforts at reform. The authors conclude that significant change requires a combination of two things: internal pressure, driven by a critical mass of party elites, and a serious external shock, such as the Liberals' election defeat of 2011. But they also note that substantial change does not always happen even in such circumstances. Like the Progressive Conservatives, many other venerable political parties in Western democracies have fallen by the wayside due to their inability to change in time, or at all.

In the case of the Liberal Party of Canada after the 2011 debacle, however, rebuilding and renewal – largely postponed for more than five years – began with a vengeance with two important decisions. The first was to delay holding a race to select a new party leader for nearly two years. The second was to postpone the party's scheduled biennial convention from fall 2011 to January 2012. These two decisions were described by Liberal insiders as crucial components of a massive rebuilding and renewal exercise that would see the party adopt major changes to its operational structure. The question for observers was whether these changes would be substantial enough, and take place soon enough, to save the party from oblivion in 2015.

Putting the Leadership Convention on Hold

One of the first and most significant changes to the party's operations came with the decision to delay a leadership race. Having endured three leaders' brief tenures in barely seven years, everyone realized that the decision on the next leader of the Liberal Party would be a crucial one. By now most partisans also recognized that the rush to find a new messiah after Paul Martin's failure had been too precipitous. Along with the subsequent coronation of Michael Ignatieff, without benefit of a leadership race of any kind, these were serious mistakes they could not afford to repeat. Grass-roots Liberals made it clear to the party executive that they wanted to take their time this time around before selecting a new leader. Yet the constitution of the party called for a leadership convention to be held by the end of October 2011. What to do?

First, the party had to select an interim leader to represent the Liberals in the House of Commons, following the resignation of Michael Ignatieff on 3 May. The national executive set conditions on potential candidates, the most important one being that they could not run for the permanent leadership if they accepted the temporary post. (Many in the executive thought this would automatically exclude Bob Rae.) In addition, only sitting MPs who were bilingual could be considered for the position (thereby ruling out Ralph Goodale, an otherwise obvious choice.) These were the same conditions that had applied when Bill Graham served as interim leader in 2006 after the resignation of Stéphane Dion, and they had worked well. However, one additional caveat, indicative of the mindset of the shell-shocked Liberal executive, was that there could be no discussion of a merger with the NDP.

On 25 May the Liberal caucus, both MPs and senators, voted in favour of Bob Rae, whose candidacy was discreetly promoted by Jean Chrétien. His only opponent, Marc Garneau, graciously supported Rae once the decision was announced. "We elected a great leader," Garneau told reporters, adding that he felt "very serene" about the decision and was "looking forward to the next steps" in party renewal.[6] Rae's selection was then confirmed by the national executive, which constitutionally had final say over an interim leader. In an interview shortly after his appointment, Rae stated that Canadians had sent Liberals a "tough message" which the party had understood. "We know that we have a lot of rebuilding to do ... [but] we have a great history as a party and I believe we have a great future. I have no hesitation in saying that the Liberal Party is here to stay."[7]

Then, in the first of many innovative moves to drag the party into the twenty-first century, the party executive proposed holding a "virtual convention" by teleconference. Its purpose (other than conserving scarce funds), was to allow delegates to debate and vote on a resolution to amend the party constitution. Responding to members' calls for delay, that resolution proposed changing the party rules to allow the executive to set a date for a leadership convention any time between 1 November 2012 and 28 February 2013

More than twenty-five hundred registered delegates participated in the unique convention exercise, moderated by former Liberal MP and speaker Peter Milliken, on 11 June. It began with a short speech by Bob

Rae, who urged delegates to support the resolution. Before accepting the post of interim leader he had made it clear that he wanted the position to be "more than a summer job" since he would be precluded from running for the permanent job. "It's important to let it have time," he said; "We need to take the time to make the right choices and to make those important strides in fundraising, organization and policy." On a personal note he concluded, "I'd like to be able to hand over to the new leader a party that's in better shape, better shape financially and generally in better shape."[8] Former leader Stéphane Dion also argued in favour of the lengthiest delay possible. Evidently speaking from personal experience, he stated that the party's fundraising and other activities should be improved first, or "the leader will be without any protection facing the Conservatives."[9]

Delegates considered not only the resolution as originally drafted, but amended versions that would provide for an earlier or a later window. As with other constitutional amendments, the resolution needed the support of two-thirds of delegates to pass. In the end, a remarkable 89 per cent of delegates supported the amended version of the resolution, which allowed the executive to delay holding the leadership convention for two years. This meant that it would now be held sometime between 1 March and 13 June 2013.

At the same time, delegates voted to delay the next biennial convention from fall 2011 to 13–15 January 2012. Four months after this virtual convention, the National Board of the Liberal Party of Canada released a discussion paper for party members titled "A Roadmap to Renewal," a comprehensive document to begin that renewal process with the January convention.

Roadmap to Renewal

As the introduction to the "Roadmap" stated, at the convention "Liberals will be called upon to meet the challenge of rebuilding and renewing the Liberal Party of Canada. The proposals contained in this document are intended to focus the debate."[10] Controversial outgoing president Alf Apps, who presided over the organization of the convention, later stressed that he was "grateful for the support of the National Board" and what he considered to be the board's "first class, thoughtful input" into the "Roadmap," its near-unanimity on the various recommendations, and its key role in the preparations for the convention.[11]

The "Roadmap" contained nineteen proposals for consideration at the convention under what, by now (after the special reports of 2006 and 2009), were the familiar four rubrics: expanding funding, engaging

Liberals and rebuilding the base, streamlining the party, and preparing for victory, along with a fifth and relatively new heading, building transparency and trust.[12] The intent of this discussion paper was to prepare the groundwork for informed debate by delegates at the convention, and to consult as widely as possible with the broader membership – whose views were to be canvassed by online commentary and/or written submissions – in advance.

In addition, in a highly unusual move, Alf Apps prepared a massive seventy-nine-page background paper, "Building a Modern Liberal Party." This second document offered the membership his candid "personal perspective" on the party's travails and detailed commentary reinforcing the various proposals of the "Roadmap to Renewal." "Because the slate has been wiped clean," Apps wrote, "the conditions required for a genuinely 'bloodless revolution' within LPC may now exist. The time for a new generation of Liberals has come. If there were ever a time for Liberals to be bold, it is now."[13]

Apps stressed that the background paper was intended to provide context and serve as a companion piece to the "Roadmap." For example, with respect to the discussion paper's proposals on fundraising, his background paper highlighted "the messaging used by the CPC about our Leader long before the campaign ever started."[14] It recognized that this "devastatingly negative" messaging "did not, in and of itself, win the election for the CPC. But our failure to understand what they were doing to us and to respond effectively ... contributed heavily to the LPC's defeat. When it came to the air war, the CPC had all the latest political artillery, very effective modern political communications. Liberals were not even playing on the same battlefield."[15] These points were designed to support the discussion paper's specific proposal "that the Convention endorse the decision to build and maintain the 'Strong Start' campaign, a special cash reserve for the purpose of promoting and defending its next permanent leader."[16]

Similarly Apps argued that, despite the real but modest progress made by establishing a national membership list and acquiring the VIN system shortly before the 2011 election, "The CPC is a generation ahead of LPC in terms of assembling the technology and data required to win a modern campaign." While Liberals continued to rely on door knocking and telephone canvassing to get out the vote on election day, with no idea as to whether the individuals they reached were actually supporters, "the CPC had not only identified its vote long before the election began, it had accumulated or extrapolated all sorts of additional information about its supporters and potential supporters ... Using highly sophisticated micro-targeting, the CPC was able to spend the entire campaign messaging its base to 'firm up' any soft or wavering support, activating its committed vote and ... suppressing the votes who did not support it – with vote pulling and vote pushing technology that put the LPC to shame."[17] These comments, in turn, were intended to provide a strong rationale for supporting the "Roadmap" recommendation "that the Convention endorse the Party's decision to fast-track the deployment, population and utilization of its universal database technology in support of LPC's national and local organization, communication and fundraising efforts."[18]

In their concluding remarks in the "Roadmap," the national board urged Liberals to give serious consideration to the proposals put forward, to contribute to the debate, and to come together in Ottawa in January 2012 for what they hoped would be a "watershed event, not only for Canadian Liberalism but for Canada's future."[19]

The Ground-Breaking January 2012 Convention

Ottawa in January is not normally an attractive proposition for visitors. Travelling to Ottawa in midwinter to attend the convention of a party on its alleged deathbed is even less likely to appeal. Yet from the moment the party elites turned their attention to preparations for this challenge, it was obvious that Liberals across the country were ready and willing to take it up. Despite near-record-low temperatures and foot-high snowdrifts, some thirty-two hundred delegates descended on Ottawa on 13 January to begin the renewal process, the largest number of participants for any non-leadership convention since 1978.

As a symbolic demonstration of party unity, former Liberal leaders John Turner, Paul Martin, and Michael Ignatieff were all present at the convention, along with former leader Stéphane Dion and interim Liberal leader Bob Rae. Numerous photos pictured the first three men and Rae sitting together chatting and joking amongst themselves, the very picture of Liberal solidarity. (At the same time, little or no mention was made of the absence of Jean Chrétien, who was "otherwise engaged.")[20]

Members of the media who attended the event repeatedly commented on the upbeat tone of the participants and the enthusiasm of delegates to debate the issues outlined in the "Roadmap."[21] Many described the atmosphere as more like a party than a funeral. Perhaps the only journalist present who was sceptical of the Liberals' optimism was Peter Newman. Resplendent in his trademark black leather trench coat and fisherman's cap, Newman was seen prowling the corridors on the second day of the convention, leading numerous delegates familiar with his recent book to refer to him as "Dr. Death."

From the point of view of the executive the convention delegates did their job, debating resolutions thoughtfully and attending workshops in droves. At the end of the weekend most of the organizational reform proposals were adopted, a scenario reminiscent of the many changes pushed through by Mike Eizenga and Steven MacKinnon in 2006, with considerable assistance from the then interim leader, Bill Graham. In this case, not only Bob Rae but also Stéphane Dion and Mike Crawley (the president-elect) spoke in favour of several of the resolutions, with positive effect.

Delegates approved the resolutions to move forward quickly with the technological innovations mentioned above, and to establish a special fund for communications to defend future leaders from targeted attacks outside of election periods. In addition, they agreed to establish a new chief fundraiser position within the party executive, and selected Alex Graham (an investment banker, long-time Liberal, and former adviser to John Turner) to be the first incumbent.

Another organizational change that delegates approved was particularly important, and in fact groundbreaking. This was to create a new class of Liberal "supporters," essentially anyone who was willing to register with the party as supporting its core values, and who would not have to become a member or pay a membership fee, but would have a say in the selection of a leader. Those who argued in favour of the change saw it as a way of attracting young Canadians to participate in politics through a political party, as well as a way of identifying possible Liberal voters in a future election campaign. Liberal Youth president Sam Lavoie told delegates "our hope is that this will send a very powerful signal of renewal ... the Liberal Party is embracing some bold new ideas." For Liberal MP Scott Brison, the move would "change the party from a club to a political movement."[22] Their views were reinforced by futurist Don Tapscott, who argued that this type of engagement was important for the future since "all political parties should fear becoming bypassed by social media tools and networks of engagement that youth are using now."[23]

For those who opposed the idea, the major problem was a concern that "supporters" would be transients who did no work at the local association level and would not be there as volunteers during campaigns. In addition, there was some concern that members of other political parties might attempt to register as supporters to influence leadership votes, but this scenario was considered less likely at the national level.

In the end the resolution passed easily. However, two tangential resolutions – to let supporters vote in candidate nominations at the local level, and to establish a type of regional primary system for leadership races – were defeated. Here, too, the concern about the potential for members of other parties or single-issue activists (such as pro-life groups) to capture the process played a key role in delegates' thinking, and with more substantial justification. Only months earlier the Harper Conservatives had engaged in a shady attempt to convince Liberal members in the riding of Liberal MP Irwin Cottler that he had stepped down, and the fear of other covert hostile takeovers loomed large in the minds of many delegates.

The adoption of the supporter category proved to be a major news draw, as did the delegates' approval of two specific policy resolutions. The first was the legalization and regulation of marijuana, a motion put forward by the youth wing that received widespread support and passed by a vote of 77 per cent.

The second major policy change was the adoption of a resolution to replace the current first-past-the-post electoral system with a preferential ballot system at the national level. Its proponents argued that this would address the concern of many Canadians that, under the current system, majority governments such as that of the Harper Conservatives could be elected with only 39 per cent of the popular vote. Under the new system parties would have to attempt to attract the support of a broader range of voters so that they would be ranked as a second choice by many voters as well, a move that Stéphane Dion argued would prevent "ugly attack ads" and lead to "more civilized debate" in Canadian politics.[24] The resolution was strongly supported by Liberal MP Justin Trudeau, who spoke at length in favour of the motion. Responding to concerns that it might be seen as a self-interested move to help the Liberal Party, Trudeau stated, "Will it help us? Me, I am a fairly polarizing figure, it might actually harm me in my own riding. But I think it is a good thing for Canada that we move toward this."[25] It was passed with the support of 73 per cent of delegates, and it too was widely reported as a major positive change, just as the party had hoped.

Last but hardly least, the convention saw the election of a new party president, a move that once again demonstrated significant change. With the term of Alf Apps drawing to a close, the party witnessed a four-person contest to replace him as president, another unprecedented display of interest in the party's organization and its future. Significantly, each of the candidates agreed that the party was in dire straits and needed to launch a rebuilding exercise immediately. Each was in favour of reform. But in their vision of reform each candidate placed the emphasis on different problems the party faced, and different aspects of that renewal process, providing delegates with a clear set of choices for the future of the party. Their surprising decision, and the issues that drove it, were a precursor of things to come.

Electing a New Party President

The first to file his papers in the surprisingly competitive race to become party president was Ron Hartling, a little-known local riding president from Kingston and the Islands.[26] In an interview Hartling, a retired academic, noted that his riding was one of only two in the country that elected a new Liberal MP despite the 2011 tsunami that defeated many established veterans. He attributed the riding's success to a detailed two-year plan he had devised to increase party membership (the riding was now the second-largest in the country) and get out the vote. And he argued that such grass-roots knowledge was the most important attribute for the next party president. Hartling made it clear that he considered local riding associations to be the basic building block in any renewal and rebuilding exercise. "The next president should have a deep understanding of the real situation on the ground in all manner of ridings across Canada," he stated, but he also advocated that each association develop its own strategic plan. "That can't be set by Liberal Party headquarters in Ottawa, because every riding has its own unique situation."[27] This position put him in direct conflict with many of the party's elites who had been trying for two decades to centralize many functions in Ottawa, including the creation of a national membership list, and suggested that his sympathies would lie heavily with the Council of Presidents so recently created, who at that point were scheduled to meet only once annually. Finally, Hartling argued that the role of party president should be an essentially anonymous one. "I'm not going to be a media star. That's important for the leader, not the president."[28]

All of these views were in stark contrast to those of the next two candidates to enter the race. The first was former Quebec Liberal MP Alexandra Mendes, who served only one term before being defeated in the 2011 "orange crush." A former riding president herself, Mendes argued that her experience as an MP was invaluable in bridging the divide between the parliamentary and volunteer wings of the party. In addition, she identified fundraising as a priority, followed closely by the need to "engage members and build a dialogue" within the party.[29] An immigrant from Portugal who arrived in Canada in her teens, Mendes also argued for greater gender equality and diversity in riding association executives, and suggested using the Charter to scrutinize party platforms and procedures. Liberal senator Grant Mitchell, who had suggested to Mendes that she throw her hat in the ring, argued that she was an ideal candidate for the times, "a fluently bilingual woman from Quebec, offering a fresh face, new energy and the perspective of someone born abroad."[30]

Both Hartling and Mendes stayed in the race until the end, but within little more than a month two other candidates had entered the contest, and from then on it was widely perceived as a two-way race between these high-profile contestants.

The first was Sheila Copps, the former Liberal MP, Chrétien cabinet minister, and deputy prime minister whose long career had been abruptly ended by the machinations of Martin organizers in 2004, when she was replaced as the Liberal candidate in her Hamilton riding. From the moment she filed her papers Copps was considered the frontrunner by the media as well as Liberal insiders, and it was generally understood that she had the support of the party elites.[31] Her public name recognition and deep roots in the party, as well as her vaunted organizational skills, made her a force to be reckoned with.

In an interview shortly after announcing her candidacy, Copps explained her "return" to active duty after seven years in the private sector. "I want to be part of the solution. I can't watch a great party disappear and see a country folded into two extremes," she said, making it clear she would never consider a merger with the NDP. Campaigning on the slogan "Strength. Determination. Grit," Copps listed her priorities for reform as membership ("I want to see a million-person march"), morale, and money. Arguing for free memberships, more communication with members by internet, and a primary-style convention model to generate greater interest in the party, Copps stressed her ability to connect and communicate with both grass-roots members and Canadians. She also highlighted her longstanding commitment to greater diversity and inclusion, as evidenced by her support from youth and minority groups such as the LGBTQ community in her failed run for the leadership against Martin in 2003.

Copps's image of the president's role was similar to that played by Iona Campagnolo, the former Liberal cabinet minister who had held the post during the dark days of the Turner leadership between 1984 and 1988, and whom many viewed as a highly successful role model. For Copps, as for Campagnolo, the post of party president was very much about maintaining a public presence, representing the party while the national director led the nuts-and-bolts reform work of the party organization at headquarters and the leader and caucus held the fort in Parliament.[32] In 2011, with only an interim leader in place for the next two years, this perception of the president's role could be seen by many as even more relevant.

However, there were others who questioned the wisdom of such a high-profile president, particularly when that individual might well be viewed as a continuation of the old guard. For these delegates, Copps's very experience and high profile worked against her, as they were committed to a symbolic change in personnel at the highest levels of the party as well as in the reform of its structure. This view was particularly strongly held, somewhat ironically, by the Young Liberals at the convention, who might otherwise have been her natural base. "I think there is a need for a certain amount of generational change," Samuel Lavoie, the Young Liberals' president, told reporters.[33] In addition there were some, albeit a small minority, who continued to see Copps as too left-wing, an opponent of business liberals and equally of Paul Martin, not only because of her 2003 candidacy for the leadership but because of her many years in Jean Chrétien's cabinet.

Primarily as a result of these concerns, and in light of the general consensus that the race was Copps's to lose, pressure was placed on a fourth individual, Toronto businessman Mike Crawley, to consider entering the contest. He ultimately did so in November 2011. The contrast between Copps and Crawley could hardly have been greater. A former president of the Ontario provincial Liberal party, Crawley was relatively well known among federal party members although a virtual unknown to most Canadians. But unlike either Hartling or Mendes, Crawley had experience at the executive level of a party. At the same time, he represented a new face and a much younger image of the Liberal Party to the public. (Last but perhaps not least, he had once worked for John Turner and been a Martin supporter.)

Crawley's initial statements made it clear that his concept of the president's role was quite different from Copps's as well. "Don't expect to see me around Ottawa much," he said or, by implication, in the news. "I won't be in the spotlight. There's a lot of work to be done in the next two years with the party ... So my interest is not to be a face on TV."[34] For him the president's role was clearly one of the nuts-and-bolts variety, keeping his head down and ensuring structural and organizational reform actually happened and fundraising improved. Similarly, although both spoke of opening up the party and of engaging the membership, Crawley took considerable pains to distinguish his analysis of the problem, and hence the remedies, from those of Copps. She argued that the party "is the author of its own misfortune," primarily because of the infighting during the Chrétien-Martin era and subsequent poor choices in leadership that destroyed its image of competence and unity, drained its financial resources, and drove away many natural supporters as well as volunteers. "My experience in the last few months travelling across the country," she said, "is that most Liberals have realized that our intense, internal naval-gazing has cost us."[35] Crawley pointedly disagreed. While he did not dispute that the party was the author of its own misfortune, he concluded there were different reasons for this. "We come from different positions on where the party is at," he said, "which is why it's not surprising we end up in different places in terms of what the party should do." Crawley instead argued that it was crucial to continue the centralization and coordination efforts begun under earlier presidents to strengthen the national party and increase cohesion. He also argued the priority should be on engaging non-Liberals as well as Liberals, non-members as well as members, rather than simply encouraging diversity among Liberal activists. Most important, he argued the party needed to rethink its policies. "We're not in government because Canadians didn't like what we had to offer, and we have got to get that through our heads … We have not, in a generation, had a chance to really open up the party, to have a broad-based debate on what we stand for. Enough of this talk that we're centrist. What does that mean? What are we standing for? What are we fighting for?"[36]

The two front-runners took differing positions on "the Rae issue" as well. By the January 2012 convention Bob Rae had been interim leader for more than seven months and in most Liberals' eyes had done well. Rumours had been flying for some time that he was reconsidering whether he should run for the leadership of the party, despite having promised he would not do so when he took the job of interim leader. Many of his supporters were pushing the idea that he should do so, and suggested that the party could simply lift the prohibition they had imposed. Other potential candidates, meanwhile, were adamant that this would provide an unfair advantage and was completely unacceptable. "He made his bed, now he can lie in it," one disgruntled delegate was overheard to say in reply to a question about Rae's future. Still others argued that at a minimum he would have to step down as interim leader immediately after the executive announced the start date of the leadership race if he intended to put his name forward. The new party executive – all of whom were being elected at the convention, and especially the new president, would have to decide what to do about this. From the beginning, Copps had said that Rae should be allowed to run if he wanted to. He would have to explain to the electors his decision to renege on his commitment to abstain and accept their judgment. Crawley, on the other hand, refused to comment directly on the issue for some time, saying only that his role as president would be to ensure a fair and open process. Eventually, however, he went so far as to say that if Rae did change his mind then he would be asked to step down as interim leader immediately, but there was no actual rule preventing him from running.

As expected, the Copps campaign was widely supported by caucus veterans and former caucus members as well as many of the elites of the voluntary wing of the party. Crawley's campaign, by contrast, was heavily supported by the Young Liberals, and also by some of the newer/younger caucus members, such as Navdeep Bains, who saw Crawley rather than Copps as the person best able to modernize the party, promote openness and transparency, and drive the renewal agenda.[37] Mark Holland, another newly defeated Liberal MP who had first been elected in 2006, concurred. He described the convention, and the election of president, as a "litmus test" of its willingness to change.[38]

In the end the race was too close to call. Even after voting had taken place on Sunday it required two official recounts before Mike Crawley was finally announced as the next president of the Liberal Party, having defeated Copps by a mere twenty-four votes. In his acceptance speech, Crawley emphasized "there is no daylight between Sheila and I" on the need for reform and rebuilding, and he referred to her as "an extraordinarily strong voice" on what the future of the party should be.[39] Still, it was clear that he viewed her defeat as a rejection of the old guard, whose time had passed. "This convention has been about change," he said. "This convention has been about openness. We Liberals have said clearly to the people of Canada that we embrace change." At the same time, he emphasized the optimism and willingness of the membership to contribute to that change by doing more than simply attending a convention. "Look at this weekend, the energy, the ideas, the debate and passion … [it] signals a party that is clearly focussed on the future and determined to bring it about."[40]

Crawley's speech to delegates was followed by closing remarks from interim leader Bob Rae, who reiterated the theme of change. "We Liberals have clearly and emphatically said to the people of Canada: 'We embrace change and we embrace all Canadians as we rebuild this great national party.'"[41]

Nuts and Bolts Reform

Mike Crawley, the national executive, and the staff at national headquarters began almost immediately to implement many of the changes approved by delegates at the January convention. By May, for example, the party was registering the first of the new "supporter" category under the direction of Ian McKay. This proved to be an innovation that appealed to Canadians. By the 2013 leadership a year later, some three hundred thousands Canadians – members and a much larger group of supporters – had signed up and were eligible to vote for the next leader of the party. Since forty thousand had been considered a high number of actual Liberal members in the past, the success of the supporter category, at least in the early days, was undeniable.

Like most of his predecessors in the recent past, Crawley had a specific list of objectives he wanted to accomplish during his term as president. As he later recalled, "We had a little more than two years to do what needed to be done if we hoped to make a difference." With limited time and resources, priorities had to be set and other issues put on hold. For Crawley the priorities, all of which were designed to "revitalise" the party, could be reduced to four: "ensuring there was an open and competitive leadership selection process with multiple candidates; breaking down silos within the party by driving cohesion across the parliamentary wing, the national party, and the provincial wings; creating a culture of engagement of party members; and modernizing the fundraising apparatus."[42]

In these priorities he was ably assisted by national director Ian McKay, whom both Crawley and interim leader Bob Rae had agreed to retain. (McKay, it will be recalled, had been appointed in 2009 by Michael Ignatieff and Alf Apps to replace Rocco Rossi after his sudden departure.) As Crawley later stated, "It was a unique time, with an interim leader, a National Director whom neither the party leader nor the party president had appointed, and a party president newly elected at a national convention with a mandate to dramatically reform the party. Given this unique circumstance, all three of us worked well together for the most part."[43]

The fundraising issue was top of mind. On the one hand, the figures had improved. From the mere $5.9 million raised in 2008, the total for 2011, most of which represented funds contributed *after* the 2 May election, had climbed to $10.3 million. This was actually ahead of the NDP at $7.5 million (despite their newfound status as the Official Opposition) but well behind the Conservatives at $23 million. On the other hand, it was barely enough to fund ongoing party operations between elections, and did little to ensure the party had the $25 million needed for a war chest to run the next election in 2015. Nor did it cover the cost of the specific fund approved at the convention to combat the Conservatives' anticipated attack ads once the new leader was selected.

Structurally an additional actor – the national revenue officer – was now involved in an oversight role. Alex Graham, who had been appointed by Bob Rae after the convention had voted to create the new post, was an active volunteer who "devoted a lot of time and energy to

modernizing LPC's fundraising with staff carrying out the actual exe-
cution."[44] The VIM software acquired under Doug Ferguson's tenure
was now applied comprehensively to modernize the party's online fundraising in order to increase the number of small donations. In particular, the party began leveraging issues-based fundraising techniques, a
model that had been mastered by the Conservatives some years before.
And, finally, the party sought to increase the number of Laurier Club
contributors (large donors who contributed the maximum allowable)
through "bundling," in which well-connected donors recruited many
others, and through intensified emphasis on a monthly payment system, rather than an annual lump sum, both of which proved quite
successful.

On the issue of increased engagement of party members a number of
innovative methods were employed with reasonably positive results.
The need was real. As one anonymous delegate at the convention put
it, "No one wants to hear from the party only when they need more
money," and this was the purpose of various initiatives undertaken
during Crawley's tenure. This lack of membership engagement, it
should be noted, had become increasingly serious since the 2006 defeat
as the party struggled to make ends meet, but it was not without precedent. As former Trudeau adviser Jim Coutts once explained, the advent
of public opinion polls and a professional public service had already
greatly reduced the perceived need for input by grass-roots members
and even riding presidents and regional executives.[45] Yet the importance of the party headquarters' interacting with the grass roots and
maintaining local linkages, particularly when that party is in opposition
and dependent on volunteers, had been clearly re-established in a 2012
study by academic Royce Koop.[46]

Moreover, the lack of a national membership list had made contact-
ing grass-roots members for their input as difficult as fundraising. But
with the recent achievement of this national list such communication
and consultation were now possible on a regular basis.

The new methods of engagement and consultation included town
hall teleconference events in which thousands of grass-roots members
participated, usually chaired or moderated by the party's parliamentary critic or point person on the topic under discussion. As well there
were online surveys of the membership's views on key emerging issues.
In addition, "Google Hangouts and other digital tools were used to connect and engage those in leadership roles within the party."[47] Lastly,
both Crawley and Rae travelled extensively to attend provincial and
territorial party meetings, a more conventional technique to engage the
membership and one frequently used in the past by national executive

members, but more recently curtailed due to lack of funds. (Here again analogies between the post-2006 era and 1984 loomed large, as Iona Campagnolo's efforts in this regard were frequently criticized as too expensive by those concerned about the party's severe lack of funds. She on the other hand defended the need for this type of personal engagement as a top priority.)[48]

The concept of "silos" within the party, which Crawley wished to "break down," was not new either. As more than one observer had remarked over the years, the party had long used descriptive terminology that was innately divisive. While both the elected executives and general membership of the party referred to the "parliamentary wing" (with a clear understanding that caucus members were temporary and therefore less significant for the party's long-term future), the caucus in turn referred to the "extra-parliamentary wing" or "voluntary wing" (with the unstated assumption that the views of those who had been elected to full-time political posts were more authoritative). This division, though always present, was likely to become far more significant when the party was out of power and the parliamentary wing was greatly reduced. In addition, the federal nature of the party structure meant that the various provincial and territorial associations (PTAs), and their respective executives, operated as semi-independent organizations with little or no coordination, as described in chapter 1.

With scarce resources, and a perceived need for party solidarity if the rebuilding and renewal exercise were to succeed, Crawley waded in where others had feared to tread, emboldened by what he perceived to be his mandate from the recent convention and the spirit of reform that had gripped the party membership. As part of the effort to "drive cohesion across all levels of the party," Crawley pushed for a consolidated budgeting and planning approach in which he required PTAs to submit financial plans to inform the allocation of scarce resources. This predictably created a greater degree of tension between the centre and the regions, since the move was part of broader cost-cutting measures also being implemented. Nevertheless, Crawley later argued it was "painful but worth it," as it gave all players the opportunity to see that the distribution of resources was rational and allowed the national office to better plan its activities. (As he also noted, one factor that assisted him in making this plan work was the fact that the powerful Quebec wing, so often a thorn in the side of the national HQ, had been essentially neutralized in the aftermath of the Gommery Inquiry revelations.)[49]

But it was the leadership issue, and Crawley's stated determination to oversee a "fair, open and competitive" process, that arguably caused the national executive most difficulty. Originally Crawley had seen Bob

Rae's possible candidacy as a "complicating factor" in his own work to renew the party, but he also described his working relationship with the interim leader as "amicable and constructive."[50] Still, with Rae continuing to muse publicly about the option of entering the leadership race despite his earlier pledge, it became increasingly difficult for the media and the Liberal executive to ignore the elephant in the room.

By April, Crawley responded to the increasing number of media queries by stating that "the whole objective is that by the beginning of the summer there will be clarity in terms of the rules for the leadership, for candidate eligibility, all those matters."[51] Another member of the executive confided that "the party's aim" was to ensure that if Rae did decide to run, "it won't be messy or dramatic."[52]

The "Rae Issue"

By May 2012 Bob Rae's followers were openly raising the possibility of his candidacy for the leadership although he himself remained more discreet. At one point in late 2011 he had even publicly suggested that it required a younger individual to change the party's image. (He was sixty-three at the time.) "It's important for the party to look to a new generation of leadership," he said.[53]

Yet the pressure to reconsider continued to build. In addition, at least one poll by Forum Research conducted during the January convention had shown Rae to be the overwhelming choice to lead the party of those random Canadians surveyed. (At the same time, since his name had been presented along with some of the other failed candidates from the 2008 leadership race, such as Gerard Kennedy, Carolyn Bennett, and Ken Dryden, as well as Mark Carney, the governor of the Bank of Canada, and Dalton McGuinty, the premier of Ontario, this was perhaps not surprising.) As Forum principal Lorne Bazinoff noted, Rae's name recognition was very high compared with the others.[54]

Certainly Rae had been exceedingly visible in Parliament, despite his status as a third party leader, and had performed exceptionally well. This too was hardly surprising, since his colleagues had expressly chosen him for his intellect and his strong communications and debating skills, which he then demonstrated in the House of Commons. His rhetoric was also on display in a fiery speech to Liberal partisans at a rally in Ottawa in April 2012. His talk there featured attacks on both Prime Minister Harper and NDP leader Tom Mulcair, the former over the government's cost overruns on the purchase of F-35 fighter jets and subsequent misleading of Parliament, and the latter over the deliberate abuse of parliamentary procedure to prevent Liberals from speaking on the

Conservative budget and then accusing them of having supported it. The speech was widely reported ("Bob Rae on Warpath against Harper and Mulcair")[55] and well received. A recent Ekos poll had also shown that Canadians gave Rae a 44 per cent approval rating for his performance as Liberal interim leader, compared with only 34 per cent who approved of the job the prime minister was doing.[56]

Clearly the Conservatives considered Rae to be a potential threat. Attack ads similar to those launched against Stéphane Dion and Michael Ignatieff had already appeared. They raised the spectre of Rae's economic "mismanagement" of the Ontario economy during his tenure as the NDP premier of that province. ("Bob Rae, if he couldn't run a province, why does he think he could run Canada?") One Conservative strategist actually stressed that Rae "is fair game because he has not ruled out running for the leadership" of the Liberals.[57]

Then on 2 May one newspaper report indicated that Rae was poised to step down as interim leader the following month, leaving the Liberals looking for an interim interim leader.[58] This was, in fact, the case. Many party insiders were now routinely referring to the problem as "the Rae issue." According to Mike Crawley, the uncertainty over Rae's intentions had become a major hindrance to planning for the leadership race. As he later confided, in order to end this speculation the party had actually negotiated an agreement with Rae that he must resign as interim leader six months before the date of a leadership vote. "And then after all that he decided not to run!"[59]

As several of Rae's supporters subsequently noted, the problem was that they had been operating on the assumption that the party by now had gone past the "knee-jerk" reaction of 2008, when Rae was seen as not really a Liberal. "We assumed because he had done so well and was obviously committed to the party, the party would now give him the chance he deserved. We were wrong."[60] The bottom line was that they found he did not have enough support to win, and they told him so. As Rae's team had learned in exploratory discussions and efforts to drum up support, too many long-time Liberals were not going to overlook his lengthy record with the NDP. For some it was clear the objection was pragmatic. They believed he could not deliver Ontario for the party in a federal election, after what they perceived as his disastrous term there as premier. For others the opposition was more fundamental; Liberals and socialists were two different things entirely. And, interestingly, it was often the more left-wing or social Liberals who felt most strongly about this, as Sheila Copps had stressed in an opinion piece.[61] "If he had been a card-carrying member when he was twenty-one, who would care?" one of his outspoken opponents stated. "We all make mistakes.

But this is ridiculous. The man was an NDP MP and the NDP premier of Ontario. In what universe did he imagine this would not matter?"[62]

The issue was particularly sensitive because of earlier ruminations by some Liberals about the possibility of a merger with the NDP. With Rae, lifelong committed Liberals reasoned, this might appear to be a reasonable option, even if it was rejected by the vast majority of party members. Indeed, at the January convention one lone delegate had approached as many participants as possible, distributing pamphlets he had printed up himself denouncing the merger idea. When some questioned why he was raising it again ("I thought we had put this one to bed," one delegate was heard to say), he pointed out that a senator had raised the issue in a workshop discussion that very morning. "We have to nip this one in the bud!" the pamphleteer warned.

On 13 June, mere hours before the national executive was scheduled to reveal their decisions about the leadership race rules, a serene-sounding Rae announced at national caucus that he would not, after all, be seeking the leadership of the party. "It hasn't been an easy decision," he said, but "I think it's best for the party and it's a decision I feel comfortable with." As one analyst noted, this was no doubt a shock but it was also a blessing for the party in many ways. It allowed Rae to stay on as interim leader, which gave the party a continuing experienced and competent parliamentary presence. Even more importantly, it prevented a bitter battle between "those who wanted Mr. Rae to lead the party into the next election and those who wanted anyone but Mr. Rae in that job."[63] At the same time, Rae's unexpected announcement "throws the race for the Liberal leadership wide open."

The 2013 Liberal Leadership Race: Choosing Another Messiah?

The national executive had already decided to allow Rae to run and his unexpected decision to withdraw was one of the reasons why their announcement on 13 June was vague. At that time they said only that the leadership vote would be held in April 2013, and a specific date would be set later in the summer. Then on 6 September they confirmed that the new leader would be announced on 14 April, with voting to take place 7–14 April. The official start of the race would therefore be 14 November 2012, and the cut off for prospective candidates to pay their $75,000 registration fee would be 14 January 2013. Both this registration fee and the spending limit of $950,000 per candidate were considerably less than those in force for the 2006 leadership race, which had already seen a lowering of both amounts from the record (and many argued unnecessary) spending of the Martin campaign during the 2003 "race" that saw Martin win in a foregone conclusion.

Once these decisions had been announced the action picked up quickly. First, a number of individuals who had been considered potential candidates began to rule themselves out if they had not already done so. This included well-known federal Liberals such as John Manley, Gerard Kennedy, Dominic LeBlanc, John McCallum, and Denis Coderre, as well as blue-sky options Frank McKenna, Jean Charest, Dalton McGuinty, and former Bank of Canada governor Mark Carney.

Then a series of leadership hopefuls quickly emerged. Most were relatively unknown and not considered to be strong candidates. Given the lack of female candidates since Sheila Copps's unsuccessful attempts in 1990 and 2003, it is undoubtedly significant that the large number of women who entered this race did so in part because of this very lack of well-known Liberal men.

First off the mark was none other than constitutional lawyer and Meech Lake opponent Deborah Coyne, who had actually announced her intentions in June. Others included Ottawa lawyer David Bertschi, Toronto lawyer Martha Hall Findlay, retired air force colonel Karen McCrimmon, and Toronto technology lawyer George Takach. Two somewhat better known and more serious contenders were BC Liberal MP and former provincial environment minister Joyce Murray and Montreal Liberal MP and former astronaut Marc Garneau. It was thought that the party's practice of *l'alternance* might in particular favour Garneau, a Quebec francophone.

Then in January, just one day before the cut-off deadline, these were joined by lawyer Martin Cauchon, the former Chrétien justice minister and Quebec Liberal MP. In a rare show of solidarity, David Bertschi had actually offered his fellow candidate some of the necessary names to sign Cauchon's nomination papers in order for him to enter the race after Bertschi learned that Cauchon might otherwise miss the deadline. (The favour was returned a year later when Cauchon attended a Bertschi fundraiser as the guest of honour and invited speaker.) Cauchon's decision to enter the race at the last minute proved to be a fatal one, despite the fact that his name had often been favourably mentioned in the past as a potential successor to Chrétien. Articulate, politically astute, and relatively young (at forty-six), Cauchon was untouched by the Gommery scandals and might well have been the Quebec candidate to beat. But his exceedingly late entry into the race, with little time to build an organization or raise funds, meant his candidacy was doomed from the start, even without the entrance into the race of another Quebec francophone candidate.

That candidate was Liberal MP Justin Trudeau. The eldest son of the legendary former prime minister, he was seen by many Liberals and ordinary Canadians as a type of reincarnation of that hugely successful brand. Unlike Michael Ignatieff, they said, he really was a Trudeau.

One Forum Research poll showed that Trudeau was extremely popular before he even declared his candidacy, something the pollster explained in terms of this phenomenon: "This is the age of the brand and you can't beat the Trudeau brand."[64]

Certainly Trudeau was photogenic and charismatic in his own right. And, as one detailed examination of the younger Trudeau by political scientist Alex Marland concluded, he was also very different from his father in many ways.[65] Not only was he not overtly intellectual, but he had a genuine populist appeal based on his obvious enjoyment of encounters with ordinary Canadians. Unlike his father he clearly relished meeting and greeting, and the nitty gritty of politics. He himself often said that he was more like his mother – the outgoing social extrovert – than his intensely private and introverted father, whose shyness was often mistaken for arrogance.

But like his father, the son also appeared to have a flair for the dramatic. Instead of a memorable pirouette behind the Queen at Buckingham Palace, the younger Trudeau engaged in a celebrity charity boxing match with one of the youngest and fittest of Stephen Harper's senate appointees, former chief of the Congress of Aboriginal Peoples Patrick Brazeau. Although Brazeau was a three-to-one favourite and Trudeau's venture, barely one year after becoming an MP, was considered politically risky, he easily prevailed. His decisive victory, seen by not only Canadians but interested spectators around the world, has been described as a "pivotal moment" in his political career,[66] heightening his name recognition and credibility as a political winner.

This image was further promoted by Trudeau's masterful use of social media, increasingly viewed in the twenty-first century as an essential element of a successful political campaign.[67] Moreover, like his father, Justin Trudeau was seen as a youthful alternative, part of a new generation of politicians who would revive a political party. (Interestingly, at forty Justin Trudeau was nearly a decade younger than his father had been when he decided to enter the leadership race, another striking example of cultural and demographic change.)

In short, Trudeau quickly proved that, like his father, he was what is now referred to by political sociologists as a political celebrity,[68] a phenomenon increasingly prevalent in many Western democracies. But was that celebrity enough on its own to lead the party to victory? And was it enough for most Liberal members, now that the vote was universal rather than in the hands of the party elites?

Since winning was so important for Liberals, another invaluable asset for Trudeau was the fact that he had demonstrated his mastery of political organization at the grass-roots level. When Stéphane Dion prevented him from running in Outremont he had proven his political skills by winning a seat for the party in a difficult contest in Papineau in 2008. And he had held that seat against the Orange Wave of 2011. Of course, he was also a fluently bilingual Quebec francophone in a race where the successor to Michael Ignatieff would most likely be chosen from that province.

In addition, Trudeau was seen by many in the party ranks as the only possible option after Bob Rae's decision to recuse himself, largely because of his well-known progressive views on many issues, revealing a son who was following in his father's philosophical footsteps. (As discussed earlier, it was already clear that Rae's aborted run for the leadership was not playing out as a business Liberal scenario, as some had feared. Simply put, most opposition to Rae was based on his NDP background, not his left-wing views.)

In the end, then, support for Trudeau appeared to be based on more than celebrity and winnability. Instead, it was due to a combination of his popular appeal, proven political smarts, and left-of-centre place on the Liberal spectrum.

But Trudeau had already declined several requests by enthusiastic Liberals to throw his hat in the ring. He had made it clear that he would never consider running if Bob Rae were in the race. Asked again about his intentions after the national caucus meeting, where Rae had informed MPs and senators of his decision, Trudeau again declined. "My decision is a sign of my own reflection and my family reflection, and my decision is a no, still."[69]

There were obvious reasons why he would not want to make the leap. At age forty Trudeau could reasonably expect to wait for several years before making a run for the leadership. With a young family, and given his own troubled family life while his father was prime minister, this reluctance could easily be understood. At the same time, since his breakout public appearance delivering a eulogy at his father's funeral, many of his friends felt it was only a matter of time before he entered public life.[70]

Shortly after, having received the blessing of his wife Sophie Gregoire, Trudeau did agree to take the plunge. But his willingness to do so, he made abundantly clear, was predicated on four assumptions: there would be no merger or arrangement of any kind with the NDP;

the divisive internecine warfare of the past twenty years must end; the next Liberal election campaign must take the high road; and, finally, the necessary modernization, restructuring, and rebuilding of the party must be accelerated. These assumptions, in turn, demonstrated not only Trudeau's commitment to change and his determination to do politics differently, but also his in-depth understanding of the state of the party's machinery. Moreover, as future developments demonstrated, his commitment to these assumptions was unwavering even after the party returned to power in 2015.

Having made the decision to run in August, Trudeau spent much of the next two months assembling a campaign organization and planning strategy. In addition to his brother Alexandre (Sacha) who served as an informal adviser and confidant, Trudeau's senior team consisted of his best friend from his student days at McGill, Gerald Butts, the former principal secretary to Ontario ex-premier Dalton McGuinty and more recently president of the World Wildlife Federation. Butts would serve as senior strategist. In addition Katie Telford, a former adviser to Stéphane Dion and Ontario minister Gerard Kennedy, would serve as campaign manager, and Cyrus Reporter, a former adviser to Alan Rock, would be the team's liaison with the party and the leadership debates. They were joined by Mike McNair (former policy adviser to Michael Ignatieff and Stéphane Dion) as policy adviser and strategist for English-language media and debate preparation, and Robert Asselin (former adviser to several Liberal cabinet ministers) as policy adviser and strategist, whose primary role was liaison with French-language media and debate preparation.

On 2 October 2012, Trudeau officially announced his candidacy at a press conference in his riding. Sounding somewhat reminiscent of Jean Chrétien, he began by stating, "I love this great country." Describing the road to success for the party as "one long, Canadian highway," he argued that Liberals needed to "reconnect with ordinary Canadians." He promoted expanding and supporting "a thriving middle class" as the best way to provide a "sense of equal opportunity and common interest for all." Then he spoke directly to the issue of political values. First he turned his attention to the Conservatives ("who promise that wealth will eventually trickle down") and the NDP ("who sow regional resentment and blame the successful"), before concluding that both "are tidy ideological answers to complex and difficult questions. The only thing they have in common is that they are both equally wrong." By contrast, he argued, Liberals believe "in an option that is not polarized ... that is not looking to ideology but is looking for the best possible ways to serve all Canadians."[71] In short, as one journalist covering the event noted, Trudeau had thrown down the gauntlet by defending the philosophical centre or "mushy middle" (so mocked by others, notably Ed Broadbent) at the same time that he was attempting to inspire young Canadians and those who had been turned off by politics during the Harper years.[72]

Trudeau then embarked on a mini cross-country tour, making appearances in Richmond, BC, Calgary, and Mississauga. It was an effort to gauge regional support in fast-growing areas that his advisers believed held the key to electoral success in 2015. Local media reported excellent turnouts, and the enthusiasm for Trudeau's candidacy appeared to be strong among Liberals across the country.

Perhaps equally important, the Trudeau team's strategy was heavily based on attracting the support of youth, women, and minorities outside of the conventional Liberal membership, many of whom also would be first-time voters. Following an approach perfected by Barack Obama's Democratic campaign team, Trudeau's organizers hoped to make heavy use of the supporter category to win the leadership, effectively bypassing the long-standing party elites. Only weeks after he had announced his candidacy there was considerable evidence that this strategy was working. Party officials indicated that of the first seventeen hundred supporters who signed up after that announcement, "more than a thousand said they had never been part of any political campaign before."[73]

Meanwhile, a total of seven additional candidates signed up for the contest by the 14 January deadline. National director Ian McKay announced that some 294,002 individuals were eligible to vote, and would now have to register if they wished to do so. This second stage, he indicated, was necessary to ensure that everyone had signed the document supporting Liberal values and stating that they were not a member of another party, as well as ensuring that all of the names on this eligible voters list had been provided by the individuals themselves rather than unknowingly by a candidate's campaign team. These precautions, Mike Crawley confirmed, were part of his plan to ensure the "fair, open and diverse" leadership race he had promised, and a "seamless transition" with no controversy for the new leader. But registration was not without its difficulties. It soon became apparent that the party had limited capacity to verify independently the names on lists provided by the various campaigns, in part because of the unexpectedly high numbers. In a sense the party was a victim of its own success. However, several camps expressed concern. One organizer said there needed to be much tighter controls in future. "You live and learn," was the response of another.

Soon after, the first leadership debate was held in Vancouver on 20 January. Held in the ballroom of the Westin Hotel, it provided the first glimpse of all of the nine candidates, assembled on stage in front of a sold-out local audience and a nationwide television audience. Well organized and tightly scripted, the event offered each candidate roughly ten minutes of air time including opening and closing statements and responses to questions by moderator Randy Boissonault, an Edmonton journalist and future Liberal MP.

In all there were five such debates, organized by Doug Kirkpatrick under the overall direction of Ian McKay. (The others were held in Winnipeg on 2 February, Mississauga on 16 February, Halifax on 3 March, and Montreal on 23 March). Kirkpatrick, who had been involved in several candidates' debates over the years, later said this was one of the most challenging given the large number of candidates, but at least "there were no real prima donnas this time."[74] McKay told reporters in a pre-debate briefing, "It's a challenge, but it's a great challenge. We have a race."[75]

Apart from the obvious difficulty faced by any candidate trying to make an impression in such a crowded field, it soon became apparent that all candidates were intent on conveying at least the impression of Liberal harmony and solidarity. Debates were polite if boring, particularly in the beginning. Few serious disagreements emerged on any policy issue in the first two rounds, but by the fourth debate in Halifax it was clear that some battle lines had been drawn. For example, Martha Hall Findlay's platform included a call to end supply management, something that was anathema to the remaining seven candidates. (George Takash had withdrawn after the third debate.)

Similarly, Joyce Murray, who had enjoyed strong fundraising success and had the support of many well-known western Liberals including Lloyd Axworthy, had consistently argued in favour of cooperation with the NDP and, more recently, the Green Party. In Montreal, Murray took credit for the decision of Green Party leader Elizabeth May to refrain from running a candidate in a Newfoundland by-election in order to avoid vote-splitting on the left, thereby ensuring that the Conservatives' candidate, Peter Penashue, would not win. Trudeau had made his opposition to Murray's electoral cooperation plan crystal clear. When Murray accused Trudeau of "old style, divisive, toxic politics" and insisted that "millions of Canadians want this change, to ensure the Conservatives are defeated in 2015," Trudeau replied that he would encourage all Green, NDP, and Bloc supporters to vote Liberal in order to defeat the Conservatives: "I am encouraging everyone to vote for a strong values-based alternative to Mr. Harper, not a hodge-podge that's about winning at all costs." Referring to that mentality as the very "definition of old school politics," he concluded: "That's what really worries me about the idea of co-operation because it's a single-minded focus, not on governing but on winning, on taking power away from people we don't like."[76] (It was this profound disagreement on such a fundamental issue, and the personal enmity that ensued, which kept Murray – an obvious choice for environment minister – out of Trudeau's cabinet for so long, despite her wealth of relevant experience, gender, and representation of a BC riding.)

Perhaps the most significant attack on Trudeau came from Marc Garneau, who repeatedly accused Trudeau of being long on rhetoric and having no policies at all. "I believe that Canadians want to see substance. They don't want empty words,"[77] Garneau said during a one-on-one exchange with Trudeau at the Halifax debate. Trudeau responded that he had staked out positions on the legalization of marijuana, the Keystone pipeline, and the long gun registry. "I've been just as specific as anybody else," he said. At the same time, he accused Garneau of negative tactics during the race: "Liberals don't want to see the party turned in on each other. That's why I'm relentlessly positive in this campaign. And that's why the top-down, backroom-heavy negative campaign that has been run by other people in this [race] is something that I don't think Liberals want to see."[78]

These disagreements did little to alter the fact that Trudeau was the front-runner. Opinion polls showed him far ahead of his opponents with both Liberals and Canadians in general, more of whom appeared to be watching these debates than might have been expected for a third party, nearly two years away from the next federal election.

However, behind the scenes some technical "glitches" were occurring. Perhaps most significantly, a controversy arose over the use of email addresses. The Trudeau campaign team, supported by several other candidates including Marc Garneau, urged the party to extend the deadline for registration – the second stage necessary in order for a supporter to vote – when it was discovered that many in the supporter category had not provided an email address when signing up (primarily for privacy reasons, and unaware that this would matter). This made it impossible for them to register online because the party could not reach them electronically. Others, it was feared, had provided an email address but did not realize that a second step was necessary in order to vote. Ironically, it appeared that it was the Trudeau camp, which had registered the greatest number of new supporters, that had the most cases in this situation and therefore had the most to lose.

Initially ballots were mailed out to address the problem, but only days before the original deadline. Candidate Deborah Coyne urged the party to use robocalls or phone banks to try to reach as many more as possible. "Otherwise, the media narrative will be that these signups were not committed … and that the supporter system is a failure. We don't want to hobble our next leader out of the gate unnecessarily." When the extent of the problem became apparent (barely one-third or roughly 93,000 of the potential 294,000 eligible voters had registered only days before the original deadline), it was agreed that the extension could take place.[79]

Shortly after, president Mike Crawley announced that some 130,774 Liberal members and supporters (or less than half of the original total) had actually registered and were eligible to vote in the upcoming leadership contest. While this number may have been a disappointment, it represented, as Crawley later stressed, a huge increase in individuals the party could interact with and potentially seek out as volunteers and donors. "We were making history," he said, "and it showed conclusively that change was possible."[80]

Nevertheless, on Friday, 6 April, the party had organized what they referred to as a "National Showcase" in Toronto, attended by the remaining six candidates. (Garneau at this point had dropped out, as had David Bertschi.) This event, which had not originally been scheduled, was a tacit admission that many Liberal grass-roots members were not entirely comfortable with the decision not to hold a convention to choose a leader. "Where is the excitement? What are we all going to do, sit in our living rooms and watch TV?" one frustrated veteran convention-going member complained. Another stated, "Conventions allow us to get together, whether to celebrate or commiserate. Without that, we are all left alone in splendid isolation. That's not a movement."[81]

Voting took place between 7 and 14 April online, and worked reasonably well, although a limited bandwidth did result in slight delays for some. Earlier technical disagreements, for example over electronic versus handheld ballots, had been resolved. Considering the large number of participants, those involved felt that it had gone as smoothly as could have been hoped for.

The Showcase was not a rousing success, primarily because it had no clearly defined purpose and appeared to be the afterthought that it was. Officials admitted that fewer than one-third of the hoped-for fifteen hundred tickets had been sold only days before the event, which featured speeches by the six remaining candidates. Since no one but those in the nearby area were likely to attend, the potential pool of Liberals was much smaller than for a delegated convention, and with no excitement of a leadership announcement there seemed little point. By contrast, the announcement of the vote result on 14 April in the ballroom of the Westin Hotel in Ottawa – which was televised – was the scene of exuberant pandemonium as supporters and campaign workers watched Justin Trudeau win the party's top job on the first ballot in a landslide. He had taken nearly 80 per cent of the vote.

In his acceptance speech on 14 April, Trudeau told Liberals they had much work to do to get ready for the next election, but he also told them that he expected the party to prevail.

> I know [Canadians] will judge us by the tenacity of our work ethic, the integrity of our efforts, and, come 2015, the clarity of our plan to make our country better. That is as it should be. So let us be clear-eyed about what we have accomplished. We have worked hard and we have had a great campaign. We are united, hopeful and resolute in our purpose. But know this: we have won nothing more and nothing less than the opportunity to work even harder. Work even harder to prove ourselves worthy of leading this great country.

8 Redemption: The 2015 Election

On October 19, 2015 the Liberal Party returned from the wilderness to form a majority government with 184 seats and 40% of the vote. Moreover, the party elected members in every region of the country, including the francophone regions of Quebec, and could now be considered once more a national party. A major victory in and of itself, the win constituted a major turnaround for a party that had been left for dead barely four years earlier.

– Brooke Jeffrey, "Back to the Future: The Resurgent Liberals," 2015

Sunny ways, my friends, sunny ways. This is what positive politics can do. This is what a causative, hopeful – a hopeful vision and a platform and a team together can make happen. Canadians – Canadians from all across this great country sent a clear message tonight. It's time for a change in this country, my friends, a real change.

– Justin Trudeau, 19 October 2015

When Justin Trudeau took over the leadership of the Liberal Party in April 2013 the party was not out of the woods, as he himself acknowledged in his acceptance speech. There was still much work to do. And there were still many pundits and academics who continued to believe the party was finished as a political force in Canada.

In a debate sponsored by the right-wing Macdonald Laurier Institute barely a month before Trudeau's leadership victory, historian Michael Bliss argued that "The Liberal Party is about to go the way of Eaton's stores. Like Eaton's the Liberal Party will live on in the history books, and maybe in the galleries at our new Canadian Museum of History." He cited two overarching reasons why the party was doomed. First, he said, "the Liberal Party has no ideas at all" and has become "the party of the mushy centre." Second, "the party's old organizational muscle, sinews that worked even as its intellect ossified, has eroded in scandal and rot."[1]

An alternative argument in favour of the party's resurgence was presented by veteran Liberal activist John Duffy, who argued that "with an enduring brand and a strong appeal to a new generation of voters, things are looking bright." In his optimistic assessment of the situation, Duffy stated, "I come to praise the Liberals, not to bury them. Praise their faith, praise their endurance, their resilience. Praise them for what they have done, and for what they are about to do. It may be too early to proclaim a Liberal spring. But it is not too soon to speak of the Liberals' long winter coming to an end."[2] Duffy was right to speak of resilience and faith, just as Trudeau was right to speak of the need for hard work. The remarkable and largely unexpected success of the Liberal Party in the 2015 election was due to all of these things.

It was a textbook example of successful reform. After the 2011 disaster the membership came together in a concerted effort to rebuild, modernize, and rejuvenate the Liberal Party, just as their predecessors had done during earlier periods of crisis. As the previous chapters have demonstrated, this was an ongoing process that actually began with the 2006 election defeat. But it was only after the near-death experience of 2011 and the reality of a Harper majority, which removed the necessity for the party elites to remain constantly on an election-readiness footing, that the efforts to bring about this change were intensified and the renewal process was completed.

What follows is the story of how the party and its members were able to achieve such significant reform in less than four years. Not surprisingly, it begins with the growing success of the Liberal fundraising machine and the implementation of new technology by the party.

Fundraising Success at Last

There can be no doubt that the various improvements to the party's fundraising techniques were bearing fruit even before the 2013 leadership race. But the entry of Justin Trudeau into the race provided an additional impetus for Liberals and interested observers to contribute, even if it was to individual candidates rather than to the party itself.

By November 2012 the Trudeau campaign had already raised more than $95,000, or far more than the $75,000 entry fee. By the end of the race in April 2013 his team reported that they had raised more than $1.3 million and even more funds were still en route. (To put this in context, it represented more than three times the amount Tom Mulcair had raised for his own successful leadership bid of the NDP, and nearly ten times more than Trudeau's nearest competitors, Martha Hall Find-lay and Joyce Murray, whose campaigns reported donations of roughly $200,000 and $175,000.)[3] In addition the Trudeau team's revenue came in small amounts (an average of $155) from more than seventy-five hundred donors, the exact model the party had been hoping to emulate for years in order to catch the Conservatives.

Equally important, Trudeau's campaign had raised far more than the amount they were allowed to spend. As a result they followed through on their plan to turn the surplus (which amounted to nearly $1 million in the end) over to the party. They earmarked this money for the special fund that delegates had approved at the January 2012 convention to defend the leader, by responding to future Conservative attack ads, a fund that until then was virtually non-existent. Speaking at the debate in Halifax, Trudeau emphasized the importance of this fund, stating that "Liberals need to tell our own story rather than have negative ads define us."[4]

Despite these positive developments, it was still true that the Conservatives had raised far more money in 2012, some $17 million compared to the Liberals' $9 million. Would the dependence on supporters make enough of a difference, and would it last beyond the 2013 leadership race year? Conservative senator and chief fundraiser Doug Finley was particularly sceptical that the Trudeau team's approach would work in the longer term. "The key to fundraising on a consistent, growing basis is the established donor relationship, constantly fed by a carefully managed network of systems and devices," Finley declared, and suggested "the Liberal Party has gone backwards in this respect" by relying on the less committed "supporter" category.[5]

But Finley's prediction was soon proven wrong, at least in the short term. By the end of the third quarter of 2013 the Liberals had surpassed the Conservatives in the total number of donors, at thirty thousand compared with twenty-one thousand. By the end of 2014 the party had raised $15.8 million, or 40 per cent more than the previous year, and this in a non-election, non-leadership race year. This amount was also double that raised by the NDP despite their Official Opposition status.

Credit for this impressive increase was due to more than the new supporter category, however. It was also the direct result of many improvements in the fundraising machinery and methods, led by two new players. These were the party's new bagman, Stephen Bronfman, the Montreal businessman and family friend who had been appointed by Trudeau shortly after he won the leadership, and Christina Topp, a professional fundraiser who had been a colleague of Gerald Butts at the

World Wildlife Federation, where she was vice-president of marketing and communications.

The fundraising progress continued in 2015, when an election was scheduled for October. Although the Conservatives continued to outdo the Liberals by a significant amount, it was also true that the Liberal Party now had a sufficient war chest to run a first-rate campaign. And, given the legal limitations on a party's total spending during a campaign, the Conservatives would not actually be able to make use of all of their massive surplus. (Evidently this was one of the drivers behind Stephen Harper's subsequent decision to call an election earlier than expected, thereby extending the campaign period to the maximum length and allowing the Conservatives to spend more. But as the election coverage that follows demonstrates, this tactic actually backfired, and it was the Liberals' ample resources that aided them in overcoming the NDP and winning the election.)

Doug Finley was nevertheless correct in arguing that a carefully managed data system was necessary to cultivate and maintain donors. It was also necessary to ensure that the party knew who its supporters were and what would motivate them, and who to target when getting out the vote on election day. Following up on the January 2012 convention's adoption of the resolution to "fast-track the deployment, population and utilization of its universal database technology," this was the very next aspect of party modernization on which the Trudeau team focused.

Modernizing the Party Machinery: Part 2

Everyone knew that the party had fallen light years behind the Conservatives in terms of technology. The VIM system acquired under Doug Ferguson, and the use of various electronic communication tools under Mike Crawley, had begun the modernization process so necessary for political parties wishing to be competitive in the twenty-first century, but they were hardly sufficient. Shortly after his leadership was confirmed, Justin Trudeau turned to Katie Telford, whom he appointed national campaign co-chair, and Gerald Butts, now his principal secretary in OLO, to make this happen. Telford had been a logistics and planning specialist with both Gerard Kennedy and Trudeau, and was known for her enthusiasm for data because "numbers never lie." Similarly, Butts had worked for pollster Mike Marzolini at Pollara before joining the World Wildlife Federation. Together with newly elected party president Anna Gainey, a long-time family friend of Trudeau and daughter of hockey great Bob Gainey, and her newly appointed national director,

Jeremy Broadhurst (a former adviser to Bob Rae), the tightknit group began to assemble a formidable team of technology gurus.

Perhaps the most striking aspect of this rebuilding exercise is the fact that hardly any of the individuals the trio recruited had previous political experience of any kind. In a scenario remarkably similar to that of the recruitment drive after the party's 1984 defeat, the Liberals were able to attract a number of young and enthusiastic experts despite their third-party status and limited prospects for career advancement. Many of these individuals accepted offers on the strength of their personal acquaintance with one of the key players. Virtually all of them subsequently referred to their interest in making a difference, working for something in which they believed, and/or having the opportunity to create something from the ground up.[6] And, once again, the image of generational change was evident, as most of the new hi-tech hires were demographically similar to Trudeau and his inner circle, in their thirties and forties.[7]

Among the first of these new recruits was Dan Arnold, a Pollara employee and, exceptionally, a former Liberal blogger from Alberta. Arnold joined the national office in March 2014 as the party's in-house pollster. This newly created position reflected the party's desire to access information on a more reliable and cost-effective basis, given that in the past ten years the it had often been forced to piggyback simple queries onto pre-existing commercial surveys due to its lack of financial resources. But the creation of the post also was motivated by the commitment to the resolution's larger scheme that would allow polling and data acquisition to interact.

To that end the party recruited someone who could get them up to speed on the fast-growing field of Big Data. Sean Wiltshire, an expert in statistics and computer modelling, was brought on board as the party's first director of analytics. A former PhD candidate in microbiology, Wiltshire was an ideal candidate for the job, enthusiastic about the potential of marrying the Liberalist information on members, and potentially on voters' lists, with a wide range of demographic data. The purpose, in the end, was to be able to tailor the Liberal message at the micro level, by focusing on communicating the party's position on subjects of interest to specific individuals, groups, or residential areas. As national director Jeremy Broadhurst explained, "Big Data can help you make better decisions about how to deploy volunteers and where to be targeting those door knockers and phone callers in a way that maximizes your chances of identifying the vote and pulling the vote on election day."[8]

At the same time, the information Arnold and Wiltshire acquired was communicated to the campaign team, and ultimately to volunteers at the riding level who were responsible for getting out the vote. As Alf Apps had noted in his background document to the convention's "Roadmap to Renewal," Liberal volunteers in 2011 had had no way of knowing if they were getting out the right vote, and might very well have facilitated votes for other parties. The Conservatives, on the other hand, had been working with Big Data programs for several years and had already achieved a high level of success at targeting their message to supporters.

In order for candidates and volunteers at the local level to be able to take advantage of this newfound data, the party created yet another new position. Hilary Leftick, an events organizer who most recently had been responsible for coordinating the POP music festival in Montreal, was engaged as director of volunteer mobilization. Broadhurst explained the need for this post as well: "You can collect all the data you want but do you have people on the ground who are trained up and know how to use it?"[9]

Leftick joined the national office in the summer of 2014. By October, a full year before the next federal election was scheduled, the party had organized innovative "Days of Action" across the country, with the ultimate objective of having volunteers canvass at the door on weekends in every one of the 308 federal ridings. Slowly but surely this led to the creation of a nationwide network of some eighty thousand volunteers, ready on the ground the day the writ was dropped. But it was not simply the advance planning that was unprecedented. As one canvasser noted, the party had made a "quantum leap" in the 2015 election in terms of its procedures. Veteran Liberal activist Nini Pal pointed out that the approach used by the party in the 2006, 2008, and 2011 elections was unchanged from decades earlier. "I campaigned like this in 1984 in Vancouver Quadra for John Turner," she said. But in 2015 the old process was transformed. "Finally, no more "LUNCH" sheets![10] The information we gathered at the door was transcribed immediately into computers using the Caravan program. It meant we could make far more use, and far better use, of what we were learning."[11]

Meanwhile, a similar exercise was taking place to create a network of phone banks, with trained volunteers calling both non-aligned individuals and supporters across the country many months before the election. Each volunteer signed up for "shifts," calling a predetermined list of individuals from the Liberalist and following a script provided by the managers of the demographic data. One dedicated volunteer reportedly placed forty thousand calls in 2015 alone.[12]

The combination of door knockers and phone calls was estimated by one insider to have led to more than 3.8 million direct contacts with voters, some 1.1 million of whom had indicated they would definitely vote Liberal. This unprecedented level of pre-election organization, unthinkable only a few years earlier, had raised the party's overall election readiness to a standard that would soon be the envy of the other opposition parties and even the Conservatives.

Then the party headquarters focused on the need to continue to engage these volunteers, along with supporters, other members, and ordinary Canadians. Here, too, there was a particular emphasis on young voters and those newly interested in politics. Following on the initial efforts undertaken during the Crawley presidency, the party hired two young media-savvy Liberals – Suzanne Cowan, daughter of Senator James Cowan, and Tom Pitfield, son of Senator Michael Pitfield – to update the Liberals' web presence and email communications and generally increase its participation in social media. Pitfield's team developed pitches for several of the Liberals' target groups, including women and the LGBTQ community. One of the most significant would prove to be a microsite aimed exclusively at issues of interest to youth that featured digital videos, several of which went viral. A few days before advance polling began on university campuses, the Liberals also made a significant purchase of advertising on Facebook, Vice, and YouTube to convey their message more widely.

In addition, Trudeau was quick to establish the structure for the upcoming election campaign itself. After appointing Katie Telford and Dan Gagnier (a Quebec businessman, lobbyist, and former senior public servant) as campaign co-chairs, he named the provincial chairs and put election readiness teams in place by mid-2014. Telford and Gagnier would run campaign committee meetings on the ground at party headquarters with Jeremy Broadhurst, while Gerry Butts, Mike McNair, and Cyrus Reporter would travel with the leader. Kate Purchase, a former Liberal press secretary during the Chrétien era, would serve as director of communications, while John Zerucelli, a former Chrétien and Ontario provincial staffer, would be in charge of the leader's tour and David Rodier would be the wagon master.

Finally, the Liberals followed past practice in establishing a Team Trudeau Candidate College as reinstituted by Doug Ferguson after the Martin era. But this time the program held briefings several months before the scheduled election date. These events, while always valuable, were an important element of election readiness in this case. The party had encountered difficulty attracting candidates in the last two elections, leaving many ridings unprepared and a large number of last-minute candidates essentially on their own. This would not happen in 2015.

Candidate Recruitment as Symbolic Change

Although it would be a gross exaggeration to say that Trudeaumania had swept the country, it was certainly true that the party had no difficulty attracting quality candidates in advance of the 2015 election. In fact, in some cases the problem was an abundance of aspiring candidates for the Liberal nomination in a riding.

One of the first tasks was to set up a screening process to ensure that those putting their names forward as potential Liberal candidates held views consistent with the party's philosophy, and also were not likely to cause the party any embarrassment. This procedure had become important for all parties in recent election campaigns, partly because of the indelible record left by individuals on social media, something that had not been an issue in the past. As a result, the Liberal Party's vetting process for candidates evolved from an informal approval process to one in which interviews were required, and eventually to the more formal "green-light committee" system, first suggested by BC election co-chair Mark Marissen in 2008 after his experience there in a provincial election.

A particular problem for Liberals in terms of candidate selection had been the increasing practice of single-issue interest groups taking control of riding associations. In the past this had led to the party's having a number of pro-life candidates and consequently MPs. Among the most notable examples was that of Tom Wappel, whose surprise victory for the Liberal nomination in Scarborough West in 1988, over star candidate Patrick Johnston (a well-known social policy expert personally recruited by leader John Turner), was orchestrated by Campaign Life. As an MP he subsequently proved to be a thorn in the side of successive leaders and the Liberal caucus until his resignation in 2008. As a result, in 1992 the party attempted to remedy this problem by authorizing the leader, through a constitutional change, to appoint or reject candidates. By 2014 this had become an even more significant issue because delegates at the January 2012 convention had for the first time taken a formal stand in favour of pro-choice.

In August 2014 Trudeau followed up the convention resolution with a formal statement declaring that all new Liberal candidates must agree to vote with the party in favour of the pro-choice option if any legislation were tabled (presumably by the Harper government.) After considerable media controversy and some internal conflict, he clarified his position to indicate that the few existing pro-life MPs, such as John McKay and Lawrence MacAulay would not be "grandfathered," but also that the requirement was "only" to vote with the party in favour of pro-choice, whatever the individual's personal beliefs might be. This would not be a problem for long, he added, since under his or any future Liberal government there would never be such legislation: "It's not for any government to legislate what happens – what a woman chooses to do with her body, and that is the bottom line." The intent of his directive, he said, was to "weed out any potential candidates looking to reopen the abortion debate" during the vetting process. "That's part of the green-light process. We check on a number of issues: How do you feel about the Charter of Rights and Freedoms, how do you feel about same-sex marriage, how do you feel about pro-choice."[13] Trudeau was unapologetic about his decision. The convention, he pointed out, had knowingly selected a "resolutely" pro-choice leader by a margin of 80 per cent.

In early 2014 Trudeau, through campaign co-chair Katie Telford, appointed Toronto lawyer and long-time party constitutional expert Jack Siegel to chair the Liberals' green-light committee for the upcoming election. At one of the first meetings of the National Election Readiness Committee they then decided on provincial and territorial green-light committee members, often a single person and never more than two, to conduct these interviews and assess the situation. Although it was agreed that the provincial campaign chairs would be kept abreast of developments in the case of rejections, it was also understood that this was an arm's-length process that would not be subject to interference.[14] At the end of the day, the ultimate purpose of the committees was to enable the party to better know its candidates, not simply to weed out "undesirables."

According to Siegel, at the interviews introduced in 2015 the party required candidates to sign on to the party's position on four issues as a bottom line: support for pro-choice, the Charter, same-sex marriage, and the Clarity Act. At the same time, Siegel was quick to note that "nobody was saying change your values or your views. It was 'not what you think but what you do' that we cared about. We wanted to be sure their public position and comments would be in line with the party's stated position."[15] Or, of course, they could be silent. Yet even with this latitude, Siegel noted that some long-time Liberals felt they could not comply and therefore did not choose to run.

Siegel also noted that the role of social media posts was "immensely challenging," but in many cases the party worked with a potential candidate to ensure that he or she could deal with an issue and still be eligible, assuming the posts did not contravene basic human rights or Liberal principles. "What was important is that they be open with us and share any potentially damaging material, so we could be prepared if necessary to respond." Yet in the end there were five Liberal candidates who were obliged to withdraw during the course of the campaign because of previously unseen earlier comments on Facebook or other social media platforms, compared with eight Conservatives, four NDP, and two Bloc Québécois candidates, proving Siegel's point about the challenges social media were posing.[16]

At the same time that the green-light committees were becoming more substantial, Trudeau had made a commitment to open nominations and said that he would not appoint candidates. Once the green-light committee had approved an individual, the process would unfold fairly and transparently according to well-established constitutional rules for nomination procedures.

Nevertheless, Trudeau and his closest advisers had definite preferences with respect to the profile of an ideal candidate. To begin with, they wanted primarily newcomers. They were concerned that a number of former Liberal MPs who had been defeated in 2008 or 2011 might choose to run again, and that their riding associations would support them. In their view this was a significant problem for at least three reasons. First, it would be difficult to demonstrate that the Trudeau Liberals were a breath of fresh air if a large number of the 2015 Liberal candidates were the same ones from earlier time periods. In addition, Trudeau was determined (some would have said obsessed) with the need to put the Chrétien-Martin wars behind him and the party. Although some of the former MPs had not been involved in that internecine warfare, it was deemed preferable to take no chances and avoid all of them at all costs. Last but hardly least, the Trudeau team wanted the election to be a watershed one in which it was clear that a "changing of the guard" had taken place, especially when it came to age. Again, the emphasis on youth was crucial, and in reality – whether consciously or not – it soon became apparent that for the most part those over forty need not apply.

Meanwhile, a variety of players, including the national campaign co-chairs and their provincial counterparts, were actively courting a number of prominent individuals with expertise in areas of particular interest. These included economics, foreign policy and defence, and criminal justice. As a result, ridings saw expressions of interest from previously non-partisan "stars" such as economic journalist and author Chrystia Freeland (Toronto: University-Rosedale) and financial adviser Bill Morneau (Toronto Centre), Air Force pilot Major Steve Fuhr (Kelowna-Lake Country) and Lieutenant General (retd) Andrew Leslie (Orleans), Francois-Philippe Champagne (St Maurice-Champlain), a lawyer and international trade expert, and Bill Blair (Toronto: Scarborough-Southwest), the former Toronto chief of police, all of whom were successful in their bids to become a Liberal candidate.

Flowing from their concern with expertise – and determined to counter anticipated Conservative charges that the leader and his party's candidates were too inexperienced and lacked the depth to form a competent cabinet – the party actually released cumulative information about the background and experience of its flag bearers, another campaign first. This information, in turn, spoke volumes about the party's concerns with Conservative perceptions of weakness. A whopping 111 Liberal candidates were listed as business people or entrepreneurs. Twenty-three were identified as military veterans or police officers, no doubt to counter the Harper government's accusations that the Liberals were "soft on crime." And seventy-three were described as teachers or professors, a number that, of course, included Trudeau himself. Despite their desire to avoid a sense of déjà vu, the Liberals were also aware that political experience was still valuable. As a result they listed one-third of their candidates as having been elected previously at some level of government.

Trudeau's team was also intent on demonstrating a high level of diversity among its nominated candidates. This was consistent with priorities Trudeau had already identified for a future cabinet, such as gender parity. In the end, the Liberals could say that eighteen candidates were of Aboriginal origin and another forty-eight were self-described visible minorities or first-generation Canadians. Although the party did not reach its goal of gender parity, slightly more than one-third of Liberal candidates were women, enhancing the possibility of Trudeau's fulfilling his cabinet promise. In addition, the Liberals were quick to highlight the number of prominent francophone candidates in Quebec, a significant point in light of the overwhelming number of francophone NDP incumbents.

Overall, the Liberals recruited an impressive roster of candidates in all regions of the country, and they did so in record time. On 2 August, when the writ was dropped somewhat prematurely by the prime minister, the Liberals had already nominated 294 of the necessary 338 candidates. In this they were far ahead of the NDP (253) and even of the Conservatives (291), who presumably knew in advance when this would happen. From the beginning, therefore, they were able to include some of their star candidates in Liberal events and in advertising, under the rubric "Team Trudeau is Ready."

Ironically, it was in the area of candidate selection that Trudeau ran into his first real controversy. Having promised open nominations, he then was faced with the prospect of losing some of his star recruits. The

first candidate conflict involved the party's disqualification of Christine
Innes (wife of former Liberal MP Tony Ianno) in a Toronto-area riding
because of alleged inappropriate activities on the part of her campaign
organizers.[17] But observers noted that her candidacy was a challenge
to star candidate Chrystia Freeland. A subsequent nomination battle
that also gained national attention took place in the east Ottawa riding
of Orleans, and again pitted one of Trudeau's star candidates (in this
case Lt. General Andrew Leslie – who did not live in the riding and had
only recently joined the party) against the riding's very well liked and
established candidate, lawyer David Bertschi, who had deep roots in
the party and the riding and an impressive set of credentials of his own.
That conflict escalated when it became apparent that the riding's executive and membership preferred Bertshi and Leslie would be unable to
win an open nomination contest. In the end Bertschi, who had been
green-lighted, was disqualified by the national campaign co-chairs and
Leslie was "acclaimed" as the Liberal candidate at a highly publicized
meeting that turned into a physically violent melee. Many believed that
if the riding had not been a long-time Liberal bastion it could have been
lost to the party over this issue.

Some observers argued that Trudeau's mistake was in having promised that he would not intervene in any nomination process in the first
place. In effect, what had been common before had now become unacceptable because of that commitment. (Several insiders confided that this
warning had been mentioned at the time but was disregarded because
of the perceived importance of demonstrating a new approach.) Others suggested that the real problem was a lack of political intelligence,
which had placed the two star candidates in the wrong ridings, that led
to the controversies.

Still, these two public relations gaffes paled in comparison to the
unexpected, and to many Liberals inexplicable, decision on Trudeau's
part to accept disgraced former Conservative MP Eve Adams as a
potential candidate. Adams, whose riding had disappeared through
redistribution, had been shopping for a winnable riding in the Toronto
area for some time, and her tactics had eventually been disowned by the
Harper Conservatives, who forbade her from running for their party
anywhere. All of this was widely known when Trudeau appeared at
a press conference in late August with Adams at his side, to announce
that she had crossed the floor to sit as a Liberal MP and been given the
green light to run for the party's nomination in the Toronto-area riding of Eglington Lawrence. Many Liberal party members in Ontario
and across Canada were appalled. So was provincial Liberal MLA Mike
Colle, whose riding overlapped the federal one. Known as a formidable

organizer who had never lost an election in his twenty-five years at Queen's Park, Colle publicly vowed that Adams would only win the nomination "over my dead body." He promptly recruited another contender, well-known local Liberal lawyer Marco Mendocino, who handily won the nomination over Adams and then went on to defeat Harper finance minister Joe Oliver in the federal election.

Nevertheless, some other Liberals saw the contest and Mendocino's victory in a more positive light, a demonstration of the openness of the process. "After all, she lost," one said. Another argued that competition was always a good thing since membership went from three hundred to five thousand because of the nomination race.[18] Certainly the numbers suggested the Liberals were seen as a viable option in the next election, despite Oliver's high profile, and the Conservatives were taking note.

The Liberals' Positive Response to Conservative Attack Ads

There was no doubt that the Conservative campaign managers were concerned about the increasing popularity of the Liberals and their new leader. They followed the same practice they had used to "frame" Dion and Ignatieff by posting negative attack ads about Trudeau. In his case, though, it was literally *minutes* after he was elected leader that they began to air their "just not ready" ads.

Trudeau's first response was to state that he would take the high road, just as Dion and Ignatieff had done. Interestingly, some polls began to suggest that this reply might have more credence than it did with his predecessors. Canadians, it appeared, had begun to tire of the relentless personal attacks. An Ipsos Reid poll conducted at the end of April found that 59 per cent of viewers "disliked" the Conservative ads and fully 74 per cent identified something they did not like about them. This included 20 per cent who did not like the very fact that it was a personal attack ad, 12 per cent who agreed it was "underhanded or tasteless," and 12 per cent who agreed it was either "propaganda" or "not credible."[19] Moreover, support for the Liberals actually rose 3 per cent from the beginning of April, to 35 per cent, although this increased support appeared to come from soft NDP supporters while the Conservatives remained at 32 per cent.

The evidence suggesting the ads were backfiring did not change the Conservatives' approach. Indeed, they rolled out more of them with the same theme of "just not ready," convinced that they would do their job in the end. But some of their supporters were not convinced. Tom Flanagan, the former Harper adviser and University of Calgary academic, argued the ads were "just not working" and urged them to adopt a different approach. Perhaps more significant was the decision of several Conservative MPs to reject the ads, which were included in Householders[20] provided to them by the party's Research Bureau and could be distributed in their individual ridings at no cost to the party since they were paid for by taxpayers. Many MPs across all regions of the country, including Alberta, indicated they felt the ads were inappropriate and even counterproductive and refused to distribute them.[21]

Even former prime minister Brian Mulroney entered the fray. He suggested Trudeau's biggest asset after nine years of the Harper government was precisely that "he's not Harper." Somewhat ironically, given his long-standing animosity towards Pierre Trudeau, the former Progressive Conservative prime minister urged Conservatives to "be very careful how you treat this fellow. Because you're not dealing with a Stéphane Dion. You're not dealing with a Michael Ignatieff here. You're dealing with a different generation, a different product of that life."[22] In a CTV interview Mulroney went further. "I've known Justin since he was a child. He's young, articulate, attractive – a flawlessly bilingual young man. What's not to like with this picture?" he said. "Anybody who … treats Justin Trudeau with scorn or derision or underestimates him, does so at his own peril. We'll see what happens in the future; it's a long way from here to there. But no one should underestimate Justin. He's a man of some consequence."[23]

Ironically, by late July at least one pollster, Lorne Bazinoff of Forum Research, told reporters the ads were not only not working but were actually having the opposite effect of the one the Conservatives were hoping for. While 81 per cent of committed Conservatives agreed that Trudeau was "just not ready," the Forum poll found that more than 67 per cent of Canadians disagreed, including 32 per cent who were more likely to vote Liberal, while some 21 per cent of NDP supporters were specifically inclined to vote Liberal because of the ads.[24]

Still the Liberals were taking no chances. They now had the money and the resources to reply and they did, releasing a series of ads in which the Conservative premise was stood on its head. In humorous vignettes showing Trudeau as a teacher they mocked the Tories' ads about lack of experience and their attempts to "frame" Trudeau as "not ready." These Liberal ads soon proved popular with Canadians generally, and especially with members of the teaching profession.

In short, it appeared that Liberals were now winning the air war, something the Conservatives had not expected. But it was also true that this early success did not prevent the Conservatives from using the same theme in later ads, with more success, primarily because some of

Trudeau's actions as leader and in the House of Commons over 2014 and early 2015 appeared to justify their message.

Trudeau in Opposition: Bold Moves and Missteps

It is the role of every opposition leader to suffer the slings and arrows of misfortune at some point. Lacking the discipline of power, with no carrots to offer or sticks to wave at recalcitrant caucus members, very few party leaders emerge unscathed from their time in opposition. This was certainly true of Jean Chrétien. Given his subsequent success, many Canadians may well have forgotten his time as opposition leader, from June 1990 to the 1993 election, when Chrétien was viewed by many of his own caucus as yesterday's man. His early performance in the House of Commons was not inspiring and he was widely criticized as a man of little policy substance.[25] And yet he hardly lacked experience.

By comparison, Justin Trudeau was unquestionably less well prepared. It should not have come as a surprise to Liberals or Canadians that there would be some inevitable missteps. But although the Conservatives downplayed Trudeau's political experience, he was hardly as unprepared as they wanted voters to believe. He had actually been an MP since 2008, for nearly five years before he was elected leader in 2013. As Cyrus Reporter, veteran ministerial adviser to Justice Minister Alan Rock and Trudeau's first chief of staff, later recalled, Trudeau had been a quick learner and had paid attention in that interval. Apart from his involvement in party reform, Reporter noted that Trudeau had been deeply engaged in a number of policy debates in caucus and in the House of Commons.[26] Former Liberal MP Mark Holland concurred. "He did an excellent job as the party's immigration critic," Holland pointed out, "yet he was continually underestimated."[27] Another former colleague noted that "he had the best set of tutorials anyone could have had. He watched and listened while his father confronted many of the same issues, and he paid close attention. He had already seen the challenges of governing from the inside."

Certainly it was clear that Trudeau had an agenda. Having set the ball in motion on election readiness, he began to stake out positions on several high-profile issues, some of which would prove of particular interest to young Canadians and recent immigrants. These announcements were also carefully considered in terms of regional appeal. For example, he chose an event in Kelowna, BC, in July 2013 to announce his commitment to the legalization and regulation of marijuana, going a step further than his original statement during the leadership race that he would be in favour of decriminalization. Referring to what he termed the failed war on drugs, "that only benefits organized crime and increases gang activity," he also stressed that legalization would need to be accompanied by regulation to ensure children were protected and health risks were minimized.[28]

Similarly, Trudeau delivered a speech to the Calgary Petroleum Club in Calgary in late October 2013 in which he reiterated his support for the Keystone pipeline project and criticized Stephen Harper's "megaphone diplomacy" in his dealings with American president Barack Obama. After eight years of Harper's Conservative government, which was often referred to as the most energy-friendly federal government the country had ever seen, Trudeau said "we are further than ever from a sensible policy to reduce carbon pollution, and the oilsands have become [needlessly] the international poster child for climate change." He also agreed that "we need to get our energy resources to the Pacific." Nevertheless, he said he could not support the Northern Gateway project based on the evidence. Presaging his later support for the Trans Mountain pipeline project, he declared, "We can find other ways to do this that will be economically viable and not have negative implications for the environment."[29]

In Montreal, meanwhile, Trudeau delivered a forty-minute speech on 9 March 2015 in which he pursued an aggressive line of attack on the prime minister regarding the latter's statements in Quebec criticizing women wearing the hijab. While Harper had attempted to justify his remarks by arguing that he wanted to liberate Muslim women from oppression, Trudeau ridiculed the idea that the prime minister was promoting liberty. "It is a cruel joke to claim you are liberating people from oppression by dictating in law what they can and cannot wear." Then he accused Harper of playing dangerous politics and dividing Canadians. "We all know what is going on here," Trudeau told his audience. "It is nothing less than an attempt to play on people's fears and foster prejudice directly towards the Muslim faith." Speaking more broadly about the Conservatives' record, which he saw as repeating this type of fear-mongering, he warned that "fear is a dangerous thing. Once it is sanctioned by the state, there is no telling where it might lead. It is always a short path from being suspicious of our fellow citizens to taking actions to restrict their liberties." Perhaps most significant, Trudeau drew a link between his comments on this issue and his plans to highlight liberal values in the coming election. "Canadians ought to know what core values will motivate their leaders' decisions, whatever events may throw at them ... It's time Liberals took back liberty. These Conservatives pretend to talk a good game about freedom, but look what they've done with it."[30]

It was no accident that Trudeau had decided to focus on the diversity issue, something that would be enhanced by his commitment to Canada's acceptance of refugees during the election campaign itself. As 2011 had revealed, even the Liberals' traditional support among various ethnocultural communities had been weakened in that election, in large part because of the concerted efforts of the Harper Conservatives to appeal to social conservative values in the outlying Toronto 905 region heavily populated by new Canadians, by attacking Liberal policies such as same-sex marriage legislation. Harper minister Jason Kenny was, in fact, given considerable credit for the 2011 majority win in light of his relentless efforts to transfer the loyalty of such communities to the Conservatives.[31]

As these various speeches demonstrated, Trudeau's team had taken a conscious decision to expose his views to as many Canadians across the country as possible, evidently not worried about a repeat of Jack Layton's attack on Michael Ignatieff for missing time in Parliament. In fact, Trudeau's spokesperson stated up front that the leader would only be in the House of Commons twice a week for Question Period. On other occasions, it would be up to the party's assigned critics, House leader Ralph Goodale and whip Dominic Leblanc, another close personal friend, to hold the fort. As a third party, this decision made perfect sense since the Liberals had far fewer opportunities to intervene than the Official Opposition NDP did.

Trudeau's team considered his forays across the country an essential element of the party's attempts to rebuild its base, just as the executive and voluntary wing of the party was working to do so by strengthening communications with the membership and increasing its efforts to develop strong riding associations in areas where those had become weak. Trudeau's repeated visits to British Columbia were a classic example of this approach, and one dictated by the leader's own commitment to having the party seen as relevant in the province.

In the summer of 2014 Trudeau also did something that Michael Ignatieff had done, but with much greater success than his hapless predecessor.[32] With the publication of *Common Ground*, Trudeau published a book that quickly became a national bestseller. Part autobiography, part manifesto, and part philosophy of governing, it was described by one reviewer as "required reading for anyone who wants to be an informed voter,"[33] while another described it as "a superior example of the genre, both deepening our sense of the politician and also the larger political landscape he inhabits."[34] In it he laid down the principles that would motivate his future policies, and the belief that diversity had strengthened rather than divided Canadians and helped them to find common ground. He also pledged that "hope and hard work" would be the mantra of his campaign and of a future Liberal government. Taken together with his various speeches, it was becoming increasingly clear that Trudeau was not just another messiah, regardless of his surname and telegenic appeal. As one former Liberal insider and initial sceptic admitted, "Deep down there really is something there after all."

Nevertheless, there were issues in Ottawa that required Trudeau's attention, and his handling of two of them in particular resulted in considerable controversy. The first was his surprise decision to expel Liberal senators from the Liberal caucus. The Senate, of course, had experienced more than two years of expense scandals at this point, including the infamous Mike Duffy affair that had mushroomed in 2013 with explosive revelations about the role of the prime minister's office. Although the vast majority of the auditor general's findings had involved Conservative senators, including two additional high-profile Harper appointees (Pamela Wallin and Patrick Brazeau, Trudeau's former boxing opponent), it was also true that a few Liberal senators had been implicated, albeit in far more minor spending irregularities. As a result, Trudeau and his team decided that the time was right to begin to implement his plan to eliminate partisan Senate appointments.

On 29 January 2014, before a regular Wednesday caucus meeting, senators and MPs were separated and sent to two different rooms. Trudeau addressed the senators first, telling them that he was removing them from the Liberal caucus and that they would now be Independents. "The Senate is broken and needs to be fixed," he told the stunned room of long-time Liberals. Then he held a press conference, at which he explained his decision in more detail. Referring to the original role of the non-elected Senate as a chamber of "sober second thought" that was intended to reflect regional concerns and offer expert input, he stated that it had increasingly become a forum for the continuation of political battles fought in the House of Commons. "Instead of being separate from political or electoral concerns, senators now must consider not just what's best for their country or their regions, but what's best for their party. At best this renders the Senate redundant. At worst – and under Mr Harper we have seen it at its worst – it amplifies the prime minister's power" rather than serving as the intended check and balance.[35]

The response to this move, both positive and negative, was immediate and substantial. The Conservatives described the move as a "smokescreen" that would see no real change take place, while the NDP continued to call for the abolition of the chamber, something that would require a (highly improbable) constitutional amendment. Academics and parliamentary procedure specialists raised numerous issues about how Trudeau's plan would work in practice. Meanwhile most of the Liberal senators were both shocked and unnerved. As key party organizers and fundraisers, many suddenly found themselves on the outside looking in when they were accustomed to being close to the centre. Still, Senate Liberal leader James Cowan stated that "what Mr Trudeau has courageously done today is to set us free to do the job we're here to do, without any interference or direction from colleagues in the other place."[36]

The controversy was not unexpected. While the move was deliberately planned to coincide with the prime minister's problems in that chamber, it was also part of a longer game plan that Trudeau had discussed with friends and colleagues for some time. As Cyrus Reporter noted, "this was an issue for him from the beginning. He really believed the Senate needed to change in order to be saved."[37] His advisers had consulted academic experts and were aware of possible difficulties, but he believed the risk was worth it. And while he knew the move would be controversial, he was convinced that his effort would be seen as showing leadership and strength. In addition, it also provided a mechanism for revealing what he considered to be an important plank in the Liberal platform for the coming election. "At our best, Liberals are relentless reformers. When public institutions fail to serve the public interest, we take bold steps to change them. We want to build public institutions that Canadians can trust, and that serve Canadians. This requires real, positive change. These proposals are the next step in our Open Parliament plan to do just that. They won't be the last."[38]

By contrast, Trudeau's response to the Harper government's controversial bill C-51, the Anti-terrorism Act, was not expected to cause problems but did. It was seen by many Canadians and quite a few Liberal militants as the opposite of showing leadership or support for liberal values. In the face of widespread criticism from legal experts, human rights advocates, and officers of Parliament (such as the privacy commissioner) that the bill's reach was too great and had the potential to violate the rights of individual citizens, the NDP, the Bloc, and the Green Party all announced that they would oppose the bill unequivocally. The Liberals instead tabled a number of amendments that they argued would address most of these concerns. But the Conservatives accepted very few of these amendments. Still the Liberals, who maintained they would make amendments to the legislation if they were elected, supported the bill. As a result it passed speedily and was in force by July 2015.

Trudeau described the Liberal approach to C-51 as "nuanced" and "balanced," arguing that it was of primary importance to enhance the security of citizens in the face of several terrorist acts that had taken place in various parts of the country in recent months. One insider confided that this was one area in which the leader did not want to take on the prime minister, for fear that Harper would use it during the election campaign to demonstrate that the Liberals were not just "soft on crime" but unable to make any tough decisions to defend Canadians. Behind the scenes some insiders also suggested that the bill's passage was viewed as important to Quebec, and that Andrew Leslie, the prime minister's defence critic, had advocated its passage. But reaction to the Liberal position was (unexpectedly) highly critical. That position was widely seen not as balanced but hypocritical or, worse still, an abrogation of the Liberals' commitment to the Charter of Rights. One Liberal insider confided that they were receiving anecdotal evidence of ripped up membership cards. "We lost volunteers over this ... Candidates were hearing about it at the doorstep. Some disgruntled party members even withdrew their financial support."[39]

Polls and the Ominous Liberal Decline

These were some of the most significant issues that Trudeau faced in opposition in terms of controversy and public criticism, but they were not the only ones. A string of minor problems had already begun to damage his seemingly Teflon image. From his flippant reference to hockey when Russia invaded the Ukraine ("It's very worrisome, particularly since Russia lost in hockey, they will be in a bad mood")[40] to his bizarre comments about Chinese democracy,[41] the numerous off-the-cuff gaffes – along with his handling of C-51 – seemed to cement concerns that the Liberal leader was, perhaps, not ready after all. By the spring of 2015 public opinion polls, so favourable for so long, began to reflect this concern and cause considerable anxiety in the Liberal trenches.

Justin Trudeau had indeed enjoyed an unprecedented honeymoon with Canadians. Days after he formally became leader of the Liberal Party (a foregone conclusion for many weeks), the party's support soared to 43 per cent in the polls, compared with 30 per cent for the Conservatives and 19 per cent for the NDP.[42] Six months later little had changed, except that the Conservatives were now at 28 per cent. For the remainder of 2013 and literally all of 2014 this heady scenario continued. "Trudeau remains golden" one frustrated media article fumed, "despite all the gaffes and setbacks ... How can this be?" The article's author concluded that "Justin Trudeau, for all that he's made mistakes, has somehow convinced a majority of Canadians that he means well."[43]

But things started to deteriorate by the beginning of 2015. By 30 April, after three months of debate and controversy over the Liberal compromise on Bill C-51 and the wrangling over the pro-choice stance for candidates, the party found itself in a virtual tie with the Conservatives, at 34 per cent to 33 per cent, and the NDP was up slightly to 21 per cent.[44]

Meanwhile the party's regional weakness continued. In the west it appeared that the party still had a long way to go. It was also clear that the campaign team was aware of this, and especially the leader. (Trudeau insisted on launching his election campaign in British Columbia, a province to which he returned many times over the course of the lengthy contest.) And in Quebec, the crucial former Liberal fortress that was unexpectedly breached by the NDP in the Orange Wave of 2011, pollster Éric Grenier had delivered sobering news. His analysis of the situation in November 2014 concluded that, although the NDP at the time was trailing badly in much of Canada, it was still "the party to beat" in Quebec.[45]

Then in May 2015 the provincial NDP in Alberta surprised the country by defeating the governing Progressive Conservatives and taking power for the first time. The success of premier-elect Rachel Notley's party led many federal NDP advisers to believe that this was a sign of things to come. That party's confidence soared even as the Liberals' began to plummet. Although experts disagreed about the potential impact of the NDP provincial victory on the federal election,[46] it was certainly true that the Liberals, for a variety of reasons, were in difficulty. By 30 July they were still in a virtual tie with the Conservatives, at 29 and 28 per cent respectively, but the NDP had rocketed to 33.7 per cent.[47]

The NDP continued to lead in the polls for more than six weeks. On 2 August, when Stephen Harper asked the governor general to dissolve Parliament, the NDP had risen to 39 per cent while the Liberals (25 per cent) were in third place, behind the Conservatives (28 per cent), and beginning to look like they were out of the running. Relative to their finish in the 2011 election four years earlier (at 19 per cent), they would need to increase their share of the popular vote by 20 per cent to win, an almost impossible feat. Worse still, although internal party polling had revealed that voters' support for change was much higher than in 2011, this was not helpful. Unhappily, and almost unthinkably, it appeared that the NDP would be the beneficiary of that desire for change. As one Liberal adviser later said, "What's a bigger change than the NDP?"

Another reason for the NDP's apparent advantage, according to one senior adviser, was that the Liberals had revealed very little of their platform at this point. In an effort to keep their powder dry they had relied on the few big announcements made by Trudeau over the past eighteen months to set the tone and tenor of their policy direction. But this was not sufficient.

Canadians did not have a sense of where Trudeau stood on major economic issues, or even on some social issues, except for his use of the term "fairness" to stress liberal values, and his generalized and repeated focus on the "hard-working middle class and those trying to join it." With so little substance, it was increasingly hard to picture him as someone who was ready to tackle the big issues of governing, even if he meant well and his heart was in the right place.

Policy Development and the Platform

Yet the Liberals had made some attempts to indicate the direction of their economic policy over the last year. In late February 2014, at the party's regularly scheduled biennial convention in Montreal, which was widely covered, they had debated options such as a national transportation policy, a national energy policy, and a basic-income strategy, as well as non-economic proposals for democratic reform, assisted suicide, and even the possible legalization of prostitution.

Meanwhile, Trudeau had released a short video discussing his views on economic reform – including the need to promote competitiveness and ensure wage and labour growth – several days before the convention. At the actual convention one of his star candidates, economic journalist Chrystia Freeland, opened the discussion with a one-on-one conversation with Larry Summers, the former US Treasury secretary who was then serving as the president of Harvard University. Both of them stressed that they were concerned with growing income disparity, and bandied about several possible options for ensuring economic growth "that benefits everyone."

After this public exposure the work of platform development continued internally. Mike McNair, an original member of Trudeau's leadership team and the former senior Dion adviser whom many considered the principal architect of the Green Shift, was in charge of this exercise. In keeping with Trudeau's commitment to engage grass-roots party members, those members were repeatedly consulted by webmail to ascertain their priorities and their reaction to a number of possible planks.

In May 2015, in response to the Conservatives' pre-election budget, Trudeau announced a "fairness" package that included a tax cut for the middle class in exchange for cancelling Harper's plan to extend the existing income-splitting provision for seniors to families, and an increased tax level for the top 1 per cent of income earners (those earning more than $200,000 a year). This plan was seen as extremely risky by several of the inner circle, but in the end it was considered a necessity if they were to have a platform that was credibly financed. In addition, the theme of reducing the burden on the middle class by "asking the wealthiest Canadians to pay a little more" was one that played well in terms of the themes of fairness and equality of opportunity.

The decision to remove Liberal senators from caucus was only one aspect of the larger plan on democratic reform, which included Trudeau's commitment to electoral reform in the form of preferential ballots, as approved at the January 2012 convention. In June 2015 he revealed the entire thirty-two-point democratic reform plan, which was seen as a way to demonstrate both change and accountability, themes that Trudeau had also been stressing from the beginning.

At the same time the party's election slogan, "Real Change," and its accompanying logo were released with considerable fanfare at a press conference in Ottawa. Yet none of these announcements appeared to have much of an impact on public opinion and did nothing to stop the Liberal's seemingly inexorable slide.

The Long Election Campaign

When Stephen Harper asked the governor general to dissolve Parliament on 2 August, for a 19 October election date, it signalled the start of what would be the longest election campaign since the first two elections after Confederation, when politicians were obliged to travel the country by train and horse and voting was staged in segments. At eleven weeks, the 2015 election would surpass even the 1926 election of seventy-four days. By contrast, most elections in the recent past had been roughly five weeks long.

Harper's timing was no accident. The longer the campaign, the more money a political party could spend. A minimum campaign was legislated at thirty-seven days by the original election expenses legislation, but there was no maximum. In 2014 the Harper Conservatives introduced a change to that legislation that provided that parties could increase their spending by one-thirty-seventh for every day that a campaign exceeded the minimum. Each party was already able to spend $25 million if it fielded a full slate of 338 candidates for a thirty-seven-day campaign, and now that amount would double, legally. There could be little doubt that these changes were designed expressly to benefit the deep pockets of the Conservatives, beginning with their approach to campaign advertising. At the same time, a variety of advocacy groups hostile to the government, such as environmentalists, would be prevented from spending on critical ads during the campaign.

The Conservatives were also hoping the unexpectedly early election call would catch the opposition parties off guard in terms of their own campaign preparations. This was true to a considerable extent with respect to the NDP. As mentioned earlier, they had fewer candidates nominated when the campaign began than either the Liberals or the Conservatives. Moreover, as later outlined by an NDP insider, the party had budgeted for a five-week campaign, so that finances would become an important underlying issue for them, unlike the Liberals. In addition, the NDP's deliberate strategy of withholding advertising until after Labour Day left the Liberals alone on the field for nearly a month, with significant impact.[48]

The Liberal ads during that time period not only began to strengthen Justin Trudeau's image as a competent manager, but criticized several of the already known NDP platform planks as well as previous statements by leader Tom Mulcair. This latter point was particularly important, since the NDP had decided to focus their entire campaign around the idea that the NDP was a government-in-waiting, and Tom Mulcair a prime minister-in-waiting. With the length of the campaign doubled by Harper's surprise call, the NDP strategists then decided to focus their efforts in August on Mulcair and a "leader's tour," an effort that actually had the effect of heightening the differences between the NDP leader and his Liberal counterpart for many Canadians, and not in a positive way.

When the NDP did finally join the air war after Labour Day this distinction continued, and was reinforced by the Liberals' unusual but highly successful approach to their own ads.

Conservative Attack Ads and the Innovative Liberal Response

The Liberals had a communications plan that was two years in the making. They would argue that their party was the *real* agent of change and that Justin Trudeau was the leader to accomplish it. Hence the slogan "Real Change," which was announced two months before the campaign began. Naturally they expected to pursue this plan in their ads. But with the polling numbers being what they were when the writ was dropped, even the Liberals' Red Leaf ad company, Bensimon Byrne, felt that their approach was "not going to work." In a memo to Gerald Butts, John Bensimon urged the Liberals to adopt a new approach as the NDP had won that battle already. He also argued that the Liberals would have no choice but to launch a negative ad campaign. Former

Martin adviser David Herle agreed, and wrote separately to Butts making the same case. Butts and national campaign co-chair Katie Telford disagreed. Their man was focused on "sunny ways" and that was to be his calling card. There would be no negative ads and they would not change their plan. Butts responded to Bensimon saying that "we will win this [election] on hope and hard work."[49]

Luckily for the Liberals, Bensimon agreed to tackle the task despite these limitations. In what would turn out to be a strategy that paid off handsomely for the Liberals, his ad team developed a series of wildly successful television ads that took on the Conservatives' "Just not ready" theme – which they had continued to promote – and beat them at their own game. This in itself was a risky tactic, since almost all communications experts would agree that repeating an opponent's ad, even if refuting it, is never a good idea. (It would most likely reinforce the opponent's case in the mind of the audience.) Yet that is exactly what the Liberal ads did.

In the first ad, released during the summer of 2015, Trudeau was featured in a close-up saying that he was "not ready" to tolerate job losses and an economic recession because of Conservative incompetence and indifference. In a second, Trudeau was shown walking up a down escalator while saying he was "not ready" to have middle-class Canadians struggle to get ahead because the Conservatives had no economic plan. This second ad reportedly attracted more than three million viewers before the election was over. (Trudeau, meanwhile, commented to aides that it was lucky he was in shape because the repeated takes of the escalator-climbing segment were apparently quite physically demanding.)

A third and final ad in the series modified the second by adding a film clip from a massive Liberal rally in Brampton Ontario near the end of the campaign. The footage showed a prime ministerial Trudeau speaking to the enthusiastic crowd and then faded to the word "Ready."

Later in the campaign, when the Liberals were making every effort to lock down their support in the Greater Toronto Area and with seniors, a different ad was presented. In it, legendary Mississauga mayor Hazel McCallion, a senior herself, appeared on camera to refute Conservative allegations that the Liberals were planning to revoke the income-splitting measure for seniors. Stating that the Conservatives were merely fear-mongering, McCallion, a long-time opponent of Harper, looked directly into the camera and said, "Do I look scared, Stephen?"

Clearly the party's plan to dedicate sufficient funds for an appropriate ad campaign to defend the leader was working. In fact, there was more than enough. As a result, when the Conservatives predictably began to attack the Liberal's economic plan and their costing, it was possible for the party to pay for full-page ads in the *Globe and Mail* on the weekend before the advance polls and again on the Thanksgiving weekend, just days before the election. The ads featured testimonials from five prominent neutral experts (including David Dodge, a former Bank of Canada governor, Ken Battle and Sheri Torjman of the Caledon Institute on Social Policy, and John Tory, the [Conservative] mayor of Toronto) praising the Liberals' platform, and in particular the proposal for massive injections of funding for infrastructure renewal and the Canada Child Benefit.

As Stephen Harper was by now no doubt realizing, his plan to extend the election campaign had backfired. Not only did the Liberals have sufficient funds to combat the Conservative attack ads, but they took advantage of the extra time he had given them with the lengthy campaign to establish Justin Trudeau's credibility. Nowhere was this more evident than in the series of leader's debates.

Trudeau's Success in the Leadership Debates

For decades a mainstay of federal elections had been two leaders' debates, one in English and one in French, at roughly the midpoint in an election campaign. Stephen Harper had not enjoyed the debates in 2008 and 2011, and by 2015 he had decided to put an end to them. Among other things, he was convinced that the consortium of broadcasters (CBC, CTV, and Global) who organized them were biased against him and his party, just as he believed the mainstream print media were all biased in favour of liberals. At the same time many observers believed he was hoping to both minimize his exposure and increase his opportunities to tackle Justin Trudeau in one-on-one debates on subjects that favoured Harper's agenda.

Initially the prime minister had simply announced that he would not participate in the consortium debates this time around. Instead, he had agreed to participate in an English-language debate organized by *Maclean's* magazine and a French debate organized by TVA. His communications director, Kory Teneycke, nevertheless said that the Conservatives would be willing to look at up to three more proposals. Among other things, these various events would have limited distribution by cable or internet, rather than nationwide coverage, which was seen as a deliberate effort to minimize any negative fallout for the Conservatives. Nonplussed, the other parties' leaders took differing positions. The NDP said it would still participate in the consortium debate, but also in the *Maclean's* event, but the Liberals were more ambivalent. They criticized Harper's decision and indicated that they would add to their democratic reform package the idea of creating an independent, non-partisan commission to organize leaders' debates in future.

In the end there were five debates, three in English and two in French, and both Trudeau and Mulcair agreed to participate in all of them. The first, the *Maclean's* event moderated by journalist Paul Wells, took place on 6 August, shortly after the writ was dropped.

The Liberals had been preparing for these debates for months. This was essential since, as one Liberal staffer admitted, Trudeau "was bad. He was overly theatrical." But he also took criticism well. Both Cyrus Reporter and Gerry Butts later stressed that he enjoyed being surrounded by strong people, worked hard, and was always trying to learn from his mistakes. He had absorbed huge piles of briefing notes and prepared the outlines of responses for various issues, which were then evaluated by his staff and improved. He was, in short, ready.

Polls demonstrated that Canadians had low expectations of Trudeau going into these events. As one Conservative commentator crudely put it, "if he comes onstage with his pants on he will probably exceed expectations."[50] Instead a fully clothed Trudeau rose to the occasion. In his first response, on economic policy, he took advantage of the opportunity to outline the Liberal economic plan in detail. And in his concluding remarks he looked directly into the camera and declared, "In order to know if someone is ready for this job, ask them what they would do with it, and why they want it in the first place." Then he went on to do precisely what Michael Ignatieff had failed to do. He explained why he wanted to be prime minister. "To lead this country you need to love this country, love it more than you crave power … I want my kids to grow up in the best country in the world. Mr. Harper and I part company on many issues, but our differences go deeper than policy … He wants you to believe that better just isn't possible … I think that's wrong. We are who we are, and Canada is what it is, because we've always known that better is always possible."

Trudeau's performance in the second debate, sponsored by the *Globe and Mail*, was arguably stronger. Most observers believed he had bested Stephen Harper while Tom Mulcair, strangely subdued and passive, trailed badly. He also did well in both French-language debates, and in particular scored points against the NDP with his adroit handling of the hijab controversy. In a dazzling pivot, he turned the issue onto Harper, arguing that Quebecers should vote to get rid of him because "you have more men in your caucus who oppose abortion than there are women in Quebec who wear the niqab."

However, it was in the fifth and final debate that Trudeau truly excelled. Held at the Munk School of Global Affairs, it was to focus primarily on foreign policy issues, not known as one of Trudeau's areas of strength. But his delivery was exceptional. As one commentator put it, "Even if you disagreed vehemently with his positions you couldn't deny that he delivered them with conviction. Throughout the night, he clearly articulated Liberal policies, [and] defended them passionately."[51] Even more striking was his spirited defence of the Charter of Rights and liberal values in response to a question from Tom Mulcair about Bill C-51, a response that resonated with the audience and with the media for several days afterwards.

Closing In

Apart from the debates, the Liberal leader was also doing well on the ground. It soon became obvious that he truly enjoyed his interactions with the general public, and they in turn were warming to him. Public opinion polls demonstrated that his popularity was increasing steadily throughout the campaign, which led organizers to schedule more events for him. One of the most striking was the massive rally in Brampton on 4 October, attended by more than five thousand enthusiastic Liberal supporters. It was this rally that the ad campaign designers chose to insert into the last of the three Liberal responses to the "not ready" ads.

There could be little doubt that his performance was a crucial element in the Liberals' rising fortunes. Coupled with the innovative ads and the solid platform, there was much to like about the party's offering in this campaign. By 6 September it appeared to be a much closer race, with the NDP at 32 per cent only two points ahead of the Liberals at 30 per cent, and the Conservatives not far behind at 26 per cent.[52]

In addition, the Liberals were helped by a number of missteps and gaffes by their opposition. Most notably, there was the almost inexplicable passivity of the NDP and their leader, Tom Mulcair, a man ordinarily known for his feisty personality and honed debating skills, who had somehow been sidelined in the actual debates. It would later emerge that this had been a deliberate strategy promoted by his closest advisers, who argued that he must above all appear statesmanlike and prime ministerial to avoid any suggestion that he and his party were radical socialists. "They were adamant that it was more important for Mulcair to calm voters than to excite them."[53]

Similarly Stephen Harper, whose handlers had attempted to enclose him in a bubble and render him as inaccessible as possible, had been instructed never to lose his temper or to look annoyed. Instead he tended to appear comatose. This was not the case with several of his ministers, however. Among them his immigration minister, Chris

Alexander, arguably committed the worst blunder by appearing completely insensitive to the suffering of migrants from war-torn regions of Africa and the Middle East who were trying to reach European countries on the Mediterranean. His apparent indifference to the fate of a small Syrian boy who had drowned, and whose image was broadcast around the world, was a key moment in the decline and fall of the Harper government when Justin Trudeau took up the cause and pledged to bring two hundred thousand Syrians to Canada before the end of the year.

Later, as the Conservatives continued to fall in the polls, it would also be Harper who would hinder his cause as he returned to the issue of the niqab with a vengeance, and appeared at events in Ontario with the controversial Ford brothers. Meanwhile his minister for the status of women, Kellie Leitch, proposed a "snitch line" for Canadians to report immigrants guilty of "barbaric cultural practices," a move that further alienated many previously uncommitted voters.

At the same time, it is important to note the support provided to the Liberals by the Ontario government of Premier Kathleen Wynne. An ardent opponent of the Harper Conservatives who had crossed swords with them on a number of files, Wynne was determined to break with tradition and campaign directly with and for Trudeau. (Provincial premiers would not normally support a political party so openly in a federal election for fear of obvious consequences if their choice was not successful. However, as the final numbers demonstrated, her support – and her party's organization – were undoubtedly a significant factor in the end in the Liberals' victory in several Ontario ridings.)

But still the numbers did not move significantly throughout that time. By early September there were increasing fears among progressives that there would be a three-way tie and that this would lead to a Conservative minority rather than either an NDP or Liberal government. Clearly it was imperative for the Liberals to break the logjam by distinguishing themselves once and for all from the NDP. With only weeks to go in the election campaign, they would need to do something dramatic, and quickly.

Breakthrough: Rejecting the Neocon Parable at Last

When the Liberals announced their plan to increase taxes on the top 1 per cent of income earners in late August they were roundly criticized not only by the Conservatives but also by the NDP. Intent on appearing responsible and safe, the NDP offered balanced budgets. They also offered a number of social program initiatives that Justin Trudeau was quick to note would not come into force for many years, when the deficit had been eliminated.

The Liberals had expected this criticism of their tax increase on the top 1 per cent and had decided that it was a risk worth taking. However, they had also offered a number of new programs of their own. Their costing document, they said, would be released only when all of their platform planks had been announced. This deliberate strategy of delay proved to be the key to their ultimate victory. It was apparent, with only a few weeks left in the campaign, that support for the NDP was not dropping, nor was their own support rising sufficiently. At this point, the team decided to implement a plan they had held in reserve. They would announce that they would run relatively small deficits for a few years in order to finance important infrastructure projects that they considered a prudent investment in Canada's economy. In other words, the Liberals had now announced that they would raise taxes *and* run deficits, in defiance of the prevailing mantra of small government championed by the Conservatives and respected by the NDP.

Pundits, Liberal insiders, and the polls themselves demonstrated conclusively that this was the breakthrough moment for the party in this campaign. Within days the Liberals had soared to 36 per cent in the polls while the NDP was at 29 per cent and the Conservatives at 24 per cent.[54] From then until the end of the campaign the Liberals maintained their lead. It would be the Liberals, not the NDP, whom voters perceived to be the agents of change.

Days before the end of the campaign it was clear that a landslide might be in the making. Even the last-minute revelation that Liberal campaign co-chair Dan Gagnier had stepped down over problematic briefings to clients did not affect the Liberal groundswell, partly because of the simultaneous news stories concerning Stephen Harper's appearance with the controversial Ford brothers in Ontario.

On 18 October the Liberal Party of Canada returned to power with a sizeable majority, having received 39.1 per cent of the vote while support for the NDP collapsed to 19 per cent. The party that had started the campaign in third place had astonished the pundits by beating the odds and standing conventional wisdom on its head.

The Liberals won 184 seats, up from the 36 they held after the 2011 election. They more than doubled their share of the popular vote. And they took sizable numbers of seats across the country, making them once more a national presence. Having swept all of the seats in the four Atlantic provinces, they took the majority of seats in Ontario and Quebec, including predominantly francophone areas of the province, and achieved pluralities in Manitoba and British Columbia. Even in Alberta, a traditional wasteland for the party, they managed to capture 4 seats.

There were many reasons for the Liberal victory. Some were immediate, as this chapter has outlined. Some depended on the actions of the party while in opposition over nearly a decade. Without question, those rebuilding and modernization efforts had paid off. This time the Liberals had won both the air war and the ground war. In addition, the polling data confirmed that the party's decision to break with the neo-conservative mantra of balanced budgets and low taxes was of paramount importance. This time the Liberals had not only put forward an appealing platform but a credible way in which to finance it. This in turn gave them the appearance of competent managers, something that had been lacking for so long.

Perhaps most important, leader Justin Trudeau had far exceeded the low expectations that the Conservatives had set for him with the general public. As polling data demonstrated, his standing in each of six categories used in surveys to evaluate "leader image" increased over the course of the campaign; he was the only leader who saw such an improvement. Most noticeable, increases occurred in the categories of "good ideas," where his rating went from 34 per cent to 41 per cent (suggesting again the importance of the platform), and "ready to be prime minister," where it increased from 29 per cent to 38 per cent.[55] In addition his image benefited from his insistence on taking the high road and stressing "sunny ways," as well as the fact that he had taken every possible opportunity to remind voters of the underlying purpose and distinctiveness of his political party, its Liberal/liberal values. The importance of this last point could be clearly seen in the data, which showed the dramatic return of the substantial number of Liberal voters who had stayed home in 2011.

An EKOS/Canada 2020 poll released a month after the election confirmed that the Liberals won in large measure because, as president Frank Graves put it, once the Liberals neutralized the Conservative parable, "the election shifted from being one about the economy to an historic one about values."[56] His findings were corroborated by a comprehensive Ensight study, "The Back to the Future Election," which found that "voters made a deliberate decision to restore the values they view as traditionally defining Canada and Canadian society ... They embraced Justin Trudeau's agenda of hope and optimism at the core of what they perceive as the values traditionally defining Canada." Moreover, the Harper Conservatives were specifically rejected for what voters described as their "Reform or Tea Party style and substance." Similarly, the study found that "Canadians reported a lack of trust in the commitments of [Tom] Mulcair, raising a nagging concern the NDP were, in fact, socialists. As a result the NDP's return to third-party status was seen as an appropriate outcome.[57]

There can be no doubt that the Liberal Party that stormed to victory in 2015 bore little resemblance to the one that fell victim to the Harper Conservatives in 2006. Virtually all of the five issues outlined in the first chapter had been addressed successfully, albeit to greater or lesser degrees. Its vibrant membership, active riding associations, state-of-the-art technology, and healthy fundraising machine once again made it the envy of the other political parties. Its broad representation across the country and healthy hold on its restored Quebec fortress, meanwhile, demonstrated the initial success of the efforts to rebuild its base. From an also-ran it recreated itself as a campaign machine role model, a new version of the Big Red Machine.

But would this be sufficient? Had the party of Justin Trudeau reinvented liberalism for the twenty-first century in a durable way? Or would the departure of Stephen Harper render some of the Liberals' selling points in 2015 obsolescent? Would the new generation of Liberal politicians, most without much relevant experience, prove capable of meeting the challenges of a particularly difficult time? Would the party's gains in regional representation withstand the inevitable strains that occur in a large and diverse federation? In short, had Canadians returned to a status quo in which the Liberal Party of Canada was once again the natural governing party?

9 Trudeau Takes Charge: Creating A New Liberal Dynasty?

Because it's 2015!
> – Rt Hon. Justin Trudeau, 4 November 2015

In Canada, better is always possible.
> – Rt Hon. Justin Trudeau, 19 October 2015

On 25 October 2018, many legendary veterans of the Liberal Party of Canada came together in the ballroom of the Chateau Laurier hotel in Ottawa. The scene of so many previous Liberal celebrations, including Pierre Trudeau's memorable return to power in 1980 ("Welcome to the 1980s") and Justin Trudeau's 2013 leadership win ("Sunny ways, hope and hard work"), the venue was once again chosen to mark a special occasion. This time, it was a by-invitation-only soirée celebrating the twenty-fifth anniversary of the party's return to power in 1993 under Jean Chrétien, after nine years in the wilderness during Brian Mulroney's two Progressive Conservative majorities. Some faces in the room were clearly too young to remember that momentous event personally, but no one was complaining. Indeed, the hundreds of Liberal faithful gathered in the room were having a wonderful time reminiscing about the many high points in an election that saw the party return to power for three straight majority governments over the next decade.

The star of the evening was, of course, Jean Chrétien. At eighty-four he showed few signs of slowing down. After an introduction by Chrétien *éminence grise* John Rae, Prime Minister Justin Trudeau added his recollections of encounters with Chrétien when his father Pierre was prime minister. Undoubtedly anxious to associate his government's prospects in the upcoming 2019 election with Chrétien's earlier success, Trudeau went on to make a number of comparisons between the achievements of the Chrétien government and his own. In particular, he drew a link between Chrétien's contributions on social progress and national unity and his more recent initiatives in the same vein. He stressed the common liberal values the two promoted during their time in office, such as tolerance and diversity, equality of opportunity, and multilateralism.

In his remarks that evening Chrétien spoke with passion about some of his government's most notable achievements that reflected those values. These included the Clarity Act, the refusal to participate in the American-led Iraq war, and the introduction of new social programs such as the Child Tax Benefit and the Millennium Scholarships. The former prime minister also underlined the importance of managerial competence and the Liberals' "balanced" approach to governing, so often derided by critics as the mushy middle. He noted that his government's elimination of the massive deficit it inherited had been followed by a widely promoted policy of devoting half of the so-called deficit dividend[1] to new program expenditures and the other half to deficit reduction and tax cuts. This popular decision, he argued, allowed the Liberals to retain the confidence of voters about their ability to manage the economy. Finally, Chrétien delivered a rousing call to arms to Liberals to maintain the momentum begun in 2015. The Liberal Party, he warned, can only win when it remains true to those liberal values.

While critics might differ with Chrétien's interpretation of his legacy,[2] they could hardly dispute the result, an unprecedented three consecutive Liberal majorities. But, as this book has demonstrated, the success of a political party can be transitory. Without the ability to adapt liberal values to new situations and changing times, and without the financial and operational resources necessary to put forward new ideas in a convincing fashion, even the once-mighty Liberal Party could lose its perceived relevance. As we have seen, political scientist Bruce Doern's statement after the 2000 election that "Jean Chrétien stands astride the Canadian political scene without much opposition at the federal level" and his further speculation concerning "the degree to which a one-party state is congealing at the federal level"[3] were soon disproven by the results of the 2004 and 2006 elections. For most of the next decade the Liberal Party was a spent force, in real danger of disappearing from the political scene.

The 2015 election confirmed that the Liberals had once again reinvented themselves. This was a major accomplishment that should not be underestimated given the difficulties the party faced and overcame in such a short period of time. Although the Liberal Party's brand was still strong after its string of defeats between 2006 and 2015, it could only succeed as a result of the major overhaul of its machinery and operating procedures that took place over that brief period, an overhaul that was long overdue.

Change took place structurally and organizationally, but values were also reinforced. Without doubt the selection of a charismatic leader was an important additional factor in the party's return to power. However, an essential element of the leader's appeal was precisely his commitment to liberal values, and his updated application of those values in new circumstances. Nor was Trudeau the one-dimensional superficial messiah some had feared, proving himself both competent and "ready."

After the 2015 election the extra-parliamentary wing of the Liberal Party continued to improve its operations and outreach to members and potential supporters. By 2018 an additional 134,000 Canadians had registered as supporters under the new membership rules discussed below. The party's fundraising was increasingly successful as well, although it continued to lag behind the Conservatives. Meanwhile, the Trudeau government immediately reinforced liberal values with a number of symbolic appointments and statements. It also delivered on many promised initiatives and performed well on a number of files. But its progress in some areas was unexpectedly slow, and it stumbled over the implementation of other promises as well as committing a number of own-goal gaffes. Some would argue the party's unfortunate tendency towards a sense of entitlement and moral superiority also re-emerged on occasion. Trudeau himself exhibited several lapses in judgment that reinforced this impression. In addition, Trudeau's government was obliged to confront a number of serious unforeseen challenges that not only posed problems in their own right, but inevitably hampered the implementation of the original Liberal agenda.

By the end of 2018 the obvious question was whether the performance of the Trudeau government would be sufficient to return the Liberal Party to power for another four years, suggesting the emergence of another Liberal dynasty.[4] Or would the combination of the government's and leader's problematic performance issues, along with the party's acknowledged failure to establish deeper roots in significant regions and demographic sectors of the country, mean that the Trudeau Liberals' stunning 2015 electoral success was a one-time event, as some scholars argued?[5]

For the pessimists Trudeau's victory was primarily the result of voters' intense desire to replace the Harper Conservatives at all costs, rather than a return to Liberal hegemony. In their view, Trudeau and his party were the beneficiaries of the same "anyone but Harper" scenario that had seen Jack Layton and the NDP vault into second place in the 2011 election, only to return to earth in 2015. Even the optimists, who disagreed with this analysis and argued that the Liberals won on their own merits, admitted that the leader and the party had become the victims of extremely high if not unrealistic expectations, something Trudeau had fostered through his optimistic pledge that "better is always possible." Both camps, however, agreed that the next election in 2019 would likely provide the definitive answer. This chapter therefore examines the record of the Trudeau Liberals during their first mandate in terms of the progress made on the underlying issues the party faced in 2006 as well as new issues that arose since 2015.

Fundraising for the Future

If there was one area in which the Liberals did not ease off on their efforts to rebuild and improve their party operations after the 2015 election, it was fundraising. With Christina Topp continuing to lead the charge as senior director, fundraising, at the Liberals' Albert Street headquarters in Ottawa, the party ceaselessly underlined to its supporters the importance of having sufficient financial resources to tackle the Conservatives' propaganda machine. By the end of 2018, although the Liberals still had not achieved parity, they had made significant strides in closing the gap. However, this progress was not linear. In 2016 the Liberal Party raised $17.2 million, a banner year – particularly since it was the year following an election campaign. But in 2017 that total fell to only $13.9 million, the party's worst showing since Justin Trudeau became leader.

By contrast, the opposition Conservatives actually increased their revenue in 2017 over 2016, to $18.8 million.[6] The Conservatives also outpaced the Liberals in terms of total number of contributions, with 94,786 individual donors compared to 64,444 for the governing Liberals. Since the Liberals had gone to great lengths to obtain more members and supporters through their various constitutional and practical changes, this was a sobering reality. With such known individuals generally forming the core of volunteers for election campaigns, or for developing targeted messaging, this gap was especially discouraging. Worse still, the Liberal Party ran a small operating deficit for the 2017 fiscal year as its expenditures exceeded revenue by roughly $425,000, and the party's war chest was reduced to only $1.6 million. What happened?

One explanation for the reversal of fortunes was the party's own decision in mid-2016 to eliminate membership fees. In 2015 this revenue source alone had produced some $2.2 million for the party's coffers. By foregoing this income the party had effectively imposed even greater demands on its direct mail and online revenue sources to make up the difference, something the Conservatives had chosen not to do. (In 2017 that party earned $3.5 million in membership fees.) In addition, Conservative coffers were enriched by some $7 million that year due to the leadership campaign that resulted in the election of Andrew Scheer, artificially increasing the revenue gap for 2017.

Still, by 2018 the Liberals appeared to have made up some of the lost revenue from membership dues. By the end of the third quarter, in October 2018, the party had raised $10.2 million, and the third quarter revenue alone was a record amount. Another positive note for the Liberals involved the increase in small donors (under $200), which had soared to 96 per cent of all contributions. The median donation, as party president Suzanne Cowan gleefully reported, was actually $10, an almost unbelievable situation given the party's dependence on large corporate and wealthy donors only a few years earlier.[7] At the same time the party continued to expand both its Laurier Club (whose members donated the maximum legally allowable individual contribution of $1,500) and Victory Fund memberships, which provided another important revenue stream.

Perhaps the most encouraging news for the Liberals was that their new fundraising practices were more efficient than those of the Conservatives. The Liberals spent only 19 per cent of their revenue on fundraising activities, whereas the Conservatives devoted fully 38 per cent of their revenue to such activities. This meant that the Liberals earned $5.14 for every dollar they spent, while the Conservatives obtained only $2.62 for each dollar expended on fundraising.

The party's communications emphasized their greatly increased revenue in the third quarter of 2018 as a positive sign of things to come. "Not only did we reach our ambitious end-of-Q3 goal," one memo trumpeted, "but we had our best Q3 ever online fundraising outside of an election campaign, with thousands of digital donors chipping in and helping us surpass our goals in July, August and September."[8] As Christina Topp said in a personal letter to major donors, "Thanks to the help of 4,200 supporters like you who helped us raise $347,127 online this past month alone, we're well on our way to closing the gap with the Conservative fundraising machine and building our strongest-ever campaign in 2019."[9]

As a further incentive the party instituted a "$400K for 400 days" fundraising campaign to highlight the time remaining until the 2019 election. The party's communications emphasized the uses to which the funds would be put, stressing preparations for the upcoming election campaign such as "building and training our campaign teams, ensuring our volunteers have the most innovative campaign tools, and equipping our regional offices and organizers with every resource they need on the road to 2019."[10]

The Liberal missives also cited the need to respond to the Conservatives' never-ending attack ads, which had become an entrenched part of their "permanent campaign" mentality precisely because they had the funds to pursue them.[11] (As an example the Liberals pointed to digital pamphlets the Conservatives had recently distributed, designed in the style of British tabloids. Their incendiary rhetoric accused the prime minister of personally ceding control of Canada's borders, abandoning the oil and gas sector, destroying full-time jobs, and allowing terrorists to wander in and out of the country at will.) Elections Canada reports indicated the Conservatives had spent more than $900,000 on such advertising in 2017 alone, despite being at the midpoint between two elections.

The Liberal Party ended 2018 with nearly $2 million more than the year before but still far short of their opponents. The significance of this situation became clear when details of the parties' activities were broken down. On the one hand the Conservatives showed an operating surplus of $3.6 million, net assets of $5.1 million, and an astonishing $9.9 million cash on hand. On the other hand the Liberals reported an operating surplus of only $4,000, net assets worth $1.7 million, and $2.3 million in cash on hand.

As aforementioned, however, an important distinction between the Liberal Party of Canada and its adversaries is the federal nature of its organization, which permits various streams of fundraising. In the past this had been the source of considerable frustration, but with the constitutional changes implemented over the past few years the situation had actually been turned to their advantage. The Liberals raised by far the most money at the riding level in comparison with the Conservatives, a direct consequence of the party's newly instituted candidate nomination criteria discussed below. While 201 local Liberal associations reported that they had raised some $4.6 million by the end of 2018, more than 262 Conservative associations were only able to raise $4 million, or roughly one-third less than the Liberals per riding.

The fundraising gap between the two parties continued in the first two quarters of 2019 (the last available before the election), despite increased pressure from the Liberals on their base. The party reported it had raised $3.9 million in the first quarter (an actual drop in revenue most Liberals attributed directly to the SNC Lavalin affair discussed below) but a record-breaking $5 million in the second, for a total of $8.9 million in the first half of 2019. However, the Conservatives raised twice as much in the same period.

Perhaps not surprisingly, Liberal party president Suzanne Cowan issued an appeal to Laurier Club members in late August, asking them to contact other potential club donors as a means of raising more funds quickly. Referring to the "action-packed" summer of activities drawing to a close, and noting that "each of the last five months has set a new record for grassroots Liberal fundraising," Cowan nevertheless stressed that much more work needed to be done to ensure the party could "invest in innovative tools and training and ... run strong competitive campaigns across the country." She concluded by asking members to pass her message on to individuals who might be potential new contributors to the Laurier Club.[12]

One area of ongoing concern for the party was the need to address growing public disapproval of the long-standing practice of political parties holding fundraisers, usually at the riding level, with senior members of government or the party as the drawing card and lobbyists in attendance. This perceived "cash for access" problem had recently plagued several provincial governments[13] and soon became a source of controversy for the Trudeau Liberals as well. After one such event in Vancouver in November 2016 (attended by the prime minister and several wealthy prominent Chinese investors) drew widespread criticism,[14] the government announced it would introduce new internal party rules governing such events. It did so in early 2017. The changes included advance public notice of fundraisers, full disclosure of attendance lists, and exclusion of lobbyists from fundraisers with the exception of "donor-appreciation events" such as Laurier Club receptions, where any lobbyists who attended were required to sign an agreement stating that they were attending in their personal capacity only. While the new rules were seen as modest progress by some, many critics, including Duff Conacher of Democracy Watch, concluded they were insufficient and in fact provided a loophole for lobbyists to circumvent the system.[15] Nevertheless Democratic Institutions Minister Karina Gould noted that the Liberals were the only party disclosing such information about their fundraisers, and pledged to expand the rules to include other political parties.[16] This was done in December 2018 with the passage of Bill C-50.

Meanwhile, as part of their 2015 democratic reform platform the Liberals introduced Bill C-76, an act to amend a number of features of the Canada Elections Act. This bill also came into effect in late 2018, in time for the 2019 election. Among the changes was the introduction of a new "pre-writ period" beginning on 30 June, when parties would be strictly limited in their expenditures on such items as advertising, over and above the existing limitations on spending during the campaign period. This move, widely discussed before the last election and recommended by the chief electoral officer, restricted but did not entirely prevent the permanent campaign activities perfected by the Conservatives.[17] It also limited third-party-advertising expenditures, an important area of concern for some time, although subsequent events would prove that these provisions in the legislation were inadequate.[18]

Given these improvements to level the playing field, many Liberal organizers were much less concerned with the Conservatives' fundraising edge this time around. "You can only spend so much. We have more than enough to finance the campaign and some pre-election ads," one insider confided. Communications experts tended to agree. While television remained the most expensive medium for advertising, it was rapidly becoming less important as a means of reaching undecided or leaning voters. By contrast, the increasing usage and importance of alternative digital media means "a relatively small amount of well-placed money can reach target voters, and in some cases messaging can spread organically with no money behind it at all."[19] In 2015 the Liberals had broken new ground in this area, and they planned to make even greater use of it in 2019.

For the Liberals, then, the more important issue now was preparing the party for the broad brushstrokes of an election campaign. This was particularly important because this time they were the government. The leader and his caucus would be on the defensive, forced to defend their record, a very different situation from 2015. Moreover, while the Conservatives' fundraising edge might be of less use in terms of advertising, it could certainly ensure a well-run and technologically advanced campaign. The Liberals had held the edge on this in 2015, but they had no real way of knowing if the Conservatives had caught up.

Taking Charge of the Big Red Machine

Many veteran Liberals had assumed the Liberal Party's constitutional reforms were over after the 2013 leadership race, at least for the foreseeable future. After all, major changes implemented in 2008 and again in 2012 had streamlined the party's organization, introduced a one-person/one-vote leadership selection process rather than a delegated convention, and opened up the party to a "supporter" category, a risky and dramatic move at the time but one that Justin Trudeau had argued was necessary to reinvigorate Canadian democracy and encourage young Canadians to participate.

Yet in late May 2016, barely seven months after his stunning electoral success, Justin Trudeau was once again pushing the envelope on party reform. This time he had the very concept of a party membership in his sights. Still concerned about the need to engage young Canadians in the political process, he referred to the success of the supporter category as a step in the right direction and argued it should now be reinforced. He took personal ownership of the plan to allow anyone who wanted to register as a Liberal to vote in leadership and nomination races and attend party conventions.

In addition to these innovations Trudeau also championed proposed amendments to the constitution that provided significantly greater discretion on the part of the leader and party executive through their ability to draft by-laws with respect to registration, policy development, riding associations, and PTAs, apparently without consultation with the affected party elites. As de Clercy has outlined, while all parties in Canada give extensive powers to the leader, the Liberals' 2012 constitutional amendments had already provided for even greater control, and these latest modifications continued the shift in that direction.[20]

Perhaps not surprisingly, these constitutional reforms were introduced and strongly supported by party president Anna Gainey, Trudeau's long-time friend and 2015 campaign adviser, demonstrating the wisdom of Trudeau's determination to avoid the problems of Chrétien and Turner by ensuring the volunteer wing of the party was led by individuals who supported him.[21] According to Gainey, all of the changes would help to further "modernize" the party. "We are trying to be more nimble, more flexible and this new constitution will do that. We are already looking to 2019 and we want to be more aerodynamic."[22]

Trudeau's plan also was strongly supported by former interim leader Bob Rae. Rae argued that "a great political party is not a club, it's not a private organization. It is an organization that is sustained by its relationship to the people around it and the people around us are the people of Canada."[23]

But this plan was a bridge too far for many long-standing party activists, who feared a serious loss of control to the executive. They organized a concerted opposition to it well in advance of the convention held in Winnipeg on 26–28 May. This opposition may have been unexpected but it was quickly addressed. Trudeau aides and party staffers fanned out to lobby members and urge support for the motion, leading some members to complain of intimidation tactics and bullying. Nevertheless, the night before the scheduled vote on the plan many party officials were not convinced that it would pass.

It required Trudeau's personal intervention, and last-minute amendments to the proposal, to achieve the required support. Speaking to delegates in advance of the vote the next morning, Trudeau tried to address their concerns. Sounding remarkably like his father, who had opened up the party more than forty years earlier by calling for a participatory democracy that included a more diverse and representative Liberal Party, Trudeau tackled the opposition to his plan head on. His rationale was particularly revealing, suggesting that in his case participatory democracy was certainly one objective, but not the only one. Calling the existing constitution a "hodge-podge" that "empowers bureaucracy and creates conflict and distance between us," Trudeau argued that "most important for me, and for any future leader of the party, it creates distance between the leader and the grassroots."[24]

But avoiding the takeover of the party apparatus by hostile forces, as had happened to Jean Chrétien when Martin supporters waged a successful campaign to replace him as leader, was clearly another. For Liberals, the path to victory had always been predicated on party unity, and the Chrétien-Martin wars had taken a huge toll on the party's image. Trudeau specifically argued that the constitution in force "is a product of the era we worked so hard, together, to put behind us: the era of factional battles and hyphenated Liberals, of regional chieftans and behind-the-scenes power-brokers, of the closed, insular thinking that almost killed this party."[25]

In the end the new constitution was adopted and the party moved on to other issues, including the election of a new executive. Anna Gainey was returned for a second two-year term as president. Her fellow staffer on the Trudeau leadership and election campaigns, Suzanne Cowan, was elected vice-president (English) while Sebastien Fassier, a digital communications specialist and former Trudeau campaign worker who had handled the leaders' debates, was elected vice-president (French). In short, Trudeau had effectively taken control of the party apparatus, ensuring there would be no repeat of the Martin palace coup on his watch.

Along with Christina Topp, the acting national director, this group was charged with consultations before the drafting of the controversial by-laws. Reiterating Trudeau's commitment to make the party "the most open and innovative movement in Canadian politics," Gainey stated that "one of our first orders of business is to consult with registered Liberals" about the by-laws. These consultations were to occur over the summer in order to enable the by-laws to be in place for the fall of 2016.[26]

The party apparatus was soon challenged to put the changes into effect. It was faced with the organization of eleven Liberal nomination meetings and campaigns for by-elections in 2017: five in April, two in October, and yet another four in December. In the first set, two Alberta ridings had long been held by the Conservatives and were expected to be retained by them. But the three ridings already held by the Liberals proved more problematic for the same reasons as had been identified during the run-up to the 2015 election. Although all three seats were ultimately retained by the party with sizeable majorities, the nomination battles proved divisive for the party. And in each case the cause was the identification of a star candidate preferred by the leader, despite the party's formal position that all nomination battles were fair and open, with no interference from the executive or the leader. Once again Justin Trudeau's earlier commitment to an arm's-length process came back to haunt him.

In Markham-Thornhill, former Kennedy adviser and Trudeau PMO staffer Mary Ng faced considerable controversy as the "star" candidate who was actually parachuted into the riding, despite the presence of another well-known local Liberal candidate. While Ng prevailed for the nomination after a tumultuous meeting, an even more damaging tussle occurred in Saint-Laurent, where the leader's candidate, former Quebec provincial cabinet minister Yolande James, was defeated by furious riding members in favour of a relative unknown, Emmanuella Lambropoulos, a twenty-six-year-old schoolteacher.

The executive's situation was particularly difficult since in each case there were other women candidates vying for the nomination and the leader could not justify intervention in the name of gender parity. Still, party communications director Braeden Caley issued a statement declaring "this is the most open political party in the country."[27] As one senior reporter covering the Markham nomination battle noted, the problem was not the decision to promote star candidates, a common practice in all parties, but the Liberals' insistence that this was not the case. "If you are going to parachute a star candidate into a riding, admit you are doing it. Don't pretend you're an open political party when patently you are not."[28]

Happily for the Liberals, the October by-elections were free of such controversy. They also produced an unexpectedly positive result for the party. Although the Alberta riding in play was retained by the Conservatives, they lost their hold on the Quebec riding of Lac-Saint-Jean. Instead, Liberal candidate Richard Hébert delivered a convincing upset victory for the party, while the Conservatives' flag-bearer finished a distant second. Since by-elections typically see the governing party suffer some defeats, this reversal of fortunes for the opposition Conservatives was particularly encouraging, as was the eventual result of the four December by-elections. Both the Liberals and the Conservatives retained their two seats each. This meant the governing Liberals not only retained all of their seats but added one in what they hoped would be their reclaimed Quebec stronghold. Perhaps even more importantly, the party's organizers and technical team believed the by-elections allowed them to test drive new add-on technology they had improved upon from 2015, and which they believed would stand them in good stead in the 2019 election.

Also in December 2017 the party announced the appointment of its new national director after a four-month search. Azam Ishmael, who had served as the party's get-out-the-vote director during the 2015 election campaign, was selected to run the party headquarters and lead preparations for the 2019 election. Described by the press release announcing his appointment as a "leading campaign mobilization expert" whose record of service included both the Nova Scotia and Ontario Liberal governments, Ishmael's appointment reflected the party's shift in focus from fundraising (job well done) to election readiness (still work to do).

These positive developments led up to the next biennial convention of the party, held in Halifax 19–21 April 2018. The agenda for that convention, which in earlier times would have concentrated on policy development, was unapologetically focused on election readiness. Of some forty workshops and panels over the three-day event, roughly half were devoted to aspects of party organization and election planning, most of which were presented by a group of Trudeau aides and advisers referred to as the "Team Trudeau Hub." These sessions covered such topics as "Campaign Planning," "The LPC Nomination Process and Recruiting a Candidate," "Grassroots Fundraising," "Organizing a Day of Action," "Party Constitution and By-laws," "Invite Her to Run and Help Her Win," "Volunteers and Growing our Movement," "Youth Engagement," and "Hope and Hard Work on the Campaign Trail." In addition, one plenary session was devoted to an in-depth conversation between Trudeau chief of staff Gerald Butts and former president Barrack Obama's chief strategist, American political consultant David Axelrod, who was credited with orchestrating Obama's stunning victory in large part by mastering new voter identification technology.

The convention also saw the election of a new slate of national officers. Suzanne Cowan, another well-connected Trudeau Liberal and daughter of Senator James Cowan, replaced departing president Anna Gainey, again emphasizing the important role women were increasingly playing in the volunteer wing of the party. In fact the executive as whole perfectly reflected the sea change that had taken place within the party since Trudeau's selection as leader. The new party leadership – a collection of forty-something or younger professionals, including several women and representatives of a variety of ethnocultural communities – epitomized the generational and cultural change that Trudeau had advocated when seeking the leadership, and in recruiting a slate of Liberal candidates for the 2015 election.

Assembling "Team Trudeau" 2019

Demographic change was clearly reflected in the team of Liberal candidates Trudeau had assembled for the 2015 election: the youngest, most diverse group with the most female candidates the party had ever fielded. Some 184 of those candidates were successful and became sitting MPs, although that number was slightly reduced, to 177, over the next four years due to deaths and resignations for a variety of reasons, including diplomatic appointments and illness in the family. In June 2018 the party announced that these incumbents would be acclaimed, providing they met certain basic conditions on fundraising and voter engagement. These included participating in at least two Day of Action engagements, where together with volunteers they would commit to a minimum of thirty-five hundred doors knocked or five thousand telephone calls made, and obtaining the signatures of 150 registered Liberals in their riding who supported their candidacy, as well as having raised at least 50 per cent of the funds required for the 2019 local campaign. For those MPS who had fulfilled these requirements the nomination meetings were expected to take place over the summer.

On 27 June 2018 Innovation and Economic Development Minister Navdeep Bains became the first MP to be acclaimed, at a meeting attended personally by the prime minister. In short order more than half of the caucus were also acclaimed, including Trudeau himself at a meeting in his riding of Papineau on 19 August. By 30 November, with less than eleven months left until the election, the Liberals had confirmed the candidacy of 150 caucus members. (By comparison, the Conservatives had nominated 161 candidates, including sitting MPs, but the NDP trailed badly with only 25 confirmed candidate nominations.)

On 31 August the remaining 155 non-held ridings were also opened up by the Liberal Party for nomination meetings. Here, too, a significant number of conditions needed to be met before the meeting date would be scheduled. These included a requirement that the local riding association have deposited in a bank account at least 15 per cent of the allowable expense limit for the election campaign, that the riding have a minimum of 150 registered Liberals, and that the local executive had conducted and documented a serious search for female candidates. Nomination meetings in those ridings the party did not hold were expected to be scheduled throughout the late fall of 2018 and early winter of 2019.

The drive to achieve gender parity was reinforced by the National Women's Liberal Commission, which held special campaign colleges across the country to encourage more women to participate as candidates and party officials. In Ontario, for example, the party held a three-hour online campaign college for prospective candidates in mid-October, providing information on the 2019 nomination procedures and inviting registrants to engage in a question-and-answer session with several experienced women candidates.

At a special caucus meeting in Saskatoon in September 2018, Suzanne Cowan concluded that the party's preparations were proceeding apace and expressed confidence in the state of their campaign planning. "We're feeling in good shape, both on the ground and here, with our caucus team," she said. "I'm feeling very optimistic about where we're at."[29]

Cowan's optimism was understandable, but the fact that the party was now in power was a two-edged sword. On the one hand the Liberals had resources they did not possess in 2015, and the added advantage of a lengthy planning period unaffected by the need for a single-minded focus on fundraising or the selection of a new leader. On the other hand, as is almost always the case when a party takes office, some of the key Liberals who had been involved in that earlier campaign were now in positions of responsibility in the government and would not be able to turn their attention to election readiness until much closer to the actual start of the campaign. This would have been true even if unexpected issues had not arisen to distract them.

For some of the new-generation Liberals, their lack of experience in government led to unrealistic expectations that the party's election readiness organization would follow a similar trajectory to that of 2015. In fact, as 2018 drew to a close there had already been murmurs of concern from some Liberal activists about what they perceived to be the party's slow start to election readiness this time. "It's critical to have the full campaign structure in place well in advance … especially when the government is expecting a tough and nasty fight in the upcoming election."[30]

One measure of the Liberals' difficulties was in full view by June of 2019, when their fast-tracking of candidate nominations appeared to have stalled. If a party wanted to field a full slate (and therefore spend the maximum allowable amount during the campaign) it would need nominated candidates in all 338 ridings. Yet by 10 June, barely five months before election day, it was the Conservatives who had nominated 277 candidates. Even more astonishing was the fact that Maxime Bernier's People's Party had chosen 217 candidates. The Liberals trailed badly, with only 197 nominated candidates, almost all of whom were sitting MPs. Yet even among these incumbents the formal nomination process dragged on. It was not until 26 August 2019, or more than a year after the process had begun, that the last of the Liberals' incumbent MPs who planned to run again – former cabinet minister Bob Nault – was formally nominated. (Quebec Liberal MP Eva Nassif [Vimy] had indicated only days earlier that she would not seek re-election, a decision that several weeks later she attributed to pressure from party headquarters over her failure to support the leader, although that accusation was strongly denied.)[31]

An important reason for the slow process in non-held ridings was the new requirement for riding associations to conduct a serious search for women candidates, as mentioned above. As national campaign director Jeremy Broadhurst noted, experience had shown that women typically are more reticent to put their names forward and it is often necessary to approach a possible candidate numerous times before they will commit. "Patience is definitely the watch word," Broadhurst said. "I can tell you that they had to go to my former boss, Chrystia Freeland, eight or nine times before she finally agreed to run."[32] (In the end 39 per cent of the party's candidates, and 48 per cent of their new candidates, were women, roughly a 10 per cent increase, as president Suzanne Cowan proudly noted.)[33]

Another major reason for the delay in ridings the party did not already hold was the unusually high number of potential candidates. With the party in power, more individuals were inclined to seek a nomination. "We have seen more potential candidates expressing interest than we've ever seen before," senior director of communications Braeden Caley explained.[34] According to Caley, more than five hundred individuals had requested nomination forms for the 141 ridings the Liberals did not already hold. The high number of Liberal hopefuls meant that far more individuals would have to be vetted by the party this time than in 2015. This vetting has become an essential element of party credibility in the age of social media, and the Liberals were determined to do everything possible to prevent embarrassing revelations once the campaign began. On 17 July 2019 they announced that a former chief of staff to MP Bill Graham, Toronto lawyer Suh Kim, would serve as the national chair of the green-light committee. (Kim had served as co-chair of the Ontario committee in 2015 when long-time party legal adviser Jack Siegel served as national chair.)

By the end of July the party had nominated a total of 258 candidates in held and non-held ridings, still leaving another eighty ridings unrepresented with little more than a month remaining before the prime minister was expected to officially begin the election campaign. Not surprisingly, the slow progress was becoming a concern for senior party organizers and those around the leader.

As a result, on 10 August the party invoked its "national electoral urgency clause," which allowed the party to bypass nomination rules and appoint candidates if necessary. According to one senior party official, this was a "long-standing" administrative measure that "always" comes into effect this close to an election "to help finalize the last few steps of the Liberal nominations process." He noted that it was triggered ahead of the 2015 election as well.[35] Nevertheless, many of the declared aspirants expressed alarm, fearing this measure had been enacted in order to ensure preferred candidates were nominated, especially in safe seats or winnable ridings. However, nomination meetings featuring several candidates continued to proceed up to and beyond the start of the election campaign on 11 September, and few were controversial. One reason was that there were only a handful of "star" candidates this time, as opposed to 2015. These included Olympic kayaker Adam van Koeverden and former provincial Liberal minister Marie-France Lalonde in Ontario and well-known environmental activist Steven Guilbault in Quebec.

Still, the Conservatives announced a full slate of candidates had been nominated by 3 September when the Liberals were eighteen short, causing another flurry of panic among some Liberal insiders. While the optics may have been problematic, as one party insider confided, this situation was primarily the result of the party's difficulties in finding individuals willing to run in ridings in southern Alberta, which were known to be unwinnable.[36]

The 2019 Liberal Campaign Team: 2015 Redux

Many of the same Liberals who were concerned with the slow pace of nominations were also anxious about what they perceived to be the delayed decisions on campaign organization and strategy. They pointed to the fact that not until fall 2018, with barely a year to go until the next election, was the composition of the national platform committee announced, including co-chairs Ralph Goodale, minister of public safety, and Mona Fortier, first-time Liberal MP. But neither the national campaign chairs nor their provincial counterparts had yet been appointed, making it difficult to proceed with nomination meetings, as they would be required to sign off on potential candidates.

Even more important for many nervous staffers was the uncertainty over who would fill the staff positions of national campaign director and the team that would serve on the ground and on the plane. As one former Liberal organizer stated, "There's been a lot of complaints and concerns right across the country … The formalization has not occurred. The PMO needs to sign off on who will be members of the national campaign committee … so we can move forward quickly.[37]

In January 2019 an unprecedented five national campaign co-chairs were announced: Intergovernmental Affairs Minister Dominic LeBlanc, Innovation Minister Navdeep Bains, former PMO adviser Brittney Kerr, and former party organizers Nikki Hipkin and Sylvie Paradis. While two co-chairs had been the norm for the Liberals in the past, the increased number for this campaign was an obvious nod to regional and gender representation. The announcement was followed up in the next few days with the appointment of provincial co-chairs, notably those for Ontario (Liberal MPs Kim Rudd and Marco Mendocino) and Quebec (Heritage Minister Pablo Rodriquez and National Revenue Minister Diane Lebouthillier.) Other provincial chairs were announced over the next several weeks.

The role of the chairs was to focus on the overall conduct of the campaign rather than day-to-day operations. Still to come was the appointment of the national campaign director and other staff who would handle the nuts and bolts of the campaign. This had been the responsibility of Katie Telford and Gerald Butts in 2015. But with the advent of the SNC Lavalin issue in February 2019 and Butts's subsequent resignation from the PMO, campaign planning and further announcements came to a halt.

Butts had been widely expected to lead the campaign team once again along with Telford, and this plan was now thrown into doubt. Not only was Butts out of the picture, but his departure forced the remaining key players in PMO, and notably Katie Telford, to put aside or significantly delay their own plans to leave the office and take over various roles with the campaign. As a result the Liberals found themselves in the unexpected position of needing a Plan B.

At a meeting of the national caucus in Ottawa on 1 May, Trudeau announced that Jeremy Broadhurst – a former Trudeau adviser and chief of staff to Foreign Affairs Minister Chrystia Freeland – would be leaving that post to serve as the national campaign director. Broadhurst had already served as the party's national director from 2013 to 2015 and was seen as both knowledgeable and competent. His appointment highlighted the depth of Liberal talent available for the campaign, a reality that was reinforced over the next several weeks as other key players in the 2015 victory, such as Christina Topp and Azam Ishmael, were again given important roles to play. Similarly, Tom Pitfield would be returning to manage the party's digital operations, including the Liberalist voter contact database that had been so successful in 2015, and Sean Wiltshire and Dan Arnold would also be in place once more to handle the increasingly important areas of data research and analytics. In addition Kate Purchase, who had served as director of communications in the early days of the Trudeau PMO, was named chief content strategist, a position that involved the supervision and coordination of advertising, leaders' debates, and platform announcements.

Then on 11 July more than sixty Liberal advisers and party workers met to finalize the party's election strategy and organize the campaign team. They learned that veteran adviser Cyrus Reporter, who had accompanied Trudeau on the plane during the 2015 election, would be taking leave from his law firm to do so again. Also on the leader's tour would be Ben Chin, Finance Minister Bill Morneau's former chief of staff, who had moved into PMO after the departure of Gerald Butts. A former adviser to BC premier Christy Clark, Chin was known to Trudeau from his earlier stint in PMO as an adviser on western issues. Finally, John Zerucelli would again be the director of the leader's tour, while David Rodier would reprise his role as wagon master – overseeing logistics and technical matters as well as liaising with media members accompanying the tour.[38]

This announcement was quickly followed by an unexpected one on 20 July confirming that Gerald Butts would be involved in the Liberal campaign after all. His role would be an informal one. At least on paper he would be serving simply as an adviser to Trudeau and the senior campaign team. Conservative leader Andrew Scheer and several of his MPs reacted swiftly to the announcement, which they described as inappropriate. "Just like that," Scheer said, "the Trudeau team that brought Canadians the SNC Lavalin scandal is right back together."[39] But Liberal insiders overwhelmingly expressed relief and satisfaction. Few considered Butts's presence a political problem. As Jonathan Scott, a Liberal activist and former director of communications for the Liberal Research Bureau, put it, few Canadians "will be animated one way or another by who is staffing the Liberal campaign."[40] Scott argued it was the Conservatives, whose campaign director Hamish Marshall was a founder and original director of the controversial far-right Rebel News, who would be vulnerable to public concern if the staffing issue was raised during the campaign.

A final and more detailed line-up of Liberal campaign staff soon followed, highlighted by the fact that Butts and Telford would be switching roles. This time Butts would be located at party headquarters, in an apparent effort to reduce his visibility, while Telford would be on the plane with the leader. Telford's team on the plane would also include two media relations officers from PMO, Cameron Ahmad and Chantal Gagnon. At party headquarters in Ottawa Olivier Duchesneau, a former ministerial chief of staff, would serve as deputy campaign director under Jeremy Broadhurst, assuming responsibility for the party's Quebec campaign. Two other ministerial chiefs of staff were given campaign responsibilities as well: Matt Stickney was named national field coordinator, in charge of getting out the vote, and Marci Surkes was assigned to coordinate policy announcements. Finally, Brian Clow, a PMO staffer who had worked closely with Telford and Butts on the NAFTA negotiations, was once again put in charge of the rapid response team (war room) for the campaign, having filled that position in 2015.

Expanding the Base

The Liberals had engaged in direct "conversations" with over four million voters in advance of the 2015 election thanks to the innovative concept of Days of Action, which were organized throughout 2014–15. In 2018 the executive of the party announced a similar plan to expand their base of supporters and volunteers and ensure election readiness. This time, the "Team Trudeau Field Program" hoped to broaden its reach even further by starting earlier and conducting more of these events.

By early 2018 a clear schedule had been laid out by party headquarters. Special Days of Action would take place on 28 April, 26 May, 16 June, 8 and 9 September, and 22 and 23 September, *in addition* to the regularly scheduled summer Days of Action held every weekend in July and August. The rationale for such days was equally clear: a combination of information exchange, voter identification, and pre-campaign training for volunteers. As the party communications stressed, "Days of Action are mass mobilizations of our supporters, on the doorstep, on the phone or at community events." By identifying specific dates far in advance, they noted, "we want to give ridings time to plan and organize their teams with specific goals in mind – to engage our movement of supporters, increase the number of active volunteers, and identify more Liberals for 2019."[41]

Party spokesman Parker Lund underlined the progress the party had already made: "Throughout 2018 the party had more field organizers on the ground than had ever been seen in a non-election year, and campaign readiness has been a major focus at special regional conventions the party continues to host across Canada."[42]

Long before the campaign began, then, it appeared the Liberals were well prepared in many key ways. They had the funds, the organization, the personnel, the technology, and a huge contingent of dedicated volunteers to deliver a well-organized and effective campaign. The Big Red Machine was definitely ready.

This effort to expand the party's base of support "one individual at a time" was then complemented by targeted efforts to reinforce the party's appeal in various regions of the country, and notably western Canada. The party increased its paid personnel and volunteer outreach efforts across the region, as well as heightening the profile of regional cabinet ministers.

Building on the efforts of Liberal predecessors Jean Chrétien and Paul Martin, Justin Trudeau was increasingly visible at Liberal and other events in western Canada in his first few years in office. He devoted particular time and effort to cultivating support in British Columbia (where he had once lived, and a region he also considered to be the most promising in terms of increasing Liberal support), regularly attending numerous events in the Vancouver area and the Okanagan. Trudeau also devoted considerable effort to reassuring Albertans that "we are all in this together," from his personal interventions during the devastating Fort McMurray fire of 2016 to federal support for the (later cancelled) Calgary Olympic bid. But his subsequent efforts to appease the oil patch with the purchase of the Trans Mountain pipeline not only failed to impress many voters in Alberta and Saskatchewan, but had the spillover effect of alienating many potential Liberal supporters in BC.

By the end of 2018 a compilation of recent public opinion polls demonstrated conclusively that these efforts had not been successful. Influenced by the increasing economic slump in the oil patch and the government's failure to speed up delivery of the Trans Mountain pipeline project, as well as the perception that Quebec issues were dominating the federal agenda,[43] neither of the two most western provinces were responding to Liberal initiatives as hoped. In British Columbia support for the Liberals, which had approached 50 per cent at the time of the 2015 election, had fallen dramatically to barely 35 per cent. Meanwhile support for the Conservatives had returned to their election strength of 30 per cent, as had that of the NDP (20 per cent) and Green Party (10 per cent), suggesting the 2019 election in that province could be problematic for the Liberals, who had obtained eighteen seats in the last election. Similarly, Liberal support in Alberta, where the party had managed to elect four MPs in 2015, had now fallen from a post-election high of 30 per cent to just under 20 per cent while the Conservatives maintained a commanding lead. Across the two prairie provinces, where the Liberals had been in a virtual dead heat of 42 per cent with the Conservatives during the 2015 election and obtained eight seats (seven in Manitoba and one in Saskatchewan), the party had plummeted to barely 27 per cent support while the Conservatives had soared to 48 per cent.[44]

Liberal efforts to reinforce their support among specific demographic groups had also had mixed results. Despite the prime minister's numerous symbolic gestures, funding increases, and restructuring of relevant departments, for example, the hoped-for new relationship with Indigenous peoples was stalled. At a meeting of the Assembly of First Nations in early December 2018 Trudeau reiterated his commitment to reconciliation, telling National Chief Perry Bellegarde and the audience that he hoped reconciliation would be his lasting legacy. "We will start from a place of partnership," he said, "the place we started all those centuries ago and then unfortunately lost our way from. That is the legacy I look forward to building with all of you over the coming years."[45] However, the difficulties posed once again by the pipeline issue, problems with the promised Truth and Reconciliation Commission, as well as government delays in delivering on campaign promises such as child welfare legislation and the Indian Languages Act, had left many Aboriginal leaders frustrated or disenchanted. The subsequent demotion and controversial resignation of Justice Minister Jody Wilson-Raybould (discussed in detail below), the first Indigenous person to hold the post, did little to improve that situation. As National Chief Bellegarde pointedly noted in his remarks to the assembled chiefs in Ottawa, "aboriginal voters were responsible for flipping 22 ridings in the 2015 federal election. You people running in the next federal election, you better listen to First Nation issues now if you want to get elected."[46]

The Liberals' efforts to retain or regain the support of many new Canadians – support that the Harper Conservatives had assiduously courted under the leadership of Immigration and Multiculturalism Minister Jason Kenney – were also in doubt. On the one hand, the Trudeau government's relentless pursuit of representational diversity, whether in candidate selection, cabinet appointments, or other order-in-council positions, had been widely publicized and well received. On the other hand, the government's promotion of other aspects of its equality agenda (such as gender parity, pro-choice, same-sex marriage, and the protection of the LGBTQ community) did not meet with the approval of some of the key demographic communities in Ontario's suburban 905 region, whose conservative social values had been exploited by the Conservatives to their political advantage. In that vein Trudeau's ill-fated India trip in early 2018, which was seen as a blatant effort to retain support among the Canadian Sikh community at the expense of foreign policy interests, only served to highlight the Liberals' difficulties in balancing their policy positions with political expediency.

By contrast, support for the Liberals among two other key target groups, women and youth, continued to be a source of strength for the party. In the case of young Canadians, Trudeau's efforts to make the party more attractive appeared to have paid off. In advance of the 2015 election, veteran pollsters such as Frank Graves of EKOS and Darrell Bricker of Ipsos had both discounted the impact of a youth vote in a federal election as "trivial." Bricker added, "If the youth voted, it would change a lot. But you first need them to show up."[47] Statistics Canada data showed that is precisely what occurred. They revealed a twelve-point increase in voter turnout among youth between eighteen and twenty-four, and a similar eleven-point increase in voters between the ages of twenty-five and thirty-four. An in-depth survey by Abacus Data reinforced this finding, concluding that young people had been instrumental in securing the 2015 Liberal majority. According to CEO David Coletto, "More young people voted for the Liberals in every region of the country, including in Alberta, than for any other party." Noting that 45 per cent of young Canadians voted Liberal, compared with 25 per cent for the NDP and 20 per cent for the Conservatives, Coletto concluded that not only was the turnout higher, but "for the first time since 1997, young people coalesced around one option."[48] With Trudeau initially assuming the portfolio of minister of youth himself, and the Liberals having implemented many of their platform commitments appealing to young voters (such as the legalization of marijuana, more financial support for post-secondary education, and initiatives to promote youth employment, as well as their strong support of the LGBTQ community and early success on the environmental file), their prospects of retaining that support in the October 2019 election appeared equally good as 2018 drew to a close.

An even more promising situation was emerging in 2018 with respect to the Liberals' support among female voters. In seven different polls conducted over the course of the year, the Liberals maintained an average twelve-point lead over the Conservatives among women, suggesting the "gender gap" among Canadian voters continued to be significant, and to favour the Liberals.[49] Here, too, Liberal platform policies that had been implemented – including pay equity, support for more female recipients of STEM post-secondary scholarships and Canada Research Chairs, additional parental leave provisions, and the use of gender-based policy analysis across all federal departments – appeared to be successfully reinforcing symbolic gestures such as Trudeau's "Because it's 2015" comment at his government's swearing-in ceremony of a cabinet with gender parity. Equally of note were the presence of a record number of female Liberal MPs (fifty) in his caucus.

Trudeau's frequent references to the importance of gender parity in his public appearances, and his noteworthy comments about feminism at international events in Davos and at the United Nations, undoubtedly heightened this positive perception of the Liberals at home and abroad. In fact, it was to some extent Trudeau's joint sponsorship of a Canada–United States Women in Business Council with Ivanka Trump, another advocate of women's rights, that led to an initially positive relationship between Trudeau and the newly elected president of the United States.[50] However, as numerous reports of their first meeting concluded, it was also the new prime minister's reputation as an international celebrity that led the mercurial American president to begin their relationship on a positive note, having demonstrated his penchant for associating with well-known celebrities long before entering politics.[51]

The Celebrity Leader's Growing Image Problems

As noted earlier, the importance of party leaders, and especially the concept of a celebrity leader, have gained increasing traction with voters in many Western liberal democracies over the past few decades. Clearly Justin Trudeau's selection as leader of the Liberal Party, and the Liberals' subsequent victory in the 2015 federal election, were in part the result of his famous name and charismatic personality. Trudeau's relative youth proved an additional asset since voters in Canada, like many other Western democracies, also seemed intent on generational change.[52] However, it was only when these various aspects of his image were combined with a clearly defined set of liberal values and beliefs that Trudeau and the Liberals ultimately prevailed in Canada.

Similarly, Trudeau's image as a progressive liberal was an important element of his appeal to his international counterparts in the early days of his mandate. Since part of Trudeau's appeal to Canadians had been his declaration that Canada was back on the world stage as a player, after years of the Harper government's more isolationist approach, this acceptance was important. This phenomenon was on full display during Trudeau's attendance at the World Economic Forum in Davos in January 2016. Media coverage of his trip was extensive and hardly run of the mill. The *New York Times* published a flattering photo of Trudeau hobnobbing with George Soros and Bono and declared "this year there is a another kind of Davos man. He is a former snowboarder and schoolteacher who now runs that country just north of the United States."[53] Business Council of Canada president John Manley reported from the event on Trudeau's "celebrity status" with media and participants, while the *Globe and Mail's* Margaret Wente summed up by saying

"Prime Minister Justin Trudeau has arrived ... Everyone wants to get a load of the hottest star in politics."[54]

Trudeau's progressive liberalism was also on display. Addressing the conference theme of industrial change and inequality, Trudeau's keynote speech concluded, "The fourth industrial revolution will not be successful unless it creates real opportunity for the billions who weren't able to join us here this week."[55] Throughout the five-day event he repeatedly underlined his support for gender equality and the need for greater diversity in government institutions, and his "I am a feminist" comment while participating in a roundtable panel led Britain's *The Guardian* to declare "Trudeau is living up to his reputation as a 21st century leader."[56] As well, from his opening salvo that "Canada is Back," Trudeau spent considerable time in Davos underlining the differences in values and priorities between himself and his Conservative predecessor, Stephen Harper, a comparison that did not go unnoticed in Canada.

After years of frosty Canada–United States relations between Harper and American president Barack Obama, Canadians quickly saw evidence of the new narrative there as well. The two leaders met briefly at the Asia-Pacific Economic Cooperation (APEC) conference in Singapore in November 2015, where they were widely reported to have formed a personal bond. The speculation was confirmed in February 2016 when Trudeau became the first Canadian prime minister in twenty years to be feted at a formal state dinner at the White House. American media coverage of the event included numerous sensationalist references to the new "young," "hunky," and "dreamy" Canadian prime minister who had been featured in the January edition of the American *Vogue* magazine. One television network proclaimed that "Justin Fever has hit America, and we don't mean the pop star."[57] Even the traditionally conventional *Washington Post* declared, "That same sort of celebrity culture that surrounded Obama, you're seeing that with the prime minister."[58] But shared liberal values were also an important element of the relationship, as Obama's national security adviser for the western hemisphere, Mark Feierstein, explained. "Both young leaders [have] similar visions. Both have a progressive vision of governing. Both are very much committed to the appropriate use of multilateral tools. Both are committed to diversity."[59] As then vice-president Joe Biden told Trudeau at a state dinner in the American's honour in Ottawa in December 2016, "The world is going to spend a lot of time looking to you, Mr. Prime Minister ... because we need you very very badly."[60]

In Europe for a G7 Summit in Sicily in the spring of 2017, Trudeau struck a chord with the newly elected French president, Emmanuel

Macron, who was his demographic double. One media outlet described them as having formed a "budding bromance." The thirty-nine-year-old Macron, a political superstar in France, was someone of Trudeau's "own age, political persuasion, and affinity," *Bloomberg News* reported, and described the two as "the true inheritors of the Kennedy charisma,"[61] rather than US president Donald Trump, who at seventy was the oldest leader present. At the event both men urged greater cooperation to reduce the growing wealth gap, promote diversity and gender equality, eliminate barriers to free trade, and ensure environmental sustainability.[62]

Meanwhile, at home Trudeau continued to benefit from an unfettered positive image, aided by his extensive use of social media. "Often referred to as the first prime minister of the Instagram age, Trudeau carefully crafts an image of positive and forceful leadership that has led to increased popularity for himself and the Liberal Party."[63] As a result the party's "honeymoon" lasted far longer than would typically have been the case. This honeymoon period is generally defined as "one in which the party polls above its vote share in the election that brought it to power."[64] In the Liberals' case, having won the 2015 election with 39.5 per cent of the vote, they continued to poll anywhere from 40 per cent to 50 per cent throughout 2016 and 2017, coming back down to earth only in early 2018 after 125 weeks.[65]

By almost any measure Canadians' love affair with the Trudeau Liberals was abnormally long, but particularly in comparison with the Harper Conservatives, who first fell below the level of their 2011 election-day support after a mere three months. Even in their first election in 2006 the Conservatives' honeymoon lasted only seven months. But Canadians' ongoing fascination with Trudeau eventually did come to an end, and largely as a result of his own perceived missteps and self-inflicted wounds.

The first of these was his family's Christmas vacation at the Aga Khan's private island in the Caribbean in December 2016. The opposition Conservatives vigorously attacked the trip as a conflict of interest, arguing it constituted accepting a gift from someone who could conceivably do business with the government. Trudeau, clearly taken aback by the charges, replied that he had not consulted the ethics commissioner about the trip because the Aga Khan was a family friend, a category specifically exempted from the newly introduced conflict-of-interest legislation.

Ethics commissioner Mary Dawson was asked to investigate and then produced a report on the issue in December 2017. It concluded that there was indeed a perception of conflict of interest and that as a result Trudeau technically had breached the act by accepting a "gift." Her decision rested primarily on her interpretation of the definition of a close[66] personal friend in the legislation, which she believed excluded the Aga Khan. In addition the commissioner argued that Trudeau should have recused himself from any cabinet discussions concerning the Aga Khan's human rights institution (the Global Centre for Pluralism) in Canada. "Mr. Trudeau must ensure that he has arranged his private affairs so that they are not incompatible with his public duties as prime minister."[67]

Trudeau's response to the report was prompt and straightforward:

> The commissioner's report this morning makes very clear that I should have taken precautions and cleared my family vacation and dealings with the Aga Khan in advance. I'm sorry that I didn't and in future I will be clearing all my family vacations with the commissioner's office.[68]

Polls in the immediate aftermath of the vacation revelations in early 2017, and even after the commissioner's report was released nearly a year later, did not reflect a noticeable decrease in the prime minister's popularity or that of his party. Many of the respondents tended to dismiss it as a minor offence being exploited by the opposition for political gain. At the same time, it did raise a subtle concern about the prime minister's judgment and his privileged background, something that would later come back to haunt him.[69]

A highly publicized trip to India in February 2018 finally broke the spell. There were myriad practical problems with the trip from the beginning. But the acknowledged diplomatic failure was compounded when a former Sikh terrorist appeared at a Canadian-sponsored dinner in Delhi. Although the invitation was apparently issued in ignorance by a BC Liberal MP to one of his constituents, the Indian government reacted with predictable outrage. Given the sensitivity of the Indian government to its domestic Sikh separatist movement, and the prime minister's well-known courting of the extensive Canadian Sikh diaspora,[70] the matter gained widespread critical coverage and a noticeably cool reception for Trudeau. Nevertheless, it was his decision to dress in formal Indian attire throughout most of the trip that led to ridicule in Canada and internationally, complete with photos. Here again, it was Trudeau's judgment that was called into question. As one media headline declared, there was a widespread perception that "Trudeau's India trip is a total disaster, and he has only himself to blame."[71]

Within a month of the ill-fated trip the polls showed a dramatic drop in support for the Liberals. According to an Ipsos poll of 2 March, not only was the party no longer running ahead of their 2015 election numbers, they were reduced to second place. At 33 per cent, or more than five points behind the Conservatives, they would have lost an election if one were held at that time. Other polls showed the Liberals either in a virtual tie with the Conservatives, or only slightly ahead. As David Coletto of Abacus Data noted, "His trip to India struck a nerve with the public and raised quite a few doubts."[72] Darrell Bricker of Ipsos agreed "there was something about this trip to India that was just a bit of a tipping point for them."[73]

Since roughly 40 per cent of those polled believed the trip had had a negative impact on Canada's international reputation, the consequences of the debacle for Trudeau's personal image were obviously significant. Shortly after his return the prime minister launched a cross-country town-hall-type tour, hoping to regain some of his lost appeal. It appeared to have an impact as the polls slowly improved. But the Liberal leader was also helped by the poor public image of his chief opponents, both new to their posts. Although Trudeau's approval rating had fallen to roughly 41 per cent by late 2018, Conservative Andrew Scheer was viewed positively by only 22 per cent of respondents, and the NDP's Jagmeet Singh by a mere 19 per cent.

By late 2018 a compilation of opinion polls suggested the Liberals were once again likely to be returned with another comfortable majority government. At 36.7 per cent (with the Conservatives at 33.8 per cent and the NDP at only 15.3 per cent), pollster Éric Grenier concluded the Liberals were on track to obtain 179 seats, far ahead of the Conservatives at 135, the NDP at 22, and the Greens and Bloc with only 1 each.[74]

Although it is often said that a week is a long time in politics, much less a year, it could also be noted that the party in the lead some twelve months before a federal election has been the one to win in three-quarters of the subsequent elections. But this optimistic prognosis was soon to be challenged by an incident that caused far more damage to Justin Trudeau's image as well as the Liberal brand.

Part of Trudeau's appeal in Canada was his commitment to bring a new approach to politics, especially in contrast to that of his predecessor. His reference to Wilfrid Laurier's famous "sunny ways" in his election-night victory speech set the tone for his government as one that would do politics differently. For Trudeau, this primarily meant reversing many of the Harper government's punitive measures in areas such as criminal justice and immigration and avoiding the Conservatives' hyperpartisan approach to policy making and governing. It meant reform of institutions, which was achieved in the case of the Senate but notably not fulfilled in the case of electoral reform. It also meant healing rifts caused by the Conservatives' tendency to pit regions of the country and various communities against each other. Trudeau's promotion of gender equality, diversity, and tolerance was an important aspect of his image as a progressive liberal, as was his commitment to reconciliation with Canada's Indigenous peoples. All of this, in turn, would be accomplished while leading a government that was seen to be open, accessible, and accountable after nearly a decade of unprecedented control of communications and heavy-handedness on the part of the Harper Conservatives. Yet almost all of these aspects of Trudeau's liberal persona were about to be challenged by an unexpected and unlikely rift within his own cabinet.

The SNC Lavalin Affair and Trudeau's Damaged Brand

In his seminal work on political branding and communications in Canada, political scientist Alex Marland concluded, "it will be interesting to see how the various brands associated with Justin Trudeau change the longer he is prime minister of Canada."[75] Whatever else Marland may have been anticipating, it is almost certain that he did not expect the developments that came to be known as the SNC Lavalin affair.

That any cabinet minister would resign shortly after accepting a new portfolio, and then spend months launching a concerted and highly public attack on their own government, in the full knowledge that these actions were doing damage to their political party in an election year, was simply inconceivable to most political insiders of whatever political stripe. That the former minister in this case would be someone who had been handpicked by the prime minister, and who had been considered a classic example of the way Liberals were doing politics differently, was for them beyond belief. In this sense both Trudeau and his advisers could be forgiven for failing to anticipate the debacle that ensued, but they alone could be held responsible for their inept handling of the affair once it erupted.[76]

Jody Wilson-Raybould was considered a star candidate for the Liberals in 2015. A lawyer by training and a member of the We Wai Kai Nation, she began her career with a brief stint as a public prosecutor in Vancouver before moving to the BC Treaty Commission, where she worked as an adviser for many years. First elected regional chief of the BC Assembly of First Nations (AFN) in 2009, she had met Justin Trudeau at the annual general meeting of the AFN in 2013, where he urged her to consider becoming a Liberal candidate.[77] Although she had no previous partisan political experience or attachment to the Liberal Party she agreed, citing the lack of progress on Indigenous rights during the Harper government's decade in power and Trudeau's own stated commitment to reconciliation with Indigenous peoples.[78] Confirmed as a Liberal candidate in 2014, she easily won her BC riding of Vancouver-Granville in the 2015 election. Within days she simultaneously became a rookie MP and the first Indigenous minister of justice and attorney general.

Perhaps not surprisingly, given her lack of relevant government experience, her performance as justice minister was questioned on numerous occasions over the next three years by stakeholders and opposition parties alike. For example, Trudeau's government was regularly criticized for falling behind in making judicial appointments – Wilson-Raybould's responsibility – thereby compounding a pre-existing backlog. With fifty-seven vacancies by early 2018, courts were routinely throwing out cases due to excessive delays. Conservative opposition critics Lisa Raitt and Rob Nicholson, and the president of the Canadian Bar Association, Ray Adlington, pointed to Wilson-Raybould's apparent desire to achieve greater diversity at the expense of efficiency as a key factor in delays. "There is no shortage of qualified candidates for these positions," Nicholson said, "and there is simply no good reason they should go unfulfilled."[79] (As if to confirm that claim, during his first five months in office Wilson-Raybould's successor, David Lametti, made more than fifty judicial appointments.)

The minister's role in appointments also came under scrutiny when it was learned she had recommended someone as chief justice of the Supreme Court even though he did not already sit on the court and, stranger still, had been a vocal critic of the Charter of Rights and judicial activism. And, after Trudeau rejected the recommendation, the minister followed up with a sixty-page memo defending her choice. As one knowledgeable insider put it, the prime minister was "puzzled" and then "seriously concerned" about the minister's judgment, which led to "significant disagreement" between the two.[80]

Meanwhile, as part of her mandate letter, Wilson-Raybould was given specific responsibility for crafting new laws on assisted dying and decriminalization of marijuana. Her handling of both, although admittedly difficult files, caused headaches for the government. In the end the implementation of the cannabis legislation was delayed until October 2018 due to the need for greater consultation with provinces, and a section of the assisted dying legislation was ruled unconstitutional only months before the start of the 2019 federal election, making it a campaign issue. She also was responsible for the amendments to the criminal code introducing the deferred prosecution agreement, a measure that she opposed in cabinet and later criticized publicly.[81] And, although it was not part of her mandate letter, the minister effected changes to the criminal code on impaired driving that many legal experts criticized as violating Charter rights.[82] At the same time, the minister failed to implement many of the easily introduced reforms promised by the 2015 Liberal platform on criminal justice, to eliminate several of the Harper Conservatives' punitive tough-on-crime measures. The views of many criminal lawyers were expressed by Daniel Brown, vice-president of the Criminal Lawyers' Association, when he wrote that "when it comes to criminal law, she dropped the ball."[83]

Meanwhile, one area in which Wilson-Raybould was increasingly attempting to intervene was Indigenous affairs, even though it was not her portfolio. As minister of Crown-Indigenous relations, it was Carolyn Bennett who was given the task of "resetting" the federal relationship with First Nations, Inuit, and Métis. But Wilson-Raybould disagreed vehemently with Bennett's go-slow consultative approach, and by her own admission attempted to wrest control of the portfolio from her cabinet colleague in the summer of 2018.[84] As one of her former colleagues noted, "Jody always kind of wanted to drive the bus from the seat behind the driver."[85]

At one point Wilson-Raybould sent what one participant called a "blistering" memo to her cabinet colleagues "tearing a strip off Carolyn's proposal in rather inflammatory language."[86] The internal power struggle preoccupied PMO, the Clerk of the Privy Council and, ultimately, the prime minister, who was obliged to meet with the two ministers and lay down the law on 17 September 2018, making it clear to Wilson-Raybould that Bennett had won.

Wilson-Raybould did not take the defeat lightly. She began making increasingly aggressive speeches criticizing her own government in a variety of public fora. On 29 November 2018 she told a group of politicians and indigenous leaders in BC that "we must be audacious. We must do what is right. And not look for a compromise."[87] Coming perilously close to breaking the long-standing Westminster conventions of cabinet confidentiality and solidarity, she continued, "Within government, when discussing matters of indigenous rights, one still finds a seemingly disproportionate focus on risk – speculation that the sky might fall – and an emphasis on the most severe, yet very remote, potential outcomes."[88] While many Indigenous leaders appreciated her viewpoint, her cabinet colleagues were not amused.[89]

Things came to a head in January 2019, when the resignation of Treasury Board president Scott Brison necessitated a cabinet shuffle. Offered the post of minister of Indigenous services, Wilson-Raybould declined and asked to remain where she was. As Gerald Butts later testified, both he and the prime minister were taken aback by this refusal, and scrambled to find an alternative. In Butt's view some change of post was essential, since allowing the minister to stay in the portfolio of her choice would have set an unfortunate precedent where the prime minister would be seen not to be in control of his own cabinet.[90] Consequently Wilson-Raybould was offered veterans affairs as part of the larger cabinet shuffle, a post she accepted even though it was more clearly a demotion from her current portfolio. On the day of her swearing in, a visibly unhappy Wilson-Raybould issued a defiant press release lauding her accomplishments in Justice. Days later she resigned from cabinet.[91]

What followed was a series of unanticipated and unprecedented events that left seasoned political observers nonplussed. A lengthy string of anonymous accusations emerged about the internal workings of the Trudeau government and its handling of the little-known procedure related to criminal charges of corporate wrongdoing, the deferred prosecution agreement (DPA). It soon became apparent that Wilson-Raybould felt it was her position on this issue (opposing the granting of a DPA to SNC Lavalin), and not the many other points of conflict with the prime minister and her cabinet colleagues, that was responsible for her removal from Justice. In short order, the demotion of a cabinet minister was transformed into a full-blown political scandal involving accusations of undue political pressure being exerted on the justice minister in her role as attorney general by the prime minister, senior PMO staff, and the Clerk of the Privy Council and inappropriate lobbying on behalf of SNC Lavalin, a Quebec business icon.

It became clear that Trudeau, who had based much of his personal appeal on his progressive views and promotion of diversity, was unwilling to take a hard line publicly with his former minister or criticize her actions. Instead he attempted to straddle a divide between doing politics differently and defending his government's actions as legitimate and appropriate. In the end this ambivalence convinced no one.

Incredibly, the government appeared to have no coherent communications strategy to deal with the affair. Veteran Liberals watched in disbelief as the scandal was allowed to carry on for two months. Trudeau issued several half-hearted apologies for what he saw as failures to communicate and reiterated his disappointment in the way things were evolving, but was unable to bring closure to the process. As one insider grumbled, "Chrétien would have had this thing shut down in days. What are these people playing at?"[92]

Instead, growing opposition party and media pressure resulted in parliamentary committee hearings, public testimony by many of the principals, and sensational nightly news coverage. In the end Trudeau's closest confidante, Gerald Butts, resigned from his post in PMO, and veteran public servant Michael Wernick resigned as Clerk of the Privy Council.

By now the actions of the former justice minister were being viewed by Liberal insiders as sufficiently damaging to the government, with an election only months away, that some began to speak about the consequences of a Liberal defeat. As the situation worsened, furious Liberal MPs asked why Wilson-Raybould, still a Liberal MP, was pursuing such a dangerous course of action for the party. How could she imagine that the Scheer Conservatives would continue the Liberals' work on reconciliation and social action, never mind gender equality and environmental protection or pharmacare?

For her part, Wilson-Raybould continued to stress publicly that she was a "truth-teller" who was merely exposing inappropriate government behaviour in order to truly change the way politics was done. And in Parliament as well as in media interviews, she increasingly focused her criticism on the prime minister personally.[93] Her position was supported by many in the media and the political sphere. For them her stance was a principled one. She was widely seen as refusing to be intimidated by power, defending the integrity and independence of the prosecutorial system – for which she was responsible in her role as attorney general – from undue political interference. From this perspective, her insistence on proceeding with the prosecution of SNC Lavalin was viewed as a victory for the rule of law and a defeat for corporate greed and corruption. As veteran journalist Andrew Coyne declared, "There is no 'middle ground' on prosecutorial independence, no room for argument on the right of the attorney general to make decisions on criminal prosecutions, free of pressure from other government officials: it is settled constitutional law, absolute and inviolable. It doesn't matter what good reasons the prime minister might think he has. Nor is the AG obliged to keep him apprised of her decisions in such matters (though she did). It's quite literally none of his business."[94]

Perhaps not surprisingly, then, when Treasury Board president Jane Philpott chose to resign from cabinet in sympathy with Wilson-Raybould (with whom Philpott had worked closely on the assisted dying legislation when she was minister of health), the prime minister who had made gender parity and gender-based analysis a signature policy was accused by his political opponents of being a "phony feminist" who fired strong women.[95]

By contrast, for many Liberal veterans and government practitioners the whole affair was really a management issue, in which two opposing views had collided on a number of subjects until finally one of them had to leave.[96] The brief eventually presented to the ethics commissioner by the prime minister's counsel reinforced that viewpoint, as it highlighted the fact that Wilson-Raybould had refused to share information with her front bench colleagues as part of a recommendation to cabinet, something that to the PMO and political veterans demonstrated that Wilson-Raybould felt co-operation or collaboration with them and the rest of cabinet was "not something that she was required to do or even should do."[97] As Michael Wernick indicated, those involved believed strongly that it was not possible to have a cabinet minister constantly at war with the prime minister. From this perspective the government's actions, while arguably heavy-handed and insensitive, were to be expected, especially in politics.[98] For those who held this view, the actions of the PMO and the clerk simply did not constitute political interference, or any threat to prosecutorial independence, but rational and responsible discussion of the issues. Andrew Cohen was one of the few senior journalists who shared this viewpoint, arguing, "This is not a scandal. Scalding conversations happen within governments, which have to make hard choices. And Wilson-Raybould and Philpott could not take the heat." Instead of ethics, he concluded, this situation "is about judgment, loyalty and realpolitik. Wilson-Raybould is a purist ... who was offended by a prime minister with a different view. But no law was broken and no one profited ... so now we have a 'crisis' over the government's ham-handed attempts to save jobs in Quebec."[99]

By now the Liberal caucus was in chaos, particularly since many Liberal insiders believed Wilson-Raybould should have been removed from cabinet much earlier. Behind the scenes some MPs, although prepared to defend the PMO's role with respect to the political interference argument and the DPA for SNC Lavalin, were nevertheless critical of what they viewed as the incompetent way in which the prime minister and his aides had handled the whole matter. In the end, it was Wilson-Raybould's secret taping of a conversation with the clerk that doomed the former justice minister and brought the crisis to an end. Both she and Philpott, who had joined in Wilson-Raybould's ongoing and highly public criticism of the prime minister and his office, were finally expelled from the Liberal caucus on 2 April, a full two months after the controversy first erupted.

Media coverage of the entire spectacle had been sensationalist and, in the view of many Liberals, heavily biased. But even among their critics there was some recognition that the "scandal" aspect was overblown – or, as one commentator succinctly put it, "seeing evil in incompetence" – particularly as no financial advantage or criminal activity was involved.[100] Eventually a number of outside experts, including Brian Greenspan, the widely respected past president of the Criminal Lawyers' Association, questioned whether Wilson-Raybould had correctly understood her role as attorney general. He also argued that she had fuelled various misconceptions with her accusations. "In a free and democratic society," he wrote, "the prosecutorial function does not operate in a vacuum ... Thoughtful reconsideration and sober second thoughts do not threaten the independence of the attorney-general."[101]

One consequence of the lengthy scandal was that the media had increasingly shifted its focus from internal cabinet relations to the merits of the little-known DPA legislation and the past behaviour of SNC-Lavalin. This was a more complicated issue for the government to explain or defend after the fact, although arguably one where a good case could have been made, as former OECD president Donald Johnston, also a former Liberal cabinet minister, pointed out. The first non-European to hold the post, the highly regarded Johnston was reappointed for a second term and it was under his watch that the DPA legislation was adopted.[102] Certainly it was clear that the government had failed to anticipate problems and communicate the rationale for the measure publicly, even though the concept of a DPA is one that has already been widely accepted and utilized in many other Western democracies, including several of Canada's key trading partners. Indeed, as financial columnist Terence Corcoran noted, "SNC Lavalin would get a deal anywhere else, why not here? Internationally, prosecuting corporations rather than negotiating settlements is a rarity."[103] But here too the government's communications efforts were feeble, as former Chrétien and Ignatieff senior adviser Peter Donolo stressed.[104] On the surface, the DPA appeared to have been introduced in an almost clandestine fashion and as such was a topic about which the public – and especially western Canadians – could easily form a negative opinion.

Another potential consequence of the whole affair was underlined by journalist Adam Radwanski. He argued Ms. Wilson-Raybould's atypical behaviour for a cabinet minister risked, rightly or wrongly, being attributed by veteran politicians to her lack of experience in partisan politics or government, thereby casting doubt on the wisdom of the prime minister's rush to incorporate diversity in his government at all costs, and potentially putting an end to whatever progress had been made on such representation.[105] (According to several sources, the prime minister was particularly concerned that these developments should not be seen as reflecting a decreased commitment to reconciliation on the part of his government. His position was reinforced by eight Indigenous senators in a publicly released statement drafted by

Independent senator Murray Sinclair, who lauded the progress made by Trudeau's government to date.)[106]

Then, on the eve of the election, a damaging report by the ethics commissioner found Trudeau guilty of ethical impropriety in his handling of the matter, although it again stressed no laws were broken. This report would be repeatedly raised by Trudeau's opponents in the upcoming election. Although experts such as University of Ottawa law professor Errol Mendes, president of the International Commission of Jurists (Canada), questioned the legal soundness of the commissioner's ruling,[107] such arguments carried little or no weight in public opinion. On the contrary, the report was widely seen as a vindication of Wilson-Raybould's position.

Indeed, from a political standpoint any such expert analysis supporting the government's actions was clearly too little too late. As political scientist Lori Turnbull concluded, "This story is sure to dominate the election campaign. In the political domain, it is up to the voters to decide whether any wrongdoing has occurred. This is where communications strategies become of critical importance."[108] Yet the Liberals still seemed to have no strategy except to let the issue run its course.

Meanwhile Wilson-Raybould, whom polls demonstrated had overwhelmingly won the battle of public opinion, announced she would run as an Independent after she was denied the Liberal candidacy in her riding. (In one of her most revealing statements at the time of that announcement, she declared, "I know who I am. I am not a party person.")[109] She also announced that she would be publishing a book of her collected speeches on Indigenous reconciliation in September, a move that many Liberals feared would inevitably raise her profile once again. Adding to Liberal woes, Trudeau's statements defending SNC Lavalin in order to protect thousands of jobs in Quebec added more fuel to the fire of western discontent.

The Liberals' lead in the polls in late December 2018, when CBC pollster Éric Grenier had predicted another majority, had disappeared. By March 2019 the party was ten percentage points behind the Conservatives. Moreover, some Liberals and pundits believed that Trudeau, who was a principal reason for the party's resurgence in 2015, was now a dubious asset if not a liability, demonstrating conclusively the perils of relying too heavily on the appeal of a celebrity leader. Meanwhile, the Conservatives took full advantage of the pre-campaign spending period to release costly television ads reprising their 2015 job interview format, with the actors this time concluding Trudeau was "never ready."

Despite the Trudeau government's inept handling of this file, the Liberals' polling numbers slowly recovered. Apart from the passage of time, a variety of strategically timed positive announcements by the government, and the ongoing strength of the Canadian economy, changed the focus of public opinion.[110] By late August the Liberals had pulled even with the Conservatives and Trudeau again enjoyed a ten-point lead over Andrew Scheer. With a minority victory now a real possibility after such bleak prospects a few months earlier (and even a majority not entirely out of the question), the Liberals' campaign strategists prepared for an election many were predicting would be extremely negative, despite Trudeau's promise to continue with sunny ways.

10 Second Chance: The 2019 Election

This campaign, even more than 2015, was a validation of the decade since 2011, the transformation of this party. It was there in 2015 but it was hard to notice because of the wave that came at the end. This election was the payoff for all that hard work. There was no wave. We won it in the trenches.

– Jeremy Broadhurst, national campaign director, 29 November 2019

We will govern for everyone. Regardless of how you cast your ballot, ours is a team that will fight for all Canadians.

– Rt Hon. Justin Trudeau, 21 October 2019

When Justin Trudeau asked the governor general to dissolve Parliament on 11 September, he was exercising one of the few advantages left to the party in power with respect to elections. The introduction of fixed election dates in 2007 meant that every party had the same opportunity to prepare since, barring a minority, they all knew when the next one would be held. But only the prime minister could decide when the election would begin. Stephen Harper's 2015 decision to arrange for the longest election campaign in modern history, at seventy-eight days, had been a serious mistake. It was not one the Liberals planned to repeat. Instead, this would be a relatively short forty-day campaign, ending as scheduled on 21 October.

By choosing this shorter period, the Liberals were hoping to avoid any serious gaffes or unexpected problems. Given that they started the campaign virtually tied with their principal opponents, the Conservatives, this was hardly surprising. They would need every possible advantage to secure a victory. But this was not where the party had expected to find itself after its convincing victory in 2015.

Still the Liberals followed through with their plan to wage a positive campaign. In August they launched their campaign slogan, "Choose

Forward." The party's national director, Azam Ishmael, later confirmed this phrase had been chosen deliberately to frame the election narrative as a contest between the Liberals, who had delivered on most of their 2015 campaign promises[1] and were proposing to continue moving forward in the same direction with more progressive initiatives, and the Conservatives, who by inference would take Canada backward with their many commitments to undo or eliminate what the Liberals had already accomplished. As Ishmael also noted, this slogan allowed the Liberals to address both their record in office over the past four years – which they felt had been overwhelmingly positive – and their plans for their next mandate. Unlike 2015, they did not have a blank slate but a four-year record the opposition could attack, and linking their earlier achievements with ongoing measures seemed the best way to remind Canadians of both.

The Government's Record: Liberal Values in Action

There can be little doubt that the Trudeau government was seized with the importance of demonstrating its commitment to liberal values, and especially the progressive social values with which Trudeau himself had been identified, from the beginning. The prime minister's symbolic commitment to gender parity in cabinet "because it's 2015" was followed up with concrete changes including the introduction of gender-based policy analysis, funding for a variety of women's groups, and the overhaul of the patronage system, which by 2018 had resulted in women being appointed to 55.5 per cent of the postings for federal boards and agencies.[2]

Shortly after the 2015 victory, platform commitments had been kept to reduce taxes for low-income individuals, introduce a Canada Child Benefit, and provide funding for housing, student aid, and Indigenous communities. The Liberals also made much of fulfilled election promises to introduce legislation on assisted dying, decriminalization of marijuana, LGBTQ rights, and the reversal of many punitive changes to the criminal code introduced by the Harper Conservatives.

Moreover, there was concrete evidence of the progress made. A February 2019 Statistics Canada report concluded the Liberals' income support policies had been highly effective. The poverty rate had fallen significantly and some nine hundred thousand individuals, including nearly three hundred thousand children, had been lifted out of poverty as a direct result of the Liberals' Canada Child Benefit.[3] Similarly, a Parliamentary Budget Office report on the impact of the Liberals' tax increase on the top 1 per cent concluded that the government's revenue had increased substantially, although it might not fully cover the amount lost through tax cuts for low-income earners.[4] And, while some

Indigenous groups complained of slow progress on specific aspects of Trudeau's signature commitment of reconciliation, AFN national chief Perry Bellegarde described the progress made by Trudeau's government after four years as "unprecedented."[5]

Then in August 2019 the Liberals received an invaluable pre-election boost when two dozen academics released a book titled *Assessing Justin Trudeau's Liberal Government*. It concluded that nearly 90 per cent of their 2015 platform commitments had been either completely (50 per cent) or partially (40 per cent) met, while the remaining 10 per cent were either unfulfilled or broken. (By contrast, using the same measurements the Harper government was found to have kept 77 per cent of its promises and broken 16 per cent.)[6]

In addition the Liberals were widely perceived to have competently handled the unexpected threat to the NAFTA free trade agreement posed by the election of US president Donald Trump. Public opinion polls consistently showed the vast majority of Canadians not only approved of the resulting deal but also of the Trudeau government's handling of the file, and notably the work of Foreign Affairs Minister Chrystia Freeland, throughout the negotiations.[7] This unexpected challenge may actually have worked to the Liberals' advantage – reinforcing their image as competent managers and making them virtually impervious to attacks by either the Conservatives or the NDP on the trade file.

Another major advantage for the Liberals going into the election was Canada's positive economic fundamentals.[8] By June 2019 the national unemployment rate, at 5.7 per cent, was at its lowest level since 1976. Statistics Canada's labour market report showed seven hundred thousand new jobs had been created in the previous two years and wages had risen a healthy 2.8 per cent over 2018. And, at 30.9 per cent, Canada's debt-to-GDP ratio was the lowest in the G7, and had actually fallen since Trudeau came to power. A *Globe and Mail* editorial concluded: "Ottawa does not have a debt crisis, or even a debt problem."[9] Public opinion polls showed Canadians generally agreed. As a result the Liberals' plan to continue to run small deficits to finance their platform – despite having failed to meet their 2015 campaign pledge to return to surplus by 2019 – was endorsed by almost all economists and left the Conservatives with little room to manoeuvre on that front either.

The Government's Record: Achilles Heels

In spite of these advantages there were two areas in which the Trudeau government's record was vulnerable. Not surprisingly, both were repeatedly raised by opponents to great effect during the campaign.

More surprisingly, in many cases they managed to overshadow the Liberals' record of accomplishments. The first, electoral reform, did not seem very important to Liberal strategists at the time. Their plan to eliminate the first-past-the-post system before 2019 had encountered opposition from the start, and an online survey conducted by the government indicated there was no public consensus on the issue. And while the NDP and Greens favoured the measure, the Conservatives did not. With opposition parties also divided, and several polls demonstrating only a minority of Canadians were concerned about electoral reform in the first place, the Liberals felt they could abandon their efforts at little political cost and instead concentrate on delivering other measures they had promised on democratic reform. But the Trudeau government's failure to deliver on this prominent campaign pledge did alienate some progressive voters who had supported the Liberals in 2015. Equally important, it ultimately allowed both the Conservatives and third-party groups to convincingly accuse them of broken promises.[10]

A far more serious problem involved a combination of the Liberals' plans for a national environmental agreement to reduce greenhouse gas emissions, and the construction of the Trans Mountain pipeline, intended to carry Alberta oil to the coast of British Columbia for transport by tanker to Asia. The two initiatives were closely linked by Trudeau, who saw the combination as exemplifying the pragmatic balancing that had long been a hallmark of the Liberal approach. On 9 December 2016 he announced a "historic national plan on clean energy and the environment" at a first ministers' conference that included representatives of Aboriginal groups.[11] The achievement also reinforced his pledge to maintain cooperative working relationships with the provincial premiers and the Liberals' reputation as guardians of national unity.

But, in a perfect storm of events largely beyond the government's control, both the environmental and energy projects began to unravel less than a year later. With the election of a minority NDP government in BC in May 2017 Trudeau lost a strong supporter of his plan in former Liberal premier Christy Clark. New NDP premier John Horgan, under pressure from his Green coalition partners, began a series of escalating measures to halt progress on the Trans Mountain pipeline over environmental concerns. With her provincial economy and her own political fortunes in danger, Alberta NDP premier Rachel Notley responded by threatening retaliatory measures. Repeated efforts by Trudeau to negotiate a resolution of the interprovincial dispute failed. With the conflict no closer to resolution after a full year, the private-sector sponsor of the pipeline, Kinder Morgan, announced it was planning to mothball the project. This in turn led the Trudeau government to announce that it was purchasing the pipeline outright for roughly $4.5 billion, a decision it justified by expressing concern that the economy would lose far more if the pipeline were not built, and reiterating its determination to proceed quickly with its completion. While the move initially was supported by a majority of Canadians, the increasingly massive costs associated with the purchase were not, despite the government's pledge to sell it back to the private sector and recoup its expenses at a later date.

Then the Supreme Court ruled the federal government could not proceed with the pipeline until it conducted proper consultations with affected Indigenous communities, something that the Harper government had neglected to do. This further delay not only exacerbated interprovincial tensions but increased dissatisfaction with the Liberals in Alberta and Saskatchewan, whose oil-dependent economies were already slumping. The situation intensified with Notley's defeat in the 2019 Alberta provincial election by the United Conservatives led by Jason Kenney, a former Harper cabinet minister and an aggressive critic of the Trudeau government.

More setbacks followed with the June 2018 defeat of the Ontario provincial Liberals. New Progressive Conservative premier Doug Ford promptly reneged on his predecessor's commitment to a cap-and-trade system with Quebec and California, and withdrew Ontario's participation in the national climate change plan that Trudeau had negotiated barely a year earlier. The Ontario withdrawal then encouraged the conservative governments of Saskatchewan (Saskatchewan Party) and Manitoba (Progressive Conservatives) to follow suit, leaving Trudeau's environmental plan in tatters.

The October 2018 victory of the Coalition Avenir Québec (CAQ) government of Francois Legault in Quebec increased the pressure on the Liberals. And Legault's controversial statements, flatly rejecting the possibility of an eastern pipeline, added fuel to western discontent. But it was his introduction of Bill 21, an act prohibiting government employees from wearing religious symbols, that would cause the most difficulty for Trudeau during the election. The bill was overwhelmingly popular in Quebec but less so elsewhere, and vigorously opposed by human rights groups. Trudeau's initial reluctance to take a position on the bill satisfied neither side.

Campaign Strategy: Sunny Ways versus Negative Attack Ads

It was increasingly evident to Liberal organizers that the government's efforts to help the oil patch had failed to make any positive impact, while the decision to buy the pipeline had alienated many voters in

BC. Since the Liberals already held all of the seats in Atlantic Canada and could not expect to duplicate that feat, they believed a win this time could only be achieved by capturing Conservative seats in suburban Ontario, as well as the sixteen seats held by the NDP in Quebec, to make up for seats lost elsewhere. With the NDP almost certain to lose all of those Quebec seats, the Liberals largely took for granted that they would come their way as the only other legitimate federalist party, given the lack of appeal of the Conservatives. With support for separation at a low point not seen since the 1970s and only ten seats in the House of Commons (not to mention a series of nondescript leaders and severe infighting that led briefly to the creation of a splinter group called Quebec Debout), the Bloc also was written off by party organizers and most observers as not a serious threat.

With the launch of "Choose Forward" on 27 August, party spokesman Braeden Caley told reporters "this theme ... speaks to Justin Trudeau's commitment to move forward with progress that helps people every day, and it highlights the choice that Canadians will make in this fall's election."[12] An accompanying video showed Trudeau riding a bus in his riding and speaking with fellow passengers. Much of the conversation revolved around the concerns of the riders and the accomplishments of the government, but it also pointedly included Trudeau "warning them that conservative politicians claim to be for the people but cut services."[13] The tone of the video was partly a response to the months of pre-election ads run by the Conservatives attacking Trudeau. Titled "Not as Advertised," they accused the Liberal leader of broken promises (electoral reform), corruption (Aga Khan and SNC Lavalin), and hypocrisy (India trip). In light of this attack on the leader's image, Liberal strategists believed the sunny ways of 2015 would have to give way, at least to some extent, to deflect this criticism in order to take seats in Ontario. Still, the Liberals argued their criticism was focused on opposition policies, not personal attacks.

The Liberals' decision to take a more aggressive stance was soon evident. Whenever possible the Conservatives were described as intolerant, and Andrew Scheer's social conservative values (including his personal opposition to gay marriage and abortion and refusal to march in Pride parades) were highlighted, despite official party positions accepting the status quo. To bolster this approach the Liberal war room had compiled a lengthy list of problematic statements by Conservative candidates reflecting racist or homophobic views. Meanwhile, the NDP and Greens were described as marginal and ineffective, in order to unite the progressive vote behind the Liberals and prevent vote splits that allowed the Conservatives to win ridings. With Ontario premier Doug

Ford's government deeply unpopular, another element of the Liberal strategy was to link him, as well as former prime minister Stephen Harper, with Andrew Scheer and the federal Conservatives. Liberal cabinet ministers from Ontario led the charge. Employment minister and Thunder Bay MP Patty Hajdu, for example, called the deep cuts in the Ford government's spring 2019 budget "cruel" and "reckless," concluding, "From my perspective Doug Ford and his cronies are trying to pull a fast one on Ontarians. It's quite clear that Andrew Scheer would take exactly the same tactic."[14]

The Liberals' Effective Advertising Campaign

The Liberals' first set of election ads of Trudeau riding a bus were released in late August along with the campaign slogan. Political advertising experts described them as "head and shoulders" above those of their opponents, technically superior and effective in terms of messaging.[15] They were also the most positive aspect of the Liberals' campaign, outlining the government's accomplishments and their positive impact on the lives of ordinary Canadians. Here too, though, Trudeau's comments straddled the divide between optimism and cautionary tale. "We've done a lot together these past four years," he said, "but the truth is, we're just getting started. So Canadians have an important choice to make. Will we go back to the failed policies of the past, or will we continue to move forward? That's the choice. It's that clear. And it's that important. I'm for moving forward for everyone."

In keeping with their ongoing efforts to attract the youth vote, the party led the way in its use of social media to communicate its message. In the previous election the party had assigned roughly 25 per cent of its advertising expenditures to this, but in 2015 it was nearly 40 per cent. In fact, the Liberals spent more money and ran more ads on Facebook than all the other parties combined.[16] The Liberals' emphasis on social media was validated by communications experts, who noted that television remains the most expensive medium but is less effective in reaching young, undecided, or leaning voters. Even more significant was the fact that the Conservatives' social media ads had conventional format and national content, while the Liberals focused on individual candidates' pages, a far more effective approach according to these experts.[17] The content again was primarily positive, highlighting government accomplishments and platform commitments, albeit tailored to local priorities and targeting whichever party posed the greatest threat to the Liberal candidate in question.

The party's ads in all formats evolved over the course of the campaign. The focus on local issues was one important innovation that would prove to be extremely significant by the end of the campaign. The Liberals realized the race was too close to call in many ridings and therefore began targeting ads related to the party's position on single issues – such as gun control, seniors, or trade – to specific local or regional audiences. Another major advertising addition responded to controversial third-party advertising by Conservative-friendly groups such as the Canada Growth Council, Canada Strong and Proud, and Shaping Canada's Future, all of which contained negative personal comments about Trudeau. One full-page ad in major newspapers by Canada Strong and Proud, for example, declared "It's Time for a New Prime Minister," describing Trudeau as a liar and "the ultimate hypocrite."[18] The Liberals responded with a series of ads featuring Trudeau alone, stating "The Conservatives want you to think this election is about me. We think it's about you." Others featured ordinary Canadians echoing this thought. Again, the messaging was effective, since committed voters had already made up their minds on the issues outlined, but undecided voters might be receptive to Liberal arguments.

Another series of Liberal ads aired late in the campaign, responding to Conservative ads falsely claiming the Liberals were planning to introduce a capital gains tax on home sales, and others in Chinese falsely accusing the Trudeau government of planning to legalize all hard drugs.[19] The Liberals denied all of the false claims and accused the Conservatives of using "the playbook of the American far right" to "spread false information to scare and mislead voters."[20] However, their response (in Chinese) was itself a classic example of negative advertising; they accused the Conservatives of opposing gun control and warned voters of potential threats to public safety.

Early Campaign Problems

As in 2015 Justin Trudeau began the campaign in earnest in British Columbia. This time his launch was more problematic, though, when a minor collision occurred on the tarmac in Victoria, damaging the Liberals' plane. However, the party organization regrouped and, having the financial wherewithal, promptly secured a second plane to carry on. As wagon master David Rodier later recounted, such incidents have the potential to negatively influence the media image of a campaign, and considerable effort is expended to avoid them. In this case, however, the accident "generated a wave of media stories and mockery on social media. For the next two weeks, we would fly unbranded planes,"[21] but it had no serious impact on the Liberal image.

The first week of the campaign then saw the party and the leader on the offensive, aggressively campaigning in non-held ridings in the province where they believed they could pick up seats, and holding several well-attended rallies of the party faithful. But the campaign's momentum came to a screeching halt on 18 September when *Time* magazine published two photos of a young Trudeau, in brownface and wearing an Aladdin costume, at an Arabian Nights fundraiser for the Vancouver school where he was a drama teacher. In short order another photo emerged, this time of an adolescent Trudeau wearing "blackface" while performing a Harry Belafonte song at a high school talent contest. Media coverage of the revelations, in Canada and abroad, was universally negative. This time the Liberal campaign was thrown into turmoil and only the leader could resolve the problem. Trudeau issued an apology immediately after the exposé appeared, stating, "I take responsibility for my decision to do that ... I should've known better. It was something that I didn't think was racist at the time, but now I recognize it was something racist to do, and I am deeply sorry."[22] A second apology followed the next day, as he told reporters he would be speaking with his candidates, opposition leaders, and his children about the incidents.

One analyst predicted the event would make the campaign "the fight of Trudeau's political life,"[23] but this did not prove to be the case. The following week revealed only a 1 per cent deviance from the virtual tie in which the Liberals and Conservatives had been locked on the eve of the bombshell incident. Liberal focus groups led by Dan Arnold also concluded these revelations were less serious than feared. In the end, pollsters concluded the majority of Canadians "either were not bothered by the scandal or had accepted Trudeau's apology."[24] This acceptance was no doubt helped by the flurry of supportive comments from Liberal candidates of colour, epitomized by the statement of Liberal MP Greg Fergus (Hull-Aylmer): "This is something that happened twenty years ago ... people are willing to cut him some slack and willing to forgive him because he has such a [positive] track record. I have confidence in the man."[25]

The same polls did find that Trudeau's personal ratings were down four points, but his opponents had fared worse. Elizabeth May's numbers were "lower than at any point since March," while "Andrew Scheer's negatives have hit a new high at 39 per cent."[26] However, the damage to Trudeau's image was potentially more significant for the Liberal campaign, since defending tolerance and diversity had been fundamental to his appeal four years earlier. Building on his earlier image problems, the revelations lent some credence to third-party advertising claims of Trudeau's poor judgment and Liberal hypocrisy. In short, both sunny ways and moral superiority – two key elements of Trudeau's original appeal – had now been abandoned or tarnished. The incident also caused problems for the broader campaign strategy of warning voters of the perils of a social conservative victory, and the Liberal war room prudently stopped releasing damaging material on opponents.

Meanwhile, the importance of the climate change issue continued to grow. Both the NDP and Greens had repeatedly criticized Trudeau's decision to buy a pipeline, rejecting his argument of a balanced approach. The Conservatives, by contrast, had cemented support on the prairies with their accusations that Trudeau was intent on shutting down the oil industry. With teenage climate activist Greta Thunberg's arrival in North America the publicity surrounding the issue – and the pressure on the Liberals – grew. Thunberg, too, had criticized the pipeline purchase, accusing Trudeau, "like all politicians," of "not doing enough."[27] When it was announced she would attend a rally in Montreal on 27 September Trudeau took the initiative. He met her in advance, declared he "was listening" to her concerns, and then participated in the rally with his family. In addition the party released another environmental platform plank promising to plant two billion trees as part of a broader ten-year, three-billion-dollar plan to "use the power of nature to flight climate change."[28] But Trudeau also unapologetically defended his balanced approach and the government's pipeline policy: "We have a "national climate plan that will reduce our emissions and hit our 2030 targets in a way that also includes getting a better price for our oil resources that allows us to put the profits directly into climate change."[29]

Then on 30 September the entire Liberal platform was released to generally positive reviews, although some specific measures (such as the proposed financial support for families to experience the outdoors) were subject to ridicule. Entitled "Forward: A Real Plan for the Middle Class," the platform as a whole was comprehensive, credible, and clearly positioned to continue the direction begun by the Liberals in 2015. Its contents were frequently in stark contrast to Conservative proposals. Liberal platform planks promoted social justice, environmental protection, Indigenous reconciliation, and economic innovation and included measures to aid students, seniors, and first-time homebuyers, a plan for net-zero emissions by 2050, and signature policies on gun control, a national pharmacare plan, and data privacy. However, virtually no one, including Liberal candidates, paid much attention to the package after its release. In a campaign characterized by mudslinging and personal attacks, and in which the Liberals were obliged to spend much of their time countering attacks on their government's record, serious policy debate took a back seat.

The Leaders' Debates Raise the Stakes

The newly created Debates Commission organized two formal debates on 7 October (English) and 10 October (French). Trudeau declined to participate in additional debates proposed by *Maclean's* and the Munk School, but did agree to a second French debate on 2 October organized by TVA.

With a complicated format, many moderators, and frequent exchanges where all the leaders spoke at once, the English debate was undoubtedly the least successful. The aggressive tone of Trudeau's opponents was set from the beginning by Andrew Scheer's personal attack on Trudeau. The Liberal leader's plan, by contrast, was to appear prime ministerial and avoid gaffes. His restrained performance did achieve that objective, but it did little to advance the Liberals' cause. Trudeau responded calmly to questions, highlighting his government's record or platform planks, but failed to make an impression. Only Jagmeet Singh appeared to have struck a chord with viewers, and notably when he attacked both Liberals and Conservatives on the environment.

In marked contrast to the English debate, the two French debates were models of organizational competence. Here it was the Bloc's Yves-Francois Blanchet who made an impact. With support for separatism near record lows, Blanchet carefully avoided the term and convinced many viewers the Bloc would be merely some sort of lobby group representing Quebec's interests in Ottawa. Trudeau was forced on the defensive, claiming the Liberals were the best choice to represent Quebec interests because they were in power, not opposition. A particular advantage for the Bloc was its unequivocal support of the CAQ's Bill 21, which Trudeau could not offer. After the debates Bloc fortunes soared and the NDP saw a glimmer of hope, while the Liberal strategy was in shambles. The party's campaign team now feared they would lose more seats outside Quebec due to a split progressive vote, while the Bloc's remarkable comeback meant they were not likely to take many of the NDP's sixteen Quebec seats to compensate. Their response was twofold: first, to double down on their narrative that a Conservative government would mean regression on climate change and cuts to programs and services, and second, to insist that they were the only ones who could stop them.

The post-debate polls showed little change. The Liberals were still tied or trailing the Conservatives, while the NDP was gaining support and the Bloc was clearly poised to win far more seats than expected. Speaking at a rally in Montreal on 16 October, Trudeau acknowledged his opponents might win. Liberal volunteers and insiders were already discouraged when reports surfaced that the Manning Centre had raised money from anonymous sources and then funded several of the major third-party groups who were attacking the Liberals, but refused to disclose its sources. While technically legal, this ploy was clearly contrary to the intent of the amendments that had been made to the Elections Act. Coupled with the various unsavoury activities to date, the revelations led Trudeau to describe the Conservative campaign as "reprehensible" and "one of the dirtiest, nastiest" in Canadian history, "based on disinformation," before concluding "it's no surprise they don't want to share whose deep pockets are funding their attacks."[30]

In the end, however, the final days of the campaign saw support gradually shifting to the Liberals. There were a number of reasons for this positive trend, most of which involved the campaign organization. Simply put, the party was able to fight the election riding by riding, due primarily to all of the advance work and technical improvements that had been developed over the past decade, and especially since 2015. To begin with, as Jeremy Broadhurst later explained, the party had more than enough boots on the ground. During the campaign itself, more than ninety thousand Liberal volunteers made fourteen million "attempts" (knocking on doors and phone calls), or nearly two million more than in the much longer 2015 election.[31] Moreover, as Azam Ishmael emphasized at an election post-mortem, these attempts were far more targeted than in 2015. Volunteers were told to focus on identifying definite Liberal supporters and to dispense with concerns about noting possible converts or undecideds. "In close races you don't want to risk getting out the vote of your opponents," Ishmael pointed out.[32]

These volunteers had even more advanced technology than in 2015, carrying iPads and a MiniVAN app with them on their rounds in order to enter data immediately. This, as both Wiltshire and Pitfield agreed, allowed the Liberals to up their game from 2015 in terms of narrowing their focus from regions to specific local and even riding-level messaging.[33] As party president Suzanne Cowan concluded, the volunteers and the focus on Liberal supporters at the riding level "made all the difference in many close ridings across the country. They got us across the line many, many times."[34]

In addition to their own actions, the Liberals were helped by the Conservatives, who released their entire platform on the Friday of the long Thanksgiving weekend, hoping to avoid scrutiny. The Liberal team quickly found numerous weaknesses. Scheer's vulnerability on climate change had already been heightened by his promise to eliminate the Liberals' carbon tax measure as one of his first acts if elected. Now the platform also confirmed Liberal accusations that the Conservatives would cut federal programs and services.[35] Liberal ads streamed out on Facebook and Twitter under the hashtag #scheercuts. Then Trudeau gave a rousing performance at the rally in Montreal, focusing on the Liberals' positive message. In addition, the Liberals released the ad showing Trudeau declaring "the election is about you," which had been filmed during a major rally in Mississauga days earlier. The late ad proved extremely timely, since a post-election study found more than two-thirds of voters did not make up their minds until the final week of the campaign.[36]

Finally, on 16 October Trudeau received a major boost from former American president Barack Obama. Although Martin Luther King III and Raptors' president Masai Ujiri also endorsed Trudeau, Liberal insiders believed Obama's ringing endorsement was a game-changer. According to one, "it recharged the base," especially those for whom the blackface incident had been a significant embarrassment.[37] The campaign distributed the endorsement widely. By election day the Liberals turned potential defeat into a sizeable minority of 157 seats.

Second Chance: From Minority to Dynasty?

An underlying factor in the Liberal win was undoubtedly the solid campaign fundamentals established in 2015 and diligently maintained over their first term in office, as Broadhurst, Cowan, and Ishmael later emphasized in an election post-mortem meeting.[38] The Big Red Machine was indeed back. Without it, there is little likelihood the party could have regrouped and overtaken the Conservatives after its dismal position in early 2019. In addition Trudeau himself, while wounded, was still a popular leader, and one far more appealing than his opponents. Unlike 2015, he was not the driving force behind the party's victory this time, but he was hardly an albatross around his candidates' necks, as Andrew Scheer so clearly was. Having adopted a more humble and realistic image than that of messiah – for example with the evidently sincere apologies on the blackface issue – he too aided in the party's eventual victory. As well, the late campaign strategy of reinforcing the "us or them" scenario had clearly worked. Post-election polls indicated that more than one-third of Canadians who voted were considering voting strategically, especially those who voted Liberal.[39] Nevertheless, with the numerous advantages the Liberals had enjoyed going into the campaign, their difficulty in securing that solid minority is a cautionary tale.

Certainly the election results were a dramatic contrast with the party's stunning 2015 election victory. Not only had the Liberals come from behind in that earlier campaign, surging from third place at the start to win a solid majority of 184 seats, but their 148-seat gain represented the largest single seat increase in Canadian electoral history. This time the Liberals lost seats in every region of the country. With only 33 per cent of the popular vote (down from 39 per cent in 2015), they formed a government with the lowest percentage of the vote ever. And, since they won no seats in Alberta or Saskatchewan, and lost their long-standing pillar of the prairies with Ralph Goodale's defeat, the regional divide between the two western oil-producing provinces and the rest of Canada was starkly evident. At the same time, the heightened importance of environmental issues throughout the campaign, especially in Ontario and Quebec, seemed to ensure the Liberals would face a significant challenge in navigating difficult policy choices in a minority Parliament. As the self-proclaimed party of national unity, the Trudeau Liberals had their work cut out for them.

The Liberals had received a substantial majority in 2015 and used their mandate to deliver on many important platform commitments. They had also presided over a period of robust economic growth. In this context, the fact they began the 2019 election in a dead heat with the Conservatives is particularly revealing. From early speculation of a new Liberal dynasty emerging,[40] the question they faced in 2019 was how to salvage a minority. What went wrong?

The 2015 victory owed much to Trudeau's personal image and commitment to a positive approach. But with the leader's image tarnished by various scandals (exacerbated repeatedly by an abject failure of Liberal communications efforts), and the party strategists' subsequent decision to "go negative," these advantages over their opponents were effectively lost. Further, unexpected developments over the course of the campaign, as well as the surge in support for the Bloc and the better-than-anticipated showing of Jagmeet Singh, all contributed to the minority result.

Still the Liberals remain in a relatively strong position. With their 157-seat minority only 13 seats shy of a majority, they should not have much difficulty obtaining sufficient support to implement the bulk of their agenda. The NDP, Bloc, and Greens are likely to approve the progressive elements of the Liberal platform and the Conservatives will have little choice but to support the controversial Trans Mountain pipeline, which the other opposition parties reject.

At a minimum the results of this election resolve the question of whether the Liberals' 2015 victory was merely the result of voters' overwhelming desire to replace the Harper Conservatives. And, with 63 per cent of the popular vote going to progressive parties, Trudeau was on solid ground when he declared the election results confirmed Canadians' rejection of Andrew Scheer and Conservative policies. In addition, despite their modest recovery the NDP's fourth-place finish at the hands of the Bloc, and loss of their Quebec foothold, suggest they are unlikely to be a credible alternative for some time.

Meanwhile, the election of Jody Wilson-Raybould as an Independent in her Vancouver riding, while certainly a rare accomplishment, must be considered a personal victory that did not appear to have any spillover effect, as the Liberals elected eleven MPs in the province and lost the other five incumbents to the Conservatives. In addition, the Liberals elected seven Indigenous MPs in total, compared with two for the NDP and none for the Conservatives. Certainly Wilson-Raybould's initial refusal to give up her ministerial office on Parliament Hill, in violation of standard practice after an election,[41] and her description of her role as an Independent MP as "lonely," suggest the former justice minister will face significant challenges in making the adjustment to the opposition, despite being named "Newsmaker of the Year." Moreover, the December settlement of the SNC Lavalin court case, with a result arguably similar to what would have emerged from the DPA process she opposed, appears to have brought that troublesome issue to a close.

The regional divide highlighted by the media in the aftermath of the election should also be placed in context. Much has been made of the Liberals' failure to win any seats in Alberta and Saskatchewan, but it must be remembered that they entered the election with only five – four in Alberta and one in Saskatchewan. Moreover, in the other two western provinces they retained fifteen seats. The party also finished in second place in three of those four provinces, well ahead of the NDP. Even more important is the fact that the electoral system, often described as favouring the Liberals, played a part in their admittedly poor results on the prairies. In Alberta, where they received 14 per cent of the vote, the Liberals won no seats, whereas in Quebec the Conservatives received only 16 per cent of the popular vote but held ten seats. In Atlantic Canada the Liberals took twenty-six of thirty-two seats; the Conservatives took no seats in PEI or Newfoundland, only one in Nova Scotia, and four in New Brunswick. Nevertheless, the results demonstrated once again that expanding their base on the prairies is still a major challenge for the Liberals, and one where progress before the next election is essential for reasons of national unity if not re-election.

While regional divisions were underlined by the election results, a Nanos poll conducted at the end of October found that some 60 per cent of Canadians (including a majority of Quebecers) were "pleased or somewhat pleased" with the election results. Perhaps more significantly, the same poll indicated nearly 50 per cent of Canadians wanted Trudeau's government to proceed with *both* the Trans Mountain pipeline and their carbon-pricing plan, thereby validating the Liberals' pragmatic balancing approach.[42]

For most voters, then, the continued pursuit of balance and positive progress based on Liberal values, along with greater humility on Trudeau's part, would appear to be the recipe for redemption for the Liberals. The prime minister's noticeably lower profile in the weeks following the election, and his widely approved, firm but measured response to the apparently accidental downing by the Iranian military of a Ukrainian Airlines plane carrying many Canadian passengers, appear to suggest that he has learned from his experience.[43] Trudeau's biggest challenge will be in calming the surging discontent in Alberta and Saskatchewan, aggressively stoked by provincial premiers based on real and perceived policy slights. At the same time, it is likely that some Liberal initiatives already in train will moderate oil patch discontent when they come to fruition. The announcement barely a week after the election that the Trans Mountain project would be hiring more than two thousand new workers is one example. The assignment of former foreign affairs minister Chrystia Freeland, a native Albertan, as deputy prime minister with special responsibility for improving federal-provincial relations with western premiers, has also been viewed as a positive initiative.

Still it would appear that greater federal consultation with provinces, and a far better communication strategy, will be necessary. In Quebec, meanwhile, with a rejuvenated Bloc Québécois ready to defend the interests of the province, the Liberals will need to re-establish their credentials as the more effective party in that province, and as an effective party of national unity in the eyes of the rest of Canada.

The results in the 2019 election could be particularly significant, not only for the Liberals but for liberal values. With the imminent departure of Germany's Angela Merkel, the ongoing Brexit saga in the UK, and the steep decline in public support for one of Trudeau's most sympathetic counterparts, French president Emmanuel Macron, following months of "yellow vest" protests, the response of Canadians to populist arguments will be closely watched by other Western liberal democracies. Trudeau himself appeared to be aware of this when he spoke at the nomination meeting for Minister of Innovation Navdeep Bains in Toronto in June 2018. "Around the world, the politics of division, of polarization, of populism are taking more and more hold," he told his audience. "We have to demonstrate here in Canada, for ourselves, our communities, for our kids – but also for the world – that those don't always work."[44] The 2019 election results' deepening divisions between the centre and the west, as well as with the Ford government in Ontario, may well prove the most significant challenge to the Trudeau Liberals in their next mandate. Reconciling the demands of climate change activists with those of the western energy-producing provinces, and the demands of Indigenous Canadians for meaningful consultation as part of a reconciliation process, will inevitably require compromise and conciliation.

It is too soon to tell whether the Liberals have learned the correct lessons from the mistakes of their first mandate and, second, whether they will have time to implement the necessary changes in policy and, equally important, attitude. Few would dispute the fact that they have already introduced a number of significant policy initiatives that are unlikely to be undone, regardless of the outcome of the next election. Their 5 December Throne Speech and ministerial mandate letters would suggest that they intend to pursue a number of their stated priorities aggressively, for as long as possible. As many commentators have noted, the situation of Justin Trudeau's Liberals in 2019 is eerily similar to the situation his father faced in 1972. As with 1974, the next election may well confirm the existence of a new Liberal dynasty or relegate the Trudeau Liberals to the margins of history as a mere interlude.[45]

Appendix A: Federal Election Results 2006–2019

National

	2006	2008	2011	2015	2019
Party	Seats/%*	Seats/%	Seats/%	Seats/%	Seats/%
Conservative	124/36.3	143/37.6	166/39.6	99/31.9	121/34.4
Liberal	**103/30.2**	**77/26.3**	**34/18.9**	**184/39.5**	**157/33.1**
NDP	29/17.5	37/18.2	103/30.6	44/19.7	24/15.9
Bloc	51/10.5	49/10.0	4/6.0	10/4.7	32/7.7
Green	1/4.48	0/6.8	1/3.9	1/3.45	3/6.5
Independent	0	2	0	0	1/0.4

* Percentage of popular vote.

Regional (Liberal Party only)

	2006	2008	2011	2015	2019
Region	Seats/%	Seats/%	Seats/%	Seats/%	Seats/%
BC	9/27.6	5/19.3	2/13.4	17/35.2	11/26.1
Prairies	5/16.5	2/13.5	2/10.6	12/28.4	4/20
Ontario	54/39.9	38/33.8	11/25.3	80/44.8	79/41.4
Quebec	13/20.7	14/23.7	7/14.2	40/35.7	35/
Atlantic	20/40	17/35.5	12/29.6	32/59	26/42
North	2/40.5	1/30.3	0/26.2	3/49.6	2/35.3

Note. Figures for the Prairies and Atlantic are an average, as the data are provided for provinces rather than by region.

National Voter Turnout (%)

2006	2008	2011	2015	2019
64.9	59.1*	61.4	68.5	65.9

* Represents the lowest turnout in Canadian electoral history.

Appendix B: Liberal Party Office Holders

Leader	President	National Director
Paul Martin (2003–6)	Mike Eizenga (2003–6)	Steven MacKinnon
Bill Graham (interim)		
Stéphane Dion (December 2006–8)	Marie Poulin (December 2006–8)	Jamie Carrol (2006–7)
	Doug Ferguson (2008–9)	Greg Fergus (2007–8)
Michael Ignatief (2009–11)	Alf Apps (2009–12)	Rocco Rossi (2009–10)
		Ian McKay (2010–12)
Bob Rae (interim)		
Justin Trudeau (2011–)	Mike Crawley (2012–14)	Jeremy Broadhurst (2013–15)
	Anna Gainey (2014–17)	Azam Ishmael (20116–)
	Suzanne Cowan (2017–)	

Appendix C: List of Interviews

Alf Apps	(former party president) 9 June 2017 & 26 Oct. 2004
Tom Ashworthy	(former adviser to Pierre Trudeau; party policy guru) April 2007
Gordon Ashworth	(veteran campaign manager) 21 Feb. 2017
Andrew Bevan	(senior Dion adviser) 10 Sept. 2018
Don Boudria	(former Chrétien minister) 23 Feb. 2018
Jeremy Broadhurst	(former party director, senior Trudeau adviser) 9 Dec. 2019*
Dan Brock	(senior Ignatieff supporter) 21 Feb. 2017
Charles Caccia	(former Trudeau minister) 2 Dec. 2006
Jamie Carroll	(senior Dion aide) 28 & 30 Nov. 2017
Suzanne Cowan	(current party president, key Trudeau organizer) 9 Dec. 2019*
Mike Crawley	(former party president) 1 June 2017
Ian Davey	(senior Ignatieff aide) 6 Sept. 2017
Peter Donolo	(Chrétien and Ignatieff adviser) 21 Feb. 2017
Mike Eizenga	(former party president) 31 May 2017
Jill Fairbrother	(Ignatieff aide) 6 Sept. 2017
Greg Fergus	(MP, former party director) 13 July 2017
Derek Ferguson	(former director, Liberal Caucus Research Bureau) 29 Oct. 2018
Doug Ferguson	(former party president) 11 Sept. 2018
Dan Hays	(former party president) 19 Dec. 2005
Mark Holland	(MP, Kennedy supporter) 29 Aug. 2018
Marlene Jennings	(former MP, Dion supporter) 9 April 2018
Don Johnston	(former minister, president OECD) 26 Sept. 2005
Lisa Kirbie Kinsella	(former Ignatieff aide) 1 June 2017
Warren Kinsella	(former Chrétien war room aide) 21 Feb. 2017

Doug Kirkpatrick   (veteran campaign organizer) 25 Aug. 2017
Sergio Marchi   (former Chrétien minister) 19 Oct. 2005
Mark Marrissen   (key Dion supporter) 22 Jan., 6 Feb., & 26 Feb.
                     2018
Gary McCauley   (former MP) 7 Dec. 2005 & 10 Dec. 2015
Steven MacKinnon   (MP, former party director) 23 June 2006 & 17 Nov.
                     2017
David Orchard   (Dion supporter) 10 Feb. 2018
Nini Pal   (veteran party volunteer) 9 Oct. 2018
Karen Redman   (former MP & Dion whip) 8 May 2018
Marjaleena Repo   (senior Orchard organizer) 9 March 2018
Cyrus Reporter   (senior Trudeau adviser) 7 Sept. 2017
Rocco Rossi   (former party director, Ignatieff aide) 21 Feb. 2017
Kathleen Rothwell   (senior caucus researcher) 13 Nov. 2018
Jack Siegel   (party legal adviser) 26 Nov. 2017
Susan Walsh   (Dion consultant) 21 Aug. 2018

* Brief conversations and email exchanges rather than formal interviews

Declined to Be Interviewed:

Johanne Senecal
Leslie Swartman

Notes

Introduction

1 John Meisel, *Working Papers on Canadian Politics* (Montreal: McGill Queens University Press, 1972).

2 Ken Carty, *Big Tent Politics: The Liberal Party's Long Mastery of Canada's Political Life* (Vancouver: UBC Press, 2015), 32.

3 Darrell Bricker and John Ibbitson, *The Big Shift: The Seismic Change in Canadian Politics, Business and Culture and What It Means for Our Future* (Toronto: Harper Collins, 2013).

4 Peter Newman, *When the Gods Changed: The Death of Liberal Canada* (Toronto: Random House, 2012).

5 Newman, *When the Gods Changed.*

6 Carty, *Big Tent Politics,* 32–3.

7 Joseph Wearing, *The L-Shaped Party: The Liberal Party of Canada 1958–1980* (Toronto: McGraw-Hill Ryerson, 1981), 235. More recently Wearing's thesis has been shown to be relevant to many European political parties of long standing. See, for example, Anika Gauja, *Party Reform: The Causes, Challenges and Consequences of Organizational Change* (Oxford: Oxford University Press, 2016).

8 Brooke Jeffrey, *Divided Loyalties: The Liberal Party of Canada 1984 to 2008* (Toronto: University of Toronto Press, 2010), especially chap. 4.

9 "Life after Ignatieff: Liberals Ponder Merger with NDP," *Waterloo Regional Record,* 3 May 2011.

10 Brooke Jeffrey, "The Disappearing Liberals: Caught in the Crossfire," in *The Canadian Federal Election of 2011,* ed. Jon H. Pammett and Christopher Dornan (Toronto: Dundurn Press, 2011), 73–4.

11 Bruce Doern, "The Chrétien Liberals' Third Mandate," in *How Ottawa Spends: 2001–02,* ed. Bruce Doern (Don Mills: Oxford University Press, 2003), 3.

12 Shawn McCarthy. "PM's Popularity at Record Low," *Globe and Mail*, 7 June 2002, https://www.theglobeandmail.com/news/national/pms -popularity-at-record-low-poll-shows/article4136070/.

1. A Party on the Brink

1 Brooke Jeffrey, *Dismantling Canada: Stephen Harper's New Conservative Agenda* (Montreal/Kingston: McGill-Queens University Press, 2015), especially 44–80.
2 Indeed, many observers have argued that the importance of party leaders (versus party ideology or platform, which had traditionally been the most significant determinant of voter intentions) increased for all political parties after the Trudeau era. See, for example, Harold Clarke, Thomas Scotto, Jason Reiffler, and Alan Kornberg, "Winners and Losers," in *The Canadian General Election of 2011*, ed. Jon H. Pammett and Christopher Dornan (Toronto: Dundurn, 2011), 293.
3 Trudeau's popularity has actually increased, and he remains one of the top choices of academics and Canadians for best prime minister. See, for example, Steven Azzi and Norman Hillmer, "Ranking Canada's Best and Worst Prime Ministers," *Maclean's*, 7 October 2016, https://www .macleans.ca/politics/ottawa/ranking-canadas-best-and-worst-prime -ministers/.
4 See the discussion of this in R. Kenneth Carty, William P. Cross, and Lisa Young, *Rebuilding Canadian Party Politics* (Vancouver: UBC Press, 2000), 76–8.
5 Jeffrey, *Divided Loyalties: The Liberal Party of Canada 1984–2008* (Toronto: University of Toronto Press, 2010), 26.
6 For a detailed discussion of the Turner era, see Paul Litt, *Elusive Destiny* (Vancouver: UBC Press), 2011.
7 For a detailed analysis see Jeffrey, *Divided Loyalties*, 89–120.
8 Jan Taber, "The Knives Came Out Quickly for Martin," *Globe and Mail*, 24 January 2006, https://www.theglobeandmail.com/news/national/the -knives-quickly-came-out-for-martin/article702284/.
9 Steven MacKinnon, interview with author.
10 Alf Apps, interview with author.
11 Ron Graham, *One-Eyed Kings* (Toronto: Collins, 1986), 284.
12 Graham, *One-Eyed Kings*, 284.
13 Iona Campagnolo, "Remarks to the First Meeting of the President's Committee for Reform," Ottawa, 17 June 1983.
14 Gary McCauley, interview with author.
15 George Perlin, *The Tory Syndrome: Leadership Politics in the Progressive Conservative Party* (Montreal: McGill Queens, 1980).

16 Campagnolo, "Remarks to the First Meeting."
17 Jeffrey, *Divided Loyalties*, 76.
18 Sergio Marchi, interview with author.
19 See, for example, K.Z. Paltiel, *Political Party Financing in Canada* (Toronto: McGraw Hill, 1970); Jansen et al., "Who Donates to Canada's Political Parties?" paper presented to the Annual Meeting of the Canadian Political Science Association, Edmonton, June 2012.
20 Paltiel, *Political Party Financing in Canada*.
21 Samara Centre for Democracy, *Lightweights? Canadian Political Participation beyond the Ballot Box*, Democracy Report #6, 2013. See also William Mishler, *Political Participation in Canada* (Toronto: Macmillan, 1979).
22 Paltiel, *Political Party Financing in Canada*.
23 Tom Flanagan and Harold Jansen, "Election Campaigns under Canada's Party Finance Laws," in *The Canadian Federal Election of 2008*, ed. Jon H. Pammett and Christopher Dornan (Toronto: Dundurn Press, 2009), 201.
24 Jeffrey, *Divided Loyalties*, 132.
25 Jeffrey, *Divided Loyalties*, 132.
26 Jeffrey, *Divided loyalties*, 162.
27 Jeffrey, *Divided Loyalties*, 256.
28 Lloyd Posno, interview with author.
29 See, for example, Jane Mayer, *Dark Money* (New York: Anchor Books, 2017). By contrast, the spectacularly successful online grass-roots funding campaign of Democrat Barrack Obama, as yet unrepeated there, provided an excellent model for future Liberal efforts, as Mayer's chapter on the Trudeau team's leadership campaign and election readiness preparations recounts.
30 As quoted in Lawrence Martin, *Harperland: The Politics of Control* (Toronto: Viking, 2010), 6.
31 Elections Canada, "Registered Parties First Quarter Financial Transaction Returns," Ottawa, 1 May 2008.
32 Carty, Cross, and Young, *Rebuilding Canadian Party Politics*.
33 Ken Carty, *Big Tent Politics: The Liberal Party's Long Mastery of Canada's Political Life* (Vancouver: UBC Press, 2015).
34 Dan Hays, interview with author.
35 Charles Caccia, interview with author.
36 Peter O'Neill, "How Martin Plans to Win the West," *Ottawa Citizen*, 10 November 2003.
37 For more details see Faron Ellis and Peter Woolstencroft, "Becoming the New Natural Governing Party?" in *The Canadian General Election of 2011*, ed. Jon H. Pammett and Christopher Dornan (Toronto: Dundurn, 2011), 15–45.

38 Gloria Galloway, Campbell Clark, and Brian Laghi, "Harper: Don't Fear a Conservative Majority," *Globe and Mail*, 18 January 2006, https://www.theglobeandmail.com/news/national/harper-dont-fear-a-majority/article965075/.
39 Clarke et al., "Winners and Losers," 300.
40 Jon Pammett, Larry LeDuc, Judith Mckenzie, and Andre Turcotte, *Dynasties and Interludes* (Toronto: Dundurn, 2010).
41 Alan Gregg and Michael Posner, *The Big Picture: What Canadians Think About Almost Everything* (Toronto: Macfarlane Walter & Ross, 1993).
42 Jeffrey Simpson, "The Trudeau Vision Won," *Globe and Mail*, 27 October 1992.
43 Chantal Hébert, "Bloc Facing Electoral Disaster," *Toronto Star*, 4 August 2003.
44 Statement by Chrétien in national caucus, according to an anonymous interviewee.

2. Unanticipated Consequences: The 2006 Leadership Race

1 Don Boudria, interview with author.
2 Don Boudria, interview with author.
3 Andrew Bevan, interview with author.
4 James Wood, "Sask. Grits Split on Leadership Race," *Saskatoon Star Phoenix*, 7 September 2006.
5 David Orchard, interview with author.
6 Marjaleena Repo, interview with author.
7 Don Boudria, interview with author.
8 "Manley Won't Seek Liberal Leadership," CBC, 26 January 2006, https://www.cbc.ca/news/canada/ottawa/manley-won-t-seek-liberal-leadership-1.622351; "McKenna Says He Won't Run for Liberal Leadership," CTV News, 30 January 2006; "Tobin Won't Be Running for Liberal Leadership," CTV News, 31 January 2006.
9 Michael Valpy, "Ignatieff Was Seen as an Outsider in the Liberal Family," *Globe and Mail*, 4 December 2006, https://www.theglobeandmail.com/news/national/ignatieff-was-seen-as-an-outsider-in-the-liberal-family/article18178928/.
10 Rae, however, had previously been a member of the Liberal Party as a young man.
11 Linda Diebel, *Stephane Dion: Against the Current* (Toronto: Viking Press, 2007), 167.
12 Jamie Carroll, interview with author.
13 Brooke Jeffrey, *Divided Loyalties: The Liberal Party of Canada 1984–2008* (Toronto: University of Toronto Press, 2010), 47–8.

14 "Don't Underestimate the Clarity Act's Value," editorial, *Globe and Mail*, 7 February 2004, https://www.theglobeandmail.com/opinion/dont-underestimate-the-clarity-acts-value/article1332101/.

15 David Herle, interview with author.

16 Diebel, *Stephane Dion*, 2.

17 Jamie Carroll, interview with author.

18 Helen Buzzeti, "Meme Dion serait de la course," *Le Devoir*, 25 January 2006, A1.

19 Andrew Bevan, interview with author.

20 Jamie Carroll, interview with author.

21 Don Boudria, interview with author.

22 Jaimie Carroll, interview with author.

23 Sean Holman, "Marissen Hitches His Horse to Dion's Wagon," *Public Eye*, 14 March 2006, http://www.publiceyeonline.com/archives/001337.html.

24 Holman, "Marissen Hitches His Horse."

25 Mark Marissen, interview with author.

26 Despite Dion's winning the leadership, his campaign was more than $3 million in debt, and it took four years for the debt to be retired.

27 Campbell Clark, "MacKay's Kingmaker Backs Dion," *Globe and Mail*, 17 August 2006.

28 David Orchard, interview with author.

29 Orchard, interview with author.

30 Orchard, interview with author.

31 Lana Haight, "Dion Welcomes Orchard's Endorsement," *Saskatoon Star Phoenix*, 16 August 2006.

32 Haight, "Dion Welcomes Orchard's Endorsement."

33 Clark, "MacKay's Kingmaker Backs Dion."

34 John Ivison, "Orchard Boosts Dion's Farm Team," *National Post*, 17 August 2006.

35 Clark, "MacKay's Kingmaker Backs Dion."

36 Marjaleena Repo, interview with author.

37 Clark, "MacKay's Kingmaker Backs Dion."

38 Mark Marissen, interview with author.

39 Statistics provided by the Liberal Party of Canada. Most are also contained in tables found at https://en.wikipedia.org/wiki/List_of_ex_officio_delegates_to_the_Liberal_Party_of_Canada_leadership_election,_2006.

40 "Stéphane Dion," stephanedion.ca, accessed 16 April 2010.

41 Don Boudria, interview with author.

42 Chantal Hébert, "Ignatieff Stumbles Out of Gate at Debate," *Toronto Star*, 12 June 2006, A13.

43 Linda Diebel, "Liberal Leadership Debates Fail to Ignite," *Toronto Star*, 11 June 2006, A3.
44 Rob Silver, "The Legend of the Delegated Convention," *Macleans*, 23 January 2013, https://www.macleans.ca/politics/the-legend-of-the -delegated-convention/.
45 Michael Valpy, "Liberal Candidates Unite to Slam Conservatives," Globe and Mail, 11 October 2006.
46 Scott Deveau, "MP Withdraws Support for Ignatieff over 'War Crimes' Comment," *Globe and Mail*, 11 October 2006.
47 Don Martin, "Ignatieff's Proposal Derailing Liberals' Leadership Race," *Calgary Herald*, 27 October 2006.
48 As cited in Brooke Jeffrey, "Missed Opportunity: The Disappearing Liberals," in *The Canadian Federal Election of 2008*, ed. Jon H. Pammett and Christopher Dornan (Toronto: Dundurn Press, 2009), 71.
49 Richard Fidler, "A Quebecois Nation? Harper Fuels Important Debate," *The Bullet*, 18 December 2006.
50 Sean Gordon, "Liberals Work to Avoid a Train Wreck," *Toronto Star*, 15 November 2006.
51 Gordon, "Train Wreck."
52 Mark Marissen, interview with author.
53 Jamie Carroll, interview with author. For more detail on the problematic SUFA, see Brooke Jeffrey, "From Collaborative Federalism to the New Unilateralism: Implications for the Welfare State," in *Continuity and Change in Canadian Politics: Essays in Honour of David E. Smith*, ed. Hans J. Michelmann and Cristine de Clercy (Toronto: University of Toronto Press, 2006), 117–46.
54 Fidler, "A Quebecois Nation?" This included such notable experts as Michael Bliss and Peter Russell, as well as respected Quebec columnist Lysiane Gagnon.
55 Tonda McCharles, "I Believe in One Nation, Undivided, Chong Declares," *Toronto Star*, 28 November 2006.
56 "Le Quebec est une nation ... sociologiquement, dit Stéphane Dion," *Le Devoir*, 27 June 2006.
57 McCharles, "I Believe in One Nation."
58 "Kennedy Takes Stand," CBC News, 27 November 2006.
59 Charles Caccia, interview with author.
60 For an interesting, albeit biased, perspective on the feud, see Jocelyn Coulon, *Une Selfie avec Justin Trudeau: Regard critique sur la diplomatie du premier minister* (Montreal: Québec Amérique, 2018).
61 Chantal Hébert, "Quebec Nation Debate Could Be Re-opened in Liberal Race," *Toronto Star*, 20 June 2012, https://www.thestar.com/news /canada/2012/06/20/quebec_nation_debate_could_be_reopened _in_liberal_race.html.
62 Hébert, "Quebec Nation Debate Could Be Re-opened."

63 Murray Campbell, "Trudeau Endorses Kennedy's Leadership Bid," *Globe and Mail*, 25 November 2006, https://www.theglobeandmail.com/news/national/trudeau-endorses-kennedys-leadership-bid/article20417090/.
64 Campbell, "Trudeau Endorses Kennedy's Leadership Bid."
65 Mark Holland, interview with author.
66 Steven MacKinnon, interview with author,
67 LPC Red Ribbon Task Force, "A Party Built for Everyone, a Party Built to Win," final report (Ottawa: 6 August 2006), 8.
68 Mike Eizenga, interview with author.
69 Mike Eizenga, "Notes for a Presentation on the Red Ribbon Task Force," presentation to the LPC (Ontario) annual general meeting, 6 May 2016.
70 LPC Red Ribbon Task Force, Final Report (Ottawa: August 2006), 5. http://www.liberal-members-matter.ca/wp-content/uploads/2016/05/redribbon_e.pdf.
71 Mike Eizenga, interview with author.
72 Mike Eizenga, interview with author.
73 Steven MacKinnon, interview with author.
74 "The Liberal Leadership: And Then There Was One," editorial, *Globe and Mail*, 1 December 2006.
75 "The Liberal Leadership: And Then There Was One."
76 Author interviews with several anonymous Kennedy team members.
77 Mark Holland, interview with author.
78 Andrew Bevan and Jamie Carroll, interviews with author.
79 Linda Diebel, "Kennedy a Charm for New Liberals; Appears to be Front-Runner in Signing Up New Members," *Toronto Star*, 13 July 2006.
80 Marjaleena Repo, interview with author.
81 Mark Marissen, interview with author.
82 Jaimie Carroll, interview with author.
83 Andrew Bevan, interview with author.
84 Don Boudria, interview with author.
85 Marrisen and Carroll, interviews with author.
86 Don Boudria, interview with author.
87 Mark Marissen, interview with author.
88 Susan Walsh, interview with author.
89 Mark Holland, interview with author.
90 This is the number frequently cited by Liberal insiders. Dion had 17.8 per cent support on the second ballot, and Kennedy 17.7 per cent. On the third ballot Dion had 37 per cent. Even after subtracting the support of Martha Hall Findlay (2 per cent) which also went to Dion, this level of support from Kennedy supporters would be required to achieve that number.
91 For a detailed description of delegate activities and convention floor antics, see Dion delegate Derek Tsang's account at http://individual.utoronto.ca/dstang/misc/liberal2006/.

92 Diebel, *Stephane Dion*, 222.
93 As quoted in Robin V. Sears, "The Liberals Stumbling Out of a Hall of Mirrors," *Policy Options*, 1 February 2007, https://policyoptions.irpp.org/magazines/the-charter-25/the-liberals-stumbling-out-of-a-hall-of-mirrors/.
94 John Duffy, "When Green Went Gold: Dion and the Greening of the Grits," *Policy Options*, 1 February 2007, https://policyoptions.irpp.org/fr/magazines/the-charter-25/when-green-went-gold-dion-and-the-greening-of-the-grits/.
95 Ian Davey, interview with author; see also Michael Valpy, "Ignatieff Was Seen as an Outsider in the Liberal Race," *Globe and Mail*, 4 December 2006, https://www.theglobeandmail.com/news/national/ignatieff-was-seen-as-an-outsider-in-the-liberal-family/article18178928/.
96 Marjaleena Repo, interview with author.
97 Mark Holland, interview with author.
98 Michael Ignatieff, *Fire and Ashes: Success and Failure in Politics* (Toronto: Vintage Canada, 2015), 86.

3. The Dion Era: Disappointment and Disarray

1 Susan Delacourt and Les Whittington, "The New Liberal Leader," *Toronto Star*, 4 December 2006.
2 Mark Marissen, interview with author.
3 Campbell Clark, Daniel LeBlanc, and Jane Taber, "Calls for Liberal Shakeup Dog Dion," *Globe and Mail*, 19 September 2007, https://www.theglobeandmail.com/news/national/calls-for-liberal-shakeup-dog-dion/article1082436/.
4 Andrew Mayeda, "Ignatieff Denies Undermining Dion," *The Province*, 8 October 2007.
5 Author interview with anonymous MP.
6 Delacourt and Whittington, "The New Liberal Leader."
7 Jane Taber, "Dion's the Leader but Who's in Charge?" *Globe and Mail*, 23 April 2007.
8 Paul Wells, "Why Dion Was Not a Leader, in His Own Words," *Macleans*, 3 November 2008, https://archive.macleans.ca/article/2008/11/3/why-dion-was-not-a-leader-in-his-own-words.
9 Author interview with anonymous former MP.
10 Marlene Jennings, interview with author.
11 Karen Redman, interview with author.
12 Marlene Jennings, interview with author.
13 As cited in Allison Crawford, "Intellect and Stubbornness Sustained and Limited Stéphane Dion's Political Career," CBC News, 10 January

2017, https://www.cbc.ca/news/politics/st%C3%A9phane-dion-profile
-1.3930011.

14 Benoit Aubin, "Ottawa's New Power Couple," *Maclean's*, 22 January 2007,
https://archive.macleans.ca/article/2007/1/22/ottawas-new-power
-couple.

15 Marlene Jennings, interview with author.

16 Don Boudria, interview with author.

17 B. Guy Peters, Carl Dahlström, and Jon Pierre, *Steering from the Centre:
Strengthening Political Control in Western Democracies* (Toronto: University
of Toronto Press, 2011), 161. See also Brooke Jeffrey, *Divided Loyalties: The
Liberal Party of Canada 1984 to 2008* (Toronto: University of Toronto Press,
2010), 451–3.

18 As cited in Linda Diebel, *Stephane Dion: Against the Current* (Toronto:
Viking Press, 2007), 215.

19 Jamie Carroll, interview with author.

20 Andrew Bevan, interview with author.

21 Author interview with anonymous senior Dion adviser.

22 Jane Taber, "Dion's the Leader."

23 Ray Heard, conversation with author, October 1987.

24 Campbell Clark and Brian Laghi, "Dion Moves to Create a New Image,"
Globe and Mail, 9 May 2007, https://www.theglobeandmail.com/news
/national/dion-moves-to-create-a-new-image/article685272/.

25 Brian Laghi, "Dion Shuffles Personal Staff," *Globe and Mail*, 22 December
2007.

26 Clark, LeBlanc, and Taber, "Calls for Liberal Shakeup Dog Dion."

27 See Justin Trudeau's autobiography, *Common Ground* (Toronto: Harper
Collins, 2014) for more details.

28 Jamie Carroll, interview with author.

29 Jamie Carroll, interview with author.

30 "Coup dur pour Stéphane Dion," editorial, *Le Devoir*, 18 September 2007,
https://www.ledevoir.com/politique/canada/157319/coup-dur-pour
-stephane-dion.

31 Campbell Clark and Daniel Leblanc, "Outremont By-election a
Test for Dion," *Globe and Mail*, 15 September 2007, https://www
.theglobeandmail.com/news/national/outremont-by-election-a
-test-for-dion/article18145262/.

32 For more details see Jeffrey, *Divided Loyalties*, 224–9.

33 David Orchard, interview with author.

34 David Orchard, interview with author.

35 David Orchard, interview with author.

36 David Orchard, interview with author. Jamie Carroll later confirmed
this.

37 Jane Taber, "Liberals at Odds over Candidate," *Globe and Mail*, 11 January 2008, https://www.theglobeandmail.com/news/national/liberals-at-odds-over-candidate/article18441786/.
38 Taber, "Liberals at Odds."
39 "Mr. Dion's Appointments," editorial, *Globe and Mail*, 25 February 2008.
40 David Orchard, interview with author.
41 David Orchard, interview with author.
42 "Dion Defends Beatty Appointment," CBC News, 9 January 2008, https://www.cbc.ca/news/canada/saskatchewan/dion-defends-beatty-appointment-1.710239.
43 Mark Marissen, David Orchard, David Karwacki, individual interviews with author.
44 Jamie Carroll, interview with author.
45 As cited in Diebel, *Stephane Dion*, 235.
46 Karen Redman, interview with author.
47 Karen Redman, interview with author.
48 Karen Redman, interview with author.
49 Jane Taber, "Liberals' 'Whipped Abstention' Preserves Minority," *Globe and Mail*, 25 October 2007, https://www.theglobeandmail.com/news/national/liberals-whipped-abstention-preserves-minority/article18148212/.
50 Taber, "Liberals' 'Whipped Abstention.'"
51 "Throne Speech Passes, Liberals Abstain from Voting," CTV News, 24 October 2007, https://www.ctvnews.ca/throne-speech-passes-liberals-abstain-from-voting-1.261372.
52 Joan Bryden, "Liberals Threaten Election over Budget," *Toronto Star*, 11 March 2008.
53 Mark Marissen, interview with author.
54 See, for example, the detailed analysis in Tom Flanagan and Harold Jansen, "Election Campaigns under Canada's Party Finance Laws," in *The Canadian General Election of 2008*, ed. Jon H. Pammett and Christopher Dornan (Toronto: Dundurn Press, 2009), 194–216.
55 Elections Canada, "Registered Parties First Quarter Financial Transaction Returns," Ottawa, 1 May 2008.
56 Elections Canada, "Registered Parties First Quarter."
57 Flanagan and Jansen, "Election Campaigns," 200, table 1.
58 Alison Crawford, "Intellect and Stubbornness."
59 Peter Woolstencroft and Faron Ellis, "Stephen Harper and the Conservatives Campaign on their Record," in *The Canadian General Election of 2008*, ed. Jon H. Pammet and Christopher Dornan (Toronto: Dundurn Press, 2009), 44.

60 Ira Basen, "A Schlemiel Is the Elephant in the Room: The Framing of Stéphane Dion," *Canadian Journal of Communications* 34, no. (2009), 297–305, https://doi.org/10.22230/cjc.2009v34n2a2215.

61 Alex Marland, *Brand Command: Canadian Politics and Democracy in the Age of Message Control* (Vancouver: UBC Press, 2016), 198–200.

62 Anonymous comments by Dion staffer and two officials at party headquarters in interviews. Significantly, while all of the individuals involved were adamant about their respective recollections, none was willing to be quoted for attribution.

63 Tom Axworthy, letter to the Hon. Stéphane Dion, 18 February 2007.

64 Tom Axworthy, interview with author.

65 Author interview with anonymous senior adviser.

66 Jamie Carroll, interview with author.

67 Jamie Carroll, interview with author.

68 "Débat sur la place des Québécois auprès de Stéphane Dion – La tête du directuer général est réclamée," *Le Devoir*, 28 September 2007, https:// www.ledevoir.com/politique/canada/158571/debat-sur-la-place-des -quebecois-aupres-de-stephane-dion-la-tete-du-directeur-general-du-plc -est-reclamee.

69 Jamie Carroll, interview with author.

70 "Dion Says Director's Comment Was Misinterpreted," CTV News, 28 September 2007. https://www.ctvnews.ca/dion-says-director-s -comment-was-misinterpreted-1.258160.

71 "Carroll Resigns as Liberal Party's National Director," CTV News, 10 October 2007; also Jamie Carroll, interview with author.

72 Greg Fergus, interview with author.

73 Doug Ferguson, interview with author.

74 Doug Ferguson, interview with author.

75 Greg Fergus, interview with author.

4. The Green Shift and the 2008 Election Debacle

1 Andrew Bevan, interview with author.

2 Author interview with anonymous Dion adviser.

3 Andrew Bevan, "Winning: The Coming Weeks and Months, and the Point of an Election," memo to the Hon. Stéphane Dion, Ottawa, 24 March 2008.

4 Karen Redman, interview with author.

5 Karen Redman, interview with author.

6 Linda Diebel, "Dion Ignored Green Shift Warnings," *Toronto Star*, 20 April 2008.

7 Diebel, "Dion Ignored."

8 Diebel, "Dion Ignored."

9 Diebel, "Dion Ignored."

10 "Dion Announces the Green Shift," Liberal Party of Canada press release, Ottawa, 19 June 2008.

11 "Dion Introduces 'Green Shift' Carbon Tax Plan," CTV News, 19 June 2008, https://www.ctvnews.ca/dion-introduces-green-shift-carbon-tax -plan-1.303506.

12 See also Susan Riley, "Dion Is Offering a Different Style of Leadership," *Ottawa Citizen*, 20 June 2008, and Frances Russell, "Which Will Canadians Prefer to Tackle?" *Winnipeg Free Press*, 25 June 2008.

13 Don Boudria, interview with author.

14 Mark Marissen, interview with author.

15 David Orchard, interview with author.

16 "Dion Hopes to Lasso Alberta Support for Green Plan," CBC News, 4 July 2008, https://www.cbc.ca/news/canada/calgary/dion-hopes-to-lasso -alberta-support-for-green-plan-1.726055.

17 "PM: Liberal Carbon Plan Will 'Screw' Canadians," CTV News, 20 June 2008, https://www.ctvnews.ca/pm-liberal-carbon-plan-will-screw -canadians-1.303683.

18 Doug Ferguson, interview with author.

19 "Green Shift Not Central Plank: Dion," CBC News, 19 September 2008, https://www.cbc.ca/news/canada/green-shift-not-central-plank-dion -1.744379.

20 "Green Shift Not Central Plank: Dion."

21 Andrew Bevan, interview with author.

22 Doug Kirkpatrick, interview with author. See also Rob Silver, "Air Canada as the Enemy," *Globe and Mail*, 11 January 2011, https://www .theglobeandmail.com/news/politics/second-reading/air-canada-as -the-enemy/article610783/. Dee also referred to Harper adviser Nigel Wright as a "good friend" and later accused Liberal governments of allowing several airlines to fail.

23 Jane Taber, "Hearing Problem Hurts Grasp of Music of English, Dion Says," *Globe and Mail*, 8 September 2008.

24 Campbell Clark and Josh Wingrove, "Liberals Left in Dark as Plane Grounded," *Globe and Mail*, 16 September 2008, https://www .theglobeandmail.com/news/politics/liberals-left-in-dark-as -plane-grounded/article1061314/.

25 Clark and Wingrove, "Liberals Left in Dark."

26 Doug Ferguson, interview with author.

27 Don Martin, "Liberal Campaign Almost Falling Down on the Job," *National Post*, 10 September 2008.

28 Doug Kirkpatrick, interview with author.

29 Gordon Ashworth, interview with author.

30 Mark Holland, interview with author.

31 Toronto Star/Angus Reid poll, 22 May 2008, reported in Allan Woods, "Dion's Approval Rating Sinks Again," *The Star*, 22 May 2008, https://www.thestar.com/news/canada/2008/05/22/dions_approval_rating_sinks_again.html.

32 Elizabeth McMillan, "What Was the Question?" *Media* 14, no. 1 (Winter 2009): 14–15.

33 CBC News, "Conservatives Jump on Dion Interview," 9 October 2008, https://www.cbc.ca/news/canada/conservatives-jump-on-dion-interview-1.765901.

34 Andrew Bevan, interview with author.

35 J. Patrick Boyer, *The Making of Senator Mike Duffy* (Toronto: Dundurn Press, 2014).

36 CBC News, "CTV Broke Ethics Code in Dion Interview: Standards Council," 8 May 2009, https://www.cbc.ca/news/entertainment/ctv-broke-ethics-code-in-dion-interview-standards-council-1.811860.

37 Andre Bevan, interview with author.

38 Brooke Jeffrey, "Missed Opportunity: The Invisible Liberals," in *The Canadian General Election of 2008*, ed. Jon H. Pammett and Christopher Dornan (Toronto: Dundurn Press, 2009), 94.

39 Faron Ellis and Peter Woolstencroft, "Stephen Harper and the Conservatives Campaign on their Record," in *The Canadian General Election of 2008*, ed. Jon H. Pammett and Christopher Dornan (Toronto: Dundurn Press, 2009), 55

40 Brooke Jeffrey, "Missed Opportunity: The Invisible Liberals," 92.

41 Jeffrey Simpson, "Harper Has a Future, Dion Is History," *Globe and Mail*, 15 October 2008.

42 Tom Flanagan and Harold Jensen, "Election Campaigns under Canada's Party Finance Laws," in *The Canadian General Election of 2008*, ed. Jon H. Pammett and Christopher Dornan (Toronto: Dundurn Press, 2009), 195–7.

43 Jane Taber, "First He Routed Liberals, and Now Harper Hopes to Bankrupt Them," *Globe and Mail*, 11 May 2011.

44 Brian Topp, *How We Almost Gave the Tories the Boot* (Toronto: Lorimer, 2010), 34–6.

45 The issue was discussed by several Liberal participants and bystanders in author interviews, but only on the condition of anonymity. As a result, most quotes in this section come from the NDP account of the event provided publicly by former party president Brian Topp some years later. Although clearly presented with that party's perspective in mind, it nevertheless reveals important information about the source of the Conservatives' advance knowledge of the plan.

46 The agreement struck between David Peterson's Liberals and Rae's NDP in 1985, after the election had delivered a tenuous Conservative minority, did last two years, a point Rae often made. However, when the agreement ended it was Peterson, whose party had been the dominant member of the accord, who won a majority in the subsequent election.

47 Topp, *How We Almost Gave the Tories the Boot*, 73

48 Rae later wrote about this experience, and his rationale, in *What's Happened to Politics?* (Toronto: Simon and Schuster Canada, 2015); see 104–7.

49 Doug Ferguson, interview with author.

50 See, for example, Andrew Coyne, "Harper's Tories Not to Blame for Political Fiasco," *Canadian Encyclopedia*, 11 February 2009, https://www.thecanadianencyclopedia.ca/en/article/harpers-tories-not-to-blame-for-political-fiasco.

51 Gary McCauley, interview with author.

52 John Geddes and Aaron Wherry, "Inside a Crisis That Shook the Nation," *Maclean's*, 11 December 2008, https://www.macleans.ca/news/canada/inside-a-crisis-that-shook-the-nation/.

53 Brian Topp, *How We Almost Gave the Tories the Boot*, 67–8.

54 A Leger poll on 4 December revealed a significant regional split over what to do if the Harper government fell. Nationally, 43 per cent of respondents preferred that a new election be held compared with 40 per cent who supported the coalition, but in western Canada respondents were sharply opposed to the coalition. Among Albertans who responded, fully 71 per cent were in favour of an election. Quebec showed the highest level of support for the coalition, with 58 per cent preferring it to a new election. This poll also showed that 60 per cent of Canadians worried the Bloc Québécois would hold the balance of power in a coalition, compared to 35 per cent that were not concerned, with the majority of respondents in every region, excluding Quebec, expressing concern.

55 Tim Naumetz, "Tories Begin Battle against Coalition," CBC News, 1 December 2008.

56 David Smith, *Across the Aisle: Opposition in Parliament* (Toronto: University of Toronto Press, 2013).

57 Several polls between 1 and 5 December consistently demonstrated that public support for the coalition was less than for another election, although there was a significant (roughly 20 per cent) number of undecideds. By 4 December, however, both Ipsos Reid and EKOS polls indicated that an election held that day would have produced a Conservative majority, with Liberal support falling several percentage points in all cases.

58 United Kingdom, House of Commons Committee on Political and Constitutional Reform, *Report*, Vol. 2, 28 January 2011.

59 For a detailed account of the important issues surrounding these events, see the excellent *Parliamentary Democracy in Crisis*, edited by Russell and Sossin (Toronto: University of Toronto Press, 2009).

60 John Manley, "The First Liberal Step: Replace Dion," *Globe and Mail*, 6 December 2008.

5. Third Try: The Ignatieff Solution

1 Alf Apps, interview with author. Coutts had been a key player in the Trudeau PMO. He was parachuted into the Toronto riding of Spadina, a previously safe Liberal seat, as the Liberal candidate in a 1981 by-election that Trudeau had expressly created by appointing MP Peter Stollery to the Senate. Coutts went on to lose the riding for the Liberals to the NDP in the by-election as well as the 1984 general election.

2 Dan Brock, interview with author.

3 Dan Brock, interview with author.

4 Michael Ignatieff, *Fire and Ashes: Success and Failure in Politics* (Toronto: Vintage Canada, 2015), 1.

5 See, for example, Michael Ignatieff, *Blood and Belonging: Journeys into the New Nationalism* (London: Farrar, Straus and Giroux, 1993).

6 Ian Davey, interview with author.

7 Ignatieff, *Fire and Ashes*, 29–30.

8 Michael Ignatieff, *The Lesser Evil: Political Ethics in an Age of Terror* (Edinburgh: Edinburgh University Press, 2004).

9 Caroline Alphonso and Jeff Sallot, "Liberals Miffed by Ignatieff's Candidacy," *Globe and Mail*, 28 November 2008, https://www.theglobeandmail.com/news/national/liberals-miffed-by-ignatieffs-candidacy/article1131539/.

10 Ignatieff, *Fire and Ashes*, 91.

11 Doug Ferguson, interview with author.

12 Doug Ferguson, interview with author.

13 "Bob Rae Gearing Up for Liberal Leadership Race," CTV News, 31 October 2008, https://www.ctvnews.ca/bob-rae-gearing-up-for-liberal-leadership-race-1.338580.

14 "Dion Done; LeBlanc Backs Iggy," CTV News, 8 December 2008, https://www.ctvnews.ca/dion-to-step-aside-leblanc-supports-ignatieff-1.349734.

15 "Rae Drops Out, Ignatieff to Be Named Liberal Leader," CTV News, 9 December 2008, https://www.ctvnews.ca/rae-drops-out-ignatieff-to-be-named-liberal-leader-1.350231.

16 "Rae Drops Out." Both men referred to the demise of their friendship in books published after their life in politics. See, for example, Ignatieff's *Fire and Ashes*.

17 Abbas Rana, "OLO Parliamentary Coffers Too Depleted to Hire Permanent Chief of Staff," *Hill Times*, 2 February 2009.

18 The Samara Blog, "How'd You Get that Job?" 28 May 2013, https://www.samaracanada.com/samarablog/blog-post/samara-main-blog/2013/05/28/how-d-you-get-that-job-samara-talks-to-michael-ignatieff's-former-speech-writer.

19 Jill Fairbrother, interview with author.

20 Jane Taber, "Ignatieff's Bay St. Brain Trust," *Globe and Mail*, 21 August 2009, https://www.theglobeandmail.com/news/politics/ignatieffs-bay-st-brain-trust/article4293129/.

21 Jane Taber, "Ignatieff's Bay Street Brain Trust."

22 "Liberal Coderre Steps Down as Quebec Lieutenant," CTV News, 28 September 2009, https://montreal.ctvnews.ca/liberal-coderre-steps-down-as-quebec-lieutenant-1.438667.

23 "Liberal Coderre Steps Down."

24 "Liberal Coderre Steps Down."

25 "New Inner Circle Surrounds Ignatieff," CTV News, 17 November 2009, https://www.ctvnews.ca/new-inner-circle-surrounds-michael-ignatieff-1.455464.

26 Ian Davey, interview with author.

27 Campbell Clark and Jane Taber, "Ignatieff Moves to Replace Top Aide," *Globe and Mail*, 27 October 2009, https://www.theglobeandmail.com/news/politics/ignatieff-moves-to-replace-top-aide/article4215183/.

28 Michael Ignatieff, *Fire and Ashes*, 137. In his account of the time in Ottawa, Ignatieff later admits that the firing of Davey was "badly handled" and something he regretted.

29 Peter Donolo, interview with author.

30 Peter Donolo, memo to Liberal colleagues, 17 November 2009.

31 Lisa Kirbie Kinsella, interview with author.

32 As cited in Brooke Jeffrey, "The Disappearing Liberals: Caught in the Crossfire," in *The Canadian Federal Election of 2011*, ed. Jon H. Pammett and Christopher Dornan (Toronto: Dundurn Press, 2011), 53.

33 Faron Ellis and Peter Woolstencroft, "The Conservative Campaign: Becoming the New Natural Governing Party?" in *The Canadian Federal Election of 2011*, ed. Jon H. Pammett and Christopher Dornan (Toronto: Dundurn Press, 2011), 31–2.

34 Mike Funston and Bruce Campion-Smith, "Ignatieff Strikes Back at Attack Ads," *Toronto Star*, 15 May 2009, https://www.thestar.com/news/canada/2009/05/15/ignatieff_strikes_back_at_attack_ads.html.

35 Rocco Rossi, interview with author.

36 Michael Ignatieff, *Fire and Ashes*, 123–4.

37 Bea Vongdouangchanh, "Liberals Want to Limit Pre-Writ Political Advertising," *Hill Times*, 1 June 2009, 32.

38 John Ibbitson, "Tory Attack Ads Pack a Punch that Leaves Liberals Reeling," *Globe and Mail*, 21 February, 2011.

39 As cited in Paul Wells, "The Untold Story of the 2011 Election," chap. 1, "The First Mistake," *Maclean's*, 4 May 2011, https://www.macleans.ca/uncategorized/politics-turned-over/.

40 Dan Brock, interview with author.

41 Jane Taber, "Handshake by Handshake the Liberals Refine Their Strategy," *Globe and Mail*, 8 September 2011, A8.

42 Harris McLeod, "Ignatieff's To-Do List," *Hill Times*, 16 November 2009, 4.

43 Taber, "Handshake by Handshake."

44 Jack Austin, *Themes in Canadian Liberalism* (Ottawa: Liberal Party of Canada, 1981).

45 Robert B. Reich, *The Resurgent Liberal and Other Unfashionable Prophecies* (New York: Penguin Random House, 1991).

46 Author interviews with Warren Kinsella and Ian Davey.

47 As cited in Jeffrey, "The Disappearing Liberals," 48.

48 Ian Davey, interview with author.

49 Program, "Canada at 150" conference, Montreal, March 2010, 4.

50 Kevin Carmichael and John Ibbitson, "Liberal Party in Danger of Losing Its Soul, Ex-diplomat Says," *Globe and Mail*, 29 March 2010, https://www.theglobeandmail.com/news/politics/liberal-party-in-danger-of-losing-its-soul-ex-diplomat-says/article1366369/.

51 Liberal Party of Canada, *Advancing Change Together: A Time to Act* (Ottawa: Liberal Party of Canada, 2009), 13.

52 Doug Ferguson, interview with author.

53 Alf Apps, interview with author.

54 As cited in John Geddes, "Ignatieff at the Liberal Convention," *Maclean's*, 21 April 2009, https://www.thecanadianencyclopedia.ca/en/article/ignatieff-at-the-liberal-convention.

55 Geddes, "Ignatieff at the Liberal Convention."

56 Geddes, "Ignatieff at the Liberal Convention."

57 Rocco Rossi, interview with author.

58 Following his loss there Rossi subsequently ran as a Progressive Conservative candidate in the Ontario provincial election of 2011, earning the considerable wrath of many Liberals, including party president Alf Apps, who wrote a scathing diatribe.

59 Susan Delacourt, "Wikileaks Reveals Liberal Tension between Ignatieff, Rae," *Toronto Star*, 1 June 2011, https://www.thestar.com/news/canada

/2011/06/01/wikileaks_reveals_liberal_tension_between_ignatieff_rae
.html.
60 Cited in Wells, "The First Mistake."
61 Wells, "The First Mistake."
62 Joanna Smith, "Committee Finds Harper Government in Contempt,"
  Toronto Star, 21 March 2011, https://www.thestar.com/news/canada
  /2011/03/21/committee_finds_harper_government_in_contempt.html.
63 See, for example, Jonathan Malloy, "Why You Should Care How
  Parliament Operates," *Ottawa Citizen*, 16 March 2011; Paul Benoit and
  Gary Levy, "Viability of Our Political Institutions Being Questioned," *Hill
  Times*, 25 April 2011.
64 Lorne Gunther, "Putting the Tories' Missteps in Perspective," *National
  Post*, 11 March 2011.
65 As cited in Dan Gardner, "The Small Matter of Contempt," https://
  dangardner.ca/article/the-small-matter-of-contempt.
66 Gardner, "The Small Matter of Contempt."
67 Smith, "Committee Finds Harper Government in Contempt."

6. The Near-Death Experience: The 2011 Election

1 See, for example, "Harper Goes Prorogue," *The Economist*, 7 January
  2010, https://www.economist.com/leaders/2010/01/07/harper-goes
  -prorogue.
2 Cited in John Ibbitson, "Few Countries Can Claim Such a Pathetic
  Parliament," *Globe and Mail*, 8 January 2010.
3 For more details, see Andre Turcotte, "Polls: Seeing through the Glass
  Darkly," in *The Canadian General Election of 2011*, ed. Jon H. Pammett and
  Christopher Dornan (Toronto: Dundurn, 2011), 195–213.
4 Gordon Ashworth, interview with author. See also Warren Kinsella, "The
  Biggest Losers," *The Walrus*, July/August 2011, https://thewalrus.ca
  /the-biggest-losers/.
5 See, for example, the many works of John Courtney, William Cross,
  Norman Ward, Conrad Winn, and John McMenemy.
6 Peter Donolo, interview with author.
7 Alf Apps, interview with author.
8 Alf Apps, interview with author.
9 Peter Donolo, interview with author.
10 Paul Wells, "Ignatieff Finds His Fight," *Maclean's*, 1 April 2011, https://
  www.macleans.ca/uncategorized/fighting-back-2/.
11 Warren Kinsella, "Secret to Ignatieff's Apparent Uptick," *London Free
  Press*, 5 April 2011.
12 Peter Donolo, interview with author.

13 Adam Radwanski, "Ignatieff's Sparkle Brightens Liberal Hopes," *Globe and Mail*, 1 April 2011.

14 Tom Kent, "First, a Few Questions for Ignatieff and the Liberals," *Globe and Mail*, 2 July 2010.

15 As cited in Althia Raj and Mike De Souza, "Liberals Release Election Platform," *National Post*, 3 April 2011, https://nationalpost.com/news /canada/canadian-politics/liberals-release-election-platform.

16 Craig Oliver, "Liberal Platform a Statement of Principles," *Craig's Take*, CTV, 3 April 2011.

17 As cited in Linda Diebel, "Exclusive: What Really Sunk Michael Ignatieff and the Liberals," *Toronto Star*, 7 May 2011.

18 Ignatieff, *Fire and Ashes: Success and Failure in Politics* (Toronto: Vintage Canada, 2015), 160.

19 Faron Ellis and Peter Woolstencroft, "The Conservative Campaign: Becoming the New Natural Governing Party?" in *The Canadian General Election of 2011*, ed. Jon H. Pammett and Christopher Dornan (Toronto: Dundurn Press, 2011), 36–7.

20 Mark Holland, interview with author.

21 Brooke Jeffrey, "Caught in the Crossfire: The Disappearing Liberals," in *The Canadian General Election of 2011*, ed. Jon H. Pammett and Christopher Dornan (Toronto: Dundurn Press, 2011), 44.

22 As cited in Paul Wells, "The Untold Story of the 2011 Election," chap. 4, "Turning Up the Heat," *Maclean's*, 8 May 2011, https://www.macleans .ca/uncategorized/politics-turned-over/.

23 L. Ian Macdonald, "Duceppe's Misplay Gives NDP Ground," *Peterborough Examiner*, 29 April 2011.

24 Peter Newman, *When the Gods Changed: The Death of Liberal Canada* (Toronto: Random House, 2011).

25 Alf Apps, interview with author.

26 Strategy Corp, "2011 vs. 2015 Federal Election, Where Did All Those Votes Come From?" 3 December 2015, https://strategycorp.com/2015/12 /total_voter_turnout_canada_2015/.

27 See, for example, Harold D. Clarke, Thomas J. Scotto, Jason Reifler, and Allan Kornberg, "Winners and Losers: Voters in the 2011 Federal Election," in *The Canadian Federal Election of 2011*, ed. Jon H. Pammett and Christopher Dornan (Toronto: Dundurn Press, 2011), 271–301.

28 StrategyCorp, "2011 vs. 2015 Federal Election, Where Did All Those Votes Come From?" https://strategycorp.com/2015/12/total_voter_turnout _canada_2015/.

29 Susan Delacourt, "What Went Wrong for the Liberals," *Toronto Star*, 30 April 2011, https://www.thestar.com/news/canada/2011/04/30/what _went_wrong_for_the_liberals.html.

30 Ellis and Woolstencroft, "The Conservative Campaign," 29–33.
31 Warren Kinsella, "The Biggest Losers."
32 CTV News, "Liberals Predict Tory Attack Ads Would Backfire," 2 March 2009, https://www.ctvnews.ca/liberals-predict-tory-attack-ads-would-backfire-1.375199.
33 As cited in Paul Wells, "The Untold Story of the 2011 Election," chap. 1, "The First Mistake," *Maclean's*, 4 May 2011.
34 See, for example, Warren Kinsella, *The War Room* (Toronto: Dundurn Press, 2007), and Allan Gregg, "The Democratic Danger of Political Attack Ads," *Toronto Star*, 18 April 2004, https://www.thestar.com/opinion /commentary/2013/04/18/the_democratic_danger_of_political_attack _ads.html.
35 Darrell Bricker, "What Were They Thinking?", presentation to the Annual CPSA Meeting, Kitchener/Waterloo, 18 May 2011.
36 Jonathan Malloy, "Why You Should Care How Parliament Operates," *Ottawa Citizen*, 16 March 2011.
37 Jeffrey, "Caught in the Crossfire," 71.
38 Steven MacKinnon, "From the Family Pack to Equal Opportunity," *Policy Options*, 1 March 2012.
39 Jeffrey, "Caught in the Crossfire."
40 As cited in John Ivison, "It's Always Sunny for Ignatieff," *National Post*, 16 December 2010, https://nationalpost.com/full-comment/john-ivison-its -always-sunny-for-ignatieff.
41 Jeffrey, "Caught in the Crossfire," 73
42 For a detailed analysis of the NDP campaign success, see P. Fournier, Fred Cutler, Stuart Soroka, and Dietlind Stolle, "Riding the Orange Wave: Leadership, Issues and Values in the 2011 Election," *Canadian Journal of Political Science/Revue canadienne de science politique* 46, no. 4 (2013): 863–97, https://doi.org/10.1017/S0008423913000875.
43 Jeffrey, "Caught in the Crossfire," 73–4.

7. Rebuilding and Renewal: Trudeau and the Liberal Way

1 George Perlin, *The Tory Syndrome: Leadership Politics in the Progressive Conservative Party* (Montreal: McGill-Queens University Press, 1980).
2 Peter Newman, *When the Gods Changed: The Death of Liberal Canada* (Toronto: Random House, 2011).
3 John Ibbitson and Darrell Bricker, *The Big Shift: The Seismic Change in Canadian Politics* (Toronto: Harper Collins, 2013).
4 Alf Apps, "Building a Modern Liberal Party," background paper, 10 November 2011, 17, https://www.liberal.ca/wp-content/uploads /2011/11/BuildingaModernLiberalParty.pdf.

5 Robert Harmel and Kenneth Janda, "An Integrated Theory of Party Goals and Party Change," *Journal of Theoretical Politics* 6, no. 3 (1994): 259–87, https://doi.org/10.1177%2F0951692894006003001.

6 Meagan Fitzpatrick, "Liberals Choose Rae as Interim Leader," CBC News, 25 May 2011, https://www.cbc.ca/news/politics/liberals-choose-rae-as -interim-leader-1.1012598.

7 Fitzpatrick, "Liberals Choose Rae."

8 Meagan Fitzpatrick, "Liberals Call in Saturday to Debate Leadership Timing," CBC News, 17 June 2011.

9 Joan Bryden "Federal Liberals Won't Pick New Leader for Full Two Years," *Globe and Mail*, 18 June 2011, https://www.theglobeandmail.com /news/politics/federal-liberals-wont-pick-new-leader-for-full-two -years/article583767/.

10 Liberal Party of Canada, "A Roadmap to Renewal," Ottawa, 2011, 1.

11 Alf Apps, interview with author.

12 Liberal Party of Canada, "Roadmap to Renewal."

13 Apps, "Building a Modern Liberal Party," 17.

14 Apps, "Building a Modern Liberal Party," 15.

15 Apps, "Building a Modern Liberal Party," 16.

16 Liberal Party of Canada, "Roadmap to Renewal," 4.

17 Apps, "Building a Modern Liberal Party," 16.

18 Liberal Party of Canada, "Roadmap to Renewal," 7.

19 Liberal Party of Canada, "Roadmap to Renewal," 8.

20 Liberal insiders were quick to note that Martin and Turner had been close allies for years, and Ignatieff owed much of his campaign organization to Martin. All three were also business liberals who had failed, where Chrétien the social liberal had succeeded, and the enmity flowing from his forced removal as leader by Martin continued. Dion was simply along for the ride. For more details see Brooke Jeffrey, *Divided Loyalties: The Liberal Party of Canada 1984 to 2008* (Toronto: University of Toronto Press, 2010).

21 See, for example, Susan Delacourt, Bruce Campion-Smith, and Les Whittington, "Liberals End Convention with Internal Changes, New President and Resolution to Legalize Pot," *Toronto Star*, 15 January 2012.

22 John Geddes, "The Liberal Crisis," *Maclean's*, 14 May 2012.

23 Jane Taber, "Delegates Divided about Creating a New Class of Liberals at Convention," *Globe and Mail*, 14 January 2012.

24 Althia Raj, "Liberal Convention 2012: Party Votes in Favour of Preferential Ballots," *Huffington Post*, 15 January 2012,.

25 Raj, " Party Votes in Favour."

26 For the past three decades the race had either been between two well-known candidates or, as in the case of Alf Apps, acclaimed.

27 Sonya Bell, "Ron Who? Would-Be President Hits the Road to Build a Base," *IPolitics*, 7 September 2011, https://ipolitics.ca/2011/09/07 /ron-who-would-be-lpc-president-hits-the-road-to-build-a-base/.

28 Bell, "Ron Who?"

29 Sonya Bell, "Defeated MP Alexandra Mendes Runs Again in Bid for Liberal President," *IPolitics*, 21 October 2011.

30 Bell, "Defeated MP."

31 Sonya Bell, "Can Anyone Touch Copps? Liberals Ponder Party Leadership," *IPolitics*, 29 November 2011, https://ipolitics.ca/2011/11/29/can-anyone -touch-copps-liberals-ponder-party-leadership/.

32 For a detailed analysis of Campagnolo's tenure, see Jeffrey, *Divided Loyalties*, 60–80.

33 Joan Bryden, "Federal Liberals Endorse Marijuana Legalization," CTV News, 16 January 2012.

34 Delacourt, Campion-Smith, and Whittington, "Liberals End Convention."

35 Megan Fitzpatrick, "Copps, Crawley Battle for Liberal Presidency," CBC News, 10 January 2012, https://www.cbc.ca/news/politics/copps -crawley-battle-for-liberal-presidency-1.1129263.

36 Sonya Bell, "Liberal President Hopeful Mike Crawley Strives for More than 'Centrist' Party," *IPolitics*, 11 October 2011.

37 Bell, "Can Anyone Touch Copps?"

38 Mark Holland, interview with author.

39 Lee Berthiaume and Jason Feteke, "Liberals Elect Mike Crawley as New Party President," *National Post*, 15 January 2012, https://nationalpost .com/news/canada/liberals-select-mike-crawley-as-new-party-president.

40 Delacourt, Campion-Smith, and Whittington, "Liberals End Convention."

41 Bryden, "Federal Liberals Endorse Marijuana Legalization."

42 Mike Crawley, interview with author.

43 Mike Crawley, interview with author.

44 Mike Crawly, interview with author.

45 For more details see Jeffrey, *Divided Loyalties*, 69–71.

46 Royce Koop, *Grassroots Liberals: Organizing for Local and National Politics* (Vancouver: UBC Press, 2012).

47 Mike Crawley, interview with author.

48 See Jeffrey, *Divided Loyalties*, 60–5.

49 Mike Crawley, interview with author.

50 Mike Crawley, interview with author.

51 Geddes, "The Liberal Crisis."

52 Anonymous interview with author.

53 Geddes, "The Liberal Crisis."

54 Forum Research polling of potential Liberal candidates, released 26 January 2012. The data are no longer available at Forum Research, but the

results are given in detail at https://nationalpost.com/news/canada /bob-rae-top-choice-to-lead-the-liberals-poll.

55 Susan Delacourt, "Bob Rae on Warpath against Stephen Harper and Thomas Mulcair," *Toronto Star*, 4 April 2012, https://www.thestar.com /news/canada/2012/04/04/bob_rae_on_warpath_against_stephen _harper_and_thomas_mulcair.html.

56 Jane Taber, "Bob Rae and Beyond: Potential Contenders for the Top Liberal Job," *Globe and Mail*, 18 January 2012, https://www .theglobeandmail.com/news/politics/ottawa-notebook/bob-rae-and -beyond-potential-contenders-for-the-top-liberal-job/article620981/.

57 Mark Dunn, "Conservative Ads Target Bob Rae's NDP Economic Record," *Toronto Sun*, 18 March 2012, https://torontosun.com/2012/03/18 /conservative-ads-target-bob-raes-ndp-economic-record/wcm/4c21fcac -f0ac-4e12-9fdf-bc7c8996d727.

58 Matt Gurney, "Bob Rae Leaves Liberals Looking for an Interim-Interim Leader," *National Post*, 2 May 2012, https://nationalpost.com/opinion /matt-gurney-bob-rae-leaves-liberals-looking-for-an-interim-interim -leader.

59 Mike Crawley, interview with author.

60 Anonymous interview with author.

61 "Seeking Liberal Presidency, Copps Vows to Fight Merger," *Globe and Mail*, 7 September 2011,.

62 Gary McCauley, interview with author.

63 John Ibbitson, "Rae Won't Seek Liberal Leadership," *Globe and Mail*, 13 June 2012, https://www.theglobeandmail.com/news/politics/rae-wont -seek-liberal-leadership/article4255399/.

64 Chris Kitching, "Trudeau-Led Liberals Find Strong Support in T.O.," CP24 News, 1 October 2012, https://www.cp24.com/news/poll-trudeau -led-liberals-find-strong-support-in-t-o-1.978589.

65 Alex Marland, *Brand Command: Canadian Politics and Democracy in the Age of Message Control* (Vancouver: UBC Press, 2016), 128–34.

66 "Justin Trudeau and Senator Patrick Brazeau Face Off in 2012 Boxing Match" (video), *The Guardian*, https://www.theguardian.com/world /video/2017/jul/28/justin-trudeau-and-senator-patrick-brazeau-face -off-in-2012-boxing-match-video.

67 See, for example, Paolo Gerbaudo, "The Age of the Hyperleader: When Political Leadership Meets Social Media Celebrity," *New Statesman*, 8 March 2019, https://www.newstatesman.com/politics/media/2019/03 /age-hyperleader-when-political-leadership-meets-social-media -celebrity; Sharon Coen, "The Age of Celebrity Politics," *The Psychologist*, vol. 28, May 2015, https://thepsychologist.bps.org.uk/volume-28/may -2015/age-celebrity-politics.

68 For the origins of this concept see, for example, Robert Michels, *Political Parties: A Sociological Study of the Oligarchical Tendencies of Modern Democracy* (New York: Free Press, 1962); Antonio Gramsci, *Selections from Cultural Writings* (Boston: Harvard University Press, 1965).

69 Ibbitson, "Rae Won't Seek Liberal Leadership."

70 Comments by Liberal candidate Mark Miller (Ville-Marie–Le Sud-Ouest–Île-des-Soeurs) at an event held at McGill University in Montreal discussing the future of Canadian liberalism, on the thirtieth anniversary of Pierre Trudeau's departure as prime minister in June 1984. The other panelists were the Hon. Marc Lalonde and the author.

71 Justin Trudeau, remarks at news conference announcing his candidacy for the Liberal leadership, Montreal, 2 October 2012.

72 Susan Delacourt, "Justin Trudeau Launches Liberal Leadership Campaign in Cross-Canada Tour," *Toronto Star*, 1 October 2012, https://www.thestar.com/news/canada/2012/10/01/justin_trudeau_launches_liberal_leadership_campaign_in_crosscanada_tour.html.

73 John Ibbitson, "Team Trudeau: Taking a Page out of Obama's Playbook," *Globe and Mail*, 12 November 2012, https://www.theglobeandmail.com/news/politics/team-trudeau-taking-a-page-out-of-obamas-playbook/article5187867/.

74 Doug Kirkpatrick, interview with author.

75 Liberal Party of Canada, press conference announcing the launch of leadership race, Ottawa, 14 November 2012.

76 Cited in Joan Bryden "Liberal Leadership Debate: 6 Candidates Face Off in Montreal," *Huffington Post*, 23 March 2013, https://www.huffingtonpost.ca/2013/03/23/liberal-leadership-debate-montreal_n_2939717.html.

77 Aly Thomson, "Justin Trudeau Shoots Back at Garneau during Liberal Leadership Debate," Global News, 3 March 2012, https://globalnews.ca/news/402021/justin-trudeau-shoots-back-at-marc-garneau-during-liberal-leadership-debate-3/.

78 Thomson, "Justin Trudeau Shoots Back."

79 Deborah Coyne, "Statement in Support of a Deadline Extension for Registration," 12 March 3013.

80 Mike Crawley, interview with author.

81 Author interviews with two anonymous delegates at the January 2012 convention who voted against the removal of a delegated leadership convention.

8. Redemption: The 2015 Election

1 Michael Bliss, "The Liberal Party Does NOT Have a Future in Canada," *Ottawa Citizen*, 23 March 2013.

2 John Duffy, "The Liberal Party DOES Have a Future in Canada," *Ottawa Citizen*, 23 March 2013.
3 Elections Canada, "Fundraising contributions/ Leadership candidates /Liberal Party," https://www.elections.ca/WPAPPS/WPF/EN/CCS /ContributionReport?returnStatus=1&reportOption.
4 Jane Taber and Daniel Leblanc, "Trudeau Compiling War Chest to Fight Tory Attack Ads," *Globe and Mail*, 22 March 2013, https://www .theglobeandmail.com/news/national/trudeau-compiling-war-chest -to-fight-tory-attack-ads/article10254429/.
5 Taber and Leblanc, "Trudeau Compiling War Chest."
6 Numerous individual author interviews.
7 A number of media articles began to mention this trend. See, for example, Leslie MacKinnon, "Justin Trudeau's Inner Circle a Reflection of the Leader," CBC News, 19 February 2014, https://www.cbc.ca/news /politics/justin-trudeau-s-inner-circle-a-reflection-of-the-leader-1.2538082.
8 Glen McGregor, "The Big Data Election," *Ottawa Citizen*, 20 October 2014.
9 McGregor, "The Big Data Election."
10 LUNCH Sheets were canvassing sheets, used for decades up to and including 1990 to identify voter preferences. These were sheets of squared paper resembling arithmetic exercise books. The top line had five categories for five columns: L = Liberal; U = Undecided; N = NDP; C = Conservative; H = Hostile. On the left-hand side were names of voters in each riding. Ridings were subdivided so each canvasser had no more than fifty voters at a time. The sheets were handed in at the end of a canvas for headquarters workers to calculate totals.
11 Nini Pal, interview with author.
12 Nini Pal, interview with author.
13 "Justin Trudeau Says Anti-abortion Candidates Can't Run as Liberals," *National Post*, 7 May 2014, https://nationalpost.com/news/politics /justin-trudeau-says-anti-abortion-candidates-cant-run-as-liberals.
14 Jack Siegel, interview with author.
15 Siegel, interview with author.
16 "Social Media Can Be Achilles Heel for Politicians, Aides," CBC News, 9 September 2015, https://www.cbc.ca/news/politics/canada-election -2015-social-media-1.3220589.
17 Innes subsequently sued the party, which also became public knowledge. The lawsuit was settled in 2017 and the terms remained confidential, but the party issued a statement saying it "regrets the circumstances that led to this lawsuit." Bertschi's lawsuit was also settled, in 2016, and while again no terms were disclosed the party did issue a statement saying that he had "answered honestly and to the best of his ability" all questions put to him by the central committee that green-lighted candidates. The

statement also praised Bertschi as a "hard-working" and respected lawyer in Ottawa.

18 "Liberals Who Helped Defeat Eve Adams Say Her Loss Will Help Trudeau," CTV News, 27 July 2015, https://www.ctvnews.ca/politics /liberals-who-helped-defeat-eve-adams-say-her-loss-will-help-trudeau -1.2489846.
19 Sean Kilpatrick, "Tory Attack Ads May Be Backfiring in Favour of Trudeau's Liberals as Support Rises, New Poll Shows," *National Post*, 7 May 2013, https://nationalpost.com/news/politics/tory-attack-ads -may-be-backfiring-in-favour-of-trudeaus-liberals-as-support-rises-new -poll-shows.
20 Householders are publications sent out by individual MPs to their constituents up to four times per year, postage free, and are intended to be used primarily to provide citizens with information on government activities and programs. Partisan commentary has always been discouraged.
21 Jennifer Ditchburn, "Further Trudeau Attack Ads Roil Conservative Ranks," 30 April 2013, https://globalnews.ca/news/523832/further -trudeau-attack-ads-roil-conservative-ranks/.
22 Mark Kennedy, "Brian Mulroney Cautions Tories to Tread Carefully with Trudeau," *Ottawa Citizen*, 5 September 2014, https://ottawacitizen.com /news/national/brian-mulroney-cautions-tories-to-tread-carefully-with -trudeau/.
23 Brian Mulroney, appearance on *Power Play*, CTV, 8 April 2013.
24 Victor Ferreira, "Conservatives' Trudeau Attack Ad Is Prompting NDP Supporters to Vote Liberal: Forum Research Poll," 30 July 2015, https:// nationalpost.com/news/canada/conservatives-trudeau-attack-ad-is -prompting-ndp-supporters-to-vote-liberal-forum-research-poll.
25 See, for example, Brooke Jeffrey, *Divided Loyalties: The Liberal Party of Canada 1984 to 2008* (Toronto: University of Toronto Press, 2010), 201–20.
26 Cyrus Reporter, interview with author.
27 Mark Holland, interview with author.
28 Erika Tucker, "Justin Trudeau Wants to Legalize Marijuana," Global News, 25 July 2013, .
29 Justin Trudeau, speech delivered to the Calgary Press Club, 30 October 2013, https://www.liberal.ca/liberal-party-canada-leader-justin-trudeaus -speech-calgary-petroleum-club/.
30 Justin Trudeau, "Canadian Liberty and the Politics of Fear," speech delivered at the McGill Institute for the Study of Canada, 9 March 2015,.
31 Faron Ellis, "Stephen Harper and the 2015 Conservative Campaign," in *The Canadian Federal Election of 2015*, ed. Jon H. Pammett and Christopher Dornan (Toronto: Dundurn, 2016).

32 Michael Ignatieff's *True Patriot Love* (Toronto: Viking, 2009) was not well received by critics or the general public.
33 Stuart Nulman, "Review of Justin Trudeau's *Common Ground*," *Montreal Times*, 1 February 2015.
34 Jeet Heer, "Memoirs from Justin Trudeau and Elizabeth May Are Superior Examples of the Genre," *Globe and Mail*, 31 October 2014.
35 "Ending Partisanship and Patronage in the Senate of Canada," speech by Justin Trudeau, 29 January 2014.
36 James Cudmore, "Justin Trudeau Removes Liberal Senators from Caucus," CBC News, 29 January 2014.
37 Cyrus Reporter, interview with author.
38 "Ending Partisanship and Patronage," speech by Justin Trudeau.
39 As cited in Jeffrey, "Back to the Future," in *The Canadian General Election of 2015*, ed. Jon H. Pammett and Christopher Dornan (Toronto: Dundurn, 2016), 73.
40 Lee-Anne Goodman, "Trudeau Apologizes after Hockey-Ukraine Joke," Global News, 25 February 2014, https://globalnews.ca/news/1171201/trudeau-apologizes-after-hockey-ukraine-joke/.
41 "Justin Trudeau's 'Foolish' China Remark Sparks Anger," CBC News, 9 November 2013, https://www.cbc.ca/news/canada/toronto/justin-trudeau-s-foolish-china-remarks-spark-anger-1.2421351.
42 Éric Grenier, "How Trudeau's Election Has Boosted the Liberals in the Polls," *Globe and Mail*, 15 April 2013.
43 Michael den Tandt, "Trudeau's Still Golden," *Ottawa Citizen*, 20 June 2014.
44 Leger Marketing, 30 April 2015. Other polls taken around this time showed similar results. For a comprehensive listing of polling data, see https://en.wikipedia.org/wiki/Opinion_polling_for_the_2015_Canadian_federal_election.
45 Éric Grenie, "NDP Still the Party to Beat in Quebec," *Hill Times*, 24 November 2014; see also Brooke Jeffrey, "Quebec Is the Liberals' Next Challenge," *Montreal Gazette*, 13 April 2013.
46 See, for example, CPAC's *Public Record* panel "Election 2015: What Does It All Mean?" http://www.cpac.ca/en/programs/public-record/episodes/45234087; and CBC's *The Current*, 1 June 2015.
47 Donovan Vincent, "NDP and Conservatives Tied, Liberals Fall to Third Place, Poll Says," *Toronto Star*, 10 July 2015, https://www.thestar.com/news/canada/2015/07/10/poll-shows-justin-trudeaus-liberals-slipping-further-behind.html. Note that all polling data in this section are based on Grenier's Poll Tracker as well: https://www.cbc.ca/news2/interactives/poll-tracker/2015/.
48 David McGrane, "From Third to First and Back to Third," in *The Canadian Federal Election of 2015*, ed. Jon H. Pammett and Christopher Dornan (Toronto: Dundurn, 2016), 90–100.

49 Quoted in Althea Raj, "Justin Trudeau's Liberals: 'We Had a Plan and We Stuck to It.' And They Won," *Huffington Post*, 25 October 2015, https://www.huffingtonpost.ca/2015/10/25/justin-trudeau_n_8382304.html.
50 Ellis, "Stephen Harper and the 2015 Conservative Campaign," 51.
51 Tasha Kheiriddin, "The Munk Debate: Mulcair Slumps, Trudeau Soars, Harper Coasts," *IPolitics*, 29 September 2015, https://ipolitics.ca/2015/09/29/the-munk-debate-mulcair-slumps-trudeau-soars-harper-coasts/.
52 CBC Poll Tracker 2015.
53 Paul Wells, "The Making of a Prime Minister: Inside Trudeau's Epic Victory," *Maclean's*, 2 November 2015, https://site.macleans.ca/longform/trudeau/.
54 Graphic demonstrations of this change can be found in CBC Poll Tracker (Grenier) and Canada 338 (Fournier) 2015 polling data. For a comprehensive listing of polling data, see https://en.wikipedia.org/wiki/Opinion_polling_for_the_2015_Canadian_federal_election.
55 Abacus Data, as cited in David Coletto, "Polling and the 2015 Election," in *The Canadian Federal Election of 2015*, ed. Jon H. Pammett and Christopher Dornan (Toronto: Dundurn, 2016), 318.
56 Mark Kennedy, "Liberal Values Won the Election Says Poll," *Ottawa Citizen*, 19 November 2015.
57 Ensight, "The Back to the Future Election" (Ottawa: 22 October 2015), 7–8. A synopsis of the report's findings was also offered by Ensight principal Jaime Watt: "Why the Liberals Struck a Chord with Voters," *Globe and Mail*, 23 October 2015.

9. Trudeau Takes Charge: Creating a New Liberal Dynasty?

1 The elimination of the long-standing deficit was seen by economists (and Liberals) as having a silver lining by making the economy more competitive and providing additional funds for government to spend on positive measures of its choosing. See, for example, Randall Palmer and Louise Egan, "Lessons from Canada's 'Basket Case' Moment," *Financial Post*, 21 November 2011, https://business.financialpost.com/uncategorized/lessons-from-canadas-basket-case-moment.
2 See, for example, Bruce Campbell and Todd Scarth, "The Real Chretien Legacy Budget," Canadian Centre for Policy Alternatives, 18 February 2003, https://www.policyalternatives.ca/publications/commentary/real-chretien-legacy-budget.
3 Bruce Doern, "The Chrétien Liberals' Third Mandate," in *How Ottawa Spends 2002–2003: The Security Aftermath and National Priorities*, ed. G. Bruce Doern (Don Mills: Oxford University Press, 2003), 3.

4 For a detailed discussion of this phenomenon see Lawrence Leduc, Jon
   H. Pammett, Judith I. McKenzie, and André Turcotte, *Dynasties and
   Interludes: Past and Present in Canadian Electoral Politics* (Toronto: Dundurn,
   2010).

5 Michael Bliss, "The Liberal Party Does NOT Have a Future in Canada,"
   Ottawa Citizen, 23 March 2013.

6 Data on party financing in this section available at Elections Canada,
   https://www.elections.ca/content.aspx?section=fin&document=index
   &lang=e. See also Éric Grenier, "Conservatives Had a Better Fundraising
   Year in 2017 than the Liberals, Filings Show," CBC, 4 July 2018, https://
   www.cbc.ca/news/politics/federal-parties-annual-filings-1.4733189.

7 Liberal Party of Canada, "Liberal Supporters Achieve New Q3
   Fundraising Record," 30 October 2018, https://www.liberal.ca/liberal
   -supporters-achieve-new-q3-fundraising-record/.

8 Liberal Party of Canada, email to Laurier Club members, 3 October 2018.

9 Christina Topp, letter to Laurier Club supporters, 6 November 2018.

10 Liberal Party of Canada, email to Laurier Club members, 3 October
    2018.

11 Éric Grenier, "Filings Show Conservatives Ended 2018 with Big Edge over
    Liberals," CBC News, 3 July 2019.

12 Liberal Party of Canada, "Full Swing," email from president Suzanne
    Cowan to Laurier Club members, 30 August 2019.

13 Ian Bailey and Justine Hunter, "B.C. Premier Christy Clark Defends
    Cash-for-Access Events," *Globe and Mail*, 27 January 2017, https://www
    .theglobeandmail.com/news/british-columbia/bc-premier-defends-cash
    -for-access-dinners-in-wake-of-federal-changes/article33801449/.

14 Robert Fife and Steven Chase, "Trudeau Attended Cash-for-Access
    Fundraiser with Chinese Billionaires," *Globe and Mail*, 22 November 2016,
    https://www.theglobeandmail.com/news/politics/trudeau-attended
    -cash-for-access-fundraiser-with-chinese-billionaires/article32971362/.

15 Bill Curry and Tom Cardoso, "Opposition Accuses Liberals of
    Maintaining 'Cash for Access' Loopholes in Spite of New Rules," *Globe
    and Mail*, 17 September 2018, https://www.theglobeandmail.com
    /politics/article-opposition-accuses-liberals-of-maintaining-cash-for
    -access-loopholes/.

16 Curry and Cardoso, "Opposition Accuses Liberals."

17 See, for example, Mr. Mayrand's testimony before the House of
    Commons Standing Committee on Procedure and House Affairs, 4 June
    2018, https://www.ourcommons.ca/DocumentViewer/en/42-1/PROC
    /meeting-109/evidence.

18 Mike Lapointe, "Early Third-Party Advertising 'Unintended Consequence'
    of Fixed Election Dates, Says Minister," *Hill Times*, 19 June 2019.

19 Adam Radwanski, "How Much Is the Conservatives' Fundraising Dominance Really Worth?" *Globe and Mail*, 17 May 2019, https://www.theglobeandmail.com/canada/article-how-much-is-the-conservatives-fundraising-dominance-really-worth/. For more details see also Mary Francoli, Josh Greenberg, and Christopher Waddell, "The Campaign in the Digital Media," in *The Canadian Federal Election of 2011*, ed. Jon H. Pammett and Christopher Dornan (Toronto: Dundurn, 2011, 219–46.

20 Cris de Clercy, "Communications as the Workhorse of Governmental Politics: The Liberal Party Leader and the Liberal Caucus," in *Political Elites in Canada*, ed. Alex Marland, Thierry Giasson, and Andrea Lawlor (Vancouver: UBC Press, 2018).

21 Detailed accounts of the acrimony between Jean Chrétien and party president Stephen LeDrew, and previously between John Turner and president Michel Robert, are provided in my earlier volume on the Liberal Party, *Divided Loyalties: The Liberal Party of Canada 1984–2006* (Toronto: University of Toronto Press, 2010).

22 Alex Bouthilier, "New Party Rules Part of Liberal Party Modernization," *Toronto Star*, 26 May 2016.

23 As cited in Joan Bryden, "Liberal Convention 2016: Liberals Vote to Adopt Controversial New Constitution," *Huffington Post*, 28 May 2016, https://www.huffingtonpost.ca/2016/05/28/liberal-convention-2016_n_10186842.html.

24 Bryden, "Liberal Convention."

25 Bryden, "Liberal Convention."

26 Anna Gainey, "Working with You for a More Open Movement," letter to Liberal members, 4 July 2006.

27 John Ivison, "Democracy, Liberal-Style, Returns in Nomination Battle for Vacant Ontario Riding," *National Post*, 27 February 2017, https://nationalpost.com/opinion/john-ivison-democracy-liberal-style-returns-in-nomination-battle-for-vacant-ontario-riding.

28 John Ivison, "Democracy, Liberal-Style."

29 Joan Bryden, "Liberal Brass Says Ruling Party in Good Shape," *IPolitics*, 18 September 2018.

30 Abbas Rana, "Some Liberals Concerned Party Hasn't Yet Named Top Campaign Officers, Compromising Election Readiness," *Hill Times*, 14 January 2019.

31 "Trudeau Denies Quebec MP Forced Out for Not Lauding Him as Feminist," Global News, 25 September 2019, https://globalnews.ca/news/5950841/trudeau-denies-quebec-mp-forced-out-for-not-lauding-him-as-feminist/.

32 Jeremy Broadhurst, comments at a Liberal election post-mortem meeting, Ottawa, 9 December 2019.

33 For more details see Sarah Boesveld, "There's a Record Number of Women Running in Election 2019. Here's Why," *Chatelaine*, 10 October 2019, https://www.chatelaine.com/living/politics/women-candidates -canada-election-2019/.

34 Samantha Wright Allen, "Conservative Party Leads Nominees, NDP Lags," *Hill Times*, 5 June 2019.

35 Abbas Rana, "Liberals Trigger 'National Electoral Urgency' Clause that Allows Party to Bypass Nomination Rules," *Hill Times*, 12 August 2019.

36 The source wishes to remain anonymous.

37 Abbas Rana, "Some Liberals Concerned."

38 For a detailed account of Rodier's experiences, see "Confessions of a Campaign Wagon Master," *Policy Options*, December 2019, https:// policyoptions.irpp.org/magazines/december-2019/confessions-of-a -campaign-wagon-master/.

39 Adam Ward, "Gerald Butts Is Back Helping the Liberals Plan for the Federal Election: Source," CTV News, 20 July 2019, https://www .ctvnews.ca/politics/gerald-butts-is-back-helping-the-liberals-plan-for -the-federal-election-source-1.4516600.

40 Cited in Ward, "Gerald Butts Is Back."

41 Liberal Party of Canada, "Day of Action" briefing note, https://www .liberal.ca/summer-of-action/.

42 Abbas Rana, "Anxious Liberals Want Grits to Fill All-Important National Campaign Director Position Soon," *Hill Times*, 22 April 2019.

43 Konrad Yakabuski, "As Trudeau Courts Quebec, the Alienation of the West Only Deepens," *Globe and Mail*, 23 January 2019, https://www .theglobeandmail.com/opinion/article-as-trudeau-courts-quebec-the -alienation-of-the-west-only-deepens/. See also "Trudeau Faces Further Western Discontent in 2019," editorial, *Toronto Sun*, 28 December 2018, https://torontosun.com/opinion/columnists/editorial-trudeau-faces -further-western-discontent-in-2019.

44 Éric Grenier, Canada Poll Tracker, Regional Breakdown, December 2018, https://newsinteractives.cbc.ca/elections/poll-tracker/canada/.

45 Janice Dickson, "Trudeau Says He Wants Reconciliation as His Legacy," *Globe and Mail*, 5 December 2018.

46 Dickson, "Trudeau Says He Wants Reconciliation."

47 Althia Raj, "Liberals Won Majority Thanks to Young Voters, Poll Suggests," *Huffington Post*, 19 April 2016, https://www.huffingtonpost.ca/2016/04 /19/liberals-young-voters-trudeau-canada-election-2015_n_9727026.html.

48 Raj, "Liberals Won Majority Thanks to Young Voters."

49 Éric Grenier, "Liberals' Budget Doubles Down on the Voters They Can't Afford to Lose: Women," CBC News, 28 February 2018, https:// www.cbc.ca/news/politics/grenier-gender-budget-1.4553911. See also

Mainstreet/Ipolitics poll, 9 September 2019, https://ipolitics
.ca/2019/09/10/liberals-have-room-to-breathe-in-latest-national
-poll-while-ndp-tumble-to-fourth/.
50 Alexander Panetta, "Canada-US Women's Group Created by Trudeau
and Ivanka Trump Issues First Proposals," CTV News, 17 January 2018,
https://www.ctvnews.ca/politics/canada-us-women-s-group-created
-by-trudeau-ivanka-trump-issues-first-proposals-1.3763474.
51 Laurence Leamer, *Mar-A-Lago: Inside the Gates of Power at Donald Trump's
Presidential Palace* (New York: Flatiron, 2019).
52 Alastair Macdonald and Noah Barkin, "Generation Macron: Young
Liberal EU Leaders Rally behind French 'Kennedy,'" Reuters, https://
www.reuters.com/article/us-france-election-eu-benelux/generation
-macron-young-liberal-eu-leaders-rally-behind-french-kennedy
-idUSKBN17Y1XT.
53 Anton Wherry, "Justin Trudeau Returns from Davos with Good Press,
Results to Be Determined," CBC, 24 January 2016, https://www.cbc.ca
/news/politics/trudeau-davos-forum-over-wherry-1.3417484.
54 Margaret Wente, "Mr. Trudeau Goes to Davos," *Globe and Mail*, 22 January
2016, https://www.theglobeandmail.com/opinion/mr-trudeau-goes-to
-davos/article28348066/.
55 Rt Hon. Justin Trudeau, "The Canadian Opportunity," speech delivered to
the World Economic Forum, Davos, Switzerland, 20 January 2016, https://
pm.gc.ca/en/news/speeches/2016/01/20/canadian-opportunity.
56 Wherry, "Justin Trudeau Returns from Davos"
57 *Good Morning America*, ABC, 11 March 2016.
58 *Washington Post* reporter Emily Heil on *NBC Nightly News*, **10 March 2016**.
59 Maya Rhodan, "Canadian Prime Minister Justin Trudeau Heads to
Washington," *Time*, 8 March 2016, https://time.com/4251661/justin-
trudeau-canada-obama-washington/.
60 Dean Dettloff, "Is Justin Trudeau's Honeymoon with Canadians Coming
to an End?" *America*, 9 December 2016, https://www.americamagazine
.org/politics-society/2016/12/09/justin-trudeaus-honeymoon-canadians
-coming-end.
61 James Wolcott, "The Bromance of Justin Trudeau and Emmanuel Macron,
Gen X Dynamos of Democracy," *Vanity Fair*, 4 August 2017, https://
www.vanityfair.com/news/2017/08/the-bromance-of-justin-trudeau
-and-emmanuel-macron-gen-x.
62 Communique of the G7 Summit, Taormina, Sicily, 25 May 2017, http://
www.g7italy.it/sites/default/files/documents/G7%20Taormina%20
Leaders%27%20Communique_27052017/index.pdf.
63 Mireille Lalancette and Vincent Raynauld, "Instagram, Justin Trudeau
and Political Image Making," *Policy Options*, 9 April 2018, https://

policyoptions.irpp.org/magazines/april-2018/instagram-justin-trudeau
-and-political-image-making/.

64 Éric Grenier, "How Long Will Justin Trudeau's Honeymoon Last?" CBC
News, 21 November 2015, https://www.cbc.ca/news/politics/grenier
-trudeau-honeymoon-1.3324631.

65 Philippe J. Fournier, "The Rise and Fall of Justin Trudeau's Political
Honeymoon," *Maclean's*, 15 August 2019, https://www.macleans
.ca/politics/ottawa/the-rise-and-fall-of-justin-trudeaus-political
-honeymoon/.

66 Fournier, "The Rise and Fall of Justin Trudeau's Political Honeymoon";
see also Éric Grenier, "How Long Will the Trudeau Honeymoon Last?"

67 Office of the Conflict of Interest and Ethics Commissioner, "Ethics
Commissioner Reports on Investigation Involving Prime Minister," press
release, 20 December 2017.

68 Rt Hon. Justin Trudeau, statement on the Ethics Commissioner's Report,
PMO, 18 December 2017.

69 Aaron Wherry, "Justin Trudeau Suffers the Political Consequences of a
Rarefied Scandal," CBC News, 20 December 2017.

70 Nearly five hundred thousand Sikhs live in Canada, primarily in BC, and
are represented in Trudeau's caucus and cabinet. The prime minister also
attended a Khalsa parade in Canada in May 2017, which was reported in
India.

71 Barkha Dutt, "Trudeau's India Trip Is a Total Disaster – and He Has Only
Himself to Blame," *Washington Post*, 22 February 2018, https://www
.washingtonpost.com/news/global-opinions/wp/2018/02/22/trudeaus
-india-trip-is-a-total-disaster-and-he-has-himself-to-blame/.

72 Abbas Rana, "Drop in Polls a Wake-Up Call for Liberals Who Need to
'Work on Their Game,' Say Leading Pollsters," *Hill Times*, 19 March 2018.

73 Abbas Rana, "Drop in Polls a Wake-Up Call."

74 Éric Grenier, "365 Days to Go – And Trudeau's Liberals Have the Edge on
the 2019 Election," CBC News, 21 October 2018, https://www.cbc.ca
/news/politics/grenier-polls-2019-election-1.4870074.

75 Alex Marland, *Brand Command: Canadian Politics and Democracy in the Age
of Message Control* (Vancouver: UBC Press, 2016), 134.

76 The voluntary resignation of a cabinet minister in Canada over policy
issues is already highly unusual, and the departure of two – over a
direct conflict with the prime minister – had not been seen in Canada
since the Conservative cabinet revolt of 1963. For more details see J.P.
Lewis, "Justin Trudeau Cabinet Resignations a Rarity in Canadian
History," *The Conversation*, 12 March 2019, https://theconversation.
com/justin-trudeau-cabinet-resignations-a-rarity-in-canadian-history
-113096.

77 Amy Smart, "Former Liberal Jody Wilson-Raybould Wins Her Vancouver Seat as Independent," *National Post*, 22 October 2019, https://nationalpost.com/pmn/news-pmn/canada-news-pmn /former-liberal-jody-wilson-raybould-wins-her-vancouver-seat-as -independent.

78 Smart, "Former Liberal Jody Wilson-Raybould Wins as Independent"; "Jody Wilson-Raybould, B.C. Aboriginal Leader, to Run for Liberals in Vancouver," CBC, 31 July 2014, https://www.cbc.ca/news/politics /jody-wilson-raybould-b-c-aboriginal-leader-to-run-for-liberals-in -vancouver-1.2724335.

79 Janice Dickson, "Wilson-Raybould Fills More Judicial Vacancies, Backlog Continues," *National Post*, 6 September 2018, https://nationalpost.com /pmn/news-pmn/canada-news-pmn/liberals-plan-to-increase-frequency -of-judicial-appointments-in-face-of-backlogs.

80 Joan Bryden, "Trudeau Rejected Wilson-Raybould's Conservative Pick for High Court, CP Sources Say," CBC News, 25 March 2019, https:// www.cbc.ca/news/politics/trudeau-supreme-court-wilson-raybould -1.5070619.

81 Marco Vigliotti, "Wilson-Raybould Had Concerns about 'Rushed' DPA Amendments: Ethics Commissioner Report," *IPolitics*, 14 August 2019, https://ipolitics.ca/2019/08/14/wilson-raybould-had-concerns-about -rushed-dpa-amendments-ethics-commissioner-report/.

82 Kyla Lee, "Jody Wilson-Raybould Did a Poor Job as Justice Minister," *Huffington Post*, 20 February 2019, https://www.huffingtonpost.ca /entry/jody-wilson-raybould-snc-lavalin_ca_5cd58951e4b07bc72978fcf7.

83 Daniel Brown, "Wilson-Raybould's Regrettable Legacy as Justice Minister," *Toronto Star*, 16 January 2019, https://www.thestar.com /opinion/contributors/2019/01/16/wilson-rayboulds-regrettable -legacy-as-justice-minister.html.

84 Randy Boswell, "The SNC Affair: What Role Did Indigenous Clash Play?" *Ottawa Citizen*, 16 April 2019.

85 John Ivison, "Trudeau Always Saw Wilson-Raybould as a Problem to Be Circumvented," *National Post*, 15 August 2019, https://nationalpost.com /opinion/john-ivison-trudeau-always-saw-wilson-raybould-as-a-problem -to-be-circumvented.

86 Ivison, "Trudeau Saw Wilson-Raybould as a Problem."

87 Boswell, "The SNC Affair."

88 Boswell,"The SNC Affair."

89 Maura Forrest, "Jody Wilson-Raybould Was the Face of Trudeau's Reconciliation Vow, 'and Now She's Gone,'" *National Post*, 1 March 2019, https://nationalpost.com/news/politics/jody-wilson-raybould-was-the -face-of-trudeaus-reconciliation-vow-and-now-shes-gone.

90 See full text of Butt's opening statement: https://www.macleans.ca
   /politics/ottawa/gerald-butts-testifies-at-justice-committee-full-opening
   -statement/.

91 Wilson-Raybould's resignation came shortly after the prime minister
   addressed a media query about her apparent unhappiness with her
   demotion by indicating that she was still in cabinet, a comment that some
   observers have suggested sparked her departure, although she has never
   acknowledged this.

92 Anonymous comment to author by a veteran Liberal MP.

93 See, for example, Rachel Aiello, "Wilson-Raybould Says She Wants
   Opportunity to 'Speak My Truth,'" CTV News, 20 February 2019,
   https://www.ctvnews.ca/politics/wilson-raybould-says-she-wants
   -opportunity-to-speak-my-truth-1.4304445.

94 Andrew Coyne, "Wilson-Raybould Recording Brings SNC-Lavalin
   Affair Crashing Back to Reality," *National Post*, 31 March 2019, https://
   nationalpost.com/opinion/andrew-coyne-wilson-raybould-recording
   -brings-snc-lavalin-affair-crashing-back-to-reality.

95 Opposition House leader Candice Bergen, for example, called Trudeau a
   "fake feminist" in the House of Commons on 8 March 2019, a term that
   was quickly taken up by several Conservative MPs and others: https://
   globalnews.ca/video/5077297/candice-bergen-calls-justin-trudeau-a
   -fake-feminist.

96 See full text of Butt's opening statement: https://www.macleans.ca
   /politics/ottawa/gerald-butts-testifies-at-justice-committee-full-opening
   -statement/.

97 Vigliotti, "Wilson-Raybould Had 'Concerns.'"

98 See Mr. Wernick's testimony before the House of Commons Standing
   Committee on Justice and Human Rights, no. 132, 21 February 2019.

99 Andrew Cohen, "Not Impressed by Saint Jody and Saint Jane," *Montreal
   Gazette*, 6 March 2019, https://www.pressreader.com/canada/montreal
   -gazette/20190306/281681141183656.

100 Andrew Cohen, "Canada's SNC Melodrama Baffles a World Facing Real
   Crisis," *Ottawa Citizen*, 2 April 2019, https://ottawacitizen.com/opinion
   /columnists/cohen-canadas-snc-melodrama-baffles-a-world-facing-real
   -crisis/.

101 Brian Greenspan, "Did Jody Wilson-Raybould Understand Her Role
   as Attorney-General?" *Globe and Mail*, 17 April 2019, https://www
   .theglobeandmail.com/opinion/article-did-jody-wilson-raybould
   -understand-her-role-as-attorney-general/.

102 See, for example, the op-ed article by Johnston, whose organization had
   promoted the use of such a mechanism: "Why Didn't SNC Lavalin Get
   a Deferred Prosecution Deal?" *Montreal Gazette*, 8 March 2019, https://

montrealgazette.com/opinion/opinion-why-didnt-snc-lavalin-get-a
-deferred-prosecution-deal. (Although Johnston had been a Liberal cabinet
minister under Pierre Trudeau, he had long since retired from active politics.)

103 Terence Corcoran, "SNC-Lavalin would get a deal anywhere else.
Why not here?" *Financial Post*, 27 February 2019, https://business
.financialpost.com/opinion/terence-corcoran-snc-lavalin-would-get
-a-deal-anywhere-else-why-not-here.

104 Peter Donolo, "Government Should Have Explained DPAs to the Public,"
Policy Options, April 2019, https://policyoptions.irpp.org/magazines
/april-2019/government-should-have-explained-dpas-to-the-public/.

105 Adam Radwanski, "Trudeau Promised Change with Fresh Cabinet
Faces. He May Regret It Now," *Globe and Mail*, 26 February 2019, https://
www.theglobeandmail.com/politics/article-jody-wilson-raybould-has
-challenged-ottawas-political-culture-in-a/.

106 "Reconciliation Outlasts Wilson-Raybould: Indigenous Senators," CTV
New, 14 February 2019, https://www.ctvnews.ca/politics/reconciliation
-outlasts-wilson-raybould-indigenous-senators-1.4297678.

107 Errol Mendes, "Did the Ethics Commissioner Misinterpret His Own Act
and Jurisdiction?" *Toronto Star*, 16 August 2019,.

108 Lori Turnbull, "Wilson-Raybould's Resignation Is an Off-Brand,
Disastrous Narrative for the Liberals," *Globe and Mail*, 13 February 2019,
https://www.theglobeandmail.com/opinion/article-wilson-rayboulds
-resignation-is-an-off-brand-disastrous-narrative/.

109 Andrew Cohen, "Wilson-Raybould and Philpott Begin Their Journey to
Obscurity," *The Guardian*, 28 May 2019, https://www.theguardian.pe.ca
/opinion/national-perspectives/andrew-cohen-wilson-raybould-and
-philpott-begin-their-journey-to-obscurity-316457/.

110 See, for example, 2019 reports by the BDC (https://www.bdc.ca/en
/blog/pages/2019-economic-outlook-canada-in-good-place.aspx) and the
OECD (http://www.oecd.org/economy/canada-economic-snapshot/).

10. Second Chance: The 2019 Election

1 Lisa Birch and Francois Petry, *Assessing Justin Trudeau's Liberal Government*
(Quebec City: Laval University Press, 2019).

2 Jordan Press, "Trudeau's Overhaul of Appointments System Has Created
Gender Parity but Minorities Still Being Left Behind," *Globe and Mail*, 21
May 2019, https://www.theglobeandmail.com/politics/article-trudeaus
-overhaul-of-appointments-system-has-created-gender-parity/.

3 "Liberals' Child Benefit Lifting Children Out of Poverty, StatsCan Says,"
Global News, 26 February 2019, https://globalnews.ca/news/5000746
/liberal-child-benefit-poverty-statcan/.

4 Bill Curry, "Tax Revenue from Canada's Richest Increased in 2017 after Liberal Reforms," *Globe and Mail*, 19 April 2019, A5. For complete details see the PBO report "Revisiting the Middle Class Tax Cut,"18 April 2019, https://www.pbo-dpb.gc.ca/en/blog/news/Revisiting_MCTC.

5 Amy Smart, "Reconciliation, Indigenous Engagement in Question ahead of Election," CBC, 13 October 2019, https://www.cbc.ca/news/politics/reconciliation-indigenous-engagement-in-question-ahead-of-election-1.5319899.

6 Birch and Pétry, *Assessing Justin Trudeau's Liberal Government*.

7 See, for example, Graham Slaughter, "Majority of Canadians Support Trudeau's Trade Tactics with Trump," CTV News, 8 July 2018, https://www.ctvnews.ca/politics/majority-of-canadians-support-trudeau-s-trade-tactics-with-trump-nanos-survey-1.4005105; John Geddes, "Liberals Enjoy Strong Support for Their Renegotiation of NAFTA," *Maclean's*, 23 November 2018, https://www.macleans.ca/politics/ottawa/liberals-enjoy-strong-support-for-their-renegotiation-of-nafta/.

8 Theophilos Argitis, "Unemployment Rate Falls to Lowest since at Least 1976," *National Post*, 8 June 2019; see also International Monetary Fund, Concluding Statement, Annual Article IV Mission to Canada, 8 June 2018, https://www.imf.org/en/News/Articles/2018/06/04/ms060418-canada-staff-concluding-statement-of-the-2018-article-iv-mission.

9 "The Debt, the Deficit – And Other Things This Election Isn't About," editorial, *Globe and Mail*, 18 September 2019, https://www.theglobeandmail.com/opinion/editorials/article-the-debt-the-deficit-and-other-things-this-election-isnt-about/.

10 See, for example, Joanna Smith, "The Liberals Broke Their Promise on Electoral Reform. Will It Hurt Them in 2019?" *National Post*, 12 October 2019, https://nationalpost.com/news/politics/election-2019/the-liberals-broke-their-promise-on-electoral-reform-will-it-hurt-them-in-2019; Conservative Party of Canada, 29 September 2019, https://www.conservative.ca/justin-trudeau-broke-his-promises-to-you-last-time-and-he-will-do-it-again-if-re-elected/; "Tories to Release Platform on Friday, Singh Sets Terms for NDP Minority Support," *National Post*, 10 October 2019, https://nationalpost.com/pmn/news-pmn/canada-news-pmn/ndp-reminds-trudeau-of-electoral-reform-promise-before-last-debate.

11 Shawn McCarthy, Robert Fife, and Gloria Galloway, "Trudeau Reaches Historic National Climate Deal with Provinces," *Globe and Mail*, 9 December 2016, https://www.theglobeandmail.com/news/politics/national-climate-deal-reached-trudeau-provinces/article33281195/.

12 Rachel Emmanuel, "Grits, Tories Release Campaign Slogans," *Globe and Mail*, 27 August 2019, A4.

13 Emmanuel, "Grits, Tories Release Campaign Slogans."
14 "Federal Grits Make Ford-Scheer Connection," *Ottawa Citizen*, 13 April 2019.
15 Peter Mazereeuw, "Liberal Election Ad 'Head and Shoulders' above Tory, NDP Offerings, Says U.S, Campaign Guru," *Hill Times*, 16 September 2019.
16 Tom Cardoso, "Liberal Campaign Has Most Ads on Facebook," *Globe and Mail*, 10 October 2019.
17 Adam Radwanski, "How Much Is the Conservatives' Fundraising Edge Really Worth?" *Globe and Mail*, 17 May 2019, https://www.theglobeandmail.com/canada/article-how-much-is-the-conservatives-fundraising-dominance-really-worth/. For more details see also Mary Francoli, Josh Greenberg, and Christopher Waddell, "The Campaign in the Digital Media," in *The Canadian Federal Election of 2011*, ed. Jon H. Pammett and Christopher Dornan (Toronto: Dundurn Press, 2011), 219–46.
18 Adam Hunter, "Regina-Based Group behind Anti-Trudeau Ad Campaign in National Newspapers," CBC News, 10 October 2019, https://www.cbc.ca/news/canada/saskatchewan/anti-trudeau-ad-campaign-1.5316341.
19 Xiao Xu and Tom Cardoso, "Conservatives Running Facebook Ads Falsely Accusing Liberals of Planning to Legalize Hard Drugs on Chinese-Language Page," *Globe and Mail*, 11 October 2019, https://www.theglobeandmail.com/canada/british-columbia/article-conservatives-running-facebook-ads-falsely-accusing-liberals-of/. See also Jonathon Gatehouse, "The Conservatives' Misleading Claims about a 'Secret' Liberal Housing Tax," CBC, 8 October 2019, https://www.cbc.ca/news/politics/the-conservatives-misleading-claims-about-a-secret-liberal-housing-tax-1.5312873.
20 David Beers, "As Scheer Falsehoods Pile Up, Postmedia Gives its Blessing," *The Tyee*, 19 October 2019, https://thetyee.ca/Opinion/2019/10/19/Scheer-Falsehoods/.
21 David Rodier, "Confessions of a Campaign Wagon Master," *Policy Options*, 16 December 2019, https://policyoptions.irpp.org/magazines/december-2019/confessions-of-a-campaign-wagon-master/.
22 "What We Know about Justin Trudeau's Blackface Photos – and What Happens Next," CBC News, 26 September 2019, https://www.cbc.ca/news/politics/canada-votes-2019-trudeau-blackface-brownface-cbc-explains-1.5290664.
23 See especially comments by Greg Lyle, Innovative Research, as quoted in Abbas Rana, "Blackface/Brownface Photos Will Make Re-Election Campaign the Fight of Trudeau's Political Life: Pollsters," *Hill Times*, 23 September 2019.

24 See, for example, Bruce Anderson and David Coletto, "Election Poll: A Sensational Week, Yet a Tight Race Remains," Abacus Data, 23 September 2019, https://abacusdata.ca/a-sensational-week-yet-a-tight-race-remains/; John Geddes, "The Blackface Photos Jolted Voters, but Maybe Only Temporarily," *Maclean's*, 23 September 2019, https://www.macleans.ca/politics/ottawa/the-blackface-photos-jolted-voters-but-maybe-only-temporarily/.
25 Greg Fergus, statement to media at press conference, Ottawa, 19 September 2019; see also Joanne Laucius, "Candidates Accept Trudeau's Apology," *Ottawa Citizen*, 20 September 2019.
26 Anderson and Coletto, "Election Poll: A Sensational Week."
27 Kathleen Harris, "Greta Thunberg Meets Trudeau, Tells Him He's Not Doing Enough to Fight Climate Change," CBC News, 27 September 2019, https://www.cbc.ca/news/politics/trudeau-greta-thunberg-climate-change-action-1.5299674.
28 Liberal Party of Canada, *Forward: A Real Plan for the Middle Class* (Ottawa: Liberal Party of Canada, 2019), 35.
29 Liberal Party of Canada, *Forward*, 35.
30 Kathleen Harris, "Trudeau Acknowledges Tories Could Win, Accuses Them of Running 'Dirtiest' Campaign Ever," CBC News, 16 October 2019, https://www.cbc.ca/news/politics/trudeau-liberal-accuses-conservatives-dirty-campaign-1.5322439.
31 Cited in Susan Delacourt, "How the Liberals Won – An Inside Look at the Targeting and Tactics That Got Trudeau Re-elected," *The Star*, 23 November 2019, https://www.thestar.com/politics/2019/11/23/how-the-liberals-won-an-inside-look-at-the-targeting-and-tactics-that-got-trudeau-re-elected.html.
32 Asham Ishmael, comments during post-mortem briefing session for Laurier Club members, Ottawa, 9 December 2019.
33 Delacourt, "How the Liberals Won."
34 Suzanne Cowan, comments during post-mortem briefing session for Laurier Club members.
35 John Ivison, "How Barack Obama Revived the Liberal Campaign," *National Post*, 13 November 2019.
36 Angus Reid Institute, "Why and When Did Uncommitted Voters Lock In? Study Shows Liberals Benefitted Most from Strategic Voting," 25 October 2019, http://angusreid.org/election-2019-exit-poll/.
37 Ivison, "How Barack Obama Revived the Liberal Campaign."
38 The author attended the meeting.
39 Joan Bryden, "Poll Suggests Plenty of Canadians Voted Strategically to Stop a Party from Winning," CBC News, 29 October 2019, https://www.cbc.ca/news/politics/poll-strategic-voting-1.5339692.

40 For a detailed discussion of the concepts of party dynasties and interludes, see Lawrence LeDuc, Jon H. Pammett, Judith I. McKenzie, and André Turcotte, *Dynasties and Interludes: Past and Present in Canadian Electoral Politics* (Toronto: Dundurn Press, 2010).

41 Aileen Donnelly, "Office Politics: Why Jody Wilson-Raybould Doesn't Really Have a Choice about Moving Offices," *National Post*, 13 December 2019, https://nationalpost.com/news/politics/jody-wilson-raybould -office.

42 Daniel Leblanc, "Liberals Have Support to Forge Ahead on Both Pipeline and Carbon Tax: Poll," *Globe and Mail*, 11 November 2019, A3.

43 Neil Moss, "Trudeau Set Right Tone in the Days after Flight 752 Downing, Say Foreign Policy Experts," *Hill Times*, 15 January 2020.

44 "Navdeep Bains Acclaimed as Liberal Candidate in 2019 Federal Campaign Kickoff," *National Observer*, 28 June 2019.

45 For an in-depth look at this concept, see Leduc, Pammett, McKenzie, and Turcotte, *Dynasties and Interludes*.

Index

ABOUT THE AUTHOR

Brooke Jeffrey is uniquely placed to provide an insider's account of the Liberal Party of Canada, having served in various official and voluntary capacities with the party since 1984. A former director of the Liberal Caucus Research Bureau (1984–90), she was secretary to the party's National Policy Committee and Platform Committee and a member of the National Campaign Committee (1988). She was appointed secretary general of the Liberal Leadership Forums in 1990. In the 1993 federal election she was the (unsuccessful) Liberal candidate in her home riding of Okanagan-Shuswap and later directed the western outreach program of the Liberals' western caucus from 1995 to 1997. She also served as policy adviser to candidates in the 2003 (Copps), 2006 (Kennedy), and 2013 (Cauchon) Liberal leadership campaigns, and was appointed to the 2008 Liberal Party of Canada Reform Committee (Federalism and the Constitution) chaired by Tom Axworthy. Dr. Jeffrey is professor of political science at Concordia University in Montreal, where she teaches courses in federalism, public administration, and political parties and for many years was the director of the MPPPA graduate program in public administration and public policy. A frequent media commentator, she is the author of five previous books on Canadian politics, including *Divided Loyalties*, the predecessor to this work.

www.ingramcontent.com/pod-product-compliance
Lightning Source LLC
Chambersburg PA
CBHW031536260326
41914CB00032B/1823/J